D1250440

2009
The Supreme Court Review

2009
The

"Judges as persons, or courts as institutions, are entitled to
no greater immunity from criticism than other persons
or institutions . . . [J]udges must be kept mindful of their limitations and
of their ultimate public responsibility by a vigorous
stream of criticism expressed with candor however blunt."
—*Felix Frankfurter*

". . . while it is proper that people should find fault when
their judges fail, it is only reasonable that they should recognize the
difficulties. . . . Let them be severely brought to book,
when they go wrong, but by those who will take the trouble
to understand them."
—*Learned Hand*

THE LAW SCHOOL

THE UNIVERSITY OF CHICAGO

Supreme Court Review

EDITED BY
DENNIS J. HUTCHINSON
DAVID A. STRAUSS
AND GEOFFREY R. STONE

 THE UNIVERSITY OF CHICAGO PRESS

CHICAGO AND LONDON

INTERNATIONAL STANDARD BOOK NUMBER: 978-0-226-36255-7

LIBRARY OF CONGRESS CATALOG CARD NUMBER: 60-14353

THE UNIVERSITY OF CHICAGO PRESS, CHICAGO 60637

THE UNIVERSITY OF CHICAGO PRESS, LTD., LONDON

© 2010 BY THE UNIVERSITY OF CHICAGO, ALL RIGHTS RESERVED, PUBLISHED 2010

PRINTED IN THE UNITED STATES OF AMERICA

The paper used in this publication meets the minimum requirements of American National Standard for Information Sciences–Permanence of Paper for Printed Library Materials, ANSI Z39.48-1984. ∞

TO

JUSTICE JOHN PAUL STEVENS

AND

JUSTICE DAVID SOUTER

Independent voices,
servants of the public

CONTENTS

HEARSAY'S LAST HURRAH   1
  David Alan Sklansky

RICCI V DESTEFANO: AFFIRMATIVE ACTION AND THE
  LESSONS OF ADVERSITY   83
  George Rutherglen

REVERSING THE ORDER OF BATTLE IN CONSTITUTIONAL
  TORTS   115
  John C. Jeffries, Jr.

QUALIFIED IMMUNITY AND CONSTITUTIONAL AVOIDANCE   139
  Jack M. Beermann

CONSTITUTIONAL AVOIDANCE AND ANTI-AVOIDANCE BY
  THE ROBERTS COURT   181
  Richard L. Hasen

AGAINST NATIONAL SECURITY EXCEPTIONALISM   225
  Aziz Z. Huq

ARIZONA V GANT: DOES IT MATTER?   275
  Barbara E. Armacost

UPDATING CONSTITUTIONAL RULES   319
  Rosalind Dixon

WHAT WAS WARREN COURT ANTITRUST?   347
  Tony A. Freyer

DAVID ALAN SKLANSKY

HEARSAY'S LAST HURRAH

Despite the encomia it has accumulated for generations, the hearsay rule gets little love today. Most lawyers, judges, and scholars, along with most laypeople who give the matter any thought, understand the dangers of secondhand testimony. They think the legal system should try to hear from witnesses directly. Nonetheless they are unlikely to defend the hearsay rule—with its esoteric formalism, its perplexing exceptions, and its arbitrary harshness—as the best way to guard against indirect evidence. Years of trial practice can sometimes give a lawyer a certain fondness for the oddities of hearsay law, but it is the kind of affection a volunteer docent might develop for the creaky, labyrinthine corridors of an ancient mansion, haphazardly expanded over the centuries. The charm arises largely from the elements of quirky dysfunctionality. Scholars, for their part, sometimes argue for preserving the hearsay rule, but almost always in a form very different from what we have today.[1] About the best that anyone has to say for the hearsay rule in its traditional con-

David Alan Sklansky is Yosef Osheawich Professor of Law at the University of California, Berkeley, and Faculty Chair of the Berkeley Center for Criminal Justice.

AUTHOR'S NOTE: I am grateful to George Fisher, Talia Fisher, Andrew Guzman, Chris Kutz, Gillian Lester, Richard Nagareda, Mike Redmayne, Eleanor Swift, Eric Talley, and Jan Vetter for criticism and guidance; to workshop participants at Berkeley, Chicago, Emory, McGeorge, Vanderbilt, Australian National University, and Hebrew University for helpful conversations; and to Laura Beckerman and Quinn Rotchford for excellent research assistance.

[1] See, for example, Eleanor Swift, *A Foundation Fact Approach to Hearsay*, 75 Cal L Rev 1339 (1987); Gordon Van Kessel, *Hearsay Hazards in the American Criminal Trial: An Adversary-Oriented Approach*, 49 Hastings L J 477 (1998); Michael L. Siegel, *Rationalizing Hearsay: A Proposal for a Best Evidence Hearsay Rule*, 72 BU L Rev 893 (1992).

figuration is that it is the devil we know and have learned to live with,[2] and that it has so many exceptions that perhaps it no longer matters.[3]

Unsurprisingly, then, the hearsay rule has long been in decline, not just in the United States but everywhere. Britain, where the rule was first formulated, largely eliminated it forty years ago in civil cases and since then has drastically limited its scope in criminal cases—allowing judges to admit, for example, any hearsay statements by witnesses who are unavailable to testify at the time of trial.[4] Other Commonwealth nations have taken similar steps.[5] In the United States, hearsay exceptions have expanded steadily for decades.[6] Civil-law countries, particularly in Europe, have been bolstering the right of criminal defendants to have their accusers questioned in court,[7] but this is a procedural right, not a rule of evidence. It operates, in the main, not to exclude statements but to allow them to be challenged.[8] The hearsay rule in its traditional form—a broad rule of evidentiary exclusion for statements made by witnesses outside of court—has been slowly withering for decades, in the United States and around the world.[9]

---

[2] See, for example, Frederick Schauer, *On the Supposed Jury-Dependence of Evidence Law*, 155 U Pa L Rev 165, 194–95 (2006).

[3] See, for example, Ronald J. Allen, *The Evolution of the Hearsay Rule to a Rule of Admission*, 76 Minn L Rev 797 (1992); Richard O. Lempert, *Anglo-American and Continental Systems: Marsupials and Mammals of the Law*, in John Jackson, Máximo Langer, and Peter Tillers, eds, *Crime, Procedure and Evidence in a Comparative and International Context: Essays in Honor of Professor Mirjan Damaška* 395, 402 (Hart, 2008); Siegel, 72 BU L Rev at 894 (cited in note 1) (noting the widespread belief "that, despite the irrational nature of hearsay law, most judges use the current rule of exclusion and its myriad exceptions to admit reliable evidence, to exclude unreliable evidence, and to achieve 'rough justice' in the majority of cases").

[4] See Criminal Justice Act, 2003, c 44, § 116 (UK); Criminal Justice (Scotland) Act, 1995, c 20, § 17 (UK).

[5] See text accompanying notes 131–40.

[6] See, for example, Richard D. Friedman, *The Confrontation Right Across the Systemic Divide*, in Jackson, Langer, and Tillers, eds, *Crime, Procedure and Evidence* at 261, 265 (cited in note 3); Allen, 76 Minn L Rev at 797 (cited in note 3).

[7] See, for example, Stefano Maffei, *The European Right to Confrontation in Criminal Proceedings: Absent, Anonymous and Vulnerable Witnesses* (Europa, 2006); Stefan Trechsel, *Human Rights in Criminal Proceedings* 291–326 (Oxford, 2005).

[8] See, for example, Friedman, *Confrontation Right Across the Systemic Divide* at 268 (cited in note 6). As developed by the European Court of Human Rights, the right to confrontation also operates as a rule of sufficiency, disallowing convictions based "solely or decisively" on government depositions of absent witnesses; this aspect of the rule is currently under challenge. See text accompanying notes 173–74.

[9] See, for example, Mirjan Damaška, *Of Hearsay and Its Analogues*, 76 Minn L Rev 425, 457 (1992).

Nor is it surprising, given how little respect the hearsay rule gets, that there has never been much support for constitutionalizing it. The Sixth Amendment right of every criminal defendant "to be confronted with the witnesses against him"[10] has long been thought to "stem from the same roots" as the hearsay rule.[11] For a quarter century, in fact, the application of the Confrontation Clause closely tracked hearsay doctrine. The Supreme Court interpreted the clause to allow the use of hearsay evidence against a criminal defendant as long as the evidence had "adequate 'indicia of reliability,'" and one way to satisfy the test—probably the most common way—was to show that the statement in question fell within a well established exception to the hearsay ban.[12] But the "indicia of reliability" test was unpopular with commentators, largely (but not only) because it seemed to yoke the content of the constitutional right to hearsay law.[13] Criticism of the test mounted steadily,[14] and the Supreme Court finally abandoned it when deciding *Crawford v Washington* in 2004.[15] As reinterpreted in *Crawford*, the Confrontation Clause broadly protects a criminal defendant against "testimonial" statements provided outside of court. The *Crawford* doctrine has since been reaffirmed and elaborated in three subsequent decisions: *Davis v Washington*,[16] *Giles v California*,[17] and—just last spring—*Melendez-Diaz v Massachusetts*.[18] In each of these cases, as in *Crawford*, Justice Scalia wrote for the Court.

---

[10] US Const, Amend VI.

[11] *Dutton v Evans*, 400 US 74, 86 (1970) (plurality).

[12] *Ohio v Roberts*, 448 US 56, 66 (1980).

[13] See, for example, Akhil Reed Amar, *The Constitution and Criminal Procedure: First Principles* 129 (Yale, 1997); Joshua C. Dickinson, *The Confrontation Clause and the Hearsay Rule: The Current State of a Failed Marriage in Need of a Quick Divorce*, 33 Creighton L Rev 763 (2000); Randolph N. Jonakait, *Restoring the Confrontation Clause to the Sixth Amendment*, 35 UCLA L Rev 557, 558 (1988); Richard D. Friedman, *The Confrontation Clause Re-Rooted and Transformed*, 2004 Cato Sup Ct Rev 439, 448.

[14] See, for example, *Lilly v Virginia*, 527 US 116, 140–43 (1999) (Breyer, J, concurring) (taking sympathetic notice).

[15] 541 US 36 (2004).

[16] 547 US 813, 824 (2006).

[17] 128 S Ct 2678 (2008).

[18] 129 S Ct 2527 (2009). There was speculation the Court might reconsider *Melendez-Diaz* when it granted review in *Briscoe v Virginia*, 78 USLW 3434 (US 2010). After briefing and argument, though, the Court released a one-sentence, per curiam opinion, vacating and remanding "for further proceedings not inconsistent with the opinion in *Melendez-Diaz*." Id. The next significant elaboration of the *Crawford* doctrine will likely come when the Court decides *Michigan v Bryant*, No 09-150, 78 USLW 3082 (US, cert granted March 1, 2010). See note 218.

Unlike the test it supplanted, the rule announced and applied in the *Crawford* line of cases has been roundly praised, in significant part because it is thought to have "detached the meaning of the Clause from the hearsay rule."[19] Not all of the reaction to the *Crawford* doctrine has been favorable, of course. The focus on "testimonial" statements has been criticized as too vague and too reductive;[20] beyond that, much of the reasoning in these cases has been originalist, and commentators have quarreled, predictably, with the Court's legal history.[21] Even critics of *Crawford* and its successor cases, though, have tended to give the Court credit for decoupling confrontation doctrine from hearsay law. Whatever the Court got wrong in these cases, at least it ended the "shotgun wedding" of hearsay and confrontation.[22] No longer "shrouded by the hearsay rule," confrontation doctrine can develop independently—and, with luck, more sensibly.[23]

That is the conventional understanding of *Crawford*, broadly shared by the doctrine's fans and by its critics. I will argue here that the truth is more complicated and less comforting. *Crawford* has, in fact, severed the *operational* link between hearsay and con-

---

[19] Friedman, *Confrontation Right Across the Systemic Divide* at 266 (cited in note 6).

[20] See, for example, Robert P. Mosteller, *Confrontation as Constitutional Criminal Procedure: Crawford's Birth Did Not Require That Roberts Had to Die*, 15 J L & Pol 685 (2007); Roger C. Park, *Is Confrontation the Bottom Line?* 19 Regent U L Rev 459 (2007).

[21] See, for example, Thomas Y. Davies, *What Did the Framers Know, and When Did They Know It? Fictional Originalism in Crawford v. Washington*, 71 Brooklyn L Rev 105 (2005); Thomas Y. Davies, *Not the Framers' Design: How the Framing-Era Ban Against Hearsay Evidence Refutes the Crawford-Davis "Testimonial" Formulation of the Scope of the Original Confrontation Clause*, 15 J L & Pol 349 (2007); Tom Harbison, *Crawford v. Washington and Davis v. Washington's Originalism: Historical Arguments Showing Child Abuse Victims' Statements to Physicians are Nontestimonial and Admissible as an Exception to the Confrontation Clause*, 58 Mercer L Rev 569 (2007).

[22] Thomas J. Reed, *Crawford v. Washington and the Irretrievable Breakdown of a Union: Separating the Confrontation Clause from the Hearsay Rule*, 56 SC L Rev 185 (2004); see also Amar, *Constitution and Criminal Procedure* at 129 (cited in note 13) (criticizing, before *Crawford*, "the Court's shotgun wedding of the hearsay rule and the confrontation clause"); Anthony Bocchino and David Sonenshein, *Rule 804(b)(b)—The Illegitimate Child of the Failed Liaison Between the Hearsay Rule and Confrontation Clause*, 73 Mo L Rev 41 (2008); Andrew King-Ries, *An Argument for Original Intent: Restoring Rule 801(d)(1)(A) to Protect Domestic Violence Victims in a Post-Crawford World*, 27 Pace L Rev 199, 200 (2007); Roger W. Kirst, *A Decade of Change in Sixth Amendment Confrontation Doctrine*, 6 Intl Commentary on Evidence, issue 2, art 5, at 21 (2009); Robert P. Mosteller, *Evidence History, the New Trace Evidence, and Rumblings in the Future of Proof*, 3 Ohio St J Crim L 523, 529–30 (2006); Deborah Turkheimer, *Crawford's Triangle: Domestic Violence and the Right of Confrontation*, 85 NC L Rev 1, 36–37 (2006); John Robert Knoebber, Comment, *Say That to My Face: Applying an Objective Approach to Determine the Meaning of Testimony in Light of Crawford v. Washington*, 51 Loyola L Rev 497, 503–15 (2006).

[23] Friedman, *Confrontation Right Across the Systemic Divide* at 265 (cited in note 6).

frontation: it has expanded the category of cases in which the hearsay rules will allow—but the Confrontation Clause will prohibit—the introduction of an out-of-court statement. By implication, the *Crawford* doctrine's focus on "testimonial" statements has also enlarged the category of hearsay violations that do not implicate the Confrontation Clause; the Court has made clear that the introduction of nontestimonial statements raises no constitutional concerns, no matter how the statements are treated under the hearsay rule.[24] In addition to this operational decoupling of hearsay and confrontation, *Crawford* has also separated the areas of law at the *argumentative* level, making clear that the pertinent factors in interpreting and applying the Confrontation Clause differ in kind from the considerations that govern the scope of the hearsay rule. But *Crawford* has left intact, and actually strengthened, the *historical* link between hearsay and confrontation: the idea that the Confrontation Clause and the hearsay rule share the same origins and the same thrust. The operational and argumentative decoupling of hearsay and confrontation has been accomplished in the *Crawford* line of cases by tying the Confrontation Clause to eighteenth-century hearsay rules, or what the Court imagines those rules to have been. Far from deconstitutionalizing hearsay, the Court has woven the hearsay rule into the Sixth Amendment more tightly than ever, but it has done so with the rule in its eighteenth-century form, or at least in its eighteenth-century form as now reconstructed by the Court.

The major difference between the eighteenth-century hearsay rule and its modern-day counterpart is that the eighteenth-century rule was less developed and subject to fewer exceptions. So *Crawford* has revived and entrenched—albeit only for evidence offered against a criminal defendant—a particularly rigid version of the hearsay rule. Furthermore, the Court has given that rule a bite it never had in the 1700s, when appellate oversight and legal publication were also less developed. Even more so than today, rules of evidence in the eighteenth century were largely subject to discretionary waiver by the presiding judge, because there was no realistic sanction for ignoring them.[25] And it was far less clear, even to a conscientious

---

[24] See *Wharton v Bockting*, 549 US 406, 420 (2007); *Davis v Washington*, 547 US 813, 824 (2006).

[25] See, for example, Julius Goebel Jr. and T. Raymond Naughton, *Law Enforcement in Colonial New York* 642 (Commonwealth Fund, 1944); T. P. Gallanis, *The Rise of Modern Evidence Law*, 84 Iowa L Rev 499, 502, 534 (1999).

judge, what the rules of evidence *were*: this was before evidence codes, before the great treatises of the nineteenth century, and before readily available case reports.[26] The rigidity of the eighteenth-century hearsay ban was tempered by its lack of clarity and by the difficulty of enforcing it. *Crawford* has constitutionalized eighteenth-century hearsay law, but without these structural limitations.

The reason the hearsay rule has so few real friends today is that it excludes too much probative evidence with too little justification. This is especially true of the uncompromising version of the hearsay rule the Supreme Court has now read into the Sixth Amendment, despite the limitation to evidence introduced against a criminal defendant. For the very reasons the hearsay rule has long been in decline throughout the common-law world, the new, constitutionalized version of the hearsay ban will almost certainly weaken over time. For the immediate future, though, *Crawford* has given the hearsay rule a new lease on life.

That should give us pause, I will argue, for three different reasons. The first and most obvious is the dysfunctionality of the hearsay rule in its traditional form. The eighteenth-century hearsay rule was not the final, polished product of centuries of common-law reworking; it was an inchoate, overly rigid version of a principle that, for good cause, was later qualified and limited by a famously long set of exceptions. For evidence introduced against criminal defendants, *Crawford* tries to freeze the hearsay rule "in 1791 . . . amber."[27] Over the long term, the effort is likely to fail, but in the short term it will generate predictable injustices. This would be bad enough if the injustices all took the form of guilty defendants escaping punishment. But the *Crawford* doctrine may also help to convict some innocent defendants. The strict application of the hearsay rule to prosecution evidence may bolster the application of the rule to evidence offered by criminal defendants—partly because it will lend credence to the idea that hearsay is too unreliable to serve as evidence in criminal cases, and partly because restrictions on defense evidence strike many judges and legislators as fairer and more reasonable when they counterbalance restrictions on prosecution evidence.

The second reason to be concerned about this effort is that it

---

[26] See, for example, Charles Alan Wright and Kenneth W. Graham, 30 *Federal Practice and Procedure* § 6344 at 393–94 (West, 1997).

[27] Amar, *Constitution and Criminal Procedure* at 44 (cited in note 13).

may stunt the development of confrontation law. The Supreme Court has never said that the Confrontation Clause protects *only* against certain forms of hearsay. On the contrary, the Court has made clear that a confrontation violation may be found when a prosecution witness testifies in court but outside the defendant's presence[28] or without the opportunity for cross-examination.[29] Nonetheless, by treating the Confrontation Clause as, first and foremost, a codification of eighteenth-century evidence rulings, *Crawford* diverts attention from dimensions of confrontation not captured by the hearsay rule—dimensions that may grow increasingly important as scientific evidence plays a larger and larger role in criminal prosecutions.[30] The Confrontation Clause could be read broadly to guarantee criminal defendants a meaningful opportunity to challenge—"to know, to examine, to explain, and to rebut"—the proof offered against them.[31] That reading would not require the Court to stray from the constitutional text and what we know of its aims, but it would require a wider inquiry into constitutional purpose, and a less wooden style of interpretation, than the Court has showed in the *Crawford* line of cases.

More to the point, it would require recognizing that the kind of "confrontation" a criminal defendant needs and deserves may in many cases have little to do with excluding hearsay evidence—or, for that matter, with sitting in court and watching a witness testify, on direct and then on cross-examination. Ironically, the best place to find traces of these larger dimensions of confrontation today may be in the rulings of the European Court of Human Rights interpreting provisions of the European Human Rights Convention that were modeled, in part, on the Sixth Amendment. Because the European Court of Human Rights explicitly disavows any concern with evidence law—that is a matter each member nation decides for itself—the emerging confrontation jurisprudence in Europe is largely decoupled from the hearsay rule, not just operationally and argumentatively, but as a matter of historical understanding, as well.

The third and final reason to be concerned about the way the

---

[28] See *Coy v Maryland*, 487 US 1012 (1988), but consider *Maryland v Craig*, 497 US 836 (1990) (making clear that the right to a face-to-face meeting is not absolute).

[29] See *Davis v Alaska*, 415 US 308 (1974).

[30] See, for example, Mirjan Damaška, *Evidence Law Adrift* 144–47 (Yale, 1996).

[31] Daniel H. Pollitt, *The Right of Confrontation: Its History and Modern Dress*, 8 J Pub L 381, 402 (1959).

Supreme Court has linked the Confrontation Clause with the hearsay rule is that it impedes the cross-fertilization between the doctrines governing out-of-court statements in criminal cases and the parallel rules in civil cases. Special rules of proof for civil or criminal cases have long been viewed with skepticism; there has been a rebuttable presumption that evidence law should apply equally across the board. That presumption has created a constructive dialectic between the rules and practices governing proof in civil cases and the parallel rules and practices in criminal cases.[32] A hearsay exception developed in civil cases might give rise to difficulties in criminal cases—and those difficulties might lead to reconsideration of the exception in civil cases, as well. Everyone recognizes that the rules in civil and criminal cases sometimes *should* be different, but it is a useful exercise to ask, repeatedly, whether that is true in particular instances, and if so, why.

Confrontation doctrine and hearsay law both used to be like evidence law more broadly in this respect: there was a regular practice of comparing practices across the civil-criminal divide. With respect to confrontation, that practice has been in decline for some time; today the Confrontation Clause is typically treated as having no implications for civil cases. Even in high-stakes civil cases—cases involving civil commitment, say, or the termination of parental rights—invocations of the Confrontation Clause are rejected out of hand.[33] Still, as long as confrontation law loosely tracked modern hearsay law, a certain sort of dialectic between civil and criminal cases was inevitable in confrontation cases, because the hearsay rule itself operated the same, for the most part, across the civil-criminal divide. This, in fact, was a standard criticism of confrontation doctrine before *Crawford*: the doctrine failed to account for the distinctive concerns raised in criminal cases. After *Crawford*, the Confrontation Clause continues to be linked to hearsay law, but to eighteenth-century hearsay law, not the modern, more lenient hearsay law applied in civil cases.

Confrontation discourse thus is now fully decoupled from the concerns raised in civil cases. Confrontation decisions have no im-

---

[32] See David A. Sklansky and Stephen C. Yeazell, *Comparative Law Without Leaving Home: What Civil Procedure Can Teach Criminal Procedure, and Vice Versa*, 94 Georgetown L J 683, 728–33 (2006).

[33] See, for example, *Cabinet for Health & Family Services v A.G.G.*, 190 SW3d 338 (Ky 2006) (termination of parental rights); *In re T.W.*, 139 P3d 810 (Mont 2006) (same); *In re Commitment of Polk*, 187 SW3d 550, 555–56 (Tex App 2006) (civil commitment).

plications, even indirectly, for civil cases, and the problems judges face in adjudicating civil cases do not inform the development of confrontation doctrine. This separation of criminal cases from civil cases has generally been viewed as all for the good, part of what makes *Crawford* such a welcome departure. But it impedes a form of doctrinal cross-comparison that in the past has helped both hearsay law and confrontation law progressively improve.

Over the long term, the cross-comparison is probably inevitable, whatever the Supreme Court says. The issues encountered in civil and criminal cases are too similar for judges and lawyers not to draw analogies. Eventually the language of confrontation will appear again in civil and administrative cases, at least where the stakes are high enough to make a comparison to criminal cases seem natural. Eventually, too, the eighteenth-century hearsay rules the Supreme Court has imported into the Confrontation Clause will be softened in response to the same pressures that have led to the worldwide, decades-long weakening of the hearsay rule. In the interim, though, the Court's new confrontation jurisprudence will insulate the hearsay rule applied to prosecution evidence in criminal cases from the exceptions that have evolved over the last two centuries. It may also, by treating civil and criminal cases as essentially incomparable, temporarily reinforce the reluctance of courts to invoke the nonhearsay dimensions of confrontation law in civil cases.

Part I of this article will discuss the hearsay rule, its long and nearly universal decline, and the reasons it has so few champions. Part II of the article will discuss the Supreme Court's dramatic refiguring of confrontation law in *Crawford v Washington* and subsequent cases, and the underappreciated manner in which these decisions have tightened rather than weakened the link between hearsay and confrontation. Part III will explore the ramifications of that development.

In the pages that follow, I will distinguish repeatedly between a categorical rule of evidentiary exclusion, barring evidence of out-of-court statements even when the people who made those statements are now dead or otherwise unavailable to testify in court, and a preferential rule of procedure, requiring live testimony when possible, but allowing evidence of earlier statements by witnesses who cannot now be brought to court. This may sound like a narrow, technical distinction. But it is precisely what distinguishes the hearsay rule in its traditional form—increasingly found only in the

United States—from a more sensible rule toward which much of the rest of the world is now converging, and which could serve as the starting point for a richer and more meaningful understanding of our own constitutional right to confrontation.

I. Hearsay's Decline

When I began teaching evidence law, my colleague Kenneth Graham warned me that the chief difficulty students have with the hearsay rule is not that they find it hard to *understand*; rather it is that they find the rule hard to *believe*. Much of what goes on in an evidence course is, in fact, acculturation. Students gradually become comfortable with a body of doctrine that initially strikes them as too weird to be true. Maybe they grow too comfortable: hearsay law is such a prominent feature of our adjudicatory system that judges, lawyers, and law professors sometimes lose sight of how odd and counterintuitive the rule is, and how unusual from a global perspective.

To appreciate the significance of the new link the Supreme Court has forged between the hearsay rule and the Confrontation Clause, we need to retrieve the sense of strangeness we had about the rule when it was first explained to us. And we need to rid ourselves of the erroneous impression, reinforced by some writing about the hearsay rule, that civil-law countries are beginning to adopt it. It is true that some civil-law systems, particularly in Europe, have been strengthening their insistence on firsthand evidence. In critical and instructive ways, though, the European rules differ from the hearsay rule as we know it.

The following overview of the hearsay rule will proceed in three stages. First, I will discuss how the rule works, what makes it distinctive, and the familiar if discomfiting fact that nothing seems to justify it. Next, I will review what is known about the history of the rule: how it arose, how it withered, and how—at least in America—it has clung to life. Finally, I will discuss the civil-law analogs to the hearsay rule, emphasizing both their similarities and their key differences from what the great treatise writer John Henry Wigmore called "the most characteristic rule of the Anglo-American law of evidence."[34]

---

[34] John Henry Wigmore, 2 *A Treatise on the System of Evidence in Trials at Common Law* § 1365 at 1695 (Little Brown, 1904).

A. THE RULE, ITS EXCEPTIONS, AND ITS JUSTIFICATIONS

Wigmore also called the hearsay rule "the greatest contribution," aside perhaps from trial by jury, of our "eminently practical legal system to the world's jurisprudence of procedure."[35] Few commentators since have been so charitable; the hearsay rule and its exceptions have become "one of the law's most celebrated nightmares."[36] At bottom, though, the rule rests on a simple, commonsensical idea: if you are trying to find out what happened, it is best to hear directly from someone who was there. Call it the principle of the horse's mouth.

There are two ways to implement that principle. The first is getting the horse into court; the second is refusing to listen to or look at any evidence of what the horse has previously said. The first is the thrust of the Confrontation Clause: every criminal defendant has a right "to be confronted with the witnesses against him."[37] The second strategy is the strategy of the hearsay rule. The two strategies are related, of course, because one way to get a witness into court is to refuse to consider evidence of his or her earlier statements. That will give any party interested in the witness's story an incentive to have the witness testify. But sometimes live testimony from the witness is impossible: the witness is dead, or cannot be found, or refuses to testify. At that point the two strategies diverge. They diverge, too, with regard to a separate question: if the witness testifies, are his or her earlier statements still inadmissible?

In the lingo of evidence law, the term "witness" is usually reserved for someone who testifies in court; someone who says something outside of court is called a "declarant." In its pure form, then, the hearsay rule bars the out-of-court statements of a declarant even if the declarant is now dead or otherwise unavailable, and even if the declarant actually testifies, becoming a witness.

A rule this sweeping threatens to exclude vast amounts of evidence that no sane system of adjudication could disregard. In a fraud prosecution, for example, suppose the government proves that the defendant's employees told customers, falsely, that the coins the customers were purchasing were made of gold. Or, in a

---

[35] Id.

[36] Peter Murphy, *Evidence and Advocacy* 24 (Oxford, 5th ed 2002).

[37] US Const, Amend VI.

tax evasion case, suppose the defendant claims good faith and testifies that the income she reported was the income her accountant told her she had earned. Imagine that the plaintiffs in an automobile collision case introduce evidence that the defendant admitted to bystanders that he had run a red light. In a homicide case, suppose that a police officer testifies that the victim told the officer, just before dying, "It was my husband. He shot me point blank." Or imagine that, to support his alibi, the defendant in a robbery case introduces records kept by his employer, showing he was at work when the crime took place.

Hearsay doctrine has made its peace with cases like this in two ways. First, an out-of-court statement counts as "hearsay" only if the party introducing the statement is asking the jury to *believe* the statement—or, as lawyers say, to take it as proof of "the truth of the matter asserted."[38] Defining hearsay in this way removes many out-of-court statements from the reach of the hearsay ban. Evidence of fraudulent claims, for example, is not barred by the hearsay rule, because it is not introduced to prove the truth of those claims: the prosecutors are not trying to show that the coins actually were made of gold.[39] Similarly, information that the tax evasion defendant received from her attorney is not hearsay if it is introduced to show that the defendant acted in good faith (although it *would* be hearsay if it was offered as proof of the defendant's actual income).

This definitional move can only take us so far, though. It does not help with the statement about the automobile accident, or the homicide victim's statement to the police officer, or the records of the robbery defendant's employers. Each of those statements,

---

[38] See, for example, FRE 801(c).

[39] See, for example, *United States v Saavedra*, 684 F2d 1293, 1297–98 (9th Cir 1982). In the 1800s and early 1900s, courts often exempted out-of-court utterances from the hearsay ban on the ground that they were part of the *res gestae*—the "things done." This phrase was applied not only to statements that were themselves part of the alleged crime or tort (because they were fraudulent, defamatory, or otherwise transgressive) but also to utterances that were essentially "verbal acts" rather than assertions (such as, "You're fired," or "I'm giving this to you."). The *res gestae* label was attached, as well, to assertions that fell within certain common-law exceptions to the hearsay rule, including the exceptions for "excited utterances" and "present sense impressions." See, for example, *Black's Law Dictionary* 1335 (West, 8th ed 2004) (Bryan A. Garner, ed); *United States v Elem*, 845 F2d 170, 173–74 (8th Cir 1988). Wigmore and other early twentieth-century commentators hated the vagueness of the term and urged its abandonment. See, for example, Judson F. Falknor, Book Review, 33 Tex L Rev 977, 982 (1955). None of the modern evidence codes employ the phrase, and it has largely—although not entirely—passed out of usage. See Chris Blair, *Let's Say Goodbye to Res Gestae*, 33 Tulsa L J 349 (1997).

though, would be admissible under one of the exceptions that have developed to the hearsay rule. These exceptions are the second way the hearsay rule has made its peace with the manifest desirability of admitting, and allowing juries to rely on, many out-of-court statements. The Federal Rules of Evidence codify some three dozen exceptions to the prohibition of hearsay.[40] They include an exception for "admissions" (i.e., statements made by the party against whom they are introduced at trial, like the statement by the defendant in the collision case),[41] an exception for "dying declarations" (like the statement by the shooting victim),[42] and an exception for regularly maintained business records, made under circumstances conducive to accuracy (like the time cards that the robbery defendant wants to introduce).[43]

The hearsay ban now has so many exceptions that it is sometimes suggested that little of the original rule remains. Cumulatively, it is said, the exceptions have turned hearsay from a "rule of exclusion" into a "rule of admission,"[44] a rule that allows the introduction of "virtually any hearsay statement that has probative value."[45] There is some truth to that characterization: on paper, at least, the hearsay rule today is a shadow of its former self. Nonetheless the rule still can show its teeth. This is notably true when criminal defendants and civil litigants seek to introduce their own, out-of-court statements.[46] Prosecutors, for their part, can find themselves barred by the hearsay rule from proving what victims said outside of court—even the victims in homicide trials, who obviously cannot be called to testify at trial. The "dying declaration" exception does not reach the statements of a homicide victim reporting attacks by the defendant, or expressing fear of the defendant, in the days or weeks preceding her death. That is why, for example, the trial judge in the murder prosecution of O. J.

---

[40] FRE 801(d) & 802–04.

[41] FRE 801(d)(2).

[42] FRE 804(b)(2).

[43] FRE 803(6).

[44] Allen, 76 Minn L Rev at 800 (cited in note 3).

[45] Ronald J. Allen and George N. Alexakis, *Utility and Truth in the Scholarship of Mirjan Damaška*, in Jackson et al, eds, *Crime, Procedure and Evidence* at 327, 343 (cited in note 3).

[46] See Eleanor Swift, *The Hearsay Rule at Work: Has It Been Abolished De Facto by Judicial Decision?* 76 Minn L Rev 473 (1992); Eleanor Swift, *Narrative Theory, FRE 803(3), and Criminal Defendants' Post-Crime State of Mind Hearsay*, 38 Seton Hall L Rev 975 (2008).

Simpson excluded evidence that one of Simpson's alleged victims, his ex-wife Nicole Brown Simpson, told relatives, friends, and a battered women's hotline counselor that Simpson was stalking her, had assaulted her, and had threatened to kill her. The "relevance and probative value" of these statements struck the judge as "obvious and compelling"; it seemed "only right and just that a crime victim's own words be heard . . . in the court where the facts and circumstances of her demise are to be presented." But the hearsay rule would not allow it.[47]

Decisions excluding statements by homicide victims were growing less common before *Crawford*, largely because of hearsay reforms aimed precisely at avoiding such results.[48] In the wake of O. J. Simpson's acquittal, for example, California adopted a new exception to the hearsay rule, allowing the introduction of certain out-of-court reports of "the infliction or threat of physical injury upon the declarant."[49] For the exception to apply, the report had to be made promptly, had to be written, recorded, or made to a medical professional or law enforcement officer, and had to be "made under circumstances that would indicate its trustworthiness."[50] But *Crawford* throws many if not most of those reforms into doubt. In 2003, for example—the year before the Supreme Court decided *Crawford*—a California jury convicted Dwayne Giles of murdering his ex-girlfriend Brenda Avie. Giles admitted he shot Avie, but he claimed self-defense. Part of the evidence against him was testimony from a police officer who responded to a report of domestic violence involving Giles and Avie three weeks before the homicide. According to the officer's testimony, Avie told him the following:

---

[47] *People v Simpson*, No BA097211, 1995 WL 21768, *4–5 (Cal Super, Jan 18, 1995). The same statements were ruled admissible in a subsequent civil trial of wrongful death claims brought against Simpson; the judge in the civil trial reasoned that the statements were relevant to Nicole Brown Simpson's "state or mind" shortly before she was killed. See Gerald F. Uelmen, *The O. J. Files: Evidentiary Issues in a Tactical Context* 104 (West, 1998). For an earlier, equally notorious example, see F. Tennyson Jesse, *The Trial of Madeleine Smith* (Hodge, 1927). Madeleine Smith was unsuccessfully prosecuted in Edinburgh in 1857 for the murder of her former lover, Emile L'Angelier, who died from arsenic poisoning. The trial court excluded, on hearsay grounds, a diary in which L'Angelier recorded that he visited with Smith just before he took ill; as a result, no evidence was presented that the two had any contact in the critical period. The jury returned a verdict of "not proven." See id at 32, 35.

[48] See text accompanying notes 141–43.

[49] Cal Evid Code § 1370(a).

[50] Id.

[S]he had been talking to a female friend on the telephone when appellant became angry and accused her of having an affair with that friend. Avie ended the call and began to argue with appellant, who grabbed her by the shirt, lifted her off the floor, and began to choke her with his hand. She broke free and fell to the floor, but appellant climbed on top of her and punched her in the face and head. After Avie broke free again, appellant opened a folding knife, held it about three feet away from her, and said, "If I catch you fucking around I'll kill you."[51]

The trial court ruled this testimony admissible under the hearsay exception California had crafted for injury reports,[52] but the Supreme Court, applying *Crawford*, threw out Giles's conviction. Since Giles never had an opportunity to cross-examine Avie, her hearsay statements could not be used against him.[53]

Another example: A Wisconsin jury convicted Mark Jensen in 2008 of murdering his wife, Julie, by poisoning her.[54] Jensen claimed Julie had killed herself. The evidence to the contrary included a letter she had given to a neighbor, setting forth her fears that her husband would kill her and insisting that she would never commit suicide. The Wisconsin courts admitted the letter, reasoning that if a defendant is responsible for the unavailability of a witness, he forfeits any right to object to the admissibility of the witness's out-of-court statements.[55] But the Supreme Court's subsequent decision in *Giles v California* throws that reasoning—and Jensen's conviction—into great doubt.[56]

The traditional justification for the hearsay rule is that out-of-court statements are so unreliable that the system is better off without them, even when it is impossible to hear directly from the declarant, and even when the declarant actually testifies in court and can be questioned about the earlier statements. As the canonical

---

[51] *People v Giles*, 2009 WL 457832, at *2 (Cal Super, Feb 25, 2009).

[52] See id.

[53] *Giles v California*, 128 S Ct 2678 (2008). The Court reasoned that the Confrontation Clause would allow the introduction of Avie's statements against Giles only if the trial court determined that Giles had killed Avie *in order to prevent her from testifying* and remanded to allow the California courts to address that question. See id at 2693; notes 219–23 and accompanying text.

[54] See Tom Kertscher, *Jensen Guilty of Homicide*, Milwaukee J Sentinel (Feb 22, 2008), at A1.

[55] *State v Jensen*, 727 NW2d 518, 521 (Wisc 2007).

[56] See Tom Kertscher, *Poison Case May Be Retried*, Milwaukee J Sentinel (June 26, 2008), at B1.

story has it, out-of-court statements pose four risks of unreliability: a *narration* risk (i.e., the risk that the declarant did not mean what he or she seemed to say); a *sincerity* risk (the risk that the declarant intentionally fabricated); a *memory* risk (the risk that the declarant misrecalled what happened); and a *perception* risk (the risk that the declarant misperceived things to begin with). Those risks are present when someone testifies in court, too—when a mere "declarant" becomes a "witness." But then the risks are subject to three safeguards: the oath the witness takes to tell the truth, the jury's ability to watch the witness's demeanor, and the opportunity for cross-examination.[57] The last of these three safeguards has long been thought especially important; Wigmore, expressing what has become the conventional view, labeled cross-examination "beyond any doubt the greatest legal engine ever invented for the discovery of truth."[58] This account has been invoked to justify not just the hearsay rule itself but also its exceptions, each of which has at some point been defended on the ground that the statements to which it applies present reduced risks of unreliability; or are subject to procedural safeguards that seem to be reasonable substitutes for the oath, demeanor evidence, and cross-examination; or ought in fairness to be admitted without regard to their reliability.[59]

A large, venerable, and steadily expanding body of commentary assesses, often quite negatively, the explanations that have been offered for various exceptions.[60] It is hard to read this literature without sensing that justifications for the hearsay exceptions have had to clear a remarkably low bar—reflecting, no doubt, mixed feelings about the hearsay ban itself. The mixed feelings are easy to understand, because the traditional story about the risks of hearsay evidence is so weak. The problem with the traditional story is not that it is implausible. To be sure, the oath is no longer thought

---

[57] For the canonical account, see, for example, Kenneth S. Broun et al, *McCormick on Evidence* § 245 at 125 (West, 6th ed 2006); Edmund Morris Morgan, *Some Problems of Proof Under the Anglo-American System of Litigation* 119–27 (Columbia, 1956); Wright and Graham, 30 *Federal Practice and Procedure* §§ 1623–27 (cited in note 26).

[58] Wigmore, 2 *Treatise on the System of Evidence* § 1367, at 1697 (cited in note 34).

[59] See, for example, Laurence H. Tribe, *Triangulating Hearsay*, 87 Harv L Rev 957, 961–69 (1974).

[60] For entertaining examples, see Robert M. Hutchins and Donald Slesinger, *Some Observations on the Law of Evidence*, 28 Colum L Rev 432, 437–39 (1928) (ridiculing the arguments for the "excited utterance" exception to the hearsay rule), and Joseph H. Levie, *Hearsay and Conspiracy*, 52 Mich L Rev 1159, 1161–66 (1954) (same for the "co-conspirator admissions" exception).

to provide much protection against perjury,[61] and some experiments suggest that demeanor evidence may mislead juries more often than it assists them.[62] Cross-examination has always had its skeptics, too; if the technique can expose the mendacious, it can also confound the honest[63] and prove clumsy against the mistaken.[64] Still, there generally is good reason to prefer live, sworn testimony, tested by cross-examination, to secondhand accounts of a witness's earlier statements. The problem is that the hearsay rule creates more than a preference. It excludes the secondhand accounts even when bringing the witness to court is impossible, and even when the secondhand accounts would supplement rather than substitute for in-court testimony.

That is to say, the problem with the traditional justification for the hearsay rule is that it gives no reason to exclude secondhand accounts when firsthand accounts are unavailable or are also being provided. Assume that hearsay can be unreliable in precisely the ways that the canonical story suggests. Judges and juries then have reason to take secondhand accounts with a grain of salt. But why deny them the evidence altogether? A wide range of evidence is routinely introduced despite the well-known dangers that it could be misleading: think about eyewitness identifications, for example, or the testimony of cooperating codefendants. The general approach of evidence law is to allow the introduction of evidence even when its probative value is only marginal, allowing the judge or the jury to give it whatever weight it deserves. Usually evidence is excluded only when its probative value is "substantially outweighed" by the danger that it will bog down the proceedings, lead the factfinders astray, or have some other bad consequence.[65] Granting that

---

[61] See, for example, John L. Watts, *To Tell the Truth: A Qui Tam Action for Perjury in Civil Proceedings Is Necessary to Protect the Integrity of the Civil Judicial System*, 79 Temple L Rev 773, 774–75 (2006).

[62] See Jeremy A. Blumenthal, *A Wipe of the Hands, a Lick of the Lips: The Validity of Demeanor Evidence in Assessing Witness Credibility*, 72 Neb L Rev 1157, 1190–94 (1993); Max Minzner, *Detecting Lies Using Demeanor, Bias, and Context*, 29 Cardozo L Rev 2557, 2559–66 (2008); Olin Guy Wellborn III, *Demeanor*, 76 Cornell L Rev 1075 (1991).

[63] See, for example, John H. Langbein, *The Origins of Adversary Criminal Trial* 246–47 (Oxford, 2003). Even Wigmore, who extolled cross-examination as "the most efficacious expedient ever invented for the extraction of truth," acknowledged parenthetically that "it is almost equally powerful for the creation of false impressions." Wigmore, 1 *Treatise on the System of Evidence* § 8 at 25 (cited in note 34).

[64] Jules Epstein, *Cross-Examination: Seemingly Ubiquitous, Purportedly Omnipotent, and "At Risk,"* 14 Widener L Rev 429, 440–41 (2009).

[65] See, for example, FRE 401–03.

hearsay can be unreliable, what reason is there to think the jury is better off without it?

One possibility is that juries are likely to give hearsay more weight than it deserves. Perhaps juries understand the dangers associated with eyewitness identifications or accomplice testimony but are apt to overlook the reasons to be skeptical of secondhand information. Perhaps, but there is little reason to think so. In fact, the best available evidence is to the contrary: mock juries do not seem to overvalue hearsay.[66] It is striking, too, that none of the hundreds of prisoners exonerated over the past few decades by DNA evidence appear to owe their wrongful convictions to hearsay evidence. Often the problem was faulty eyewitness identifications; in other cases there were false confessions; sometimes there was sloppy or fraudulent lab work.[67] But it is difficult to find even a single case in which hearsay evidence has been blamed for the conviction of a defendant later exonerated by DNA evidence—and that despite the well-known proliferation of exceptions to the hearsay ban in the decades leading up to *Crawford*.[68]

Another possibility is that excluding hearsay, even when the out-of-court declarant is unavailable to testify in court, is the best way, in the long run, to produce more reliable evidence: if not in-court testimony, then at least some more reliable or better documented form of hearsay, which can be made admissible under an exception to the hearsay rule.[69] But no one has ever explained why those purposes require excluding hearsay when the party offering it has

---

[66] See Friedman, *Confrontation Right Across the Systemic Divide* at 264 (cited in note 6); Peter Miene, Roger C. Park, and Eugene Borgida, *Juror Decision Making and the Evaluation of Hearsay Evidence*, 76 Minn L Rev 683 (1992); Richard F. Rakos and Stephan Landsman, *Researching the Hearsay Rule: Emerging Findings, General Issues, and Future Directions*, 76 Minn L Rev 655, 664 (1992); Roger C. Park, *Visions of Applying the Scientific Method to the Hearsay Rule*, 2003 Mich St L Rev 1149; consider Margaret Bull Kovera, Roger C. Park, and Stephen D. Penrod, *Jurors' Perceptions of Eyewitness and Hearsay Evidence*, 76 Minn L Rev 703, 703 (1992) (reporting that "mock jurors are more skeptical of hearsay testimony than eyewitness testimony").

[67] See, for example, Edward Connors et al, *Convicted by Juries, Exonerated by Science: Case Studies in the Use of DNA Evidence to Establish Innocence After Trial* 15–20 (Natl Inst J, 1996); Brandon L. Garrett, *Judging Innocence*, 108 Colum L Rev 55, 122 (2008); Samuel R. Gross et al, *Exonerations in the United States 1989 Through 2003*, 95 J Crim L & Criminol 523 (2005).

[68] A false confession introduced against the defendant who made it qualifies, technically, as hearsay, but the hearsay rule will never keep it out; it falls squarely within the "admissions exception." See, for example, FRE 801(d)(2); text accompanying note 41.

[69] See, for example, Damaška, 76 Minn L Rev at 458 (cited in note 9).

done everything we could want them to do.[70] My colleague Eleanor Swift, for example, suggests the justification for the hearsay rule is that it forces a party to prove the facts necessary to trigger one of the rule's exceptions[71]—say, that the statement in question is a regularly maintained business record, made under circumstances conducive to accuracy.[72] But those purposes could be served just as well if the hearsay ban were replaced with a requirement that contextual evidence of this sort accompany out-of-court statements offered into evidence. Professor Swift has in fact argued for just such a rule.[73]

Even Wigmore ultimately concluded that the hearsay rule, as a rule of exclusion, should give way to a simple rule of a preference. The "spirit of the rule," he thought, was "to insist on testing all statements by cross-examination, *if they can be*"; accordingly, "if the person has passed beyond the power of the law to procure him, the test may be dispensed with."[74] Wigmore thought any stricter application of the hearsay rule was senseless:

> No one could defend a rule which pronounced that all statements thus untested [by cross-examination] are *worthless*; for all historical truth is based on un-cross-examined assertions; and every day's experience of life gives denial to such an exaggeration. What the Hearsay rule implies—and with profound verity—is that all testimonial assertions *ought to be* tested by cross-examination, as the best attainable measure; and it should not be burdened with the pedantic implication that they must be rejected as worthless if the test is unavailable.[75]

---

[70] A rigid hearsay rule, despite its over- and underinclusiveness, might plausibly produce better results than letting all-too-human judges decide case by case whether excluding an out-of-court statement will produce more benefits than costs. See Schauer, 155 U Pa L Rev at 195–97 (cited in note 2). But that is an argument for having a rule, not for having a rule that operates even when witnesses are unavailable and even when they actually testify.

[71] See Eleanor Swift, *Abolishing the Hearsay Rule*, 75 Cal L Rev 495 (1987).

[72] See FRE 803(6).

[73] See Swift, 75 Cal L Rev (cited in note 1).

[74] John Henry Wigmore, *A Supplement to a Treatise on the System of Evidence in Trials at Common Law* xxix (Little Brown, 2d ed 1915).

[75] Id. Nonetheless, Wigmore continued to classify hearsay as an "analytic" rule rather than a "preferential," "prophylactic," "simplificative," or "synthetic" rule. John Henry Wigmore, 1 *Treatise on the Anglo-American System of Evidence in Trials at Common Law* xliii, lxxxv (Little Brown, 2d ed 1923). By an "analytic rule," Wigmore meant a rule that subjects evidence "to a scrutiny or analysis calculated to discover and expose in detail its possible weaknesses, and thus to enable the tribunal to estimate it at no more than its actual value." Id 2 § 1360 at 1. Wigmore thought hearsay was the only rule of this kind, and the "scrutiny

The American Law Institute took the same view of hearsay when it promulgated its Model Code of Evidence in 1942. Drafted by the evidence scholar Edmund Morgan, the Model Code declared hearsay admissible whenever the declarant either was "unavailable as a witness" or was "present and subject to cross-examination."[76] But the ALI itself conceded the "radical" nature of this proposal,[77] and "professional reception . . . varied between chilliness and heated antagonism."[78] The hearsay provisions of the Model Code of Evidence helped ensure that it was never adopted anywhere.[79] Reformers took note.[80] Later efforts to codify evidence law, culminating in the 1975 adoption of the Federal Rules of Evidence, kept hearsay as a categorical rule of exclusion and not just a rule of preference, albeit a categorical rule riddled with a labyrinthine series of exceptions.[81]

Wigmore's view—that hearsay should be a rule of preference, not a rigid rule of exclusion—has continued to attract scholarly support. Often this support takes the form of an explicit appeal to the "best evidence rule," once said to be the organizing principle of Anglo-American evidence law.[82] Eighteenth- and nineteenth-century treatises commonly identified, as the first and most important canon of evidence law, the requirement that litigants put forward the best evidence available on any contested issue.[83] There seems little doubt that this principle was "at the very least one of the basic

---

or analysis" he had in mind consisted of "Cross-examination and Confrontation." Id. Cross-examination, he thought, was "the essential and indispensable feature"; confrontation was "subordinate and disposable." Id § 1362 at 3.

[76] American Law Institute, Model Code of Evidence Rule 503 (1942).

[77] Id, Rule 503 comment a.

[78] John MacArthur Maguire, *Evidence: Common Sense and Common Law* 153 (Foundation, 1947).

[79] See, for example, James H. Chadbourn, *Bentham and the Hearsay Rule—A Benthamic View of Rule 63(4)(C) of the Uniform Rules of Evidence*, 75 Harv L Rev 932, 945 (1962).

[80] See, for example, Wright and Graham, 30 *Federal Practice and Procedure* § 6336 at 126–27 (cited in note 26); John H. Maguire, *The Hearsay System: Around and Through the Thicket*, 14 Vand L Rev 741, 741 (1961).

[81] See, for example, Michael Ariens, *A Short History of Hearsay Reform, with Particular Reference to Hoffman v. Palmer, Eddie Morgan and Jerry Frank*, 28 Ind L Rev 183, 223–25 (1995).

[82] See, for example, George F. James, *The Role of Hearsay in a Rational System of Evidence*, 34 Ill L Rev 788, 797–98 (1940); Dale A. Nance, *The Best Evidence Principle*, 73 Iowa L Rev 227 (1988); Siegel, 72 BU L Rev 893 (cited in note 1).

[83] See, for example, John H. Langbein, *Historical Foundations of the Law of Evidence: A View from the Ryder Sources*, 96 Colum L Rev 1168, 1173 (1996); Nance, 73 Iowa L Rev at 248 (cited in note 82) (citing sources).

elements in the early development of the rule of hearsay exclusion."[84] By the early twentieth century, though, the influential evidence scholar James Bradley Thayer—Wigmore's teacher—had rejected the best evidence rule as a true principle of Anglo-American evidence law; instead, he argued, relevant evidence is and should be admissible, regardless of its strength, unless a specific rule of evidence calls for its exclusion.[85] Thayer's view won out, and today the best evidence rule survives only as a narrow requirement that a party seeking to prove the content of a document must, in certain circumstances, produce the original.[86]

Even before Thayer, moreover, the hearsay rule was commonly described, including by champions of the best evidence rule, as a flat prohibition rather than simply a rule of preference. For example, Simon Greenleaf—the leading American evidence scholar of the nineteenth century, and the author Thayer identified most closely with the best evidence rule—associated the hearsay prohibition with the recognition that "every living witness should, if possible, be subjected to the ordeal of a cross-examination."[87] But he took pains to make clear that exclusion of hearsay was not premised solely on the fact that "this species of testimony supposes something better, which might be adduced in the particular case"; on the contrary, "its intrinsic weakness, its incompetency to satisfy the mind as to the existence of the fact, and the frauds, which may be practised under its cover, combine to support the rule, that hearsay evidence is totally inadmissible."[88]

Greenleaf was quoting here, and the source—Chief Justice Mar-

---

[84] James, 34 Ill L Rev at 796 (cited in note 82).

[85] James Bradley Thayer, *A Preliminary Treatise on Evidence at the Common Law* 264–66, 484–507 (Little Brown, 1898). Regarding Thayer's influence, see Nance, 73 Iowa L Rev at 248 (cited in note 82); David A. Sklansky, *Proposition 187 and the Ghost of James Bradley Thayer*, 17 Chicano-Latino L Rev 24, 24–25 (1995).

[86] See, for example, FRE 1001–1002; *United States v Gonzales-Benitez*, 537 F2d 1051 (9th Cir 1976). But see Nance, 73 Iowa L Rev at 227 (cited in note 82) (arguing, "against the tide," that "there exists, even today, a principle of evidence law that a party should present to the tribunal the best evidence reasonably available on a litigated factual issue").

[87] Simon Greenleaf, 1 *A Treatise on the Law of Evidence* § 98 (Little Brown, 1842). Thayer, too, thought the basic problem with hearsay was that "something which should come through an original witness is sought to be put in at second hand," effectively "nullify[ing] the requirement that witnesses should personally appear and testify publicly in court." Thayer, *Preliminary Treatise on Evidence* at 501 (cited in note 85).

[88] Greenleaf, 1 *Treatise on the Law of Evidence* § 99 (cited in note 87).

shall's opinion for the Supreme Court in *Queen v Hepburn*,[89] probably the most widely cited American hearsay case of the early nineteenth century—warrants a brief digression. Mima Queen was a slave suing to emancipate herself and her child on the ground that her ancestor, Mary Queen, was brought to the United States as a free woman. Mary and those who knew her history firsthand were no longer alive, so Mima supported her claim with deposition testimony recounting what Mary and others who knew her had said.[90] The federal trial court excluded the depositions as hearsay, and in 1813 the Supreme Court affirmed.[91]

The ruling in *Queen v Hepburn* struck Justice Gabriel Duvall as so senseless and so unjust that he issued the only significant dissent of his twenty-four years on the Supreme Court.[92] Duvall was from Maryland, and he wrote that Maryland law—under which Queen's petition was tried—recognized a hearsay exception for cases where a slave claimed that a long-dead ancestor had been free. Excluding hearsay in such cases, Duvall stressed, would effectively make them impossible to pursue. Hearsay was admissible here for the same reason it was admissible, under well-recognized exceptions, to prove ancestry or land boundaries: "because from the antiquity of the transactions to which these subjects may have reference, it is impossible to produce living testimony."[93] But the Court saw the equities differently. Chief Justice Marshall reasoned that the death of the speaker could not justify the admission of hearsay; otherwise "no man could feel safe in any property, a claim to which might be supported by proof so easily obtained."[94]

Queen v Hepburn seems to have had precisely the impact Justice Duvall warned it would have, closing the door to emancipation

---

[89] 11 US (7 Cranch) 290 (1813). For brief discussions of the case, see Wright and Graham, 30 *Federal Practice and Procedure* § 6321 at 18 (cited in note 26); Robert M. Cover, *For James Wm. Moore: Some Reflections on a Reading of the Rules*, 84 Yale L J 718, 725–26 (1975); Jason M. Gillmer, *Suing for Freedom: Interracial Sex, Slave Law, and Racial Identity in the Post-Revolutionary and Antebellum South*, 82 NC L Rev 535, 584–85 (2004); Donald M. Roper, *In Quest of Judicial Objectivity: The Marshall Court and the Legitimation of Slavery*, 21 Stan L Rev 532, 533 (1969).

[90] 11 US at 293–95.

[91] Id at 293, 296.

[92] See William L. Reynolds, *Maryland and the Constitution of the United States: An Introductory Essay*, 66 Md L Rev 923, 931–32 (2007); Norman R. Williams, *Gibbons*, 79 NYU L Rev 1398, 1425 n 148 (2004).

[93] 11 US at 297 (Duvall, J, dissenting).

[94] Id at 296 (opinion of the Court).

petitions like Mima Queen's.[95] It also came to stand, authoritatively, for the view that hearsay was such "intrinsically weak" evidence that it was banned even when the speaker could not come to court and testify.[96] As Thayer explained, "[n]either the original speaker's death, alone, nor the highly probative character of the circumstances under which he spoke, alone, are enough" to make hearsay admissible—"and not the two together except in special cases."[97] As we have seen, even Simon Greenleaf, the great American champion of the best evidence principle, accepted this view of hearsay, largely on the authority of *Queen v Hepburn*. This remains the accepted view; indeed, it was largely the departure from this orthodoxy that doomed the Model Code of Evidence. And it is largely the adherence to this orthodoxy that makes the hearsay rule today so hard to defend, and so weakly defended.

B. HISTORY OF THE RULE

What can explain the development and persistence of a rule so famously difficult to defend? It is hard to read *Queen v Hepburn*, with its nearly obscene solicitude for the repose of "property" owners, and not suspect that class interests may be part of the story. One of the things that case underscores is that the hearsay ban handicaps litigants who are unable to track down live witnesses and bring them to court—and all things being equal, poor litigants are more likely than rich litigants to suffer that disability. Moreover, the established exceptions to the hearsay rule may themselves reflect class bias. *Queen v Hepburn*, for example, refused to recognize a hearsay exception for statements regarding the free status of someone long dead, but it did nothing to throw into doubt the established hearsay exception for statements regarding land boundaries. Under the "business records" exception to the hearsay rule, commercial enterprises can introduce their records, rather than suffer the inconvenience of calling a series of their present and former employees into court, because—as Wigmore explained—such records are relied upon "in the most important

---

[95] See *Davis v Wood*, 14 US (1 Wheat) 6 (1816); Gillmer, 82 NC L Rev at 585–86 (cited in note 89).

[96] See, for example, Morgan, *Some Problems of Proof* at 111–12 (cited in note 57). The case is still cited for this proposition. See, for example, *United States v Florex*, 985 F2d 770, 778 (5th Cir 1993); *United States v Gomez-Lemos*, 939 F2d 326, 333 n 2 (6th Cir 1991); *Valmain v State*, 2009 WL 863471, *7 (Miss 2009) (Kitchens dissenting); *Garza v Delta Tau Delta Fraternity National*, 948 So2d 84, 91 (La 2006).

[97] Thayer, *Preliminary Treatise on Evidence* at 501 (cited in note 85).

undertakings of mercantile and industrial life"; they are "expedi-
ents which the entire commercial world recognizes as safe."[98]
There is no parallel exception, it goes without saying, for records
or statements routinely relied upon by laborers, the unemployed,
or the illiterate.

Once you start looking, it is easy to find other signs of class
bias in the development of hearsay law. *Wright v Tatham*[99]—the
English case in which "the scope of the hearsay rule reached its
high water mark"[100]—threw out a will leaving a large country estate
to the testator's servant; the evidence excluded as hearsay would
have rebutted the suggestions of mental incompetence successfully
advanced by the testator's well-born cousin.[101] The Supreme
Court's famous decision in *Mutual Life Insurance Co. v Hillmon*[102]
pushed back the other way, crafting a novel exception to the hearsay rule and, not coincidentally, helping to protect insurance companies against claims they suspected were fraudulent.[103]

In these ways and in others, the interests of the wealthy may
well have influenced the development of hearsay law. It would be
surprising if they had not. But class interests of this kind cannot
be the whole story, or even most of the story. They do not explain,

---

[98] Wigmore, 2 *Treatise on the System of Evidence* § 1530 at 1895–96 (cited in note 34);
see also, for example, Wright and Graham, 30 *Federal Practice and Procedure* § 6321 at 15
(cited in note 26) (observing that "[t]he role of business interests in the development of
the business-records exception is well-known").

[99] 7 Adolph & E 313, 112 Eng Rep 488 (Ex Ch 1837), and 5 Cl & Fin 670, 47 Rev
Rep 136 (HL 1838).

[100] Friedman, *Confrontation Right Across the Systemic Divide* at 263 (cited in note 6).

[101] The best account of the case remains Maguire, 14 Vand L Rev at 749–60 (cited in
80). The disputed evidence consisted of letters sent to the testator and addressing him in
a manner that suggested that the letter writers thought he was mentally competent. One
letter, for example, discussed the settlement of a legal dispute with the testator. The English
courts treated the letters as "implied assertions" of the testator's competence and reasoned
that the hearsay rule should apply to implied assertions as well as explicit assertions. The
weight of authority is now to the contrary, on both sides of the Atlantic: the hearsay rule
is generally restricted to statements (verbal or otherwise) that are offered into evidence
to prove the facts they were intended to communicate. See, for example, FRE 801(a), (c)
& Advisory Committee Note; Criminal Justice Act, 2003, c 44, § 115(3) (UK); *United
States v Zenni*, 492 F Supp 464 (ED Ky 1980). But consider, for example, *State v Dullard*,
668 NW2d 585, 595 (Iowa 2003) (noting and adopting minority position that "uninten-
tional assertions in speech" should be treated as hearsay).

[102] 145 US 285 (1892).

[103] See Brooks W. MacCracken, *The Case of the Anonymous Corpse*, Am Heritage (June
1968), at 51; John MacArthur Maguire, *The Hillmon Case—Thirty-Three Years After*, 38
Harv L Rev 709 (1925). For an extended, fascinating argument that the insurance com-
panies, rather than the claimant, may have been guilty of fraud, see Marianne Wesson,
The Hillmon Case, the Supreme Court, and the McGuffin, in Richard Lempert, ed, *Evidence
Stories* 277 (Foundation, 2006).

for example, why the hearsay rule gained hold at a particular time—nor why simpler and more reliable ways for protecting wealth and power did not develop, instead. Any complicated and obscure area of legal doctrine is likely to favor the wealthy more than the poor, simply because the continuous battle over the contours of legal doctrine favors those with better access to lawyers and more in common with judges and legislators. But why a ban on *hearsay*? Recent work in legal history places the credit—or blame—not with a socioeconomic class, but with a particular professional class: lawyers.

To be sure, this was no part of Wigmore's explanation. Wigmore traced the origins of the modern hearsay rule in England to the seventeenth and early eighteenth centuries.[104] He thought the hearsay rule arose as a slow but natural response to the shift away from self-informing juries in the 1500s and early 1600s: once witnesses began to testify in court, the system began to recognize the great value of cross-examination and to distrust statements not subject to that check.[105] As we have seen, Wigmore came to view the hearsay rule as essentially a rule of preference: whenever possible, witnesses should be brought to court and cross-examined.[106] He recognized, however, that the hearsay rule had expanded to ban out-of-court statements even by declarants who were now dead or otherwise unavailable,[107] and to ban the earlier statements of witnesses who actually come to court and testify.[108] These struck him as "pedantic" results in tension with "the great spirit of the rule."[109] What had happened, he thought, was that the hearsay rule had been "overworshipped and overworked."[110]

---

[104] See John Henry Wigmore, *The History of the Hearsay Rule*, 17 Harv L Rev 437, 445, 448 (1904). Wigmore incorporated this article into his treatise, the first edition of which appeared two years later. See Wigmore, 2 *Treatise on the System of Evidence* § 1364 (cited in note 34).

[105] See Wigmore, 17 Harv L Rev at 443, 451–52, 454–58 (cited in note 104). Wigmore thus located the origins of the hearsay rule about a century before the emergence of modern evidence law as a "consciously and fully realized" system of rules; that happened, he thought, between 1790 and 1830. See Wigmore, 1 *Treatise on the System of Evidence* § 8 at 26–27 (cited in note 34).

[106] See notes 74–75 and accompanying text.

[107] See, for example, Wigmore, 17 Harv L Rev at 452–53 (cited in note 104).

[108] Wigmore, *Supplement* at xxviii–xxix (cited in note 74).

[109] Id at xxix.

[110] Id at xxviii. Wigmore is often said to have attributed the rise of the hearsay rule to distrust of lay juries. See, for example, Gallanis, 84 Iowa L Rev at 501 (cited in note 25); Frederick W. J. Koch, *The Hearsay Rule's True Raison D'Etre: Its Implications for the New Principled Approach to Admitting Hearsay Evidence*, 37 Ottawa L Rev 249, 252 (2005–06). It is true that Wigmore's teacher, James Bradley Thayer, saw the jury as "the occasion of

Wigmore did see a connection between the rise of the hearsay rule and the growing role of lawyers in criminal trials, but he thought the rule influenced the role, not vice versa. Once the hearsay rule firmly established the importance of cross-examination, Wigmore explained, pressure grew to allow defense attorneys to question prosecution witnesses in all felony trials—a practice that, before the middle of the eighteenth century, was permitted only in treason trials.[111] As the practice spread, it spurred rapid developments in "the art of interrogation," as well as in certain procedural rules.[112] The increased use of cross-examination pushed aside, for example, "the old fixed tradition that a criminal trial must be finished in one sitting," and it spurred changes to "the various rules of evidence naturally most applicable on cross-examinations—particularly, the impeachment of witnesses."[113] It did not occur to Wigmore that the expanding role of trial lawyers might have contributed to the growth of the hearsay rule. The story of the hearsay rule, he thought, was the story of a rule that arose naturally, as a logical reaction to the demise of the self-informing jury, but then was unthinkingly taken a little too far.

More recent historical work casts doubt on Wigmore's account. An emerging consensus dates the hearsay rule—as a genuine rule, honored more in the observance than in the breach—to the late eighteenth century and early nineteenth century.[114] There are earlier cases invoking the rule; that is what misled Wigmore. But through the mid-1700s, the "rule" was flagrantly flouted, typically

---

our law of evidence"; the whole point of the rules, he thought, was to prevent jurors "from being confused and misled." Thayer, *Preliminary Treatise on Evidence* at 2, 3 (cited in note 85). It is true, as well, that Wigmore acknowledged his debt to Thayer's treatment of evidence law as "directly appurtenant to jury trial." Wigmore, 1 *Treatise on the System of Evidence* at xii (cited in note 34). But Wigmore in fact placed much less emphasis than Thayer on the need to protect jurors from misleading evidence and, in particular, did not stress that theme when reviewing the history of the hearsay rule. For that matter, even Thayer's treatment of the history of the hearsay rule downplayed concerns about jurors' gullibility, instead highlighting "the necessity of discriminating the office of a witness from that of a juror." Thayer, *Preliminary Treatise on Evidence* at 500 (cited in note 85). The central impetus for the rule's development, Thayer explained, was that "repeating hearsay was not regarded as legitimate testifying." Id at 499.

[111] See Wigmore, 17 Harv L Rev at 45 (cited in note 104).

[112] Id at 457–58.

[113] Id.

[114] See Langbein, *Origins of Adversary Criminal Trial* at 234, 238–42 (cited in note 63); Friedman, *Confrontation Right Across the Systemic Divide* at 263 (cited in note 6); Gallanis, 84 Iowa L Rev at 512–15, 535–36 (cited in note 25).

without discussion.[115] Moreover, until the late 1700s, even judges who disparaged out-of-court statements as "no evidence" appear to have generally allowed it when the declarants were unavailable to testify, or when the declarants actually did testify and their prior statements were introduced as "corroboration."[116] Beginning in the 1780s, though, the hearsay rule grew more prominent: lawyers invoked it more often, judges applied it more strictly, and treatises discussed it more extensively.[117] By the end of the eighteenth century, "the contours of the modern rule against hearsay were largely in place."[118]

T. P. Gallanis suggests that the hearsay rule took root in the 1780s because of the increasing prevalence of defense counsel in criminal cases. Old Bailey judges began allowing defense lawyers to participate in felony trials in the 1730s,[119] but relatively few defendants employed trial counsel until the 1780s, when the practice began to expand.[120] Until the early nineteenth century, defense lawyers in criminal cases were not allowed to address the jury; their role was largely restricted to questioning of prosecution witnesses.[121] So defense counsel focused their energies on cross-examination—and, Gallanis suggests, on evidentiary objections, and more particularly on objections to forms of evidence that denied them the opportunity for cross-examination.[122] Gallanis argues that aggressive cross-examination and aggressive invocation of the hearsay rule emerged hand-in-hand in criminal cases in the 1780s and then migrated to civil cases. The chief vectors, he proposes, were lawyers who appeared both in civil and in criminal cases: "[a]s lawyers began working more and more in criminal trials it

---

[115] See Langbein, *Origins of Adversary Criminal Trial* at 239–40 (cited in note 63); Gallanis, 84 Iowa L Rev at 501 n 11, 512, 536 (cited in note 25). Langbein and Gallanis focus on English trials, but the same laxity was found on this side of the Atlantic. See, for example, Goebel and Naughton, *Law Enforcement in Colonial New York* 642–43 (cited in note 25).

[116] See Langbein, *Origins of Adversary Criminal Trial* at 238–39 (cited in note 63); Goebel and Naughton, *Law Enforcement in Colonial New York* 651–52 (cited in note 25).

[117] See Gallanis, 84 Iowa L Rev at 536 (cited in note 25).

[118] Id at 535; see also Langbein, *Origins of Adversary Criminal Trial* at 242 (cited in note 63).

[119] See Langbein, *Origins of Adversary Criminal Trial* at 167–77 (cited in note 63).

[120] See Gallanis, 84 Iowa L Rev at 544 (cited in note 25), citing John M. Beattie, *Scales of Justice*, 9 Law & Hist Rev 221, 227 (1991).

[121] See Langbein, *Origins of Adversary Criminal Trial* at 171, 296–318 (cited in note 63).

[122] See Gallanis, 84 Iowa L Rev at 545–46 (cited in note 25).

is natural that the skills and techniques needed for success in that arena would, over time, be deployed on the civil battlefield as well."[123] As Gallanis acknowledges, the evidence for his account is suggestive rather than conclusive.[124] But no serious challenge has emerged to his narrative, and there appears to be an emerging scholarly consensus that the hearsay rule, in its modern form, took root in the late 1700s, and that this development owed much to the "lawyerization" of criminal trials during the same period.

In the early 1800s, the hearsay ban stiffened and grew more firmly entrenched.[125] By 1813, as we have seen, the Supreme Court thought it obvious that the "intrinsic weakness" of hearsay warranted its exclusion even when the declarant was no longer alive.[126] *Wright v Tatham*,[127] the hearsay ban's "high water mark,"[128] reached the House of Lords in 1838. As the rule rigidified, exceptions proliferated—but not without limits, as Mima Queen discovered. By the late nineteenth century, hearsay doctrine had assumed its modern appearance: a strict rule of evidentiary exclusion, accompanied by a long and confusing set of exceptions. American judges and lawyers grew accustomed to the rule, and proposals for radical reform—for example, turning the hearsay ban into a rule of preference, applicable only when live testimony could be substituted—were rebuffed.[129] Throughout the twentieth century, though, the overall course of hearsay doctrine was toward liberalization, chiefly through the steady expansion of the exceptions to the hearsay ban.[130]

Outside the United States, the liberalization went further, and it picked up pace in the last decade of the twentieth century and the first decade of the twenty-first.[131] By statute, England made firsthand hearsay admissible in civil trials in 1968,[132] abolished the

---

[123] See id at 549–50.

[124] See id at 550.

[125] See id at 535.

[126] See *Queen v Hepburn*, 11 US (7 Cranch) 290 (1813); text accompanying notes 89–97.

[127] 7 Adolph & E 313, 112 Eng Rep 488 (Ex Ch 1837), and 5 Cl & Fin 670, 47 Rev Rep 136 (HL 1838); see notes 99–101 and accompanying text.

[128] Friedman, *Confrontation Right Across the Systemic Divide* at 263 (cited in note 6).

[129] See text accompanying notes 74–81.

[130] See Allen, 76 Minn L Rev at 797 (cited in note 3).

[131] See id at 811–12.

[132] Civil Evidence Act, 1968, c 64, § 2 (UK).

rule entirely for civil cases in 1997,[133] and in 2003 created a broad exception in criminal cases for firsthand hearsay from declarants unavailable to testify at trial.[134] This last exception was borrowed from Scotland, where it had been in place since 1995.[135] Like England, Scotland had earlier abolished the hearsay rule in civil cases.[136] Meanwhile the Supreme Court of Canada, in a series of decisions over the past two decades, declared hearsay admissible whenever it is "reliable" and "necessary," and made clear that hearsay is "necessary" when the declarant is now dead or otherwise unavailable.[137] Legislation in Australia in the 1990s created a series of sweeping exceptions to the ban on firsthand hearsay, including one that applies across the board in civil cases, and another that applies in criminal cases to any statement "made in circumstances that make it likely [to be] reliable."[138] New Zealand followed suit in 2006, statutorily exempting from the hearsay rule all prior statements by testifying witnesses, and any statement by an unavailable witness, so long as "the circumstances relating the statement provide reasonable assurance that the statement is reliable."[139] The story has been similar in other common-law jurisdictions.[140]

Much of the impetus for these reforms came from heightened concern, over the past several decades, with criminal victimization of women and children, especially in cases of domestic violence, child abuse, and sexual molestation. There was a widespread sense

---

[133] Civil Evidence Act, 1995, c 38, § 1 (UK).

[134] Criminal Justice Act, 2003, c 44, § 116 (UK).

[135] Criminal Justice (Scotland) Act, 1995, c 20, § 17 (UK).

[136] Civil Evidence (Scotland) Act, 1988, c 32, § 2(1) (UK); see David Field and Fiona Raitt, *Evidence* 180 (Green, 2d ed 1996).

[137] See, for example, Bruce Archibald, *The Canadian Hearsay Revolution: Is Half a Loaf Better Than No Loaf at All?* 25 Queen's L J 1 (1999); Hamish Stewart, *Khelawon: The Principled Approach to Hearsay Revisited*, 12 Can Crim L Rev 95, 96–97 (2007).

[138] Commonwealth Evidence Act, 1995, §§ 63, 65 (Australia). The Act applies only in federal and territorial courts, but similar reforms were enacted by some state legislatures. See Marian K. Brown, *Reform and Proposed Reform of Hearsay Law in Australia, New Zealand, Hong Kong, and Canada, with Special Regard to Prior Inconsistent Statements* at 8 (unpublished paper presented at 2007 Annual Conference of the International Society for the Reform of Criminal Law), online at http://www.isrcl.org/Papers/2007/Brown.pdf.

[139] Evidence Act, 2006, § 18 (NZ). The legislation followed a series of liberalizing decisions by the New Zealand Court of Appeal. See Elizabeth McDonald, *Going "Straight to Basics": The Role of Lord Cooke in Reforming the Rule Against Hearsay—From Baker to the Evidence Act 2006*, 39 Vict U Wellington L Rev 143 (2008).

[140] See, for example, Brown, *Reform and Proposed Reform of Hearsay Law* at 16–20 (cited in noted 138) (regarding Hong Kong).

that criminal justice systems offered too little protection and too little justice to vulnerable victims. A prominent part of the problem was that the hearsay rule often left victims "voiceless" in court, even when they had made earlier statements that seemed to cry out for legal consideration.[141] The same considerations drove hearsay reforms in the United States, as well.[142] Traditional exceptions—particularly those for "state of mind" and for statements to medical personnel—were stretched both by legislators and by courts, often controversially, to facilitate the introduction of statements by victims, especially when the victims were unavailable, unable, or simply frightened to testify at trial.[143]

In the United States much of this reform agenda has been stalled, at least for the time being, by the Supreme Court's reinterpretation of the Confrontation Clause in *Crawford v Washington* and later cases. I will discuss *Crawford* and its consequences below. First, though, I want to provide some additional framing for that discussion by examining the treatment of out-of-court statements in civil-law jurisdictions.

C. THE CIVIL-LAW COMPARISON

The hearsay rule has long been understood as a distinguishing mark of common-law trials, one of the key features setting those trials apart from their counterparts in civil-law jurisdictions. Often the hearsay rule has been tied to another distinguishing feature of common-law trials, the jury system. The hearsay rule has been seen as a consequence of the commitment to trial by jury; the notion has been that the Anglo-American legal tradition developed the hearsay rule, and should retain it, because lay jurors (in contrast to professional judges) are ill-equipped to evaluate secondhand

---

[141] Id at 2–3.

[142] See, for example, Andrea Dworkin, *In Nicole Brown Simpson's Words*, LA Times (Jan 29, 1995), at M1, M6; text accompanying notes 47–50.

[143] See, for example, *White v Illinois*, 502 US 346 (1992); *United States v Joe*, 8 F3d 1488 (10th Cir 1993); Richard D. Friedman and Bridget McCormack, *Dial-In Testimony*, 150 U Pa L Rev 1171, 1173–92 (2002); Tom Lininger, *Evidentiary Issues in Federal Prosecutions of Violence Against Women*, 36 Ind L Rev 687, 708–17 (2003); Cynthia Jennings, Comment, *Accommodating Child Abuse Victims: Special Hearsay Exceptions in Sexual Offense Prosecutions*, 16 Ohio N U L Rev 663, 665–68, 672–77 (1989); Note, *The Problem of Using Hearsay in Domestic Violence Cases: Is a New Exception the Answer?* 49 Duke L J 1041, 1044–58 (2000).

testimony.[144] The common-law jury trial has thus served both to explain the hearsay rule and to justify it.[145]

Both the explanation and the justification have fallen from favor, for reasons I have already discussed. Recent work in legal history links the rise of the hearsay rule not to the rise of jury trial—a much earlier development—but to the emergence of the adversary, lawyer-driven criminal trial.[146] And experiments with mock juries have produced no evidence that lay adjudicators are prone to over-value hearsay;[147] few scholars today suggest that the hearsay rule is a necessary accommodation to the use of lay adjudicators in common-law trials. Even scholars relatively sympathetic to the hearsay rule, or to some conceivable permutation of it, tend to shy away from the claim that jurors, in particular, need to be protected from hearsay.[148]

Sometimes it is suggested that the jury system—or more precisely the division of authority between the judge and the jury—creates the necessary conditions for the hearsay rule, and for other rules of evidentiary exclusion, by allowing the decision about exclusion to be made by someone uninvolved in the ultimate weighing of the evidence.[149] The "'unitary' character of the adjudicative body" in civil-law trials is said to render a ban on hearsay impractical: when "the same persons decide the admissibility of evidence and the weight it deserves," the exclusion of probative evidence "[i]nevitably . . . acquire[s] a more pronounced aura of psychological unreality."[150] Whether the hearsay rule really depends on a bifurcated tribunal is debatable. As a formal matter, evidence law assumes that it does not: the hearsay ban and other rules of evidentiary exclusion apply in bench trials just as in jury trials.[151] And even if this assumption is mistaken—even if the hear-

---

[144] Wigmore is often blamed, unfairly, for this account of the hearsay rule. See note 110.

[145] See, for example, Damaška, *Evidence Law Adrift* at 31 (cited in note 30) (calling this the conventional justification).

[146] See text accompanying notes 114–24.

[147] See note 66 and accompanying text.

[148] See, for example, Damaška, *Evidence Law Adrift* at 31 (cited in note 30); Schauer, 155 U Pa L Rev 165 (cited in note 2).

[149] See, for example, Damaška, *Evidence Law Adrift* at 46–52 (cited in note 30).

[150] Damaška, 76 Minn L Rev at 427–28 (cited in note 9).

[151] But see Schauer, 155 U Pa L Rev at 166–67 (cited in note 2) (noting that American trial judges frequently ignore the hearsay rule when sitting without a jury, and that some scholars have suggested this informal practice should be officially authorized).

say rule cannot meaningfully be applied without a bifurcated court—that is an argument, at best, against exporting the hearsay rule to civil-law jurisdictions. It is not an argument for retaining the hearsay rule in common-law countries. Not everything feasible is desirable.

Over the last decade, though, a different suggestion has surfaced about the hearsay rule and civil-law trials. The new claim is that the hearsay rule not only is *feasible* in civil-law jurisdictions, but that it is increasingly being *adopted*—or at least that civil-law countries have analogs to hearsay that are all but indistinguishable from the Anglo-American ban. Thus, for example, Richard Lempert asserts that "differences in the treatment of hearsay" in common-law and civil-law jurisdictions are "[i]n practice . . . not that great."[152] This "convergence" is partially due, he suggests, to the many exceptions to the hearsay ban in Anglo-American law, and to the fact that "even where exceptions do not neatly fit statements offered," Anglo-American trial judges "will often find some way to admit hearsay that [they] think is reliable."[153] But Lempert claims there is convergence from the other side as well: "Continental systems . . . often treat hearsay with suspicion, discounting it when it is not corroborated with other evidence, and in one Continental system, Italy, theoretical barriers to admitting hearsay appear similar to what they are in the United States and England."[154]

There has in fact been a long-term weakening of the hearsay ban in common-law jurisdictions.[155] It is wrong, though, to suggest that the American hearsay ban has no bite, or to lump together hearsay barriers in the United States and in England—particularly after *Crawford*. Preventing a criminal defendant from offering evidence of his own out-of-court statements, or preventing the prosecution from proving that a homicide victim had earlier complained about threats by the defendant, is virtually inconceivable anywhere outside the United States. It is a mistake, also, to suggest that there is no practical difference between excluding hearsay and

---

[152] Lempert, *Anglo-American and Continental Systems* at 402 (cited in note 3). For roughly similar observations, see, for example, Allen and Alexakis, *Utility and Truth* at 343, 346 (cited in note 45).

[153] Lempert, *Anglo-American and Continental Systems* at 402 (cited in note 3).

[154] Id.

[155] See text accompanying notes 130–43.

treating it with suspicion. Everyone agrees that secondhand evidence is less reliable than firsthand evidence, all else being equal. The question is whether to use it cautiously—as we do or should do with, say, eyewitness identifications—or to exclude it entirely. The murder prosecutions of Dwayne Giles and Mark Jensen throw the difference into sharp relief.[156] Finally, it is wrong, it turns out, to suggest that Italy, or any other civil-law country, has adopted a hearsay rule similar to what is found in the United States.

Continental legal systems have long recognized the advantages of hearing from witnesses directly, but they have never adopted a rule of exclusion as rigid as the traditional Anglo-American ban on hearsay. Roman canon law addressed the deficiencies of secondhand evidence with what amounted to corroboration requirements and related rules of sufficiency, specifying the circumstances in which oral hearsay, in conjunction with other evidence, could provide the basis for factual findings.[157] These were restrictions on relying on hearsay, not on considering it, and, like the rest of the Roman canon rules of evidence, they started out malleable and "hedged in with numerous qualifications."[158] By the late seventeenth century, though, the system of proofs was rigidifying, and by the eighteenth century it had become a prominent target of Enlightenment attack.[159] In the wake of the French Revolution, Continental legal systems moved sharply away from the medieval system of evidence; the new ideal was free proof.[160] The hearsay rule, of course, could hardly be more alien to that ideal.

Nonetheless modern Continental legal systems have, in fact, erected barriers to certain uses of derivative proof. These barriers have two sources: the principle of "immediacy" embraced by Continental legal systems since the nineteenth century, and the fair trial guarantee in the European Human Rights Convention. The principle of immediacy requires that witnesses testify orally at

---

[156] See text accompanying notes 51–56.

[157] See Damaška, 76 Minn L Rev at 440 (cited in note 9). "Although a general approach to derivative proof [whether written or oral] can . . . be detected, submerged, in Roman-canon law, a terminology limiting 'hearsay' to its oral form became habitual and survives on the Continent to the present day." Id at 439.

[158] Id at 441.

[159] See id at 441–44.

[160] See, for example, id at 445.

trial.[161] As a formal matter, it bars only the medieval practice of having witnesses testify before one official, with another official then deciding the case. "Narrowly conceived as a weapon against 'official' mediation, the principle does not apply to hearsay witnesses, although they also 'mediate' between the factfinder and original sources of information."[162] Nonetheless the principle of immediacy is occasionally invoked in support of a broader disapproval of relying on hearsay when the original witnesses are available to testify.[163] Even this broader, intermittently applied version of the principle, though, does not amount to a ban on hearsay; it is strictly a rule of preference.[164] This is true even in Italy, often said to have adopted a version of the hearsay rule closely approximating the traditional common-law rule, along with other elements of "adversarial" criminal trials. Recent amendments to the Italian constitution do in fact restrict the admissibility of out-of-court statements, but the restrictions do not apply when "examination of the witness is impossible for objective reasons independent of the parties' will."[165]

The same may be said of the limitations imposed on hearsay by the fair trial provisions of the European Human Rights Convention. Adopted in the aftermath of World War II, the Convention provides, among other things, that every criminal defendant "is entitled to a fair and public hearing" and "to examine or have examined witnesses against him."[166] Over the past two decades, the European Court of Human Rights (ECHR)—charged with

---

[161] See, for example, id at 446–48; Sarah J. Summers, *Fair Trials: The European Criminal Procedure Tradition and the European Court of Human Rights* 47–58 (Hart, 2007). Summers suggests that the requirement that proof be presented orally is separable, strictly speaking, from the requirement that proof be presented directly to the adjudicator, but she notes that the two ideas "are frequently referred to together or interchangeably" in European discussions of criminal procedure. See Summers, *Fair Trials* at 48.

[162] Damaška, 76 Minn L Rev at 447 (cited in note 9).

[163] See id at 447.

[164] See, for example, id; Stefano Maffei, *European Right to Confrontation* at 183–84 (cited in note 7) (discussing French case law); Antonio Pablo Rives Seva, *El Testimonio de Referencia en la Jurisprudencia Penal*, Revista Peruana de Jurisprurdencia, R196 4 no 11:LXVII-LXXIII (2002), online at http://noticias.juridicas.com/articulos/65-Derecho%20Procesal%20Penal/200001-testimoniojpenal.html (discussing Spanish case law).

[165] Michele Panzavolta, *Reforms and Counter-Reforms in the Italian Struggle for an Accusatorial Criminal Law System*, 30 NC J Intl L & Comm Reg 577, 611–12 (2005); see also William T. Pizzi and Mariangela Montagna, *The Battle to Establish an Adversarial Trial System in Italy*, 25 Mich J Intl L 429, 462 (2004).

[166] European Convention for the Protection of Human Rights and Fundamental Freedoms, § I, arts 6, 3(d), Nov 4, 1950, 213 UNTS 221.

implementing the Convention[167]—has interpreted these provisions
to require, as a general matter, that evidence "be produced at a
public hearing, in the presence of the accused" and that "the accused . . . be given an adequate and proper opportunity to challenge and question a witness against him, either when he makes
his statement or at a later stage."[168] These are procedural requirements, not rules of admissibility.[169] The ECHR has repeatedly
stressed that "the admissibility of evidence is primarily a matter
for regulation by national law"; the court understands its task as
"not to give a ruling on whether statements of witnesses were
properly admitted as evidence, but rather to ascertain whether the
proceedings as a whole, including the way in which evidence was
taken, were fair."[170] Accordingly, the ECHR has found violations
of the Convention when informants have been questioned but
their identities not disclosed to the defense,[171] and when alleged
victims of child sexual abuse have been questioned by police officers but not by magistrates.[172] It has also ruled, more recently,
that the Convention does not permit government depositions of
witnesses who do not testify at trial to be the "sole or decisive
basis" for a criminal conviction, even if the witness' absence is
beyond the prosecution's control.[173] The "sole or decisive" rule is
currently under challenge,[174] and it operates, in any event, as a

---

[167] Id § IV; see also John D. Jackson, *Transnational Faces of Justice: Two Attempts to Build
Common Standards Beyond National Boundaries*, in *Crime, Procedure and Evidence* at 221, 227
(cited in note 3); Diane Marie Amann, *Harmonic Convergence? Constitutional Criminal Procedure in an International Context*, 75 Ind L J 810, 826–30 (2000).

[168] *P. S. v Germany*, App No 33900/96, para 21 (Eur Ct H R, Dec 20, 2001), online at
http://cmiskp.echr.coe.int/tkp197/search.asp?skin=hudoc-en; see also *Kostovski v Neth-
erlands*, App No 1145/85, 12 Eur H R Rep 434, 447, para 41 (1989). For helpful overviews
of the case law, see Stefan Trechsel, *Human Rights in Criminal Proceedings* at 291–326
(cited in note 7); Roger W. Kirst, *Hearsay and the Right of Confrontation in the European
Court of Human Rights*, 21 Quinnipiac L Rev 777 (2003); and Sarah J. Summers, *The Right
to Confrontation After Crawford v. Washington: A "Continental European" Perspective*, 2 Intl
Commentary on Evidence, issue 1, art 3, at 1 (2004).

[169] See, for example, Friedman, *Confrontation Right Across the Systemic Divide* at 268–69
(cited in note 6).

[170] See, for example, *P. S. v Germany*, para 19.

[171] See *Saidi v France*, App No 14647/89, 17 Eur H R Rep 251, 268, para 44 (1993).

[172] See *P. S. v Germany*.

[173] See *Al-Khawaja v United Kingdom*, App Nos 26766/05 & 22228/06, 49 Eur H R Rep
1, 59, para 23 (2009).

[174] The Supreme Court of the United Kingdom has declined to follow the decision, and
the Grand Chamber of the European Court of Human Rights has agreed to review it.
See *Regina v Horncastle*, 2 WLR 47, 53, 74, 96, 98 (2010); Ian Dennis, *The Right to Confront*

rule of sufficiency, not a rule of admissibility. The ECHR has never disapproved the mere introduction of hearsay statements by witnesses who are dead or otherwise unavailable at the time of trial.[175] Nor is it clear whether the European Human Rights Convention imposes any restrictions at all on the introduction of hearsay evidence through "intermediaries" other than government officials.

The bottom line is that the hearsay rule—as a categorical rule of exclusion, rather than a procedural principle of preference or a rule of evidentiary sufficiency—remains alien to civil-law legal systems. It is also, as we have seen, on the decline in most common-law nations. The lone exception is the United States. Until recently the hearsay rule was in decline here, too. What has changed that, ironically, is the line of cases beginning with *Crawford* and extending, most recently, to *Melendez-Diaz v Massachusetts*—decisions widely applauded, even by their detractors, for *decoupling* constitutional law from the hearsay rule.

II. Hearsay and Confrontation

The irony of the *Crawford* line of cases is that these decisions, celebrated for taking evidence law out of the Bill of Rights, have in fact given the hearsay rule a new, constitutionally protected lease on life. To understand how that has happened, we need to explore not just the *Crawford* doctrine itself but the tradition against which it has taken shape, because confrontation doctrine and hearsay law have a long history of mutual entanglement. This part will therefore begin with a discussion of confrontation law pre-*Crawford*, before continuing with an examination of *Crawford*, *Davis*, *Giles*, and *Melendez-Diaz*, paying particular attention to the various ways in which these cases have altered the relationship between the Confrontation Clause and the hearsay rule. The Supreme Court's new approach to confrontation has, in fact, weak-

---

Witnesses: Meanings, Myths and Human Rights, 2010 Crim L Rev 255, 271; *Al-Khawaja v United Kingdom*, App Nos 26766/05 & 22228/06 (Eur Ct H R, Mar 8, 2010) (accepting referral to Grand Chamber), online at http://cmiskp.echr.coe.int/tkp197/view.asp?item = 1 & portal = hbkm & action = html & highlight = & sessionid = 48342600 & skin = hudoc-pr -en.

[175] Consider *Ferrantelli & Santangelo v Italy*, App No 19874/92, 23 Eur H R Rep 288, 309, para 52 (1996) (finding no error in introduction of accomplice's confession against defendants, in part because the confession was corroborated, and in part because "the judicial authorities . . . cannot be held responsible for" the accomplice's death before the defendants' trial).

ened some links between hearsay doctrine and the Sixth Amendment, but at the same it has strengthened other connections between the two bodies of law.[176]

A. BACKGROUND

The Confrontation Clause of the Sixth Amendment entitles every criminal defendant "to be confronted with the witnesses against him." There are two key terms here: "confronted" and "witnesses." The Supreme Court has interpreted "confronted" to mean, more or less, "cross-examined in the defendant's presence."[177] We will return later to the merits of that reading, but it has been largely settled for decades. There is controversy only at the edges, about the limits that can be placed on cross-examination[178] and the circumstances in which the questioning may occur outside the defendant's presence.[179]

Most of the controversy about the Confrontation Clause has involved its scope rather than its content; it has involved, that is to say, the proper definition of the term "witnesses." One way to read that term, of course, is as a reference to people who come to court and testify. The Confrontation Clause, on this interpretation, has nothing to say about hearsay. It simply governs trial procedures, giving defendants a right to "confront"—by cross-examination or otherwise—the individuals who testify against them at trial. This was Wigmore's reading of the Confrontation Clause. He thought the clause meant only that "*so far as testimony is required under the Hearsay rule to be taken infra-judicially*, it shall be taken in a certain way, namely, subject to cross-examination,—

---

[176] Portions of the following discussion expand on David Alan Sklansky, *Anti-Inquisitorialism*, 122 Harv L Rev 1634, 1643–52 (2009).

[177] See, for example *Dutton v Evans*, 400 US 74, 95 (1970) (Harlan, J, concurring in the result) (suggesting that "[i]f one were to translate the Confrontation Clause into language in more common use today, it would read: 'In all criminal prosecutions, the accused shall enjoy the right to be present and to cross-examine the witnesses against him.'"); *Davis v Alaska*, 415 US 308, 316 (1974) (quoting with approval Wigmore's statement that "[t]he main and essential purpose of confrontation is to secure for the opponent the opportunity of cross-examination").

[178] See, for example, *Davis v Alaska*, 415 US at 316–17.

[179] See, for example, *Maryland v Craig*, 497 US 836, 850 (1990) (holding—on a 5–4 vote—that a prosecution witness can testify by closed-circuit television, without physically "confronting" the defendant, if the procedure is "necessary to further an important public policy" and "the reliability of the testimony is otherwise assured").

not secretly or 'ex parte' away from the accused."[180] This was also the position reached ultimately by the second Justice Harlan,[181] and it is the position taken by some scholars today.[182]

But it has never been the Supreme Court's view. The Court has consistently reasoned that the Confrontation Clause protects criminal defendants against some uses of hearsay evidence. In fact the vast majority of the Supreme Court's Confrontation Clause cases have involved challenges to hearsay evidence.[183] Repeatedly, the Court has said that the hearsay rule and the Confrontation Clause "protect similar values"[184] and "stem from the same roots."[185]

In the traditional telling, the roots of the Confrontation Clause lie in grievances about prosecutions based on affidavits and depositions taken ex parte from the defendants' accusers—especially in the infamous English treason trials of the 1500s and early 1600s, and most particularly in the 1603 trial of Sir Walter Raleigh. Raleigh was convicted of joining the so-called Main Plot to depose James I and to place Arabella Stuart on the throne. The core evidence against him consisted of a written examination of the plot's alleged leader, Lord Cobham, and a letter Cobham later wrote. Raleigh asked repeatedly, but unsuccessfully, for Cobham to be brought from his cell to the courtroom. The trial ended in a sentence of execution, which was eventually carried out.[186] Widespread revulsion at the conduct of Raleigh's trial has been credited with helping spur development of the common-law right to con-

---

[180] Wigmore, 2 *Treatise on the Anglo-American System of Evidence* § 1397, at 101 (cited in note 75). Wigmore explained that "[t]he Constitution does not prescribe what kinds of testimonial statements (dying declarations, or the like) shall be given infra-judicially,—this depends on the law of Evidence for the time being,—but only what mode of procedure shall be followed—*i.e.* a cross-examining procedure—in the case of such testimony as is required by the ordinary law of Evidence to be given infra-judicially." Id.

[181] See *Evans*, 400 US at 94 (Harlan, J, concurring).

[182] See, for example, Amar, *Constitution and Criminal Procedure* at 94 (cited in note 13).

[183] See, for example, Penny J. White, *Rescuing the Confrontation Clause*, 54 SC L Rev 537, 555–91 (2003) (reviewing pre-*Crawford* case law).

[184] See, for example, *Ohio v Roberts*, 448 US 56, 66 (1980); *California v Green*, 399 US 149, 155 (1970).

[185] See, for example, *Roberts*, 448 US at 66; *Evans*, 400 US at 86.

[186] See, for example, Catherine Drinker Bowen, *The Lion and the Throne: The Life and Times of Sir Edward Coke* 190–217, 414–16 (Atlantic, 1956); Allen D. Boyer, *The Trial of Sir Walter Raleigh: The Law of Treason, the Trial of Treason and the Origins of the Confrontation Clause*, 74 Miss L J 869, 895 (2005).

frontation, later codified in the Sixth Amendment.[187] It has also been suggested that the case may have helped motivate English courts to develop the modern ban on hearsay evidence,[188] but that does not quite fit the timing: recent historical work indicates that the hearsay rule did not take shape in its modern form until the late eighteenth century.[189]

Regardless, the Court has thought it plain that the Confrontation Clause excludes some hearsay.[190] At the same time, the Justices have been wary of treating *all* prosecution hearsay as a violation of confrontation; that would "abrogate virtually every hearsay exception" and be "too extreme."[191] Over a century ago, in its first case applying the Confrontation Clause, the Supreme Court warned that "general rules of law of this kind, however beneficent in their operation and valuable to the accused, must occasionally give way to considerations of public policy and the necessities of the case."[192] The Court retained this pragmatic perspective on the Confrontation Clause throughout the 1900s. The trick was deciding where to draw the line.

Thirty years ago, in *Ohio v Roberts*, the Court drew the line at reliability. The Justices reasoned that the "underlying purpose" of confrontation was "to augment accuracy" by "ensuring the defendant an effective means to test adverse evidence." So prosecution hearsay was barred by the Confrontation Clause unless it carried "adequate 'indicia of reliability'"—either because the statements

---

[187] See, for example, *Green*, 399 US at 157 n 10; Francis Howard Heller, *The Sixth Amendment to the Constitution of the United States: A Study in Constitutional Development* 104–06 (Kansas, 1951); Boyer, 74 Miss L J at 895–901 (cited in note 186); Randolph N. Jonakait, *The Origins of the Confrontation Clause: An Alternative History*, 27 Rutgers L J 77, 81 n 18 (1995). For skeptical assessments of this received understanding, see Kenneth W. Graham Jr., *The Right of Confrontation and the Hearsay Rule: Sir Walter Raleigh Loses Another One*, 8 Crim L Bull 99, 100 (1972); Frank R. Herrmann and Brownlow M. Speer, *Facing the Accuser: Ancient and Medieval Precursors of the Confrontation Clause*, 34 Va J Intl L 481 (1994). Even the Supreme Court has begun to back away from the Raleigh story. Writing for the majority in *Melendez-Diaz*, Justice Scalia stressed that "[t]he right to confrontation was not invented in response to the use of the *ex parte* examinations in *Raleigh's Case*," although he reiterated that the case involved "a paradigmatic confrontation violation"—which was precisely why, Justice Scalia said, Raleigh's conviction "provoked such an outcry." 129 S Ct at 2534.

[188] See, for example, James W. Jennings, *Preserving the Right to Confrontation—A New Approach to Hearsay Evidence in Criminal Trials*, 113 U Pa L Rev 741, 746 n 31 (1965).

[189] See text accompanying notes 114–18.

[190] See, for example, *Roberts*, 448 US at 63.

[191] Id.

[192] *Mattox v United States*, 156 US 237, 243 (1895).

at issue fell, by statute or common law, within a "firmly rooted" exception to the hearsay ban, or because they bore "particularized guarantees of trustworthiness."[193] The Court eventually made clear that it deemed all of the myriad hearsay exceptions codified in the Federal Rules of Evidence and adopted by most of the states to be "firmly rooted." This amounted to allowing the Confrontation Clause to track the Federal Rules of Evidence, because most states have copied the Federal Rules of Evidence virtually verbatim.

The only exceptions a majority of the Court ever found *not* to qualify were the catchall provisions in the Federal Rules of Evidence and most state evidence codes for statements "not specifically covered" by other exceptions "but having equivalent circumstantial guarantees of trustworthiness"; the Court reasoned that "ad hoc" assessments of reliability did not deserve the weight given to "longstanding judicial and legislative experience" in evaluating particular categories of extrajudicial statements.[194] Statements admitted under the catchall exceptions could still survive a Confrontation Clause challenge, but only if they had "particularized guarantees of trustworthiness," which the Court interpreted *not* to include corroboration. "To be admissible under the Confrontation Clause," the Court explained, "hearsay evidence used to convict a defendant must possess indicia of reliability by virtue of its inherent trustworthiness, not by reference to other evidence at trial."[195]

B. FROM CRAWFORD TO MELENDEZ-DIAZ

Partly because it seemed odd to hitch constitutional doctrine to the twists and turns of evidence law, the *Roberts* approach to the Confrontation Clause was never popular with commentators, and by the time the Court decided *Crawford v Washington* in 2004,

---

[193] *Roberts*, 448 US at 66. *Roberts* also suggested that when a prosecution witness was available to testify in court, the Confrontation Clause "normally" called for the exclusion of the witness's out-of-court statements even in the face of "indicia of reliability." Id. But the Court made clear that "[a] demonstration of unavailability . . . is not always required," id at 65 n 7, and even the qualified requirement later fell by the wayside, applied only to statements admitted under hearsay exceptions that themselves required a showing of unavailability. See *White v Illinois*, 502 US 346, 355–56 (1992); *United States v Inadi*, 475 US 387, 394 (1986); Robert P. Mosteller, *Confrontation as Constitutional Criminal Procedure: Crawford's Birth Did Not Require That Roberts Had to Die*, 15 J L & Pol 685, 694 n 28 (2007).

[194] *Idaho v Wright*, 497 US 805, 817 (1990).

[195] Id at 822.

it was ready for a new approach. Michael Crawford was convicted of stabbing a man who allegedly tried to rape Crawford's wife, Sylvia. The evidence against him included a tape-recorded police interrogation of Sylvia Crawford, in which she described the stabbing. Sylvia declined to testify against her husband at trial, invoking spousal privilege, but the prosecutors introduced her tape-recorded interrogation. Based in part on that evidence, the jury rejected Crawford's claim of self-defense. The trial judge found no violation of the Confrontation Clause, because Sylvia's statements appeared reliable. The statements did not fall within a firmly rooted exception to the hearsay rule, but they had "particularized guarantees of trustworthiness": they were based on direct observation, they were made soon after the events in question, they did not seek to shift blame, they were made under questioning by a "neutral" law enforcement officer, and they "interlocked" with Michael Crawford's own statements to the police. The intermediate appellate court reversed, finding the statements insufficiently reliable, but the state supreme court reinstated the conviction, relying chiefly on the manner in which the statements by Michael Crawford and Sylvia Crawford "interlocked."[196]

The United States Supreme Court reversed. Writing for the majority, Justice Scalia made clear he agreed with Washington's intermediate court of appeals about the reliability of Sylvia Crawford's statements to the police, but he declined simply to "reweigh[] the 'reliability factors' under *Roberts*."[197] Instead, he took the occasion to revisit *Roberts* and to reject its entire approach, at least as applied to statements made in a police interrogation, or to other hearsay that seemed "testimonial." For those statements, "the only indicium of reliability sufficient to satisfy constitutional demands is the one the Constitution actually prescribes: confrontation."[198] That meant that testimonial hearsay was inadmissible against a criminal defendant unless the defendant actually received an opportunity to cross-examine the witness, either at trial or in an earlier proceeding. And even then, statements by a witness who did not appear at trial would be inadmissible if the witness were available and could in fact be called to the stand.[199] The only

---

[196] 541 US at 38–42.

[197] Id at 67; see also id at 68.

[198] Id at 68–69.

[199] See id at 53–54, 68.

exceptions the Court signaled it would accept to these imperatives were the equitable principle of "forfeiture by wrongdoing"[200] and, possibly, the venerable rule admitting dying declarations[201]—doctrines that the Court has since made clear are to be applied narrowly, with strict adherence to their contours in eighteenth-century common law.[202]

The Court declined in *Crawford* to offer any precise definition of "testimonial" hearsay or any comprehensive set of criteria for distinguishing it from nontestimonial hearsay. The point, though, was to focus constitutional attention on "the principal evil at which the Confrontation Clause was directed," namely, the practice of questioning prosecution witnesses in ex parte, pretrial examinations, in lieu of having them testify at trial allowing the defendant to cross-examine them.[203] The Confrontation Clause, Justice Scalia suggested, was both narrower and broader than the hearsay rule:

> [N]ot all hearsay implicates the Sixth Amendment's core concerns. An off-hand, overheard remark might be unreliable evidence and thus a good candidate for exclusion under the hearsay rules, but it bears little resemblance to the civil-law abuses the Confrontation Clause targeted. On the other hand, *ex parte* examinations might sometimes be admissible under modern hearsay rules, but the Framers certainly would not have condoned them.[204]

"Testimonial" hearsay, then, was hearsay that raised "the Sixth Amendment's core concerns," the concerns raised by questioning prosecution witnesses the way Lord Cobham was questioned— before trial and away from the defendant, instead of at trial, in the defendant's presence, and subject to cross-examination. Instead of defining the category of cases that raised these concerns, the Court took note of three alternative definitions and declined to choose among them. One possibility, suggested Crawford's lawyers, was "*ex parte* in-court testimony or its functional equivalent—

---

[200] Id at 62.

[201] See id at 56 n 6 (suggesting that if "an exception for testimonial dying declarations . . . must be accepted on historical grounds, it is *sui generis*").

[202] See *Giles v California*, 128 S Ct 2678 (2008); text accompanying notes 222–24.

[203] *Crawford*, 541 US at 50.

[204] Id at 51. Regarding the Court's association of ex parte examinations with civil-law systems of adjudication, see Sklansky, 122 Harv L Rev 1634 (cited in note 176).

that is, material such as affidavits, custodial examinations, prior testimony that the defendant was unable to cross-examine, or similar pretrial statements that declarants would reasonably expect to be used prosecutorially."[205] Another possibility, floated by Justice Thomas in an earlier case, was "extrajudicial statements . . . contained in formalized testimonial materials, such as affidavits, depositions, prior testimony, or confessions."[206] Still another possibility, suggested by amici in *Crawford*, was "statements that were made under circumstances which would lead an objective witness reasonably to believe that the statement would be available for use at a later trial."[207] Any of these definitions, the Court reasoned, would make statements given during a police interrogation "testimonial."[208]

Nor did the Court say in *Crawford* whether the *Roberts* test, or any other requirements derived from the Confrontation Clause, would continue to apply to *nontestimonial* hearsay introduced against a criminal defendant. The Court answered the latter question two years later, though, in *Davis v Washington*. Writing again for the Court, Justice Scalia explained that the focus on testimonial statements was "so clearly reflected in the text" of the Confrontation Clause that it "must fairly be said to mark out not merely its 'core,' but its perimeter."[209] *Davis* thus makes clear that the Confrontation Clause now applies only to testimonial hearsay. *Davis* also threw some limited, additional light on the key term "testimonial," at least in the context of questioning by police officers, 911 operators, or other law enforcement personnel. In that context, the Court held, statements are testimonial only if "the circumstances objectively indicate . . . that the primary purpose of the interrogation is to establish or prove past events potentially relevant to later criminal prosecution," rather than to respond to "an ongoing emergency."[210] The Court therefore found no con-

---

[205] *Crawford*, 541 US at 51.

[206] Id at 51–52, quoting *White*, 502 US at 365 (Thomas, J, concurring in part and concurring in the judgment).

[207] *Crawford*, 541 US at 52, quoting Brief for National Association of Criminal Defense Lawyers et al as amici curiae.

[208] *Crawford*, 541 US at 52.

[209] 547 US 813, 824 (2006).

[210] Id at 822. *Davis* said nothing about statements not in response to law enforcement questioning, other than to disavow any suggestion that they were "necessarily nontestimonial." Id n 1.

stitutional violation in the evidence used to convict Adrian Davis of assault: statements his former girlfriend, Michelle McCottry, made after calling 911 to report that he was attacking her. Those statements included the name of her attacker, provided in response to questions from the 911 operator. But the Court thought that even the questions about the assailant's identity appeared "necessary to resolve the present emergency," because police dispatched to the scene would want to "know whether they would be encountering a violent felon."[211] The heart of the matter was that "[a]lthough one *might* call 911 to provide a narrative report of a crime absent any imminent danger, McCottry's call was plainly a call for help against bona fide physical threat. . . . She simply was not acting as a *witness*; she was not *testifying*."[212]

In this respect the Court thought McCottry's statements contrasted sharply with the statements at issue in *Hammon v Indiana*, a case consolidated for decision with *Davis*. Herschel Hammon was convicted of battery based on statements his wife, Amy Hammon, had made to police officers who came to the Hammons' house in response to a "domestic disturbance" report.[213] The Court found these facts essentially indistinguishable from the circumstances in *Crawford*. "There was no emergency in progress," so it was "entirely clear . . . that the interrogation was part of an investigation in possibly criminal past conduct."[214] Amy Hammon's statements were therefore testimonial, unlike Michelle McCottry's statements. Justice Thomas, concurring in *Davis* but dissenting in *Hammon*, could not see the difference: neither the 911 call in *Davis* nor the at-the-scene questioning in *Hammon* looked to him much like formal, "*ex parte* examinations."[215] But this turned out to be too much originalism even for Justice Scalia, who warned that "[r]estricting the Confrontation Clause to the precise forms against which it was originally directed is a recipe for its extinction."[216] Amy Hammon's statements were formal enough—either (as the Court suggested at one point) because she was questioned

---

[211] Id at 827.

[212] Id at 827–28.

[213] Id at 819–21.

[214] Id at 829–30.

[215] Id at 835 (Thomas, J, concurring in part and dissenting in part), quoting *Crawford*, 541 US at 50.

[216] Id at 830 n 5.

away from her husband, in a separate room, "with the officer receiving her replies for use in his 'investigat[ion],'"[217] or (as the Court suggested elsewhere) because "lies to [police] officers are criminal offenses."[218]

Given the outcome in *Hammon*, it is understandable that the state of California did not even try to convince the Supreme Court that Brenda Avie's statements to a police officer about Dwayne Giles were nontestimonial,[219] and it is unsurprising that on remand in *Giles* the California Court of Appeal concluded with little discussion that the statements were, in fact, testimonial.[220] Avie, like Hammon, was questioned by a police officer responding to a domestic violence call, after the police had separated her from her alleged assailant and at a point when "[t]here was no emergency in progress."[221] The central question in *Giles v California* was whether the Confrontation Clause allowed a testimonial statement to be used against a criminal defendant when the reason the declarant could not testify in court and be cross-examined was that the defendant had killed her. The California courts thought yes, but the Supreme Court disagreed. Writing once again for the Court, Justice Scalia explained that there *is* an exception to the Confrontation Clause for "forfeiture by wrongdoing," but that it applies only when the defendant has culpably rendered the declarant unavailable *for the purpose of preventing her from testifying against him.*[222] The Court also took the occasion of deciding *Giles* to suggest that there is a separate Confrontation Clause exception for "dying declarations," but that this exception, too, is to be narrowly construed, in conformity with its contours at common law.[223]

---

[217] Id at 830.

[218] Id at 830 n 5. The Court has agreed to review a lower court decision concluding, under *Davis*, that a homicide victim's statement to the police, shortly after he had been shot, was "testimonial," because "the 'primary purpose' of the questions asked, and the answers given, was to enable the police to identify, locate, and apprehend the perpetrator," rather than to help the police respond to an "ongoing threat." See *People v Bryant*, 768 NW2d 65, 67, 71 (Mich 2009), cert granted, 78 USLW 3082 (2010).

[219] *Giles v California*, 128 S Ct 2678, 2682 (2008).

[220] *People v Giles*, 2009 WL 457832, at *3 (Cal Super, Feb 25, 2009).

[221] *Davis v Washington*, 547 US at 829–30; see *People v Giles*, 2009 WL at *4; text accompanying note 51.

[222] *Giles v California*, 128 S Ct at 2693.

[223] Id at 2682–83. In *Crawford*, the Court had noted that there was founding-era authority for admitting dying declarations, even in cases where the declarations were plainly tes-

Because the Court now reads the Confrontation Clause to preserve "the right of confrontation at common law, admitting only those exceptions established at the time of the founding,"[224] most of Justice Scalia's majority opinion in *Giles*—and a large portion of Justice Breyer's dissent—was devoted to discussion of common-law decisions from the seventeenth, eighteenth, and early nineteenth centuries. One striking feature of these cases is that they rarely if ever use the term "confrontation" or speak of a right to face or to challenge one's accuser in court. They do not use the term "hearsay" either, but they are very plainly cases about the admissibility of proof: the question in each was whether a certain statement, made by a witness who is no longer available to testify, should be treated as evidence.[225] In *Giles*, as in *Crawford* and *Davis*, the Court assumed that at the time of the adoption of the Bill of Rights these cases—or at least the evidentiary principles on which they relied—were understood to be part of the right to "confrontation" secured by the Sixth Amendment.

The Court assumed, in other words, that the Confrontation Clause was intended, or was originally understood, to incorporate and to codify common-law strictures against prosecutorial reliance on "testimonial" hearsay. But there is little evidence in support of that assumption—or, for that matter, against it. It amounts to a leap of faith. Like the rest of the Bill of Rights, the Sixth Amendment lacks the kind of legislative history that would throw appreciable light on its meaning.[226] The debates over the ratification of the Constitution itself help explain why the Bill of Rights *as a whole* was adopted, but those debates do little to clarify the meaning of key terms such as "confront" or "witnesses." If anything, those debates suggest that the Bill of Rights was understood at the time of its adoption to codify not particular legal rules but general principles that could and were expected to evolve over time.[227]

---

timonial. But *Crawford* expressly declined to decide "whether the Sixth Amendment incorporates an exception for testimonial dying declarations." 541 US at 56 n 6.

[224] 128 S Ct at 2682, quoting *Crawford*, 541 US at 54.

[225] See, for example, *Lord Morley's Case*, 6 How St Tr 769 (H L 1666); Harrison's Case, 12 How St Tr 833 (H L 1692); *King v Woodcock*, 1 Leach 500, 168 Eng Rep 352 (1879); *Queen v Scaife*, 117 QB 238, 117 Eng Rep 1271 (KB 1851); *State v Moody*, 3 NC 31 (Super L & Eg NC 1798).

[226] See, for example, Epstein, 14 Widener L Rev at 430 (cited in note 64).

[227] See, for example, Saul Cornell, *The Original Meaning of Original Understanding: A Neo-Blackstonian Critique*, 67 Md L Rev 150 (2007); Larry Kramer, *Two (More) Problems*

The originalist reasoning in *Crawford*, *Davis*, and *Giles* has been challenged on two main grounds. The first is that originalism is a mistaken approach to constitutional interpretation; the second is that the Court is wrong about what kind of evidence was commonly allowed by eighteenth-century common law. There is much to be said for each of these objections, but the point I want to flag here is different. For the sake of argument, grant that originalism is a coherent and attractive approach to constitutional interpretation.[228] Grant even the more specific and more dubious claim that the right to confrontation, as incorporated against the states by the Fourteenth Amendment, should be interpreted as it was understood when the Sixth Amendment was adopted.[229] Finally, grant for the sake of argument that certain forms of hearsay were flatly inadmissible against criminal defendants at the time that the Sixth Amendment was framed and adopted, even in cases where the declarant was dead or otherwise unavailable at the time of trial. It still does not follow that hearsay of that kind is constitutionally inadmissible. There is a missing premise: that the Sixth Amendment right to be confronted with adverse witnesses was understood by its framers and adopters to include all the restrictions that had developed by the late eighteenth century on the use of hearsay against criminal defendants.

The same unsupported assumption—that the right to "confrontation" was understood in the late eighteenth century to mean, at least in significant part, a right against prosecution hearsay—underlies the Court's most recent confrontation decision, *Melendez-Diaz v Massachusetts*. Luis Melendez-Diaz was convicted of drug trafficking based partly on laboratory results showing that bags seized from Melendez-Diaz and two codefendants contained cocaine. No one from the state laboratory testified in court; instead, pursuant to a state statute, the prosecution submitted notarized "certificates" from analysts at the laboratory, indicating that the materials in question had been examined and determined to

---

with Originalism, 31 Harv J L & Pub Pol 907 (2008); H. Jefferson Powell, *The Original Understanding of Original Intent*, 98 Harv L Rev 885 (1985).

[228] But see, for example, Mitchell N. Berman, *Originalism Is Bunk*, 84 NYU L Rev 1 (2009).

[229] But see, for example, Sklansky, 122 Harv L Rev at 1674–77 (cited in note 176) (suggesting there is little evidence the Framers and adopters of the Fourteenth Amendment "aimed to extend to the states not only the restrictions imposed by the Bill of Rights, but also the way those restrictions were understood by eighteenth-century common law judges").

contain cocaine.[230] The Massachusetts courts saw no confrontation problem, because the certificates bore little resemblance to the kind of "*ex parte* examinations" the Confrontation Clause was intended to bar; instead, they were "akin to business or official records"[231]—and the Supreme Court itself had opined that business records, like most other statements covered by hearsay exceptions at common law, "by their nature were not testimonial."[232]

On a 5–4 vote, the Supreme Court reversed and remanded. Writing once again for the majority, Justice Scalia found the case "straightforward." It involved, he said, "little more than the application of our holding in *Crawford v. Washington*."[233] There was "little doubt" that the laboratory certificates fell "within the 'core class of testimonial statements,'" under any of the alternative definitions described in *Crawford*: the certificates were, in essence, affidavits, made for the express purpose of providing evidence for use at trial.[234] Accordingly, they could not substitute for live testimony "[a]bsent a showing that the analysts were unavailable to testify at trial *and* that the petitioner had a prior opportunity to cross-examine them."[235] The Court reasoned that traditional hearsay exceptions for business records and official records did not apply to statements produced for use at trial. And even if they *did* apply, it would not matter: they were still testimonial. The Court explained that business records and public records

> are generally admissible absent confrontation not because they qualify under an exception to the hearsay rules, but because—having been created for the administration of an entity's affairs and not for the purpose of establishing or proving some fact at trial—they are not testimonial. Whether or not they qualify as business or official records, the analysts' statements here—prepared specifically for use at petitioner's trial—were testimony against petitioner, and the analysts were subject to confrontation under the Sixth Amendment.[236]

---

[230] *Melendez-Diaz*, 129 S Ct at 2531.

[231] *Commonwealth v Verde*, 827 NE2d 701, 706 (Mass 2005). The Appeals Court of Massachusetts relied on *Verde* in affirming Melendez-Diaz's conviction, 2007 WL 2189152, *4 (July 31, 2007), and the Supreme Judicial Court denied review, 874 NE2d 407 (2007).

[232] *Crawford*, 541 US at 56.

[233] 129 S Ct 2527, 2533, 2536 (2009).

[234] Id at 2532.

[235] Id.

[236] Id at 2539–40.

The Court's discussion of what it called "the business-and-official-records hearsay exceptions"[237] papered over some long-standing controversies. It is true, as Justice Scalia pointed out, that in 1943 the Court ruled that an accident report prepared by a railroad employee fell outside the traditional business records exception, because the report was "calculated for use essentially in the court, not in the business"; its "primary utility" was "in litigating, not in railroading."[238] Subsequently, though, an influential ruling by the Second Circuit, construing a successor statute, limited exclusion to situations in which the author of the accident report was himself potentially liable and therefore had a "motive to fabricate."[239] The Federal Rules of Evidence intentionally skirted the issue, which the drafters characterized as a "source of difficulty and disagreement" that did not lend itself to "[t]he formulation of specific terms which would assure satisfactory results in all cases."[240] The business records exception in the Federal Rules of Evidence applies to *any* records made "in the course of a regularly conducted activity," whether made with litigation in mind or not,[241] but it also calls for exclusion, on a case-by-case basis, if "the source of information or the method or circumstances of preparation indicate lack of trustworthiness."[242] *Government* records are treated more restrictively: reports of "police officers and other law enforcement personnel" made in the course of official duty are generally inadmissible in criminal cases.[243] But there has been continued disagreement about who counts as "law enforcement personnel": medical examiners, for example, are often excluded.[244] And federal appellate courts have repeatedly found the limitations on the admissibility of reports by "police officers and

---

[237] Id at 2539.

[238] *Palmer v Hoffman*, 318 US 109, 114 (1943) (construing Act of June 20, 1936, 49 Stat 1561, codified until repeal at 28 USC § 695); see *Melendez-Diaz*, 129 S Ct at 2538. On the background of the case and its role in the broader story of hearsay reform, see Ariens, 28 Ind L Rev at 191–224 (cited in note 81).

[239] *Lewis v Baker*, 526 F2d 470, 473 (2d Cir 1975) (construing the Federal Business Records Act, June 25, 1948, 62 Stat 945, codified as amended at 28 USC 1732).

[240] Advisory Committee Note, FRE 803(6).

[241] Id.

[242] FRE 803(6).

[243] FRE 803(8); see *Melendez-Diaz*, 129 S Ct at 2538.

[244] See, for example, *United States v Rosa*, 11 F3d 315 (2d Cir 1993); Carolyn Zabrycki, Comment, *Toward a Definition of "Testimonial": How Autopsy Reports Do Not Embody the Qualities of a Testimonial Statement*, 96 Cal L Rev 1093, 1123–24 (2008).

other law enforcement personnel" inapplicable to "routine" or "non-adversarial" records.[245]

Presumably, the majority in *Melendez-Diaz* felt comfortable ignoring these complexities—and the dissent did not mention them, either—because under *Crawford* they were irrelevant: modern exceptions to the hearsay rule do not override restrictions imposed by the Confrontation Clause. What mattered was whether a forensic lab report would have been admissible against a criminal defendant when the Sixth Amendment was adopted in 1791. Of course there were no forensic lab reports in 1791. So the majority and the dissenters in *Melendez-Diaz* reached for analogies. The dissent, by Justice Kennedy, said lab reports were like copyists' certifications—routinely relied upon in eighteenth-century courts—declaring that copies of public records were true and accurate.[246] Justice Scalia's majority opinion said they were more like a certification by a clerk that a particular record could *not* be found—which Justice Scalia suggested was inadmissible at common law.[247]

Justice Kennedy did not challenge the Court's assumption that the right to "confrontation" at the time of the framing was understood to include a criminal defendant's right against hearsay statements by an absent witness, but he did complain, repeatedly and at length, that the Court was turning confrontation law into a "formalistic," "wooden," and "pointless" set of rules, unmoored from "common sense," from earlier case law, and from goals of the Sixth Amendment.[248] He also warned that extending *Crawford* from "ordinary" witnesses to forensic analysts threatened serious disruption of criminal prosecutions nationwide, and was "unjustified by any demonstrated deficiency in trials."[249] Justice Scalia

---

[245] See, for example, *United States v Brown*, 9 F3d 907, 911–12 (11th Cir 1993); *United States v Orozco*, 590 F2d 789, 793–94 (9th Cir 1979).

[246] *Melendez-Diaz*, 129 S Ct at 2552–53 (Kennedy, J, dissenting).

[247] Id at 2538–39 (opinion of the Court). The earliest authority Justice Scalia cited for this proposition was a Louisiana case decided in 1917, but he also referenced the third edition of Wigmore's treatise, which in turn cited, inter alia, Tennessee cases decided in 1796 and 1806. See Wigmore, 2 *Treatise on the System of Evidence* § 1678, at 753 n 3 (cited in note 34). Wigmore, like Justice Scalia, took it as "certain" under common law "that the only evidence receivable would be the testimony on the stand of one who had made the search" and that a "certificate of *due search* and *inability to find* was not receivable." Id at 752–53. He predicted, though, that this would "someday be reckoned as one of the most stupid instances of legal pedantry in our annals." Id at 754.

[248] *Melendez-Diaz*, 129 S Ct at 2544, 2547 (Kennedy, J, dissenting).

[249] Id at 2543, 2550–51.

doubted that the Court's ruling would prove unduly disruptive, partly because some states had already adopted the rule announced in *Melendez-Diaz*, and there was "no evidence that the criminal justice system" in those states had "ground to a halt."[250] Justice Scalia doubted, too, that "confrontation will be useless in testing analysts' honesty, proficiency, and methodology,"[251] and he pointed out that "[s]erious deficiencies have been found in the forensic evidence used in criminal trials."[252] Ultimately, though, *Melendez-Diaz* treated utilitarian considerations of this kind as beside the point. "The Confrontation Clause may make the prosecution of criminals more burdensome," but that was the nature of constitutional rights. The clause required what it required, and the Court lacked the power to modify it.[253] Similarly, there might be "other ways—and in some cases better ways—to challenge or verify the results of a forensic test," but the Confrontation Clause "guarantees one way":[254] the "crucible of cross-examination."[255]

Justice Kennedy was surely right to call this reasoning "formalistic," but the formalism started with *Crawford*, not with *Melendez-Diaz*. Justice Scalia had a point in claiming that he was "faithfully applying *Crawford*" in *Melendez-Diaz*, and that the dissenters were seeking to resurrect the pragmatism of the old "indicia of reliability" approach to the Confrontation Clause, "a mere five years after it was rejected in *Crawford*."[256] The formalism so apparent in *Melendez-Diaz* is the formalism of *Crawford*.

Melendez-Diaz made other things clear, as well. It underscored, as I have already suggested, the particular "form" of *Crawford*'s formalism: the equation of "confrontation" with "cross-examination," and the rigid insistence that "confrontation" means freedom from any prosecution hearsay that would have been officially disapproved in the late eighteenth century. And the alignment of votes in *Melendez-Diaz* served as a reminder that the formalism of *Crawford* cannot be understood as "conservative" or "liberal," at least not as those terms are generally understood in the context

---

[250] Id at 2541 (opinion of the Court).

[251] Id at 2538.

[252] Id at 2537.

[253] Id at 2540.

[254] Id at 2536.

[255] Id at 2536, quoting *Crawford*, 541 US at 61–62.

[256] *Melendez-Diaz*, 129 S Ct at 2533.

of constitutional criminal procedure. Justice Scalia's majority opinion in *Melendez-Diaz* was joined by Justice Stevens, Justice Souter,
Justice Thomas, and Justice Ginsburg. Dissenting with Justice
Kennedy were Chief Justice Roberts, Justice Breyer, and Justice
Alito. The debate was not between "law and order" Justices and
"civil rights" Justices. The debate, to a great extent, was between
formalism and pragmatism, between Justice Scalia's famous insistence on "the rule of law as a law of rules"[257] and the kind of
"consequential" approach to constitutional interpretation championed by Justice Breyer.[258]

C. DECOUPLING AND RECOUPLING CONFRONTATION AND HEARSAY

What can be said, then, about the relationship between the
Confrontation Clause and the hearsay rule after *Crawford, Davis,
Giles*, and *Melendez-Diaz*? These cases have been applauded, even
by their critics, for detaching confrontation doctrine from evidence law. There is a broad consensus that, whatever its flaws, at
least the rule announced in *Crawford* has ended the "shotgun wedding" of hearsay and confrontation;[259] at least the Sixth Amendment is no longer "shrouded by the hearsay rule."[260] The reality
is more complicated.

The *Crawford* line of cases have certainly weakened the *operational* link between confrontation and hearsay. That is to say, they
have made it easier for an out-of-court statement to be barred
under the Sixth Amendment even though it falls within an exception to the hearsay rule, and—conversely—easier for evidence
to be inadmissible hearsay without also violating the Constitution.
Before *Crawford*, the Court reasoned that statements falling within
any established, categorical exception had sufficient "indicia of
reliability" to satisfy the demands of the Confrontation Clause.
After *Crawford*, things are different. As Justice Scalia made plain

---

[257] Antonin Scalia, *The Rule of Law as a Law of Rules*, 56 U Chi L Rev 1175 (1989).

[258] Stephen Breyer, *Our Democratic Constitution*, 77 NYU L Rev 245, 247 (2002). It is
no coincidence that Justice Blackmun, who articulated the "indicia of reliability" test in
his opinion for the Court in *Ohio v Roberts*, 448 US 56 (1980), shared Justice Breyer's
concern for "real-world consequences," Breyer, *Our Democratic Constitution* at 249. See,
for example, Linda Greenhouse, *Becoming Justice Blackmun* (Times, 2005); Harold Hongju
Koh, *Justice Blackmun and the "World Out There*," 104 Yale L J 23 (1994); Note, *The
Changing Social Vision of Justice Blackmun*, 96 Harv L Rev 717 (1983).

[259] See notes 19 and 22.

[260] Friedman, *Confrontation Right Across the Systemic Divide* at 265 (cited in note 6).

for the Court in *Melendez-Diaz*, forensic lab reports are constitutionally inadmissible against a criminal defendant, absent cross-examination of the analyst, regardless of whether the reports fall within the "business records" or "public records" exception to the hearsay rule. And just as satisfying the hearsay rule no longer means that evidence satisfies the Confrontation Clause, prosecution evidence that *violates* the hearsay rule does not automatically violate the Sixth Amendment. *Davis* made explicit what *Crawford* had strongly suggested: only "testimonial" hearsay implicates the Confrontation Clause. In many ways, the line between testimonial and nontestimonial hearsay remains indistinct, but the Court has made reasonably clear that certain kinds of hearsay—casual remarks among friends, for example—are nontestimonial and therefore raise no constitutional problems, even when their introduction violates the hearsay rule.

In addition to weakening the *operational* link between confrontation and hearsay, the *Crawford* doctrine has also loosened the *argumentative* connection between the two bodies of law. Writing for the Court in these cases, Justice Scalia has stressed again and again that confrontation questions are not to be decided by assessing the reliability of particular kinds of hearsay, the hardships that would be caused by its exclusion, or even the reasons for believing that cross-examination would actually serve a useful purpose. This kind of weighing, he has said, has already been done for us by the Framers and adopters of the Bill of Rights. The Confrontation Clause of the Sixth Amendment codifies and makes mandatory a particular, across-the-board balancing of the advantages and disadvantages of allowing testimonial hearsay to be introduced against criminal defendants without the safeguard of cross-examination. The Constitution does not allow us to revisit that balancing. Therefore the kinds of inquiry that are routine in hearsay cases—inquiries into the risks of unreliability attendant to particular kinds of hearsay, and the grounds for thinking that cross-examination is or is not essential—have no place in rigorous application of the Sixth Amendment. Rather, the proper inquiries are historical and analytic. What matters fundamentally is what the Confrontation Clause meant to the people who framed and adopted it. And since the Court thinks the answer to *that* question is that the Confrontation Clause was originally understood to codify common-law restrictions on the use of testimonial hearsay against criminal defendants, deciding a confrontation case today requires an analytic inquiry into the nature of the hearsay involved—is it testimonial or nontestimonial?—as well as a historical inquiry into any common-law doctrines that might have allowed the use of the evidence against criminal defendants in the late eighteenth century. The inquiry is resolutely and self-consciously nonconsequentialist—one might say legalistic.

This is where the chief complication lies in describing the link between confrontation and hearsay after *Crawford*. For although *Crawford* and its successor cases have weakened the operational and argumentative connections between the Sixth Amendment and evidence law, they have done so by strengthening another kind of link between the two bodies of law. Call it the *historical* link. Confrontation doctrine is now bound more tightly than ever to a particular *stage* of hearsay law: hearsay doctrine as of the time of the drafting and adoption of the Sixth Amendment. Indeed, the chief job of the Confrontation Clause has become preserving and enforcing eighteenth-century protections against prosecution hearsay. The Court has decoupled confrontation doctrine from *modern* hearsay law by yoking it to the hearsay law of the late 1700s, or—more accurately—to the Court's idealized version of the hearsay law of the late 1700s, a version far tighter and more consistent than what was actually applied in founding-era criminal trials.

The story of hearsay law since the late 1700s is a story of harmonization followed by decline. Over the course of the nineteenth century, the rules of evidence were applied with new consistency, uniformity, and predictability; the hearsay rule became a real rule. Almost as soon as that happened, though, exceptions to the rule began proliferating and expanding, and over the past century the hearsay rule has grown progressively weaker, in the United States and throughout the common-law world. It was hard to find any examples of hearsay exceptions being narrowed or eliminated; the process was "one of ever-increasing scope for the exceptions."[261] If anything, that process accelerated as the twentieth century drew to a close. So linking the Confrontation Clause to the *modern* hearsay rule, as the Court did before *Crawford*, meant that in criminal cases as in civil cases, restrictions on the use of out-of-

---

[261] Allen, 76 Minn L Rev at 799 (cited in note 3).

court statements steadily loosened. Linking the Confrontation Clause to *eighteenth-century* hearsay law—and to the law on the books, not the law in practice—does something very different. It resurrects and preserves the hearsay rule in a particularly inflexible and relatively undeveloped form. The *Crawford* doctrine is not "conservative" or "liberal" in traditional criminal justice terms, but it is "conservative" in an older, less specialized sense. If by the end of the twentieth century the hearsay rule seemed to be in "death throes,"[262] the Supreme Court now has given it—or an (imagined) eighteenth-century version of it—a new lease on life.

III. RAMIFICATIONS

Resurrecting and preserving an old legal rule can be a good thing. Not all change is for the better. The whole point of a constitution, on one view, is to insulate certain rules from the vicissitudes of politics and public opinion.[263] Nonetheless there are at least three reasons to be concerned about the way the Supreme Court has now read eighteenth-century hearsay rules into the Constitution—wholly apart from whether the Court's originalist reasoning is convincing.[264] First, the long-term decline of the hearsay rule has been well deserved. The uncompromising version of the rule dusted off and constitutionalized by the Court has little to recommend it and will lead to predictable injustices. Second, the *Crawford* doctrine, with its antiquarian focus on eighteenth-century rules of evidence, has diverted attention from what should be the central question under the Confrontation Clause today: how to guarantee twenty-first-century criminal defendants a meaningful opportunity to meet and to challenge the evidence against them. Third, by creating two bodies of hearsay law—one, still evolving, for use in civil cases and to evidence introduced by criminal defendants, and a second, frozen in eighteenth-century amber and applicable only to evidence introduced by prosecutors—the Court has stifled a form of doctrinal cross-comparison

---

[262] Id at 798.

[263] This is, of course, Justice Scalia's view. See, for example, Antonin Scalia, *Common-Law Courts in a Civil-Law System: The Role of United States Federal Courts in Interpreting the Constitution and Laws*, in *A Matter of Interpretation: Federal Courts and the Law* 3 (Princeton, 1997).

[264] On the latter question, see Sklansky, 122 Harv L Rev at 1670–77 (cited in note 176); note 21.

that could lead to progressive improvement of the rules governing the use of out-of-court statements both in civil cases and in criminal cases.

A. THE CELEBRATED NIGHTMARE

The reason that the hearsay rule has long been in decline throughout the Anglo-American world is that it is dysfunctional—something that became apparent as soon as it began to be applied in earnest. The archaic, uncompromising version of the rule that the Supreme Court has now read into the Sixth Amendment excludes too much probative evidence with too little justification. This is true even when the rule is applied only to evidence offered against criminal defendants. In a limited but important group of cases, it generates predictable injustices.

We have already touched on the most conspicuous subcategory of those cases: murder prosecutions in which the victim, in the days or weeks leading up to her death, complained about threats, assaults, or other incriminating behavior by the defendant. I say "her death" because the defendants in these cases tend to be men, and the victims tend to be women.[265] Much of the liberalization of the hearsay rule over the last twenty years—in the Commonwealth and, before *Crawford*, in the United States—has been part of a more general movement to make the criminal justice system more responsive to violence against women, especially violence committed by intimates, former intimates, and would-be intimates. The legal system still struggles to protect women against domestic violence, and the hearsay rule makes it harder—especially in cases where the victim's death prevents her from repeating in court the complaints she earlier made about the defendant. Judge Lance Ito, who presided over O. J. Simpson's murder trial, was right: "It seems only just and right that a crime victim's own words be heard . . . in the court where the facts and circumstances of her demise are to be presented."[266]

The hearsay rule can hinder domestic violence prosecutions even when the victim is still alive, because women abused by their domestic partners often do not want to testify at trial. Sometimes

---

[265] Madeleine Smith and Emile L'Angelier notwithstanding. See note 47.

[266] *People v Simpson*, No BA097211, 1995 WL 21768, *4–5 (Cal Super, Jan 18, 1995); see note 47 and accompanying text.

they fear retaliation, and sometimes they simply have a change of heart. Either way, prosecutors often want to use, in lieu of live testimony, statements that victims of domestic violence have previously provided to the police or to 911 operators. The hearsay rule will typically make the earlier statements inadmissible, and some of the liberalization of the rule over the past two decades has been aimed squarely at allowing prosecutors to get around this obstacle. The exceptions for "excited utterances" and "present sense impressions" have been stretched, and new exceptions have been created for reports of abuse or threats of abuse. *Crawford* and its successor cases, particularly *Davis* and *Giles*, have rendered most of those efforts unconstitutional—except, possibly, in cases where the doctrine of equitable forfeiture applies. Justice Scalia stressed in *Davis* that "one who obtains the absence of a witness by wrongdoing forfeits the constitutional right to confrontation," and he strongly suggested that the "wrongdoing" could include scaring a witness into silence.[267] Although *Giles*, as we have seen, limited the doctrine of equitable forfeiture to cases involving conduct *aimed* at preventing a witness from testifying,[268] that condition may well be satisfied in many cases in which a victim of domestic violence declines to testify against her abuser. Nevertheless, it remains to be seen how often domestic violence prosecutors will actually be able to demonstrate the factual predicate necessary for invoking the doctrine of equitable forfeiture.

In cases where prosecutors cannot make that showing, it will often be debatable whether the *Crawford* doctrine has advanced or set back the interests of justice. Substituting prior statements of victims for courtroom testimony in domestic violence cases— notwithstanding that the victims were alive and locatable—was a controversial practice, and criticism of the practice provided some of the impetus for the Court's decision in *Crawford*.[269] Part of the intuitive appeal of the confrontation right is the idea that accusers should have to look into the eyes of the person they are accusing. More than once, Justices of the Supreme Court have invoked President Eisenhower's reported description of the code he learned growing up in Abilene, Kansas: "In this country, if some-

---

[267] *Davis v Washington*, 547 US 813, 833–34 (2006).

[268] See notes 219–23 and accompanying text.

[269] See, for example, Friedman and McCormack, 150 U Pa L Rev at 1171 (cited in note 143).

one dislikes you, or accuses you, he must come up in front. He cannot hide behind the shadow."[270] This idea has little force when there is no possibility of bringing the defendant face to face with his accuser, because his accuser is dead, but it may be good reason to insist on courtroom testimony when it can, in fact, be obtained. Or then again, it might not be. Perhaps the whole idea of looking your accuser in the eye is itself a gendered privileging of physical force and intimidation, an artifact and an instrument of patriarchy.[271] If so, then virtually every case of domestic violence that cannot now be prosecuted because of *Crawford*, *Davis*, and *Giles*— and there appear to be a great many[272]—is a case of justice impeded.

For present purposes, we need not go that far. Even without a strict version of the hearsay rule, like the one the Supreme Court has now read into the Constitution, a rational legal system—especially one with a constitutional clause guaranteeing a right of "confrontation"—might well require accusers to meet the person they are accusing face to face. That is, in fact, precisely the kind of rule many legal systems around the world seem to have adopted, while abandoning or rejecting the hearsay rule in its traditional form. Where the American hearsay rule, now constitutionalized, goes beyond these overseas analogs is in excluding statements by witnesses who are now dead or otherwise unavailable, possibly because of the defendant's own wrongdoing, but not because of wrongdoing that can be proven to have had the *goal* of preventing testimony. This is not a large category of cases, but neither is it merely hypothetical. Cases of this kind recur with some regularity, and they tend to attract attention. Every time the statements of a homicide victim like Nicole Brown Simpson, Brenda Avie, or Julie Jensen are ruled inadmissible, a toll is taken.

It is a toll that may not be measured only in terms of justice left undone. Even when a conviction can be secured without use

---

[270] *Coy v Iowa*, 487 US 1012, 1017–18 (1988), citing 1953 speech by President Eisenhower quoted in Pollitt, 8 J Pub L at 381 (cited in note 31); see also *Coy*, 487 US at 1017 ("The phrase persists, 'Look me in the eye and say that.'"); *Jay v Boyd*, 351 US 345, 372 (1956) (Frankfurter, J, dissenting) (invoking President Eisenhower's 1953 description of the Abilene code); id at 374–75 (Douglas, J, dissenting) (same).

[271] For a thoughtful argument along these lines, see Mark Egerman, *Avoiding Confrontation* (unpublished manuscript, 2010) (on file with author).

[272] See, for example, Tom Lininger, *Prosecuting Batterers After Crawford*, 91 Va L Rev 747, 749–50 (2005).

of the victim's statements, but especially when it cannot, refusing to allow the jury to hear the victim's own words can erode the "moral credibility" of the criminal justice system—its ability to build consensus and to secure compliance.[273] More particularly, it may send a signal about the seriousness with which the state takes domestic violence, and the degree to which it can be relied upon to protect the victims of domestic violence and to bring the perpetrators to account.

Nor will these tolls be paid only when statements from dead victims are excluded in homicide cases. Similar costs may arise when chemists, medical examiners, or other forensic analysts die or otherwise become unavailable before trial, and their reports become inadmissible. The majority and the dissenters in *Melendez-Diaz* argued at length about how difficult it will be for prosecutors to call laboratory analysts to the stand instead of relying on their reports, but virtually all of the discussion assumed that the analysts *could* be called to testify, at least in theory. In cases of that kind, the Court may well be right that requiring live testimony will not be burdensome, because in the vast run of cases defendants will waive the requirement.[274] But when calling the witness is impossible, waivers are much less likely. It is one thing for defense counsel to waive the right to live testimony when calling the analyst seems like an empty exercise; it is quite another thing—in many cases it would probably be malpractice—to waive that right when the analyst is dead, and insisting on live testimony means keeping the lab results out of the trial altogether.

It is rare, fortunately, for forensic chemists to die before trial, but it happens more often with medical examiners.[275] Autopsies typically are conducted shortly after death, but it can sometimes take years for a homicide case to be charged, let alone come to trial. Partly because autopsies are often conducted when it is not yet clear that there will be a criminal investigation—or even when it is reasonably clear that there will not be one—autopsies could in theory be distinguished from chemical analysis of seized substances, the kind of forensic analysis involved in *Melendez-Diaz*. Autopsy reports can also be distinguished from the laboratory

---

[273] Paul H. Robinson and John M. Darley, *The Utility of Desert*, 91 Nw U L Rev 453, 457, 471–78 (1997); see also Tom R. Tyler, *Why People Obey the Law* (Princeton, 1990).

[274] See *Melendez-Diaz v Massachusetts*, 129 S Ct 2527, 2542 (2009).

[275] See, for example, *People v Geier*, 41 Cal 4th 555, 602 (2007).

analyses in *Melendez-Diaz* on the ground that medical examiners typically do not submit their results in a formal statement signed under oath: part of the majority's reasoning in *Melendez-Diaz* was that the certificates at issue in that case were "quite plainly affidavits: 'declaration[s] of facts written down and sworn to by the declarant before an officer authorized to administer oaths.'"[276] It is hard to believe, though, that the result in *Melendez-Diaz* would have been different had the certificates been unsworn. The critical point for the Court seemed to be that the certificates were "functionally identical to live, in-court testimony," because they provided "the precise testimony the analysts would be expected to provide if called at trial,"[277] and they were "'made under circumstances which would lead an objective witness reasonably to believe that the statement would be available for use at a later trial.'"[278] Much the same could be said about autopsy reports, even if it will often be less clear whether the facts found in an autopsy will ultimately prove relevant in a criminal trial.

And, in fact, the majority opinion in *Melendez-Diaz* strongly suggested that autopsy reports, like the reports of forensic chemists, are "testimonial" for purposes of the Confrontation Clause. Responding to an argument raised by the dissent—which suggested that coroners' reports were admissible at common law without the coroner's testimony, and that modern-day forensic laboratory results should be treated similarly—Justice Scalia insisted that "whatever the status of coroner's report at common law in England, they were not accorded any special status in American practice."[279]

Before the Supreme Court decided *Melendez-Diaz*, every court that had considered the status of autopsy reports under *Crawford* had deemed them nontestimonial—sometimes on the ground that autopsies are not carried out in anticipation of litigation, sometimes on the ground that coroners are not allied with law enforcement, sometimes on the ground that they are "descriptive" or "factual," and sometimes on the ground that they fall within

---

[276] See *Melendez-Diaz*, 129 S Ct at 2532, quoting *Black's Law Dictionary* at 62 (cited in note 39).

[277] Id at 2532.

[278] Id at 2531, quoting *Crawford v Washington*, 541 US 36, 52 (2004).

[279] *Melendez-Diaz*, 129 S Ct at 2538.

the business records exception to the hearsay rule.[280] These arguments seemed dubious even before *Melendez-Diaz*. Nevertheless, it is worth taking seriously the unanimous sentiment by courts that autopsy reports should not be deemed testimonial.

Carolyn Zabrycki argues persuasively that those decisions have been driven by the pragmatic recognition that excluding an autopsy report in a case where the medical examiner is not available to testify can derail a murder prosecution without advancing any significant, countervailing goal. She points out that autopsies, unlike lab tests, generally cannot be redone: "The body decomposes and exhumation poses multiple difficulties."[281] Meanwhile the practical benefits of cross-examining the medical examiner will typically be slight: examiners "rarely remember the details of an individual autopsy at the time of trial," and if the goal is to expose deviations from standard practice or discrepancies in the report, questioning another examiner from the same office will likely be as helpful as questioning the examiner who carried out the autopsy.[282] Beyond that, medical examiners—like the state laboratory analysts in *Melendez-Diaz*—are formally independent of the police and the prosecutors. They are at low risk of being caught up in what the Supreme Court has memorably called "the often competitive enterprise of ferreting out crime."[283]

None of this is to say that cross-examination of medical examiners will never be valuable, nor even that medical examiners should be excused from testifying. It is to say, though, that excluding an autopsy report because the author is dead or otherwise unavailable to testify is the sort of thing that has given the hearsay rule such a bad name. Constitutionalizing results of this kind should give us pause.

The injustices caused by excluding prosecution evidence will involve, by definition, erroneous acquittals rather than erroneous injustices, but that should provide little comfort. In the first place,

---

[280] See Zabrycki, 96 Cal L Rev at 1101–13 (cited in note 244).

[281] Id at 1114.

[282] Id at 1116.

[283] *Johnson v United States*, 333 US 10, 14 (1948). Zabrycki suggested that the Supreme Court should deem a statement testimonial only if the statement was generated or elicited with the participation of "adversarial governmental officials" responsible for investigating or prosecuting the defendant. Zabrycki, 96 Cal L Rev at 1137–38 (cited in note 244). Justice Kennedy noted this suggestion with approval in his *Melendez-Diaz* dissent, see 129 S Ct at 2552, but the majority was unreceptive.

wrongful acquittals are a form of injustice. There was once a fashion in legal scholarship to dismiss pro-defense errors as socially inconsequential. The idea was that criminal trials serve solely to protect individuals against the state, and that it "inflicts no tangible harm on anyone when a criminal evades punishment."[284] That sentiment is less common today, and for good reason: it trades too obviously on a picture of the criminal justice system in which "victims do not appear."[285]

In any event, the Court's new approach to confrontation threatens unjust convictions as well as unjust acquittals. Partly this is because the *Crawford* line of cases have diverted attention from other, better ways to give meaning to the Confrontation Clause— a matter I will take up below. And partly it is because constitutionalizing the hearsay rule for prosecution evidence inevitably, if indirectly, bolsters the rule's application to evidence offered by criminal defendants, too. On a rhetorical level, it lends respectability to the old idea that hearsay's "intrinsic weakness" justifies keeping it from the jury, even when live testimony cannot be substituted. On a practical level, restrictions on prosecution hearsay make it easier to defend rules that "level the playing field" by blocking defense hearsay.

Thus, for example, the Federal Rules of Evidence contain an exception to the hearsay ban for statements by an unavailable declarant that were so plainly contrary to the declarant's interest that no reasonable person would be expected to make them unless they were true.[286] Absent corroboration, though, that exception is unavailable for statements "tending to expose the declarant to criminal liability and offered to exculpate the accused."[287] The thinking is that evidence of this kind is too unreliable: there is too large a risk of "fabrication either of the fact of the making of the confession or in its contents."[288] Before *Crawford*, this rule was sometimes defended on the ground that it blocked the defense from using unreliable hearsay analogous to some of the unreliable

---

[284] David Luban, *The Adversary System Excuse*, in David Luban, ed, *The Good Lawyer: Lawyers' Roles and Lawyers' Ethics* 83, 91 (Rowman, 1983); see also Murray L. Schwartz, *The Zeal of the Civil Advocate*, 1983 Am Bar Found Res J 543, 553 (suggesting that "the basic purpose" of criminal procedure is "to avoid one type of error").

[285] William H. Simon, *The Ethics of Criminal Defense*, 91 Mich L Rev 1703, 1708 (1993).

[286] FRE 804(b)(3).

[287] Id.

[288] Advisory Committee Note to FRE 804(b)(3).

hearsay the Confrontation Clause stopped the prosecution from introducing. Now that the Supreme Court has suggested that the Confrontation Clause provides no protection against any form of prosecution hearsay, so long as it is "nontestimonial," amendments are pending to re-level the playing field—not by removing the corroboration requirement for statements against penal interest offered by the defense, but by statutorily extending that requirement to the prosecution.[289]

B. OTHER APPROACHES TO CONFRONTATION

On its face, the Sixth Amendment does not make testimonial hearsay inadmissible against criminal defendants. It gives a defendant the right "to be confronted with the witnesses against him." A major cost of the *Crawford* doctrine, beyond the injustices it will generate directly by excluding probative evidence offered by the prosecution, and indirectly by bolstering the exclusion of probative evidence offered by criminal defendants, is the distraction it will provide from more promising ways to interpret the Confrontation Clause.

It says something about the state of constitutional interpretation today that virtually all of the opinions in *Crawford, Davis, Giles*, and *Melendez-Diaz*—the dissents included—have assumed, at least for the sake of discussion, (*a*) that the Confrontation Clause should be interpreted today the same way it was interpreted in 1791, (*b*) that the clause was understood in 1791 to codify the then-existing law of hearsay as it applied to evidence offered against criminal defendants, and (*c*) that "to be confronted with" means, essentially, to have your lawyer cross-examine. Not all of these assumptions are new: the third, as we have seen, dates back at least to Wigmore, and the first reflects the strong version of originalism that Justices Scalia and Justice Thomas have long championed. The second

---

[289] See Report of the Advisory Committee on Evidence Rules (May 12, 2008). The proposed Committee Note explains that "[a] unitary approach to declarations against penal interest assures both the prosecution and the accused that the Rule will not be abused and that only reliable hearsay statements will be admitted under the exception." Id, attachment at 2; see also, for example, Letter to Peter G. McCabe, Secretary of the Committee on Rules of Practice and Procedure, Judicial Conference of the United States, by Professor David P. Leonard, Loyola Law School, Los Angeles, at 3 (Feb 14, 2009) (commenting that "it is sensible and fair to level the playing field by imposing the same restrictions on the prosecution as are imposed on the accused").

assumption is the only one added by *Crawford*. Nonetheless, all three assumptions are leaps of faith.

Suppose we did not make them. How might we give meaning to the Confrontation Clause? One well-pedigreed strategy, which might be called liberal originalism, seeks to understand what a clause signified when it was adopted—what evils it aimed to prevent, and why—and then asks how we can best be faithful to those purposes today.[290] The guiding thought, once commonplace but today increasingly contrarian, is that a constitutional right "must be capable of wider application than the mischief which gave it birth"; otherwise principles "declared in words might be lost in reality."[291] A related strategy—less frequently endorsed than the first, but perhaps more often practiced—focuses not so much on the wording of the a constitutional clause but on the set of evolving, common-law principles for which it has served as a focal point. The question under this approach would be, not what purposes the Confrontation Clause was originally intended to serve, but what purposes our constitutional tradition suggests that it should serve today. David Strauss, who champions this second approach, calls it "common law constitutional interpretation."[292] Fortunately, we do not need to choose between the two approaches, because either would produce the same result: an understanding of the Confrontation Clause less tethered to hearsay and cross-examination, and aimed more broadly at providing criminal defendants with a meaningful opportunity "to know, to examine, to explain, and to rebut"[293] the proof offered against them.

Start with liberal originalism, which takes as its touchstone the

---

[290] See, for example, Jeb Rubenfeld, *Revolution by Judiciary* (Harvard, 2005); James Boyd White, *Justice as Translation: An Essay in Cultural and Legal Criticism* (Chicago, 1990); Lawrence Lessig, *Fidelity in Translation*, 71 Tex L Rev 1165 (1993); David A. Sklansky, *The Fourth Amendment and Common Law*, 100 Colum L Rev 1739, 1743, 1746–47, 1763–64 (2000).

[291] *Weems v United States*, 217 US 349, 373 (1910); see also, for example, *Harmelin v Michigan*, 501 US 957, 1015 (Kennedy, J, concurring in part); *Browning-Ferris Industries of Vt v Kelco Disposal*, 492 US 257, 276 (1989); *Thompson v Oklahoma*, 487 US 815, 821 n 4 (1988); *Glass v Louisiana*, 471 US 1080 (1985) (Brennan, J, dissenting); *Rummel v Estelle*, 445 US 263, 307 (1980) (Powell, J, dissenting); *Gregg v Georgia*, 428 US 153, 171 (1976) (opinion of Stewart); *Estes v Texas*, 381 US 532, 564 (1965) (Warren, J, concurring); *Poe v Ullman*, 367 US 497, 551 (1962) (Harlan, J, dissenting); *Olmstead v United States*, 277 US 438, 473 (1928) (Brandeis, J, dissenting).

[292] See David A. Strauss, *Common Law Constitutional Interpretation*, 63 U Chi L Rev 877 (1996).

[293] Pollitt, 8 J Pub L at 402 (cited in note 31).

broad underlying aims of the Confrontation Clause when it was adopted. To "confront" meant, in the late eighteenth century, essentially what it means today: to face or to challenge. Thus Alexander Hamilton, writing as Publius, complained that the anti-Federalist pamphleteer Cato had made claims about the Constitution that were refuted by the plain text of the document, and he called for Cato to be "confronted with the evidence of this fact," so that he could try to "justify or extenuate the shameful outrage he has offered to the dictates of truth and to the rules of fair dealing."[294] Similarly, James Madison argued that the Articles of Confederation could be dissolved without the unanimous consent of the states, because a breach by any party to the pact absolved the others from their continuing obligations, and any state that objected to dissolving the Confederation would have difficulty answering "the MULTIPLE and IMPORTANT infractions with which they may be confronted."[295] Another anti-Federalist, the Federal Farmer, wrote that the "unalienable or fundament rights in the United States" included the rights of a criminal defendant "to have witnesses face to face" and "to confront their adversaries before the judge."[296] It was common, in the context of court proceedings, to speak of confronting "accusers" as well as "witnesses";[297] several of the state bills of rights, for example, gave criminal defendants the right to be confronted with "accusers and witnesses."[298] Noah Webster's dictionary defined "confronted" as "[s]et face to face, or in opposition; brought into the presence of."[299] Webster offered several definitions of the root word "confront," including: (1) "[t]o stand face to face in full view; to face; to stand in front"; (2) "[t]o stand in direct opposition; to oppose";

---

[294] Federalist 67 (Hamilton), in Ian Shapiro, ed, *The Federalist Papers* 340, 341 (Yale, 2009).

[295] Federalist 43 (Madison), in *The Federalist Papers* 219, 226 (cited in note 294).

[296] Letters from the Federal Farmer, No VI (Dec 25, 1787), reprinted in Herbert Storing, ed, 2 *The Complete Anti-Federalist* 262 (Chicago, 1981).

[297] See, for example, The Address and Reasons of Dissent of the Minority of the Convention of Pennsylvania to their Constituents (Dec 12, 1787), reprinted in Storing, 3 *The Complete Anti-Federalist* at 151 (cited in note 296); The Impartial Examiner, No I, Virginia Independent Chronicle (March 5, 1788), reprinted in Storing, 5 *The Complete Anti-Federalist* at 183 (cited in note 296).

[298] North Carolina Declaration of Rights § VII (1776); Vermont Declaration of Rights Ch I, § X (1777); see also Delaware Declaration of Rights § 14 (1776) ("accusers or witnesses").

[299] Noah Webster, 1 *An American Dictionary of the English Language* (Converse, 1828).

and (3) "[t]o set face to face; to bring up in the presence of; as an accused person and a witness, in court, for the examination and discovery of the truth; followed by with." And he defined "confrontation" as "[t]he act of bringing two persons into the presence of each other for examination and discovery of truth."[300]

There is little reason to suppose, therefore, that the phrase "confronted with the witnesses against him" would have been understood in 1791 as simply a way of referring to cross-examination and nothing more. Instead, the phrase likely carried the two broad connotations it does today: to meet the witnesses face to face; and to oppose them, to challenge their testimony. Both connotations can be found more explicitly in precursors to the Sixth Amendment. The Massachusetts Declaration of Rights and the New Hampshire Bill of Rights, for example, both gave a criminal defendant the right "to meet the witnesses against him face to face,"[301] while the North Carolina Declaration of Rights guaranteed the right "to confront the accusers and witnesses with other testimony."[302]

The language and the background of the Confrontation Clause suggest that the paradigmatic evil against which it took aim—what Jed Rubenfeld would call its "core, actuating application" or "foundational paradigm case"[303]—was, in fact, a case like Raleigh's: a case, that is to say, where state authorities questioned the key witness against a defendant outside his presence, and the defendant then requested but was denied the opportunity to face and to challenge the witness.[304] As the Court pointed out in *Crawford*, the revolutionary generation had close and bitter familiarity with proceedings of this kind, because a 1769 act of Parliament allowed customs cases to be brought in vice-admiralty courts, which historically relied on depositions and on oral testimony taken by the judge in private.[305] The language and history of the Confrontation Clause suggest something else, as well: that the underlying value the Confrontation Clause sought to protect was not, first and

---

[300] Id.

[301] Massachusetts Declaration of Rights § XII (1780); New Hampshire Bill of Rights § XV (1783).

[302] North Carolina Declaration of Rights § VII (1776).

[303] Rubenfeld, *Revolution by Judiciary* at 119, 134 (cited in note 290).

[304] See text accompanying notes 186–87.

[305] See *Crawford*, 541 US at 47–48; Pollitt, 8 J Pub L at 395–97 (cited in note 31).

foremost, the specifics of cross-examination but the broader ability of an accused to test and to challenge the state's proof.

That is a value that runs deep in the Anglo-American legal tradition (and, as we have seen, in the Continental legal tradition).[306] It is also a value that is plainly worth caring about. Protecting a defendant's ability to probe the evidence offered against him serves, in fact, three more basic goals. It helps to ensure the accuracy of verdicts. It guards against authoritarian abuse of the criminal justice system—a particular concern, obviously, of the Revolutionary generation. And it accords the defendant a degree of dignity, allowing him some agency in the adjudication process and treating his input and his objections as worthy of respect. For all of these reasons, fidelity to the Framers' purposes is not the only route to this broader view of confrontation—the view that confrontation means more than cross-examination, that it means a meaningful opportunity to test and to challenge the prosecution's evidence. That is also the understanding of confrontation likely to be generated by a more open-ended assessment of how best to extend our evolving constitutional traditions.[307]

Attending to the broad values underlying the Confrontation Clause does not require ignoring its narrower aims. There are at least two reasons to interpret the Confrontation Clause today to prohibit, at a minimum, what happened to Raleigh—to require, that is to say, that the state call witnesses to testify at trial, in the defendant's presence and subject to in-court challenge, rather than rely on testimony taken in private or statements given outside of court. The first applies only to the strategy of liberal originalism. Fans of that strategy often distinguish between, on the one hand, extending a constitutional clause beyond "the mischief which gave it birth" and, on the other hand, ignoring that mischief or treating its prohibition as up for grabs. Jed Rubenfeld, for example, draws a sharp line between the "fundamental commitments" made by the Constitution and the "mere intentions" of the framers and ratifiers.[308] But he thinks that the "foundational applications" of

---

[306] Consider Dennis, 2010 Crim L Rev at 271 (cited in note 174) (arguing that the confrontation rights protected under UK and European law should be understood to rest, first and foremost, on a defendant's interest in "test[ing] the probative value of the evidence").

[307] See Strauss, 63 U Chi L Rev 877 (cited in note 292).

[308] Rubenfeld, *Revolution by Judiciary* at 15 (cited in note 290).

a constitutional provision—the core, paradigmatic cases in which it was expected to apply—are themselves "definitive of the Constitution's commitments"; they are part of (but decidedly not all of) what the Constitution binds the nation to do or not to do.[309] They differ in this respect from expectations that a constitutional provision would *not* apply in a particular way: *those* understandings, "even if held by every framer and ratifier, are not commitments."[310] So "American judges are free to determine, and in fact have determined, that the Constitution's commitments require considerably more than was originally contemplated—but not less."[311]

This kind of appeal will mean little to believers in common-law constitutional interpretation. But there is a second, more pragmatic reason to think the Confrontation Clause should continue to prohibit the paradigmatic evil of Raleigh's trial—the evil, that is to say, of denying a defendant the right to meet and to challenge the key witnesses against him face to face. There may be times when the "foundational applications" of a constitutional provision no longer seem necessary, or even helpful, for securing the broader, "fundamental commitment" to which the provision seems to point, or for which it serves as a useful reminder. Those are test cases for modified, one-way-ratchet originalism of the kind that Jed Rubenfeld defends. They are also test cases, of a kind, for common-law constitutional interpretation: they force us to decide how free we really are from what might be thought the hard nucleus of original intent. The Second Amendment might present a test case of this kind; certainly there are many people who think that it does. But the Confrontation Clause is not in that category. Virtually no one thinks that what happened to Raleigh should be allowed to happen today: nobody suggests that it should be permissible to question a criminal defendant's alleged coconspirator outside the defendant's presence, introduce the results in court, and refuse to allow the defendant to question the witness himself or through his attorney.

The reason no one argues for that procedure is that it seems as threatening today as it did in the eighteenth century—or, for that matter, in Raleigh's time—to the underlying value protected

---

[309] Id; see also id at 119, 134.

[310] Id at 15.

[311] Id at 147.

by the Confrontation Clause, the ability of a defendant to test the prosecution's evidence. That is why the procedural right of a criminal defendant to challenge prosecution witnesses in open court, when they are available to testify, is so widely recognized as fundamental today, not just in common-law systems but also in civil-law countries and as a matter of international law.[312] The American hearsay rule—barring indirect evidence even when, through no fault of the government, direct proof is impossible—is more and more a global anomaly. But the procedural right to have informants and alleged accomplices questioned in open court has much broader support.

We can therefore safely bracket the question whether, at some point in the future, there might be grounds for thinking that procedure an obsolete means to the underlying goals of the Sixth Amendment. We are nowhere near that point today. I want to bracket, as well, certain recurring questions about how the courtroom confrontation should proceed: what limits should be allowed on cross-examination,[313] and whether some vulnerable witnesses, such as a young child the defendant is accused of abusing, should be permitted to testify outside the defendant's presence.[314] These are important questions, but they are tangential to the issue at the heart of this article: the Supreme Court's use of the Confrontation Clause to constitutionalize the hearsay rule. And they cast no doubt on the continued prohibition, under the Confrontation Clause, of the procedures followed in Raleigh's trial, and in the smuggling cases that so rankled the American colonists.

The Supreme Court was right in *Crawford* to treat those cases as the paradigmatic abuses targeted by the Confrontation Clause. The Court was right, also, to infer from those "foundational applications" that the Confrontation Clause bars some prosecution hearsay: that it is not limited, as Wigmore suggested, to governing the mode of testimony for any witness that the state chose to call at trial.[315] Construed that narrowly, the clause would prohibit ex parte taking of testimony at trial—the kind of thing permitted in vice-admiralty courts—but not the procedures followed in cases

---

[312] See text accompanying notes 161–75.

[313] See, for example, *Olden v Kentucky*, 488 US 227 (1988); *Delaware v Van Arsdall*, 475 US 673 (1986); *Davis v Alaska*, 415 US 308 (1974).

[314] Compare *Coy v Iowa*, 487 US 1012 (1988), with *Maryland v Craig*, 497 US 836 (1990).

[315] See note 180 and accompanying text.

like Raleigh's. As Justice Scalia pointed out for the Court in *Craw-ford*, Raleigh was "perfectly free to confront those who read Cob-ham's confession in court."[316] That option plainly did not give Raleigh what the Confrontation Clause aimed to provide: a mean-ingful opportunity to test and to challenge the state's proof. Given how powerfully the procedures in Raleigh's case threatened the underlying goals of the Confrontation Clause, and given the no-toriety of the case from the seventeenth century on, restricting the clause as Wigmore suggested has little to recommend it.

For similar reasons, it makes little sense to read the Confron-tation Clause to bar evidence of out-of-court statements only when they are obtained through some kind of formal, judicial or quasi-judicial procedure. Justice Thomas has suggested the provision should be interpreted in this way,[317] but the Court has been right to reject the suggestion. Even if Cobham's interrogation is thought sufficiently formal to satisfy Justice Thomas's test, the modern analogs of that interrogation are typically carried out by police officers, in settings that have few trappings of procedural formality. Letting prosecutors rely on those statements, and denying criminal defendants a chance to question the witnesses who make them, straightforwardly abridges defendants' right to test and to chal-lenge the evidence against them. Criticizing Justice Thomas's po-sition, Justice Scalia reasoned sensibly in *Davis* that "[r]estricting the Confrontation Clause to the precise forms against which it was originally directed is a recipe for its extinction"[318]—a nice way of saying that the provision "must be capable of wider application than the mischief which gave it birth."[319]

So the Court was right in *Crawford*—and in *Davis*, *Giles*, and *Melendez-Diaz*—to focus on the paradigmatic abuses targeted by the Confrontation Clause, and it was right to generalize from those abuses. The problem was how the Court generalized. Instead of seeing, in the Confrontation Clause, a fundamental commitment to let criminal defendants test and challenge the state's proof, the Court saw a provision aimed, above all, at barring "the civil-law mode of criminal procedure."[320] *That* was "the principal evil at

---

[316] *Crawford*, 541 US at 51.

[317] See *Davis v Washington*, 547 US 813, 835–36 (2006) (Thomas, J, dissenting in part).

[318] Id at 830 n 5 (opinion of the Court).

[319] *Weems*, 217 US at 373.

[320] *Crawford*, 541 US at 50.

which the Confrontation Clause was directed"[321]—the alien procedural system of Continental Europe. The *Crawford* line of cases
are part of a broader, recently revived pattern in constitutional
criminal procedure: the treatment of "civil-law traditions"[322] and
their "magistrate-directed, inquisitorial legal system,"[323] as a kind
of constitutional bogeyman, a negative polestar against which our
system can be defined. Elsewhere I have argued, on general
grounds, that this approach to constitutional criminal procedure
is unjustified and misguided.[324] Here I want to stress the way in
which it clouded the Court's view of the Confrontation Clause.

Because the Court has treated the Confrontation Clause as
aimed, first and foremost, at entrenching the common-law system
of criminal adjudication and warding off the rival, civil-law system,
the Justices have found it easy to suppose that the confrontation
the Sixth Amendment guarantees must have to do, at bottom, with
promoting cross-examination (long celebrated as the common
law's most important and most distinctive contribution to criminal
adjudication) and prohibiting hearsay (the best known and most
characteristic feature of the Anglo-American law of evidence). The
Court's fixation on the divide between common-law systems and
civil-law systems pushed it away from any understanding of the
Confrontation Clause that would tie it to values shared by the
common-law and civil-law traditions—such as protecting a defendant's broad ability to test and to challenge the state's proof.

Suppose we took seriously the idea that the fundamental aim
of the Confrontation Clause is not guarding against civil-law taint
but instead safeguarding the ability of a defendant to probe and
to fight back against the evidence offered against him. What would
safeguarding that ability mean, in our day—beyond barring the
kind of ex parte testimony that made Raleigh's trial so infamous?

Melendez-Diaz is a nice point of entry for that inquiry, because
the laboratory analyses at issue in that case are part of an epochal,
ongoing transformation of criminal adjudication: the rapidly increasing importance of scientific evidence. In a variety of ways,
the "scientization of proof"[325] has rendered traditional ways of

---

[321] Id.

[322] *Blakely v Washington*, 542 US 296 (2004).

[323] *Sanchez-Llamas v Oregon*, 548 US 331, 357 (2006).

[324] See Sklansky, 122 Harv L Rev 1634 (cited in note 176).

[325] Damaška, *Evidence Law Adrift* at 147 (cited in note 30).

challenging the prosecution's case—including cross-examination—flagrantly inadequate.[326] Defense attorneys lack the technical training to assess scientific evidence and to spot its potential weaknesses.[327] They lack connections with independent experts and the resources to hire them.[328] They lack access to the computerized databases upon which the most advanced forms of forensic science, such as DNA typing, heavily rely.[329] Even if they could mount a meritorious challenge to the scientific evidence offered by the prosecution, they generally lack an audience—on the bench or in the jury box—with the background to understand it.[330] Beyond all this, an individual defense attorney, bound by tradition and professional ethics to a single-minded focus on the representation of a particular client, lacks the time, the incentive, and the organizational platform needed to oversee forensic laboratories in the systematic way that legal scholars and scientists increasingly say is required.[331]

There is growing recognition that these deficiencies have allowed shoddy and sometimes fraudulent forensic science to go unchallenged, leading in a distressing number of cases to wrongful convictions.[332] Justice Scalia's majority opinion in *Melendez-Diaz* cited a review by Brandon Garrett and Peter Neufeld of the first 220 convicted defendants subsequently exonerated by DNA testing; their findings make clear that "invalid forensic science" was involved in a significant fraction of these cases.[333] What Justice

---

[326] See, for example, id; Brandon L. Garrett and Peter J. Neufeld, *Invalid Forensic Science Testimony and Wrongful Convictions*, 95 Va L Rev 1, 33, 89 (2009); Erin Murphy, *The New Forensics: Criminal Justice, False Certainty, and the Second Generation of Scientific Evidence*, 95 Cal L Rev 721 (2007).

[327] See, for example, Murphy, 95 Cal L Rev at 753–56, 770–71 (cited in note 326).

[328] See, for example, id at 771–72; Garrett and Neufeld, 95 Va L Rev at 33–34 (cited in note 326).

[329] See Murphy, 95 Cal L Rev at 751–53, 772–74 (cited in note 326).

[330] See, for example, Damaška, *Evidence Law Adrift* at 144–47 (cited in note 30); National Research Council, Committee on Identifying the Needs of the Forensic Sciences Community, *Strengthening Forensic Science in the United States: A Path Forward* 85 (National Academies, 2009); Murphy, 95 Cal L Rev at 768–70 (cited in note 326).

[331] See, for example, National Research Council, *Strengthening Forensic Science* at 214–15 (cited in note 330); Murphy, 95 Cal L Rev at 761–63 (cited in note 326).

[332] See, for example, Pamela R. Metzger, *Cheating the Constitution*, 59 Vand L Rev 475, 491 (2006).

[333] See Garrett and Neufeld, 95 Va L Rev 33 (cited in note 326). Justice Scalia read the study to conclude that "invalid forensic testimony contributed to the convictions in 60% of the cases," *Melendez-Diaz v Massachusetts*, 129 S Ct 2527, 2537 (2009), but this exaggerates the findings. Out of the 220 cases of exoneration they reviewed, Garrett and

Scalia glossed over is that all of these cases of bad forensics con-
tributing to wrongful convictions appear to have involved live, in-
court testimony by forensic analysts.[334] Garrett and Neufeld did
not identify *any* cases in which hearsay from forensic analysts contributed to the conviction of innocent defendants. (Indeed, as I
noted earlier, none of the exoneration cases to date involve trials
in which hearsay exceptions of any kind seem to have played a
significant role.) Instead, what they found was that cross-examination of the analysts was rarely effective in disclosing flaws in
their work or their reasoning;[335] that defense counsel rarely retained their own experts, because "courts routinely denied funding";[336] and that even when defendants *did* present testimony from
their own experts, the experts were sometimes "inexperienced"
and lacked "access to the underlying forensic evidence."[337] The
result was that there was rarely a "meaningful challenge" to "invalid forensic science testimony."[338]

The Court acknowledged in *Melendez-Diaz* that there might be
"other ways—and in some cases better ways—to challenge or verify
the results of a forensic test," but it reasoned that "the Constitution
guarantees one way: confrontation."[339] That is surely true, but the
Court also assumed that "confrontation" was synonymous with
"testing in the crucible of cross-examination"[340]—an assumption
that, for reasons that I hope are becoming clear, has little to recommend it. The text says "confronted with," not "cross-examine."
The framers and ratifiers of the Sixth Amendment do not appear
to have used those terms interchangeably. And reading the Confrontation Clause as narrowly focused on cross-examination and

---

Neufeld identified 156 in which forensic evidence was presented—71% of the total. See
Garrett and Neufeld, 95 Va L Rev at 12 (cited in note 326). They obtained trial transcripts
for 137 of those 156 cases, and concluded that 60% of those 137 cases—a total of 82—
"involved invalid forensic science testimony." See id at 12–14. Their findings thus suggest
that bad forensics were involved in somewhere around 43%—i.e., 60% of 71%—of the
220 cases of exoneration that Garrett and Neufeld reviewed.

[334] See Garrett and Neufeld, 95 Va L Rev at 12 (cited in note 326). Some of the cases,
though, did involve one examiner reporting work carried out by another. Telephone interview of Brandon Garrett, July 30, 2009.

[335] See Garrett and Neufeld, 95 Va L Rev at 10–11, 89 (cited in note 326).

[336] Id at 11.

[337] Id at 90.

[338] Id.

[339] *Melendez-Diaz*, 129 S Ct at 2536.

[340] Id, quoting *Crawford*, 541 US at 61.

the exclusion of hearsay increasingly disserves the underlying goal of the provision by diverting attention from what defendants require, today, in order to mount a meaningful challenge to the state's proof.

In the case of forensic science, meaningful confrontation likely requires a good deal more than disclosure of the results reached by the prosecution's analysts and their methodology. At a minimum, defendants probably need access to independent experts, to the underlying databases on which the state relies, and—where feasible—to samples and materials that will allow them to carry out their own tests.[341] The Supreme Court has rejected, in other contexts, the argument that effective confrontation may require pretrial access to certain categories of critical information,[342] but that position deserves reconsideration. It may also be that defendants cannot challenge forensic proof effectively on an individual, case-by-case basis; to make the Confrontation Clause more than an empty formalism in the increasing number of criminal cases that rely heavily on scientific proof, it may be necessary to put into place certain systemic protections—for example, regulatory oversight of forensic labs, and facilitation of information-pooling by defense attorneys.[343]

In addition to creating new challenges for criminal defendants, scientific advances have also changed our understanding of what defendants need in order to confront more traditional forms of state proof. For example, evidence has been accumulating for almost a century that eyewitness identifications are far less reliable than jurors (and many judges) tend to think they are, that they are prone to certain predictable forms of error, and that cross-examination offers limited protection against these risks. The evidence has grown much more compelling over the past few decades, partly because of a steadily growing body of research by experimental psychologists, partly because a broad consensus has emerged among experts about what that research shows, and partly because a majority of the wrongful convictions exposed by subsequent DNA testing have involved erroneous eyewitness testi-

---

[341] See, for example, Murphy, 95 Cal L Rev at 753, 790–91 (cited in note 326).

[342] See *United States v Ritchie*, 480 US 39 (1987); *United States v Bagley*, 473 US 667 (1985); Wayne R. LaFave et al, 6 *Criminal Procedure* § 24.3(a), at 341–43 (3d ed 2007).

[343] See Murphy, 95 Cal L Rev at 777, 788–91 (cited in note 326).

mony, against which cross-examination proved ineffective.[344]

An emerging consensus among psychologists and legal experts familiar with the problems of eyewitness identifications supports the use of expert testimony to inform the jury about those problems. Expert testimony of this kind is now widely accepted—but far from universally accepted.[345] Many courts continue to reason that expert testimony about the hazards of eyewitness identifications is unnecessary and inappropriate, and that cross-examination can be relied upon as a sufficient check against error. This is particularly common when eyewitness identification testimony is corroborated by other evidence, even when the other evidence is itself questionable. Courts often reason that cross-examination, followed and supported by defense counsel's arguments to the jury, is the historic and time-tested way for criminal defendants to expose the weakness in prosecution evidence, including eyewitness identifications.[346] They assume, in other words, what the Supreme Court assumed in *Crawford* and its successor cases, echoing Wigmore: that confrontation means cross-examination and nothing more. But perhaps a right to confront eyewitness testimony in the twenty-first century should mean more than an opportunity for cross-examination, at least in any case in which an eyewitness identification plays an important role. Perhaps it should entail some properly circumscribed entitlement to challenge the prosecution's proof through expert testimony on the hazards of eyewitness identifications. Precisely how such an entitlement should be circumscribed is a question for another article. The important point for present purposes is that the Supreme Court has closed off this avenue of inquiry as a matter of constitutional doctrine by reading the Confrontation Clause as, effectively, a codification of eighteenth-century hearsay doctrine.

In theory, analysis of this kind could be conducted without reference to the Confrontation Clause; instead, courts could ask whether a particular kind of assistance in confronting the state's proof is included in the right to present a defense—a right the

---

[344] See Jules Epstein, *The Great Engine That Couldn't: Science, Mistaken Identifications, and the Limits of Cross-Examination*, 36 Stetson L Rev 727 (2007).

[345] See, for example, id; Richard S. Schmechel et al, *Beyond the Ken? Testing Jurors' Understanding of Eyewitness Reliability Research*, 46 Jurimetrics J 177 (2006).

[346] See, for example, *Ford v Dretke*, 135 F Appx 769, 772 (5th Cir 2005); Epstein, 36 Stetson L Rev at 727–28 (cited in note 344).

Supreme Court has derived "in significant part" from "the Fourteenth Amendment's due process guarantee of fundamental fairness."[347] Two decades ago, in *Ake v Oklahoma*, the Court relied
upon this right in concluding that the state needed to provide a
court-appointed psychiatrist to an indigent capital defendant who
made clear before trial that his sanity would play a large role in
his defense.[348] The Court reasoned in *Ake* that fundamental fairness required giving a criminal defendant access to the "basic tools
of an adequate defense."[349] The same language could be used in
asking what resources, access, and organizational support a defendant needs in order to meaningfully challenge forensic science
evidence or an eyewitness identification.[350]

In practice, though, the right recognized in *Ake* has proven
narrow. Some lower courts have explicitly limited *Ake* to the context of court-appointed psychiatrists. Others have reached essentially the same result by refusing to treat anything as a "basic tool
of an adequate defense" if the defense could be raised without
it.[351] As David Harris has pointed out, "the presence of a psychiatrist in *Ake* was an all-or-nothing proposition": insanity was the
only defense raised, and it was inconceivable that the defense could
be raised without a psychiatrist.[352] When a resource requested by
the defense is not "a virtual necessity"[353] in this sense—because,
for example, forensic science or eyewitness testimony is only part
of the prosecution's case, or because cross-examination is thought
to be the classic, "most basic" way to challenge the prosecution's
evidence—courts often find *Ake* inapplicable.[354]

The problem is twofold. First, confrontation is not always

---

[347] *Ake v Oklahoma*, 470 US 68 (1985).

[348] Id at 86–87.

[349] Id at 77, quoting *Britt v North Carolina*, 404 US 226, 227 (1971).

[350] See, for example, Jay A. Zollinger, Comment, *Defense Access to State-Funded DNA Experts: Considerations of Due Process*, 85 Cal L Rev 1803 (1997).

[351] See, for example, David A. Harris, *The Constitution and Truth Seeking: A New Theory of Expert Services for Indigent Defendants*, 83 J Crim L & Criminol 469, 484–87 (1992).

[352] Id at 486.

[353] *Ake*, 470 US at 81, quoting Martin R. Gardner, *The Myth of the Impartial Psychiatric Expert—Some Comments Concerning Criminal Responsibility and the Decline of the Age of Therapy*, 2 Law & Psychol Rev 99, 113–14 (1976).

[354] *Ford*, 135 F Appx at 772; see Epstein, 14 Widener L Rev at 439 (cited in note 64); Paul C. Ginnelli, *Ake v. Oklahoma: The Right to Expert Assistance in a Post-Daubert, Post-DNA World*, 89 Cornell L Rev 1305, 1356 (2004); Harris, 83 J Crim L & Criminol at 484–86 (cited in note 351); Zollinger, 85 Cal L Rev at 1810–15 (cited in note 350).

treated as an integral part of the right to present a defense. Second, when confrontation *is* treated as an integral part of the right to present a defense, it tends to be understood narrowly as a right to cross-examination, rather than more robustly as an opportunity "to know, to examine, to explain, and to rebut"[355] the state's evidence. The first half of the problem could be addressed by understanding the right to present a defense the way a number of scholars have urged that it be understood: as a kind of interpretive synthesis of a criminal defendant's Sixth Amendment rights to confrontation "with the witnesses against him" and to "compulsory process for obtaining witnesses in his favor"—and perhaps also of the Sixth Amendment right to "the Assistance of Counsel."[356] The second half of the problem, though, requires reading the right to confrontation less woodenly than the Supreme Court has done. It requires a construction of the clause attendant to its broad, underlying purposes, and not just to the specific "mischief which gave it birth."[357]

C. CIVIL AND CRIMINAL CROSS-COMPARISON

Beyond the predictable injustices that will result from the exclusion of probative evidence, and beyond the distraction the *Crawford* line of cases provide from more productive ways to interpret the Confrontation Clause, there is a third reason to be concerned about the manner in which the Supreme Court has now constitutionalized the hearsay rule. We have seen that the damage caused by recent confrontation cases may be aggravated by the ramifications the decisions will have outside the area of their direct application: restrictions on prosecution hearsay are likely to bolster restrictions on hearsay offered by criminal defendants. At the same time, though, *Crawford* will make a different, more helpful kind of doctrinal cross-comparison *less* likely.

---

[355] Pollitt, 8 J Pub L at 402 (cited in note 31).

[356] US Const, Amend VI; see, for example, Harris, 83 J Crim L & Criminol 469 (cited in note 351); Jonakait, 27 Rutgers L J 77 (cited in note 187); Peter Westen, *The Compulsory Process Clause*, 73 Mich L Rev 72, 182–84 (1974); consider *California v Green*, 399 US 149, 176 (Harlan, J, concurring) (suggesting that "the confrontation guarantee may be thought, along with the right to compulsory process, merely to constitutionalize the right to a defense as we know it"); Amar, *Constitution and Criminal Procedure* at 130, 244 n 189 (viewing the Confrontation Clause and the Compulsory Process Clause as "fraternal twin[s]").

[357] *Weems*, 217 US at 373; see note 291 and accompanying text.

Because the version of the hearsay rule the Supreme Court has read into the Confrontation Clause is the eighteenth-century version—or at least what the Justices take to have been the eighteenth-century version—the Court has effectively frozen the hearsay rule, as applied to the evidence offered against criminal defendants, in the 1790s. The hearsay rule operating in civil cases, meanwhile, can continue its evolution—and gradual decline. The rhetorical support that *Crawford* and subsequent cases have provided for the hearsay rule—the credence these decisions lend to the traditional treatment of hearsay as too unreliable to count as evidence—might be expected to spill over to civil cases, just as it has to evidence offered by criminal defendants. But while judges and legislators often seek to "level the playing field" between prosecutors and criminal defendants, there is no similar instinct to equalize the restrictions on civil and criminal litigants. They are not on the same playing field to begin with.

In the wake of *Crawford*, for example, the Advisory Committee on Evidence Rules has sought to equalize the restrictions placed on the prosecutors and criminal defendants invoking the hearsay exception for declarations against penal interest, but it has made no effort to have the same rule apply in civil and criminal cases. The committee has proposed that both prosecutors and criminal defendants—but not civil litigants—be required to supply corroboration for any hearsay they seek to introduce under the exception for declarations against penal interest. The inconsistency between the rule in criminal cases and civil cases does not trouble the committee, given "the different policy questions that might be raised with respect to declarations against penal interest offered in civil cases"[358]—an oblique reference, presumably, to the fact that neither side in a civil case is bound by the Confrontation Clause. Nor is the committee alone in its approach; as far as the committee could tell, only one court had ever suggested that the corroboration requirement should be extended to civil cases.[359] In contrast, appellate courts have repeatedly and uniformly applied the corroboration requirement to all statements against penal interest offered in criminal cases, even though the explicit language

---

[358] Report of the Advisory Committee on Evidence Rules 2 (May 12, 2008); see note 289 and accompanying text.

[359] Id.

of the rule applies only to evidence offered by the defense.[360]

It was once much more common to compare the rules governing hearsay and confrontation in criminal cases with the parallel rules in civil cases. There was a kind of informal, rebuttable presumption that the rules should be similar, absent some special reason for them to differ. That presumption also operated—and continues to operate—for evidence law more generally. As a result there has long been a continual and constructive dialectic between the rules and practices governing proof in civil cases and the parallel rules and practices in criminal cases.[361] A hearsay exception developed in civil cases might give rise to difficulties in criminal cases—and those difficulties might lead to reconsideration of the exception in civil cases, as well.

Confrontation doctrine and hearsay law both used to be like evidence law more broadly in this respect; there was a regular practice of comparing practices across the civil-criminal divide. Like the rest of evidence law, the hearsay rule is framed the same for criminal and for civil cases, and so are most (but not all) of the exceptions to the rule. The Confrontation Clause, in contrast, is limited by its terms to criminal cases. But there is, or was, a tradition of treating the rule as pointing toward a broader principle of fairness applicable not just in criminal prosecutions but in civil and administrative proceedings as well—particularly those civil and administrative proceedings with stakes arguably as important as those in many criminal cases.

In the 1950s, for example, the procedures followed in employment cases involving alleged "security risks" were forcefully and sometimes successfully challenged on the ground that, as a matter of logic and basic fairness, the right to confrontation set forth in the Sixth Amendment "applies with equal vigor to civil proceedings."[362] Here is the Supreme Court in 1959, for example, striking down procedures used to revoke the security clearance of an engineer employed by a government contractor:

---

[360] See Edward J. Imwinkelried, *Rethinking the Limits of the Interpretive Maxim of Constitutional Avoidance: The Case Study of the Corroboration Requirement for Inculpatory Declarations Against Penal Interest (Federal Rule of Evidence 804(b)(3))*, 44 Gonzaga L Rev 187, 189, 200–01 (2009).

[361] See Sklansky and Yeazell, 94 Georgetown L J at 728–33 (cited in note 32).

[362] Pollitt, 8 J Pub L at 401 (cited in note 31); see also, for example, Robert B. McKay, *The Right of Confrontation*, 1959 Wash U L Q 122, 128–67.

Certain principles have remained relatively immutable in our jurisprudence. One of these is that where governmental action seriously injures an individual, and the reasonableness of the action depends on fact findings, the evidence used to prove the Government's case must be disclosed to the individual so that he has an opportunity to show that it is untrue. While this is important in the case of documentary evidence, it is even more important where the evidence consists of the testimony of individuals whose memory might be faulty or who, in fact, might be perjurers or persons motivated by malice, vindictiveness, intolerance, prejudice, or jealousy. We have formalized these protections in the requirements of confrontation and cross-examination. They have ancient roots. They find expression in the Sixth Amendment which provides that in all criminal cases the accused shall enjoy the right "to be confronted with the witnesses against him." This Court has been zealous to protect these rights from erosion. It has spoken out not only in criminal cases, but also in all types of cases where administrative and regulatory actions were under scrutiny.[363]

Eleven years later, the Court quoted this language when ruling that welfare recipients facing a termination of their benefits have a due process right "to confront and cross-examine the witnesses relied upon by the department."[364] But *Goldberg v Kelly* proved to be the beginning of the end—not just of welfare rights as a branch of due process, but of the idea that the Confrontation Clause could meaningfully be invoked in civil cases as well as criminal cases. Nowadays invocations of the Confrontation Clause are rejected out of hand in civil cases, no matter how high the stakes.[365]

The legal historian S. F. C. Milsom has stressed the productive use the common law has made of the dialectic—the confrontation, if you will—between "lines of reasoning" that develop "in separate compartments" but on occasion "come sufficiently close for a situation which has traditionally fallen under the one to be represented as within the other."[366] This is a method of development that draws strength from redundancy and inconsistency. In order for it to work, sets of rules need to develop separately, but not entirely separately; there needs to be periodic cross-comparison,

---

[363] *Greene v McElroy*, 360 US 474, 496–97 (1959).

[364] *Goldberg v Kelly*, 397 US 254, 270 (1970).

[365] See note 33.

[366] S. F. C. Milsom, *Reason in the Development of the Common Law*, in *Studies in the History of the Common Law* 149, 152 (Hambledon, 1985).

but not full coordination, between two or more bodies of law that address similar problems.

Some areas of constitutional law have precisely this character, and have developed in much the way Milsom described. First Amendment law is a good example, and so is Fourth Amendment law. Each of these fields has developed a hodgepodge of overlapping doctrinal boxes that develop semiautonomously. First Amendment law has separate rules for commercial speech, for public forums, for campaign finance, and so forth; Fourth Amendment law has specially tailored doctrines for automobile searches, for border searches, for searches incident to arrest, for "special needs" searches, and on and on. In each case, there are regular complaints (mostly from scholars, not from judges or lawyers) about doctrinal disorder, but there is reason to think the redundancy and inconsistency have facilitated the progressive improvement of the law: "overall disorder" is the price paid for "logical strength in detail."[367] Equal protection doctrine, by contrast, is much more unified, and the uniformity may well have stunted its development.[368] Various aspects of civil and criminal procedure have historically had the opposite problem: the separate sets of rules for civil cases and for criminal cases have been kept *too* isolated from each other, and there has been too little cross-comparison.[369]

Evidence law, to its benefit, has been different. Special rules of proof for civil or criminal cases have been viewed with skepticism, and that skepticism has proven useful.[370] Everyone recognizes that the rule governing proof in civil and criminal cases sometimes *should* diverge, but it is has proven productive to ask whether that is true in particular instances, and if so, why. Confrontation doctrine and hearsay law both used to be like evidence law more broadly in this respect, but over the past few decades confrontation has come to be seen, more and more, as a concern in criminal cases only.

The *Crawford* line of cases promises to accelerate that process.

---

[367] Id at 166; see also, for example, David A. Sklansky, *The Private Police*, 46 UCLA L Rev 1165, 1271–72 (1999).

[368] See David A. Sklansky, *Cocaine, Race, and Equal Protection*, 47 Stan L Rev 1283, 1312–15 (1995).

[369] See Sklansky and Yeazell, 94 Georgetown L J at 696–727 (cited in note 32).

[370] See id at 728–33.

When confrontation law loosely tracked *modern* hearsay law, a degree of cross-fertilization between civil and criminal cases was inevitable, because the hearsay rule itself operated the same, for the most part, across the civil-criminal divide. After *Crawford*, the Confrontation Clause continues to be linked to hearsay law, but to eighteenth-century hearsay law, not the modern, more lenient hearsay law applied in civil cases. As a consequence, confrontation discourse thus is now fully decoupled from the concerns raised in civil cases: confrontation decisions do not implicate civil controversies, and the problems judges encounter in civil cases do not inform the development of confrontation doctrine. For the most part, *Crawford*'s decoupling of the criminal and civil rules for out-of-court statements has been warmly applauded. I have tried to suggest here why the applause may not be warranted. By yoking the Sixth Amendment to eighteenth-century hearsay law, the recent confrontation decisions have impeded a form of doctrinal cross-comparison that in the past has helped both hearsay law and confrontation law progressively improve.

Over the long term, the cross-comparison is probably inevitable, whatever the Supreme Court says. The issues encountered in civil and criminal cases are too similar for judges and lawyers not to draw analogies. Over the long term, the hearsay rule is probably doomed, in criminal as well as civil cases. It keeps out too much probative evidence, with too little justification. There are good reasons to insist on live testimony, when it can feasibly be procured. When direct proof is unavailable, though, flatly barring secondary evidence makes little sense. That is why the hearsay rule has long been in decline around the globe, and that is why its days are likely numbered in the United States, as well.

For the time being, though, *Crawford* has given the hearsay rule a final day in the sun. The results will be predictable injustices, in the form both of guilty defendants escaping conviction and innocent defendants found guilty; a diversion of judicial and legislative attention from other, more promising ways to bring meaning to the Confrontation Clause; and less appreciation than ever before for the respects in which out-of-court statements in criminal and civil cases raise similar concerns.

GEORGE RUTHERGLEN

RICCI v DESTEFANO: AFFIRMATIVE
ACTION AND THE LESSONS OF
ADVERSITY

This last Term, the Supreme Court revisited the issue of affirmative action, in the heavily cloaked guise of the technical rules governing claims of intentional discrimination and disparate adverse impact under Title VII. In *Ricci v DeStefano*,[1] the Court held the city of New Haven liable for discarding the results of two civil service tests because of their adverse effects on African-Americans and Hispanics. Before *Ricci*, the Court had rendered over twenty decisions across more than three decades on affirmative action and related issues. So, it is natural to ask what this latest decision adds to an already complex body of law, one marked from its inception by fundamental ambivalence over the need for affirmative action and doubts about whether it compounds existing discrimination. Against this complicated and contested background, only a sweeping decision could reshape the law of affirmative action. *Ricci* does not. It takes the law in a direction skeptical of race-conscious decision making, but one that might be only the latest in a series of zigzags rather than a fundamental change of course.

Ricci concerned two promotion tests administered by the city of

George Rutherglen is John Barbee Minor Distinguished Professor and Edward F. Howrey Research Professor, University of Virginia School of Law.

AUTHOR'S NOTE: Thanks to John Jeffries, Liz Magill, Jim Ryan, and other colleagues who commented on an earlier draft of this article.

[1] 129 S Ct 2658 (2009).

New Haven for the positions of lieutenant and captain in the city fire department. Although African-Americans and Hispanics were well represented among those who took the tests—making up over a third of applicants—only two Hispanics and no African-Americans scored high enough to be eligible for promotion under the applicable civil service rules; in effect, all but two Hispanics failed the tests. The city therefore discarded the test results, at least partly to avoid liability for disparate impact under Title VII of the Civil Rights Act of 1964. This decision led most of the firefighters who scored high enough to be promoted—seventeen whites and one Hispanic—to sue the city for intentional discrimination in violation of the Constitution and Title VII. The Supreme Court upheld their claim under Title VII, finding that the decision to discard the test results constituted a race-based decision that could be justified only if the city had a "strong basis in evidence" for believing that it would otherwise be held liable for disparate impact.[2]

The Court's decision was based entirely on Title VII and it was mostly concerned with the uneasy relationship between the two principal theories of liability under that statute: intentional discrimination (or disparate treatment, as it is sometimes called) and disparate impact. The Court explicitly reserved all the constitutional questions in the case, although it recognized that several influenced its decision, because the Constitution prohibits intentional discrimination in virtually the same terms as Title VII. The tension between disparate impact and intentional discrimination under Title VII could as well be between Title VII and the Constitution: insofar as Title VII prohibits practices with disparate impact, and gives employers incentives to engage in affirmative action, it might contradict the constitutional restrictions on race-conscious decision making. The Court's narrow interpretation of liability for disparate impact under Title VII, and its strained holding that the city had no good reason to fear such liability, avoided the constitutional question. The decision nevertheless signaled a discernible tightening of the standards both for liability for disparate impact and for permissible forms of affirmative action. The city could have taken race into account in some circumstances, but not in this case.

What do we make of the Supreme Court's prolonged ambivalence toward affirmative action? This is the most important question

---

[2] Id at 2676–77.

posed by *Ricci*. In order to understand it, the narrow confines from which the decision arose must first be explained. This is the subject of Part I. Part II turns to the contours of the Supreme Court's decision. Technically, it is only that the city of New Haven engaged in intentional discrimination under Title VII. The decision assumes general significance only as it bears on broader issues of affirmative action. Explaining how it does so is the subject of Part III. If any general principle emerges from *Ricci*, it is a hostility to zero-sum racial politics—justifying affirmative action for some groups at the expense of others without any showing of collective benefit to the community as a whole.

Whether fairly or not, the city of New Haven invited precisely this interpretation of its actions in giving the tests and then refusing to accept the results, taking away the benefits to the identifiable individuals who passed, who were overwhelmingly white, and re-distributing them to include a greater number of African-Americans and Hispanics, who mainly failed. The city steadfastly refused to argue, although it could readily have done so, that discarding the test results would have been in the interests of the community as a whole because the tests failed to measure the leadership necessary in a large, urban fire department. Neither the Supreme Court nor the public—if polls on affirmative action are taken to be reliable—has been willing to accept race-conscious decision making in these circumstances. *Ricci* might be doctrinally intricate, as many earlier decisions on affirmative action have been, but it boils down to a simple cautionary tale. Affirmative action plans never will escape scrutiny. The only question is how much they receive. Precautions must be taken accordingly, and, in particular, precautions to distance such plans from divisive racial politics. This is an old and salutary lesson from the cases on affirmative action, but one especially suited to the times in which we now live.

I. WHAT LED TO THE DECISION

Ricci represents a familiar conflict between testing under state and local civil service laws and liability for disparate impact under Title VII. Like the debates over affirmative action, this conflict goes back several decades and initially reached the Supreme Court in *Washington v Davis*.[3] That case concerned a verbal ability test for

---

[3] 426 US 229 (1976).

police officers in the District of Columbia. Like *Ricci*, it involved claims that the test in question had a disparate impact upon African-Americans, in violation of both the Constitution and statutes that applied to the District of Columbia. The Court rejected both claims, holding that the Constitution did not support claims for disparate impact, independent of proof of intentional discrimination, and that the applicable statutes had been satisfied by the defendant's evidence that the test was job related. The constitutional holding has had momentous consequences by cutting off further development of disparate impact as a means of enforcing constitutional equality.[4] This holding at once made a finding of intentional discrimination more important and more ambiguous, more important because everything turned on it and more ambiguous because it could still be proved by evidence of adverse impact. These complexities were compounded by the statutory holding that the plaintiffs had also failed to make out a claim of disparate impact under standards similar to those under Title VII. The tests, although they had an adverse impact upon African-Americans, nevertheless were found to adequately measure the verbal ability skills needed by a police officer.

All of these features of *Washington v Davis* bear directly upon *Ricci*, most immediately, by posing the central conundrum faced by cities like New Haven: compliance with civil service laws might lead to liability because of the discriminatory effects of civil service tests. Public employers subject to such laws cannot avoid exposure to liability under the theory of disparate impact by the simple expedient of adopting other selection procedures. The command of civil service laws to avoid political favoritism and nepotism collides with the suspicion of tests with racially adverse impact under Title VII. This regulatory bind becomes all the tighter when unions representing incumbent employees impose further restrictions by way of collective bargaining agreements, leaving the city with still less room to maneuver. Add the constraints imposed by political decision making in local government and you have the situation faced by the city of New Haven in *Ricci*. Whatever the city did, it was likely to be embroiled in controversy and litigation.

The city charter required promotions to be made according to

---

[4] See, for example, David A. Strauss, *Discriminatory Intent and the Taming of Brown*, 56 U Chi L Rev 935 (1989); Daniel R. Ortiz, *The Myth of Intent in Equal Protection*, 41 Stan L Rev 1105 (1989).

civil service tests, allowing the selection of any of the three highest-scoring applicants for each vacancy. It therefore made little difference who officially passed the tests—about a third of the minority applicants did so. It was scoring at the top of the list that was crucial—and only two Hispanics and no African-Americans scored this high. After each test, the city's Civil Service Board certified the results and provided the names from which selections could be made. Since only a limited number of positions were open—eight for lieutenant and seven for captain when the tests were administered—the city had little flexibility in composing the pool of those eligible for promotion. The city was further constrained by its collective bargaining agreement with the firefighters' union, which required the tests to be scored according to a formula that gave 60 percent to the written portion of the tests and 40 percent to the oral portion. The crucial decision for the city was how to formulate the tests that it administered. From that point on, its discretion was severely limited by local law and the collective bargaining agreement.

The city therefore insisted upon an elaborate process for devising the tests to be used, retaining an independent firm to undertake this task. Most of this evaluation concerned an analysis of the duties of lieutenant and captain in the fire department, development of the test questions, and an assessment of the connection between the two. With the benefit of hindsight, we now know that the evaluation process already narrowed the range of positions that the city could take in litigation. After it decided to administer the tests, the city was faced with the embarrassing prospect of discrediting the validity of the evaluation process that it had itself commissioned. Having decided that the tests validly measured applicants for the job, the city took a long step toward defending the tests on this ground.

The issue of validity was crucial to the city's liability for disparate impact under Title VII. The minority applicants who failed the tests could easily establish adverse impact. Only two Hispanics were eligible for the positions immediately open in the department (although three African-Americans might have been eligible for positions that subsequently came open). These results left the city with two choices, both of which exposed it to litigation: either accept the test results and face a claim of disparate impact or reject the test results and face a claim of intentional discrimination. The former choice required the city to defend the tests on the ground that they were, in the terms used in Title VII, "job related for the position in question and consistent with business necessity."[5] The entire burden of proving this defense fell upon the city, and it was made all the heavier by the doubts surrounding the written parts of the tests. Such tests, as amici pointed out in the Supreme Court, are notoriously unreliable measures of general abilities, such as leadership.[6] They are still more unreliable when they are given an automatic 60 percent weighting, as required by the collective bargaining agreement, and when they are used to rank order candidates, as required by the city's civil service rules. Alternatively, if the city chose to reject the test results, it faced the risk of the lawsuit actually brought in *Ricci*, for intentional discrimination by those who scored high enough to be eligible for promotion.

As Judge Wisdom pointed out many years ago, employers caught in this situation—between liability for disparate impact and liability for disparate treatment—find themselves on a "high tightrope without a net beneath them."[7] What is remarkable in *Ricci* was how soon the city of New Haven found itself out on this tightrope. It was forced there by its obligations under the city charter and the collective bargaining agreement. The case then seems to have unfolded with a kind of tragic inevitability. The city had to study the validity of the tests before it adopted them. Having financed a study to devise valid tests, the city then decided to adopt them. Administering the tests, however, led to the racially disparate results, which caused the city to reject the tests and led to the lawsuit in *Ricci*. When the case reached the Supreme Court, the city could not reject the tests as invalid, because it had accepted their validity at the outset of the process. Looking back, the case was over before it had even begun. The city was foreordained to fall from the tightrope on which it was precariously balanced.

Of course, such a deterministic narrative leaves out crucial steps in the story, where it might have come out differently. Yet these contingencies just heighten the tragedy that it did not. The first

[5] § 703(k)(1)(A)(i), codified as 42 USC § 2000e-2(k)(1)(A)(i) (2006).

[6] Brief of the Society for Human Resource Management as Amicus Curiae in Support of Respondents 22–24; Brief of Industrial-Organizational Psychologists as Amici Curiae in Support of Respondents 8–21.

[7] *Weber v United Steelworkers*, 563 F2d 216, 230 (5th Cir 1978) (Wisdom, J, dissenting), rev'd, 443 US 193 (1979).

was the decision to adopt these tests, instead of some alternative selection procedure, the most promising being "assessment centers." These comprise a range of exercises and tests, such as participation in discussion groups, simulations of performance in the position in question, interviews, and personality tests—all of which are evaluated by multiple raters who are specially trained for this task.[8] Assessment centers allow greater flexibility in evaluation than tests with written questions and predetermined answers, and they have a more plausible connection to the job. If an assessment center includes significant parts of the job itself, it can be proved to be "content valid": its relationship to the job just depends upon how faithfully it reproduces the important parts of the job itself.[9] The city of New Haven did not choose this alternative, most probably because it was more expensive than the tests it used and because it did not conform to the terms of its collective bargaining agreement with the firefighters' union.

A second turning point occurred when the city Civil Service Board, which heard extensive testimony on the adverse impact of the tests and on their validity, refused to certify the test results. With one member recused, a motion to certify the results failed by a tie vote of two-to-two. Some evidence, emphasized by Justice Alito in his concurring opinion and vehemently disputed by Justice Ginsburg in her dissent,[10] supports the conclusion that the mayor's office worked behind the scenes for racially discriminatory reasons to ensure that the board discarded the test results. The evidence attributes the mayor's position to attempts to assuage the concerns of a politically prominent black pastor who assailed the adverse impact of the tests. Whatever the force of this evidence, the tie vote by the Civil Service Board reveals how close the question was. In any case, if the city had acted on the test results, it might well have faced the disparate-impact claim that it tried to avoid.

A third alternative ending to *Ricci* might have occurred if the judgment of the lower courts in favor of the city had become final because the Supreme Court denied certiorari. The district court

---

[8] Michelle A. Dean, Philip L. Roth, and Philip Bobko, *Ethnic and Gender Subgroup Differences in Assessment Center Ratings: A Meta-Analysis*, 93 J App Psych 685 (2008).

[9] Uniform Guidelines on Employee Selection Procedures § 14C, 29 CFR § 1607.14C (2009).

[10] *Ricci*, 129 S Ct at 2684–88 (Alito, J, concurring); id at 2690–95, 2707–09 (Ginsburg, J, dissenting).

granted summary judgment for the city and the court of appeals affirmed summarily, in a per curiam order relying upon the district court's lengthy opinion.[11] The Second Circuit's order attracted great attention because then-Judge Sotomayor sat on the three-judge panel. Her participation in the summary affirmance was much discussed at her confirmation hearings. A petition for rehearing en banc was denied, but only after it received the votes of six of thirteen judges on the Second Circuit. Of the seven judges concurring in the denial of rehearing en banc, five recognized that it presented "difficult issues" for the Supreme Court, almost inviting the Court to hear the case.[12] Moreover, the district court's grant of summary judgment for the city itself was problematic, prompting even the dissenters in the Supreme Court to express a willingness to remand the case to receive further evidence.[13] The grant of summary judgment presupposed that the only reasonable inferences from the record supported the city's characterization of its decision as race-neutral because it was designed solely to achieve compliance with Title VII. This remained a point of contention throughout the case.

A final road not taken in *Ricci* involved the city's refusal to abandon the validity of the tests. Apparently because of continuing fear that it might be held liable for disparate impact, the city never contended that the tests failed to measure applicants for the job. Instead, it carefully articulated its position in terms of the sufficiency of the evidence before the Civil Service Board. The city contended only that the board could have found that the tests were invalid, not that they were actually invalid. The nuances of this position came out in oral argument, when the Chief Justice asked whether

---

[11] *Ricci v DeStefano*, 554 F Supp 2d 142 (D Conn 2006), aff'd 530 F3d 87 (2d Cir 2008) (per curiam), rev'd 129 S Ct 2658 (2009). The Second Circuit originally affirmed the district court's judgment with a one-line order, 264 Fed Appx 106 (2d Cir 2008), but this was withdrawn and the two-paragraph per curiam opinion was substituted for it after the Second Circuit voted to deny rehearing en banc. 530 F3d 88 (2d Cir 2008).

[12] These judges, including then-Judge Sotomayor, concurred in Judge Katzmann's opinion, which stated: "The Supreme Court now has before it a petition for certiorari in this case, which I recognize presents difficult issues." 530 F3d at 90 (Katzmann, J, concurring). Judge Calabresi also filed a concurring opinion, offering a subtle and complex argument to the effect that the case was too subtle and complex to be taken en banc. Id at 88–89 (Calabresi, J, concurring).

[13] In her dissent, Justice Ginsburg said that she "would not oppose a remand for further proceedings fair to both sides." 129 S Ct at 2707 (Ginsburg, J, dissenting). See also id at 2702–03 and nn 9, 10, 2707. The Obama administration took the same position in its amicus brief. Brief for the United States as Amicus Curiae Supporting Vacatur and Remand 32.

the city was changing positions on this issue from what it had argued in the lower courts. The city's attorney responded, "No, not at all. The ultimate validity of the test, our position below, was not relevant; the question is what was before the board."[14] If the ultimate validity of the tests was irrelevant, then so were the advantages to the city in discarding the tests, not in terms of exposure to liability or in assuring racial balance, but in terms of the efficiency of the fire department and in protecting the citizenry as a whole. As it is, the city left a full-scale attack on the validity of the tests to amici, whose arguments, no matter how powerful, lacked the political commitment that would have come from arguments by the city itself.

The city's tactical decision on validity did not predetermine the outcome of the case, which, after all, was decided five-to-four in the Supreme Court (although the dissenters might have joined in a unanimous decision to remand for further evidence). Nevertheless, the city's position set the stage for a decision that was all the more poignant because it came so close to being different—if the city had adopted different tests, if the Civil Service Board had certified the test results, if certiorari had been denied, if the city had rejected the validity of its own tests. Observers of the Supreme Court would also add a last contingency—if Justice Kennedy had voted differently, since he has been the swing Justice on so many issues recently before the Court. His opinion for the majority is discussed in the next part of this article.

II. WHAT THE COURT DECIDED

Justice Kennedy has become the key vote on affirmative action, taking the place of Justice O'Connor and, before her, Justice Powell.[15] In fact, he turned to opinions by these Justices in framing

---

[14] Transcript of Oral Argument at 57. For the statement of the city's position in its brief, see Brief of Respondents 27–33. The city also contended that there was evidence of alternatives with less disparate impact than the tests used. Id at 33–37.

The city's fear of a lawsuit by minority applicants who failed the tests has since materialized in the aftermath of *Ricci*. *Briscoe v City of New Haven* (D Conn, filed Oct 15, 2009). The merits of this lawsuit now seem to be foreclosed by the opinion in *Ricci*, which gives the city the same "strong basis in evidence" defense to a claim of disparate impact as it has for one of disparate treatment. 129 S Ct at 2681. Even before the decision, however, a decision by the city to discard the test results because the tests were invalid would have protected it from a lawsuit by minority applicants. In the absence of any promotions based on the tests, there would have been nothing for the minority applicants to attack.

[15] See John C. Jeffries, Jr., *Bakke Revisited*, 2003 Supreme Court Review 1.

the standard for judging the city's action in *Ricci*. He went back to *Richmond v J. A. Croson Co.*[16] and *Wygant v Jackson Board of Education*,[17] two constitutional decisions striking down affirmative action plans, to find the standard of a "strong basis in evidence" to justify race-conscious action under Title VII. These two earlier decisions also concerned action by local government, but they relied entirely on constitutional grounds, while *Ricci* relied only on Title VII. Justice Kennedy went out of his way to avoid the constitutional questions, while at the same time acknowledging their implications for the statutory issues. Hence the cumulative uncertainties surrounding affirmative action, and their dependence often on the vote of a single Justice, all figured in *Ricci*.

The fundamental source of uncertainty is to be found in the concept of discrimination, which is common both to the Constitution and to Title VII. Under the seemingly redundant heading of "intentional discrimination," both sources of law generally prohibit any decision that takes account of race, subject to limited exceptions, chiefly for permissible forms of affirmative action. The first step in the Court's decision was therefore to find intentional discrimination in the city's decision to discard the test results. This finding created a presumptive violation of Title VII. At a literal level, it was hard to avoid this conclusion. The city, or, more precisely, the Civil Service Board, refused to certify the test results because so few minority applicants passed the tests with sufficiently high scores. This was a decision based on race, whether it was motivated by efforts to avoid liability under Title VII or by efforts to placate the minority constituencies in New Haven. The city, of course, fought to avoid any characterization of this decision as race-based, framing it simply as a neutral attempt to comply with Title VII in order to gain the rhetorical advantage of acting in a completely neutral fashion.

That strategy, however, does not work in the doctrinal and conceptual terms in which it was framed, and it may, in the end, have done the city more harm than good. It may have deflected the city from a full-fledged attempt to justify its decision in terms of permissible affirmative action and left it only with the vagaries of contradictory characterizations of what it did decide. The decision to

---

[16] 488 US 469, 500 (1989).

[17] 476 US 267, 290 (1986) (O'Connor, J, concurring in part and concurring in the judgment).

discard the test results cannot be equated to an action based merely on awareness of race. The city, like most employers, knew the race and national origin of most of its employees, and it certainly knew of the racially adverse effects of the tests. But it did not act *despite* those effects. It acted *because of* them. By its own account, it implicated race far more deeply in its decision than simply acting with awareness. It acted with intent to avoid the adverse effects of the tests.[18]

The argument advanced by the city, that it acted neutrally, depends upon characterization: that it discarded the test results for all applicants, whether white or minority, in an attempt to comply with Title VII.[19] According to the city, it was acting neutrally to avoid liability under Title VII, as if it had, for instance, discovered that one of its minority firefighters was about to be denied a promotion because of his race. If it had then taken action to prevent the promotion of a white firefighter in his place, and started the promotion process all over again, it would not have violated Title VII. This analogy works, however, only because the neutral characterization in the example proceeds from the need to take remedial action—not the other way around. The city's action in the example could be characterized as race-based—preventing the promotion of a white firefighter—but nevertheless justified by the need to assure compliance with Title VII. The bare characterization of the city's action—whether on the facts of *Ricci* or in the example—has undoubted rhetorical force but little argumentative value. Everything depends upon the reason offered for describing the action one way or the other.

This question lies at the heart of *Ricci*: what reasons justify actions,

---

[18] This feature of the case distinguishes it from *Personnel Administrator v Feeney*, 442 US 256 (1979), in which the Supreme Court upheld a state veteran's preference statute despite its obvious adverse impact upon women. The Court held that the state had not engaged in intentional sex-based discrimination. Although the state legislature was aware of the preference's adverse impact on women, it did not enact the preference for that reason. "'Discriminatory purpose,' however, implies more than intent as volition or intent as awareness of consequences. It implies that the decisionmaker, in this case a state legislature, selected or reaffirmed a particular course of action at least in part 'because of,' not merely 'in spite of,' its adverse effects upon an identifiable group." Id at 279 (footnotes and citations omitted). By contrast, the city of New Haven was both aware of and acted on the adverse effects of the promotion tests.

[19] These efforts appear at various points in its brief: "On the contrary, Title VII and the Constitution permit, indeed favor, the City's limited and reasoned race-neutral action." Brief for Respondents 2. "This case does not involve racial classification but rather race-neutral action—the noncertification applied to all candidates of all races." Id at 14. Compliance with Title VII is "a legitimate nondiscriminatory reason." Id at 24 n 16.

which might be characterized as race-conscious, in order to avoid liability? In the example, it is avoiding liability for intentional discrimination. In *Ricci*, it is avoiding liability for disparate impact. This leads, in turn, to deeper questions about the relationship between claims of intentional discrimination and claims of disparate impact, including the purposes that liability for disparate impact serves and how these purposes implicate questions of affirmative action. A problem with the opinion in *Ricci*, and with the parties' arguments, is that they do not squarely confront these questions. The plaintiffs argued for proof of actual liability, or, failing that, a "strong basis in evidence." The city proposed a weaker standard, or, in the alternative, that it had a "strong basis in evidence" for its decision. The Court settled on the intermediate standard but applied it far more harshly than the city intended. According to the Court, the risk of allowing practices with disparate impact must be subordinated to the risk of encouraging intentional discrimination.

In the key passage in the opinion, rejecting a defense based simply on a good faith fear of liability for disparate impact, the Court made its order of priorities clear:

> A minimal standard could cause employers to discard the results of lawful and beneficial promotional examinations even where there is little if any evidence of disparate-impact discrimination. That would amount to a *de facto* quota system, in which a "focus on statistics . . . could put undue pressure on employers to adopt inappropriate prophylactic measures."[20]

This is the only passage in the opinion that refers directly to affirmative action, by pointedly using the pejorative term "quota." The fear of liability for disparate impact cannot be invoked as a pretext, as the Court says later in the same paragraph, for "obtaining the employer's preferred racial balance." An employer cannot rely solely on the numbers, in this case, of minority and white applicants who pass a test, in deciding whether to abide by its results. Since the city did not impugn the validity of the tests themselves, it was left only with the numbers to support its position and no further reason for relying on the numbers alone.

Having gone so far to limit the theory of disparate impact, the Supreme Court nevertheless hesitated to go any further. The Court

---

[20] 129 S Ct at 2675 (quoting *Watson v Fort Worth Bank and Trust*, 487 US 977, 992 (1988) (opinion of O'Connor, J)).

instead issued a fact-specific ruling, taking the district court's grant of summary judgment *for* the city and turning it into a grant of summary judgment *against* the city. The Court found no reasonable inference that the tests were invalid, despite substantial arguments to the contrary by amici. Justice Ginsburg forcefully advanced these arguments in her dissent: paper-and-pencil tests are dubious measures of leadership, the rank ordering in the test had not been validated; neither had the weighting of the written test as 60 percent of the total score.[21] The Court's harsh interpretation of the record, however, limited the scope and precedential effect of its decision. Because the Court entered judgment for the plaintiffs on their Title VII claims, it did not reach their constitutional claims and it stopped short of calling the theory of disparate impact in its entirety into question.

Yet the Court stopped short at points that appear to be more arbitrary than logically compelling. If, as the Court reasoned, the city engaged in intentional discrimination by rejecting the test results because of their racially adverse impact, then why allow a defense of a "strong basis in evidence" for finding disparate impact? The Court allows the *certainty* of intentional discrimination to be offset by the *probability* of an illegal disparate impact. How can the Court, on its view, allow the certainty of the greater harm to be justified by the probability of the lesser? Moreover, the Court was careful to distinguish decisions made before any test is given. As the Court said, "Title VII does not prohibit an employer from considering, before administering a test or practice, how to design that test or practice in order to provide a fair opportunity for all individuals, regardless of their race."[22] Employers have considerably greater freedom to take account of the potential adverse effects of a test before it is administered than they do to consider the actual effects afterward. If the Court is suspicious of disparate impact as a pretext for quotas, why does it allow employers to rely on the numbers earlier rather than later?

These questions go to the ultimate significance of *Ricci*, but they presuppose an understanding of the progression among several preliminary questions, from the relationship of disparate impact to intentional discrimination, to the purposes of liability of disparate

---

[21] Id at 2703–07.

[22] Id at 2677.

impact, to the connection between disparate impact and affirmative action. Otherwise, the arguments tend to slip from professed certitudes about the different forms of liability under Title VII to entrenched positions on the desirability of affirmative action. In fact, the legal issues at every stage are rife with inherent tensions and ambiguities that are all related to one another.

To begin with the first question, disparate impact has to be distinguished from intentional discrimination, but in a way that preserves the relationship between these two theories of liability. Intentional discrimination is the dominant conception of discrimination *simpliciter* because most instances of "discrimination" already presume the requisite intent. "Intentional discrimination" has an irreducible element of redundancy about it. "To discriminate" simply means to make a distinction, and insofar as the discrimination involves action, it means relying upon that distinction.[23] Calling discrimination "intentional" just draws attention to the intentional feature of discrimination generally. On this view, disparate impact is a form of discrimination only in an extended sense. It is like discrimination because discriminatory effects might be the consequence of discriminatory action, or they might support an inference of discriminatory intent, or they might be thought to be as bad as discrimination. For all these reasons, the law might prohibit disparate impact along with intentional discrimination.

So far from assimilating disparate impact to intentional discrimination, however, these reasons presuppose the difference between the two. One requires intent and the other provides some substitute for it. Even psychological theories of "implicit discrimination" do not bridge this gap. These theories find widespread forms of discriminatory action by individuals who are not fully aware of their own mental processes, but they presume that there are mental processes at work.[24] The nuances of this psychological mechanism do not fit liability for disparate impact, which is imposed regardless of an employer's mental processes (or those of its agents). Effects alone matter.

This was precisely the distinction emphasized by the Supreme

---

[23] For the most recent analysis to make this point, see Deborah Hellman, *When Is Discrimination Wrong?* 13 (2008) ("Descriptively, to 'discriminate' is merely to draw distinctions among people on the basis or absence of some trait.").

[24] David Faigman et al., *A Matter of Fit: The Law of Discrimination and the Science of Implicit Bias*, 59 Hastings L J 1389 (2008).

Court when it defined "disparate treatment" under Title VII to mean intentional discrimination and then distinguished it from "disparate impact."[25] The difference lies in the elusive additional element of intent, which is difficult both to define and to prove, particularly when applied to the institutional defendants typically found in employment discrimination cases. Plaintiffs with claims of disparate impact are relieved of this unwieldy burden. They get the benefit of a broader theory of liability and one thought to be more favorable to them. Of course, in any particular case, the plaintiff might find it much easier to prove intentional discrimination, for instance, through a supervisor's remarks, than to undertake a complicated empirical inquiry into the general effects of an employer's overall policies. The theory of disparate impact does not always work to the plaintiff's advantage.

The fundamental reason why it does not arises from the close connection between intent and fault.[26] Proof of discriminatory intent provides a ready basis for attributing fault to the employer. If an employer acted against the plaintiff because of his race, then it knew what it was doing, it could easily have done something else,

---

[25] *International Bhd. of Teamsters v United States*, 431 US 324, 335 n 15 (1977). In a forthcoming article, Professor Richard Primus offers a novel and different account of how the distinction between intentional discrimination and disparate impact evolved. Richard Primus, *The Future of Disparate Impact*, 108 Mich L Rev draft at 22–23 (2010). He argues that *Teamsters* signaled a radical departure from how the distinction was understood when it was first advanced by the Supreme Court and that *Ricci* has perpetuated this departure. He contends that "intentional discrimination and disparate impact were not yet rigorously distinguished from each other" in the early 1970s, and, in particular, in *McDonnell Douglas Corp. v Green*, 411 US 792 (1973), and, by inference, in *Griggs v Duke Power Co.*, 401 US 424 (1971). Yet in both *McDonnell Douglas* and *Griggs* the Court made precisely this distinction. In *McDonnell Douglas*, the Court reversed a decision that treated the case as one of disparate impact, because it should have been treated as one of intentional discrimination, 411 US at 805–06; and in *Griggs*, the Court reversed a decision that treated the case as one of intentional discrimination, because it should have been treated as one of disparate impact, 401 US 428–29.

Professor Primus also argues that "intentional discrimination and disparate treatment were considered two separate categories" at this time. Primus, 108 Mich L Rev draft at 22. Only in the mid-1970s, on his view, did the Supreme Court equate "intentional discrimination" with "disparate treatment," after it had demoted disparate impact to a secondary theory of liability in *Washington v Davis*, 426 US 229 (1976). This point about the usage of "disparate treatment," however, demonstrates only that the Supreme Court did not use terminology that was then to be found only in a few obscure decisions, mainly by the EEOC. As Professor Primus candidly acknowledges, "[w]hen *Griggs* was decided in 1971, no appellate court had yet spoken of 'disparate treatment' in a Title VII case," Primus, 108 Mich L Rev draft at 22–23 and n 100, and no Justice used the term in *Griggs*, *McDonnell Douglas*, or *Washington v Davis*.

[26] For the role of fault in civil rights law, see John C. Jeffries, Jr., *In Praise of the Eleventh Amendment and Section 1983*, 84 Va L Rev 47 (1998).

and it transgressed a widely known and broadly accepted legal norm. "Discriminatory intent," of course, is a notoriously elastic concept, which can be proved by a variety of means, including the very same statistical evidence that is used to prove disparate impact. The concept can be readily extended to apply to any evidence that supports a finding of fault, even if no single individual's intent can be readily ascertained and attributed to the employer. The "inexorable zero" of no minority representation is one basis for finding intentional discrimination, most often in combination with individual instances of discrimination that bring "the cold numbers convincingly to life."[27]

Liability for disparate impact operates differently. Where it has been recognized in the law, it results from specific statutory prohibitions[28] and it tends to be imposed only when the disparity is extreme and the justification for it is weak.[29] Its effective operation remains confined to cases in which fault can be easily attributed to a defendant who was subject to a specific well-known statutory prohibition, who followed a seemingly neutral practice with obvious adverse effects, and who had little justification for doing so. These elements accurately describe, respectively, the codification of disparate impact under Title VII (and, before 1991, the Supreme Court's interpretation of the statute), the plaintiff's burden of proving that the defendant "uses a particular employment practice that causes a disparate impact," and the defendant's burden of proving that "the challenged practice is job related for the position in question and consistent with business necessity."[30] The quoted provisions clearly exclude the need for any formal finding of intent, but they leave intact the need to find some form of fault. Assimilating disparate impact to discrimination generally requires this step. An employer who has engaged in prohibited discrimination has done something wrong. Why else should liability be imposed upon that

---

[27] *International Bhd. of Teamsters v United States*, 431 US 324, 339, 342 n 23 (1977).

[28] For instance, under the Voting Rights Act, Title VI of the Civil Rights Act of 1964, the Age Discrimination in Employment Act, and the Americans with Disabilities Act. For a summary of these provisions and the decisions interpreting them, see George Rutherglen, *Disparate Impact, Discrimination, and the Inherently Contested Concept of Equality*, 74 Fordham L Rev 2313, 2317–19 (2006).

[29] See note 34 below.

[30] § 703(k)(1)(A)(i), codified as 42 USC § 2000e-2(k)(1)(A)(i). A third stage of proof in disparate-impact cases involves the plaintiff's burden of proving an alternative employment practice with less adverse impact. § 703(k)(1)(A)(ii), codified as 42 USC § 2000e-2(k)(1)(A)(ii). Few cases, apparently, reach this stage.

employer rather than someone else? The extended sense of "discrimination" in the law dispenses with the need to prove intent, but it does not dispense with the need to prove fault.

This observation takes us to the next question, about the purpose of the theory of disparate impact. A range of purposes have been proposed, but they can be grouped into two broad categories: "smoking out" hidden forms of intentional discrimination that cannot be directly detected, and encouraging forms of affirmative action necessary to achieve actual equality of opportunity.[31] The first, narrower goal seeks to close the gap between intentional discrimination and disparate impact, while the second, broader goal leaves the gap open. The first makes it harder for plaintiffs to win claims of disparate impact and, conversely, harder for employers in the city's situation in *Ricci* to establish a "strong basis in evidence." The second goal has the opposite effect, imposing a lighter burden of proof upon the plaintiff and a heavier one on the defendant. The opinion in *Ricci* definitely inclines toward the first set of goals, although for reasons which are not quite consistent with the Civil Rights Act of 1991.

On the first view, the theory of disparate impact remains conceptually distinct from claims of intentional discrimination—because it assigns different burdens of proof to the parties—but it is instrumentally related—because it is directed to the same goal of preventing intentional discrimination. The theory transfers some of the burden of proof from the plaintiff to the defendant: the plaintiff needs to prove only adverse impact, and if the plaintiff does so, the defendant then has to justify the disputed practice. These shifting burdens of proof contrast with the structure of proof of intentional discrimination, which, under Title VII, requires the plaintiff to bear the entire burden of persuasion on the question whether race was "a motivating factor" in the disputed employment decision.[32] The theory of disparate impact results in some over-enforcement of the prohibition against intentional discrimination, but it yields the corresponding advantage of avoiding underenfor-

---

[31] See 129 S Ct at 2682 (Scalia, J, concurring).

[32] § 703(m), 42 USC § 2000e-2(m) (2006). Under *McDonnell Douglas Corp. v Green*, 411 US 792, 803–04 (1973), the defendant bears only the burden of production, and only of producing "a legitimate, nondiscriminatory reason" for the disputed decision. The structure of proof in class claims of intentional discrimination is much the same, because the plaintiff still must persuade the trier of fact to find discrimination even after making out a prima facie case. See *Hazelwood School Dist. v United States*, 433 US 299, 309–13 (1977).

cement. Some innocent employers are held liable, but some who engaged in hidden forms of intentional discrimination are caught.

This instrumental view of the theory of disparate impact has many consequences, but all of them adapt the requirements of the theory to the goal of uncovering hidden discrimination. Many of the decisions under the theory of disparate impact bear out this general correlation, among them, *Griggs v Duke Power Co.*,[33] the seminal decision recognizing the theory under Title VII. The employer there, a utility company in North Carolina, had engaged in pervasive discrimination against African-Americans before the effective date of Title VII, segregating them in its lowest-level department. But when Title VII took effect, it replaced the color bar with ostensibly neutral tests and education requirements. By the time the case reached the Supreme Court, only a single African-American had been promoted from the lowest-level department. The evidence of discriminatory intent, while not as overwhelming as under Jim Crow, was nevertheless powerful. Most of the decisions imposing liability for disparate impact—but not all—follow a similar pattern.[34] The more evidence of hidden discrimination that can be found in the record, the less the plaintiff should have to prove to challenge a disputed employment practice and the more the defendant should have to establish to justify it. Conversely, in the absence of such evidence, an employer should be able to easily carry a light burden of justifying a disputed practice. There is less need to "smoke out" hidden discrimination when there is less reason to believe it is there in the first place.

The metaphor of "smoking out" hidden intentional discrimination reveals one of the several connections between the theory of disparate impact and affirmative action. The metaphor was first used in the analysis of legislative motive generally and then applied to affirmative action plans, supporting strict scrutiny to distinguish benign racial classifications from prohibited reverse discrimination.[35] The "strong basis in evidence" standard in *Ricci* is a direct

[33] 401 US 424 (1971). For instance, the Court stated that Title VII "proscribes not only overt discrimination but also practices that are fair in form, but discriminatory in operation." Id at 431.

[34] Michael L. Selmi, *Was the Disparate Impact Theory a Mistake?* 53 UCLA L Rev 701, 738–46 (2006). For an analysis of earlier cases, see George Rutherglen, *Disparate Impact Under Title VII: An Objective Theory of Discrimination*, 73 Va L Rev 1297, 1320–23 (1987).

[35] *City of Richmond v J. A. Croson Co.*, 488 US 419, 493 (1989) (opinion of O'Connor, J); John Hart Ely, *Democracy and Distrust: A Theory of Judicial Review* 146 (1980); John

descendant of these constitutional decisions. The Court weighs the risk of one form of prohibited discrimination—hidden discrimination against minorities by the city—against the risk of another—discrimination against whites in the guise of permissible affirmative action. From this perspective, *Ricci* becomes an exercise in risk assessment, weighing the risk of direct discrimination against the risk of reverse discrimination.

Unfortunately for the city, it had little evidence of hidden discrimination, apart from the adverse impact of the tests. Just as the city was understandably reluctant to submit evidence that the tests were invalid, it was also reluctant to admit to any form of recent discrimination. There was no evidence that the city discriminated against minorities in selecting and formulating the promotion tests, and the only discrimination documented in the record occurred decades earlier.[36] Hence the Supreme Court easily concluded that an employer in the city's situation, faced with a choice between liability under one theory or liability under the other, should avoid the greater evil of obvious discrimination in discarding the test results rather than the lesser evil of hidden discrimination accessible only through liability for disparate impact.

This approach to the case casts a different light on the heated exchange between Justices Alito and Ginsburg over the extent to which the Civil Service Board's deliberations were tainted by racial politics. Race inevitably plays a role in public controversies in cities, like New Haven, which have large blocs of white, African-American, and Hispanic citizens. It is unrealistic to expect heated public controversies to be resolved without regard to racial divisions, as the Supreme Court has recognized in its decisions on redistricting, allowing a role for racial politics so long as it does not play a "predominant" role.[37] Whether race played too great a role in the city's decision in *Ricci* probably remains unfathomable. An extended judicial inquiry into the intricacies of political deliberations creates the risk of judicial entanglement in the same racial divisions that it seeks to discourage. On the narrow version of the theory of disparate impact, the problem in *Ricci* was not too much evidence of dis-

---

Hart Ely, *The Constitutionality of Reverse Racial Discrimination*, 41 U Chi L Rev 723, 736 (1974).

[36] Justice Ginsburg thoroughly examined all the evidence in the case and cited only instances of intentional discrimination in the New Haven fire department dating from the 1970s. 129 S Ct at 2690–91 (Ginsburg, J, dissenting).

[37] E.g., *Miller v Johnson*, 515 US 900, 916–17 (1995).

crimination *in favor of* racial minorities when the test results were discarded, but too little evidence of discrimination *against* them before the test results were known.

In order to prevail, the city therefore had to appeal to the second, broader version of the theory. This version of the theory frees it from a completely instrumental role in detecting hidden discrimination by providing employers with additional incentives to avoid practices that result in underrepresentation of minority and female employees. The city implicitly relied on this version of the theory in arguing that it was entitled to engage in affirmative action in order to avoid liability for disparate impact; and the plaintiffs, in arguing to the contrary, sought to restrict the theory of disparate impact to its narrower version. Hidden beneath all the formalism in the parties' arguments and in the Court's opinion lies the decision whether to endorse the broader version of the theory, giving employers an incentive to adopt affirmative action plans in order to preempt a plaintiff's ability to prove adverse impact. If this strategy is successful, the employer avoids the need to carry the burden of proving that the disputed practice is "job related for the position in question and consistent with business necessity." On this version of the theory, this burden is more than simply dispelling the inference that the employer has engaged in hidden discrimination. Significantly diminished opportunities for minorities and women require a correspondingly significant justification.

This version of the theory goes beyond preventing hidden intentional discrimination, although it is important to note that it does do that as well. Employers who implement affirmative action plans generate evidence that counteracts claims of intentional discrimination, by negating statistical evidence that could otherwise be used by plaintiffs and by providing background evidence of a general absence of discriminatory intent. But employers who adopt affirmative action plans also do more, and the more affirmative action they engage in, the more they do. They open up jobs to minorities and women who have been previously excluded from them. Because of the heavier burden of proof imposed upon them once adverse impact is found, under this version of the theory, employers take greater precautions against practices that have such an impact. They are exposed to greater liability, regardless of any independent evidence that they engaged in hidden discrimination.

This analysis in terms of risks and incentives might be thought to be compromised by a decision from two decades ago that bears a disturbing resemblance to *Ricci*. In *Connecticut v Teal*,[38] the Supreme Court addressed another instance of belated affirmative action by a public employer, also involving civil service tests, and also, curiously, from Connecticut. The state government administered a civil service test and discovered that too few African-Americans and Hispanics passed. After charges of discrimination were filed, the city instituted an affirmative action plan that eliminated the adverse effects of the test by increasing the proportion of minority applicants ultimately hired from among all those who passed. The Supreme Court found this step inadequate to counteract the initial adverse impact of the test and required the state to justify the test as valid. Although *Teal* does not confer a formal defense upon employers who adopt affirmative action plans, it still leaves them with substantial reasons to institute such plans. The plan can be made an inseparable part of the selection procedure, and even if it is not, the proportional representation of minorities among those hired might well deter a plaintiff, or, more realistically, her attorney, from suing in the first place.

The problem in *Teal*, as in *Ricci*, stemmed from the employer's attempt to counteract the adverse effects of the test only after it was administered. This resemblance between the cases might be simply an ironic coincidence, since the cases otherwise are a study in contrasts. A group of minority employees prevailed in *Teal*, not a group composed mostly of white employees, as in *Ricci*, and the theory of disparate impact received an expansive interpretation, not the theory of disparate treatment. The one common feature of the two decisions is the suspicion attached to after-the-fact attempts to compensate for test results, particularly when they work to the disadvantage of identifiable individuals. Despite the focus of the theory of disparate impact upon groups, the Court appealed to the same principles of individualized evaluation that can be found throughout the decisions on affirmative action.[39] In both *Teal* and

---

[38] 457 US 440 (1982).

[39] "The statute speaks, not in terms of jobs and promotions, but in terms of *limitations* and *classifications* that would deprive any individual of employment *opportunities*." Id at 448 (footnote omitted). For constitutional decisions that follow this principle, see *Regents of the University of California v Bakke*, 438 US 265, 316–18 (1978) (opinion of Powell, J); *Gratz v Bollinger*, 539 US 244, 270–75 (2003). Both decisions struck down easily administered numerical standards for admission to programs of higher education, insisting instead on individualized treatment of each applicant.

Ricci, the Court forced the case to be decided on the issue of the tests' validity; the employer could not rely on its attempt to eliminate adverse impact alone.

"Eliminating adverse impact" can be just a euphemism for engaging in affirmative action, which goes directly to the third question: how does the theory of disparate impact relate to permissible forms of affirmative action? This question permeates the opinion in *Ricci*, even if it only once comes to the surface. The technicalities of the theory of disparate impact take on significance only as they relate to affirmative action; only as the focus shifts from the procedures that employers use, to the results for different groups that those procedures yield. In purely doctrinal terms, the question is whether the threat of liability for disparate impact augments the reasons and conditions under which affirmative action plans can be adopted. Does an employer have better reasons, available in a wider range of circumstances, to engage in affirmative action because it might otherwise be held liable under the theory of disparate impact? If so, an affirmative action plan that was questionable absent the threat of such liability would become permissible when it was present. If not, it would have to be justified by the standards for affirmative action, both statutory and constitutional, supplied elsewhere.

The answer to this question depends upon more than the idiosyncrasies of a single Justice. Justice Kennedy, like Justices O'Connor and Powell before him, has recently cast the deciding vote on issues of affirmative action. If he had sided with the dissenters in *Ricci*, he would have transformed them into the majority, and he would, in all likelihood, still have written the decisive opinion, as he did in the recent case on voluntary school integration.[40] The close division on affirmative action does not result from the preferences of a single swing Justice. On the contrary, it is what makes the views of one Justice decisive. Nor is the close division a product only of ambivalence within the Supreme Court. Congress has legislated on affirmative action in similarly ambivalent terms, especially under Title VII. Opinion polls express a similar unwillingness to offer a definitive resolution of this issue, with respondents both condemning "racial preferences" and supporting "affirmative

---

[40] *Parents Involved in Community Schools v Seattle School District No. 1*, 551 US 701, 783–98 (2007) (Kennedy, J, concurring in part and concurring in the judgment).

action."[41] The significance of *Ricci* depends on how the opinion navigates the treacherous currents on this issue and whether it channels them into a clearer course.

III. Implications of the Decision

The consequences of *Ricci* proceed from direct doctrinal implications for proof of intentional discrimination and disparate impact, to shifting attitudes toward affirmative action, to the lessons that employers can draw from the decision. If the opinion begins by confirming the priority of intentional discrimination over disparate impact, it is hardly the first opinion of the Supreme Court to do so. Like much else in *Ricci*, it was anticipated several decades ago.[42] This is no accident, but one way of imposing some constraints on the theory of disparate impact. If claims for disparate impact could routinely be brought by any group, including white males, then employers would be subject to some form of liability for any practice that did not result in racial and gender balance. If the practice were intentionally discriminatory, they would be liable to the victims of such discrimination, but if it were neutral, they would be liable to any group that suffered from the resulting imbalance. In order to preserve some range of managerial discretion, the theory of disparate impact has to be constrained in some way.

These constraints come in two forms. First, the adverse effects must be significant. Minor deviations in the representation of different groups might be the result of chance, and, even more so, they would not rise to the difference in selection rates recognized as a disparate impact by the Equal Employment Opportunity Commission (EEOC). Under the Commission's "four-fifths rule," the success rate of any group must be less than four-fifths of the selection rate of the most successful group to trigger a finding of

---

[41] Jeffrey M. Jones, *Race, Ideology, and Support for Affirmative Action* (Aug 23, 2005) at http://www.gallup.com/poll/18091/Race-Ideology-Support-Affirmative-Action.aspx. "Support for affirmative action has been known to vary depending on how the question is worded, particularly when the question describes the programs in more detail. Surveys conducted in the past five years by the major polling firms show a range of support from as low as 38% (when the term 'racial preferences' is used) to as high as 64%."

[42] In *City of Los Angeles, Dep't of Water & Power v Manhart*, 435 US 702 (1978), a case concerned with sex-based actuarial tables, the Court rejected the argument that sex-neutral actuarial tables would have a disparate impact upon men. "Even a completely neutral practice will inevitably have *some* disproportionate impact on one group or another. *Griggs* does not imply, and this Court has never held, that discrimination must always be inferred from such consequences." Id at 710 n 20 (emphasis in original).

disparate impact.[43] Although not strictly binding on the courts, this rule approximates the results that courts achieve using more elaborate methods of statistical analysis. Note that there is no corresponding restriction on claims of intentional discrimination. Even the slightest adverse result supports a plaintiff's right to recover.

Ricci says little about limiting the theory of disparate impact to significant adverse effects because the effects in this case were so stark. Twenty-five African-Americans took the tests, but none was immediately eligible for promotion, and of eighteen Hispanics, only two were eligible. From the Court's point of view, however, these disappointing results were part of the problem, not part of the solution. They led the city to engage in a form of racial balancing that required some form of justification. The source of this justification was the second limitation on the theory of disparate impact. It prohibits only practices that cannot be shown to be "job related for the position in question and consistent with business necessity."

This particular language was codified in amendments to Title VII made by the Civil Rights Act of 1991.[44] Congress picked up and combined phrases from the seminal opinion in *Griggs*, which used them to formulate one version of the employer's defense (among others): "The touchstone is *business necessity*. If an employment practice which operates to exclude Negroes cannot be shown to be *related to job performance*, the practice is prohibited."[45] This passage points in opposite directions: toward a heavy burden of proving business necessity and toward a light burden of proving some relationship to the job. The italicized phrases were incorporated into Title VII, but with the crucial difference that the statute only requires a test to be *consistent* with business necessity, not *required* by it. Proving that a test is required by business necessity would involve a showing that the business could not live *without* it. Taken literally, "consistent with business necessity" requires only proof that the business could live *with* it.

Congress undoubtedly meant to require something more than such a weak showing. Why would an employer adopt a test that would cause it to go out of business? But exactly how much Con-

---

[43] Uniform Guidelines on Employee Selection Procedures § 4D, 29 CFR § 1607.4D (2009).

[44] § 703(k). The actual language first appeared in the Americans with Disabilities Act, passed a year before the Civil Rights Act of 1991.

[45] 401 US at 431 (emphasis added).

gress required remains uncertain. The particular language adopted by Congress just perpetuates the ambiguity that can be found throughout the opinion in *Griggs* and, it is fair to say, in every opinion of the Supreme Court on the theory of disparate impact. It goes to the question whether the employer's burden of justifying a practice with adverse impact is a light burden—to prove only some relationship to the job—or a heavy burden—to prove that it is a matter of business necessity.

This question has been left open, just like the questions surrounding affirmative action, to which it is intimately related. As noted earlier, the heavier the burden of justifying practices with adverse impact, the more likely an employer is to respond to the threat of liability by eliminating the adverse impact, and the easiest way to do this is by engaging in affirmative action. That is precisely what the city of New Haven did in *Ricci*. Beneath the Court's entire analysis is the assumption that the city did not have to take this step because the burden of justifying the tests was light. This assumption accords with its concern that the employer might otherwise be encouraged to adopt a "*de facto* quota system" and its ultimate conclusion that there was no reasonable dispute that the promotion tests were valid. On the spectrum between heavier and lighter burdens of justification, the Court came down decidedly in favor of a lighter burden.

The Supreme Court has done this once before, as Justice Ginsburg pointed out in her dissent.[46] In *Wards Cove Packing Co. v Atonio*,[47] the Court watered down the employer's burden of justification. The employer no longer had the burden of persuasion; it only had to present evidence that a test "serves, in a significant way," its legitimate employment interests; and a court could only engage in "reasoned review" of this justification.[48] In the Civil Rights Act of 1991, Congress specifically rejected this holding, and singled out *Wards Cove* by name for criticism. The Court therefore can no longer rely on this holding in *Wards Cove* as an authoritative interpretation of Title VII. In *Ricci*, however, the Court cited a still

---

[46] 129 S Ct at 2698.

[47] 490 US 642 (1989).

[48] Id at 659–60. The Court also said that the court could only engage in "reasoned review" of the question whether the test "serves, in a significant way, the legitimate employment goals of the employer." Id at 659.

earlier opinion that anticipated this holding in *Wards Cove*,[49] calling into question the attempt by Congress to enact superseding legislation.

Congress, of course, would have the last word on what Title VII means, but the Court would have the last word on whether Title VII, as so amended, conforms to the Constitution. Only Justice Scalia thought that such a conflict was inevitable. He thought that the theory of disparate impact was vulnerable to constitutional attack to the extent that it imposed a heavy burden of justification upon the employer.[50] The other four Justices in the majority were unwilling to precipitate a constitutional conflict with Congress, most likely because there was no need to do so.[51] The statutory defense that the disputed practice is "job related for the position in question and consistent with business necessity" just repeats, in the context of the theory of disparate impact, the ambivalence over affirmative action that Congress expressed elsewhere in the Civil Rights Act of 1991. Thus, Congress explicitly prohibited "race norming" of test scores: adjusting the scores of one group to compensate for poor performance relative to another group.[52] On the other hand, Congress also limited collateral attacks on judicially ordered or approved affirmative action plans,[53] and in a particularly delphic passage, made the following declaration: "Nothing in the amendments made by this title shall be construed to affect court-ordered remedies, affirmative action, or conciliation agreements, that are in accordance with the law."[54] This passage, in a provision buried in the uncodified sections of the act, studiously refuses to address the central question of what is "in accordance with the law." Even with respect to *Wards Cove*, Congress approved of the decision

[49] The Court went back to the opinion of Justice O'Connor in *Watson v Fort Worth Bank and Trust*, 487 US 977, 992 (1988) (opinion of O'Connor, J), 129 S Ct at 2675. In this respect, however, Justice O'Connor spoke only for four Justices in a case in which the Court was equally divided.

[50] 129 S Ct at 2682 (Scalia, J, concurring). In making this argument, he prominently cited Richard Primus, *Equal Protection and Disparate Impact: Round Three*, 117 Harv L Rev 493 (2003). See also Charles A. Sullivan, *The World Turned Upside Down? Disparate Impact Claims by White Males*, 98 Nw U L Rev 1505 (2004).

[51] In another decision last Term, under the Voting Rights Act, the Court expressed a similar unwillingness to declare landmark civil rights legislation unconstitutional. *Northwest Austin Municipal Utility District Number 1 v Holder*, 129 S Ct 2504 (2009).

[52] § 703(*l*), codified as 42 USC § 2000e-2(*l*) (2006).

[53] § 703(n), codified as 42 USC § 2000e-2(n) (2006).

[54] Pub L No 102-166, § 116, 105 Stat 1071 (1991).

in other respects, so that its attitude toward the decision as a whole is ambivalent.[55]

Congress also preserved the ambiguity inherent in the theory of disparate impact, from its inception in *Griggs* onward. Congress confined the rejection of *Wards Cove* to the issue of job relationship and business necessity, and even on that issue, it only turned the clock back to the day before *Wards Cove* was decided.[56] Against this background, *Ricci* emerges as one of a series of decisions unsuccessfully seeking to dispel the ambiguities surrounding the theory of disparate impact. This continued failure, perhaps, is only to be expected in the absence of a clearer political resolution of the acceptability of affirmative action. The only lesson that can be drawn from the Civil Rights Act of 1991 is a negative one. Congress refused to limit the theory of disparate impact to "smoking out" intentional discrimination, as *Wards Cove* had done. It did not reject other limits on the theory.

These limits derive from disparate impact as a form of discrimination. Congress rightly extended the concept of discrimination to include disparate impact and, with some ambivalence, to promote some forms of affirmative action. It could not, however, escape the confines of the concept of discrimination altogether, and, in particular, the requirement of fault. Congress did not transform disparate impact into an all-purpose cure for the deficiencies in the concept of discrimination. If it did, it would have compromised the moral force of the theory as a ground for imposing liability upon employers. To get the benefit of disparate impact as a form of prohibited discrimination, Congress had to accept the accompanying requirement of proof of some form of fault. The limits on the concept of discrimination turn out to be more difficult to escape than first appears.

Advocates for an expansive interpretation of the theory often invoke as an alternative the concept of equal opportunity, defined more broadly than nondiscrimination alone. To use the terminology of John Rawls, the goal is not formal equality of opportunity—

---

[55] In particular, on the issue of adverse impact, the act followed *Wards Cove*, which in turn echoed the earlier decision in *Connecticut v Teal*. § 703(k)(1)(B), codified as 42 USC § 2000e-2(k)(1)(B) (2006). On proof of an alternative employment practice with less adverse impact, Congress set the clock back before *Wards Cove*, but the opinion only relied upon preexisting law on this issue, which apparently remains intact. § 703(k)(1)(C), codified as 42 USC § 2000e-2(k)(1)(C) (2006). See *Wards Cove*, 490 US at 660.

[56] Pub L No 102-166 §§ 2(2), 3(2), 105 Stat 1071.

according to neutral rules that do not discriminate against any protected group—but fair equality of opportunity—designed to give members of every group an equal chance to succeed according to those rules.[57] This step has much to be said for it by way of connecting concrete prohibitions against discrimination to abstract theories of justice. Yet it preserves the concept of discrimination rather than discarding it. On Rawls's view, prohibitions against discrimination serve as an essential component of a just society, but they are only one among many, such as distribution of initial entitlements, rights to individual liberty, guarantees of the basic capacities of citizenship, and social insurance against catastrophic losses.

Few advocates of expanded liability for disparate impact actually articulate its goals in these terms, because a Rawlsian approach reveals how limited any prohibition against employment discrimination really is. It fails to capture many of the additional features of a general theory of justice. Thus, the theory of disparate impact, so long as it is confined to the employment relationship, comes too late in an individual's career to compensate for a variety of inequalities earlier in life—in upbringing, education, or health care. Regulation of employment can make up for these deficits only in some manner related to what the employer can control. Because disparate impact also remains a form of liability for discrimination, it retains an unavoidable element of fault. Employers are not strictly liable for all the adverse effects of their employment practices and they do not have to take drastic steps to counteract such effects. They do not have to redress the cumulative disadvantages that individuals face from discrimination elsewhere in society. That is why they are liable only for employment practices that have substantial adverse effects and that have no significant justification. The ambitions and effects of employment discrimination law are themselves limited by its subject matter.

The legal and political resources available to the theory of disparate impact reflect these limitations. As currently configured, the theory cannot be reformulated to require employers to adopt affirmative action plans, as opposed to providing them with the opportunity and incentives to do so. Neither are they allowed to meet the adverse effects of tests with simple readjustment of test scores. These forms of race-conscious action are too coercive, and perhaps

[57] John Rawls, *A Theory of Justice* 63 (rev ed, 1999).

too clear, to fit the long-standing consensus on affirmative action. The first restriction is reflected in the disclaimer in Title VII that "[n]othing in this title shall be interpreted" to require affirmative action and the second in the prohibition against race norming in Title VII.[58] Justice Kennedy emphasized both of these provisions in his opinion,[59] but even a Justice as sympathetic to affirmative action as Justice Brennan had to recognize their force.[60] They constitute fixed boundaries that exercise a pervasive influence over even the broadest versions of the theory of disparate impact. Strict numerical limits, as well as government coercion, displace the individualized judgment that the Court has deemed essential to permissible affirmative action. Whatever the logical defects in the Court's reasoning to this conclusion, it is entirely consistent with the compromises endorsed by Congress and the public as a whole.

In *Ricci*, the city defended this step as a race-neutral effort to comply with Title VII, but reliance on adverse effects alone cannot be race-neutral, for reasons discussed earlier. Compliance with Title VII could still be a sufficient reason for the city's action, but only to the extent that the theory of disparate impact encourages permissible affirmative action. The theory is limited to *permissible* forms of affirmative action, which must be identified in terms other than simply complying with the theory of disparate impact. To do otherwise is to engage in circular reasoning. The city could not justify the decision to discard the test results by arguing, first, that it was necessary to avoid liability for disparate impact; second, that such race-conscious action is a permissible form of affirmative action; and, third, that it is permissible because it was necessary to avoid liability for disparate impact.[61] The glaring omission in the city's reasoning is the absence of any reason, other than counteracting adverse impact, to justify its decision. The theory of disparate impact does not provide a self-sufficient, freestanding reason for licensing forms of affirmative action not otherwise permitted by Title VII.

The city could have broken out of this circularity by several means, most readily by adopting a more flexible form of testing,

[58] § 703(j), (*l*), codified as 42 USC § 2000e-2(j), (*l*) (2006).

[59] 129 S Ct at 2675–76.

[60] *Johnson v Transportation Agency*, 480 US 616, 636–37 (1987); *Local 28 of Sheet Metal Workers Intern'l Ass'n v EEOC*, 478 US 421, 475–76 (1986) (opinion of Brennan, J).

[61] Judge Easterbrook has forcefully made this point. *Biondo v City of Chicago*, 382 F3d 680, 684 (7th Cir 2004).

such as an assessment center (assuming it was consistent with state law and with the collective bargaining agreement). Once the decision to administer the tests was made, however, the city had to challenge the validity of its tests. Its half-hearted concession that the tests might have been invalid resulted in more than logical problems over doctrinal technicalities. Such tentative doubts about the test forsake any attempt to demonstrate some advantage for everyone in race-conscious action. If the tests used by the city really did not measure the leadership skills for officers in the fire department, then the entire city would have been better off if some alternative selection procedure had been used instead. As it is, the city put itself in the worst possible position by discarding the test results, victimizing those who passed the test, and conferring only the most diffuse benefit on those who failed. There were no identifiable winners—only those applicants who stood a chance under an alternative selection procedure—but several identifiable losers. Most of them were white, sharpening the racial conflict that broke out into the open in the civil service commission hearings. This debate quickly degenerated into a zero-sum calculation over what was in the interest of one group at the expense of another. A serious look at whether the tests were in anyone's interests would not have eliminated the acrimony, but it would have offered a way out of it.

The Court characterized what the city did as a form of strict numerical balancing, equivalent to "race norming," a conclusion that appears to be little more than the mirror image of the city's attempt to characterize its own actions as "race-neutral." Neither characterization is persuasive by itself; each depends on the alternatives available to the city to achieve the undeniably legitimate goals of its promotion process. In retrospect, the city could have either decided not to give the tests at all, or after it had given them, rejected the tests as invalid. As it is, the city transgressed the elusive distinctions that mark the boundary between permissible affirmative action and illegal reverse discrimination. The city had every reason to assure the integrity of the promotion process for reasons of public safety. Promoting only the applicants genuinely qualified for leadership positions would have directly contributed to the effectiveness of the fire department. An assessment center could have conformed to the existing strictures on affirmative action, which recently have emphasized the need for individualized assessment of each candidate and the general benefits of affirmative action for everyone.[62] Counteracting the adverse effects of the tests alone without impugning their validity did not meet these requirements.

This perspective on *Ricci* explains the Court's emphasis on the timing of the city's decision. The city waited too long when it acted only on the numbers without also acting on the content of the test. The city argued that it was caught in a bind once the adverse impact of the tests was established, and it was, to the extent that it had to take a position on the validity of the tests. At that point, it either had to accept the tests as valid and make promotions accordingly, or reject the tests because they were invalid. The city would have been forced into the latter alternative and coerced into affirmative action only if it had faced a heavy burden of validation. Historically, the Supreme Court has resisted any interpretation of the theory of disparate impact with this consequence—not for reasons internal to the theory, but for external reasons based on the law of affirmative action. Even on its broadest interpretation, the theory of disparate impact can do no more than encourage permissible forms of affirmative action.

In *Ricci*, the Court confirmed this principle. Perhaps the Court went too far in presupposing that the city could meet its burden of validation, but the city invited this step by holding open the possibility that the tests were valid, leading the Court to find no "strong basis in evidence" for concluding otherwise. The city could not invoke adverse impact alone to claim that it was coerced into after-the-fact racial decision making.

IV. CONCLUSION

Cities subject to civil service requirements remain particularly vulnerable to claims of disparate impact. The movement toward more flexible standards of evaluation, such as assessment centers, without the rigid scores of civil service exams, has to overcome the obstacles imposed by civil service laws and labor contracts. *Ricci*

---

[62] An exception to this proposition is *United Steelworkers v Weber*, 443 US 193 (1979), which was conspicuously not cited in any of the opinions in *Ricci*. That case upheld a one-to-one ratio in training for skilled craft positions. Moreover, it did not require a prima facie case of prior disparate impact on minority employees as a prerequisite for upholding this program. Where *Weber* did not find a prima facie case of disparate impact to be necessary, *Ricci* did not find it to be sufficient. The cases can be reconciled only on the ground that the preference in *Weber* was necessary "to break down old patterns of segregation and hierarchy," 443 US at 208, while no such showing was made in *Ricci*.

will no doubt accelerate this movement. Private employers have not operated under any such constraints and have demonstrated a notable reluctance to box themselves into the dilemma faced by the city of New Haven. The decision will have its greatest practical consequences in inducing employers to take still further precautions to avoid binding themselves to test results that they cannot anticipate.

The doctrinal consequences of the decision could be more far-reaching, signaling the end of the decades-long equivocation over affirmative action and the intimately related issue of disparate impact. Despite the legitimate worries of those who regard affirmative action as a necessary complement to prohibitions against discrimination, such a general retrenchment is likely to be based on more than judicial decisions. A shift in political attitudes, coalitions, and agendas is necessary. Much has been made of the election of President Obama, both for affirmative action because his strongest base of support is in the liberal wing of the Democratic Party, and against it because his remarkable rise to power suggests that it is no longer necessary. These contradictory conclusions tend to cancel themselves out, but his election does not detract from the long-term trend toward greater scrutiny of affirmative action plans. If anything, it shows that an election in which race could not be disregarded still could be decided on other and better grounds. So, too, the justification for affirmative action cannot rest on the desirability of considering race alone, but on a showing that it is in the public interest. At this fundamental level, the city of New Haven failed to carry its burden of proof.

JOHN C. JEFFRIES, JR.

REVERSING THE ORDER OF BATTLE IN CONSTITUTIONAL TORTS

Few Supreme Court decisions have been as completely unsurprising as *Pearson v Callahan*.[1] *Pearson* overturned *Saucier v Katz*, which required courts to reach the merits of constitutional tort claims before addressing qualified immunity.[2] Since qualified immunity precludes damages unless defendants violate "clearly established" rights,[3] *Saucier* mandated some merits adjudications incapable of supporting damages judgments in those particular cases, because the rights violated had not been "clearly established" at the time of the defendants' actions. These "unnecessary" merits adjudications had been criticized by sitting Justices[4] and prominent

---

John C. Jeffries, Jr., is David and Mary Harrison Distinguished Professor, University of Virginia School of Law.

AUTHOR'S NOTE: Thanks go to James McKinley, Gregory Mitchell, George Rutherglen, and Jim Ryan for helpful criticism and to Kristin Glover, Wells Harrell, and Mary Robinson for exceptional research assistance.

[1] 129 S Ct 808 (2009).

[2] 533 US 194, 201 (2001) ("A court required to rule upon the qualified immunity issue must consider, then, this threshold question: Taken in the light most favorable to the party asserting the injury, do the facts alleged show the officer's conduct violated a constitutional right? This must be the initial inquiry.").

[3] *Harlow v Fitzgerald*, 457 US 800, 818 (1982).

[4] See *Brosseau v Haugen*, 543 US 194, 201–02 (2004) (Breyer, J, with whom Scalia and Ginsburg, JJ, joined, concurring) (expressing concern at a rule that "rigidly requires lower courts unnecessarily to decide difficult constitutional questions when there is available an easier basis for the decision (e.g., qualified immunity)"); *Bunting v Mellen*, 541 US 1019, 1019 (2004) (Stevens, J, joined by Ginsburg and Breyer, JJ, on denial of certiorari) (criticizing the "unwise judge-made rule under which courts must decide whether the plaintiff

---

appellate judges.[5]

In the lower courts, discontent sometimes edged toward defiance.[6] And the Supreme Court itself, when given the opportunity to demonstrate its devotion to *Saucier*, chose not to do so, resolving *Brosseau v Haugen*[7] on qualified immunity without ever reaching the supposedly prior question whether the police had used unconstitutionally excessive force. Not only did *Saucier* have its critics, but the critics had a point. They successfully identified circumstances (about which, more later) where the merits-first, immunity-second "order of battle" proved genuinely awkward. Given this background, the Supreme Court's directive that the parties in *Pearson* address whether *Saucier* should be overruled made a change in course seem preordained. And so it proved. "[W]hile the sequence set forth in [*Saucier*] is often appropriate," said the Court, "it should no longer be regarded as mandatory."[8]

The specific question in *Pearson*—whether the merits of constitutional tort claims should be adjudicated, even when they do not control immediate outcomes, in order to achieve "clearly established" rights capable of enforcement in the future—is discussed in Part I below. That question is important and interesting. Although the Court unanimously endorsed the watering down of *Saucier*'s categorical imperative, there is more to be said for the merits-first order of battle and for a systemic approach to constitutional enforcement than *Pearson* suggests.

---

has alleged a constitutional violation before addressing the question whether the defendant state actor is entitled to qualified immunity"). For more recent expressions of the same views by some of the same Justices, see *Morse v Frederick*, 551 US 393, 425–33 (2007) (Breyer, J, concurring in the judgment in part and dissenting in part) (emphasizing that "often the [*Saucier*] rule violates the longstanding principle that courts should 'not . . . pass on questions of constitutionality . . . unless such adjudication is unavoidable'"); *Los Angeles County v Rettele*, 550 US 609, 616–17 (2007) (Stevens, J, joined by Ginsburg, J, concurring in the judgment) ("disavow[ing] the unwise practice of deciding constitutional questions in advance of the necessity for doing so").

[5] See, for example, *Lyons v City of Xenia*, 417 F3d 565, 580–84 (6th Cir 2005) (in which Judge Sutton wrote a concurrence to his own opinion so that, having correctly followed *Saucier*, he could then criticize it); Pierre N. Leval, *Judging Under the Constitution: Dicta About Dicta*, 81 NYU L Rev 1249, 1275–81 (2006) (criticizing *Saucier* as a "new and mischievous rule").

[6] For citations to such cases, see *Pearson*, 129 S Ct at 817; Leval, 81 NYU L Rev at 1275 n 81 (cited in note 5).

[7] 543 US 194 (2004) (per curiam). The lower court had followed *Saucier*, ruling that Officer Brosseau had used excessive force before determining that he lacked qualified immunity. *Haugen v Brosseau*, 339 F3d 857 (9th Cir 2003).

[8] *Pearson*, 129 S Ct at 818.

At a broader level, *Pearson* reminds us that different constitutional rights require different remedies. The role of money damages—or indeed of any mechanism for vindicating constitutional rights—depends on the alternatives. The point is obvious, and yet the lesson needs learning. There is no way to craft a sensible and effective scheme of constitutional enforcement if remedies are considered in isolation. There must be comparison among options if remedial choices are to be made wisely. And comparison among remedies *requires* differentiation among rights. The remedial options available for one kind of constitutional violation are not the same as those for another.

It follows that the effectiveness of a particular remedy varies from right to right. For some rights, money damages are relatively unimportant, and the costs of foreclosing merits-first adjudication will be low. For other rights, money damages are central. For those rights, refusal to reach the merits of constitutional tort claims will cut to the bone. Going directly to qualified immunity will not only inhibit the development of constitutional doctrine, but will also degrade existing rights to a least-common-denominator understanding of their meaning.

As it is obviously not necessary that every constitutional violation trigger every conceivable remedy, limiting or foreclosing any particular remedy is in principle not objectionable. If, however, constitutional rights are to function as operational limits on government rather than mere figures of rhetoric, there must be an adequate *structure* of enforcement. Even though some wrongs go unrighted, there must be a generally effective remedial structure if constitutional law is to have functional meaning. Choices about specific mechanisms for enforcing constitutional rights cannot be made in isolation. The difference between foreclosing *a* remedy and foreclosing *the* remedy is only visible in comparison with other remedies, and the availability of other remedies varies across rights. Despite the Court's reluctance to particularize remedial doctrine, effective enforcement of constitutional rights demands it. *Pearson v Callahan* shows the need for reconceptualization of the law of constitutional torts.

I

The rationale for *Saucier* rests on the law of qualified immunity. That doctrine protects government officers from damages liability unless they violate "clearly established" rights.[9] The rights must be "clearly established" not merely at the lofty level of abstraction where uncertainties fade away, but at a level of particularity that provides practical guidance: "The contours of the right must be sufficiently clear that a reasonable official would understand that what he is doing violates that right."[10]

Pearson is illustrative. At issue was the sufficiency of the theory of "consent-once-removed" to justify the warrantless search of a house whose occupant sold drugs to a police informant and the subsequent arrest of that individual.[11] As described by the Supreme Court, consent-once-removed "permits a warrantless entry by police officers into a home when consent to enter has already been granted to an undercover officer or informant who has observed contraband in plain view."[12] The original consent to the undercover agent suffices despite the pretense of wanting to purchase drugs. "Once-removed" kicks in when the inside agent calls on outside officers to enter and make the arrest. Several circuits have endorsed this theory,[13] and none has squarely rejected it. In *Callahan v Millard County*,[14] as the case was then styled, a split panel of the Tenth Circuit ruled that consent-once-removed suffices when outside forces are summoned by an undercover *officer* who is invited into the premises and sees contraband in plain view, but does not extend to similar actions by a confidential *informant*.[15] Of course, the target of the investigation is not aware that he is dealing with either an

---

[9] *Harlow v Fitzgerald*, 457 US 800, 818 (1982).

[10] *Anderson v Creighton*, 483 US 635, 640 (1987).

[11] The facts are described in *Pearson*, 129 S Ct at 813–14, and more fully in *Callahan v Millard County*, 494 F3d 891, 893–94 (10th Cir 2007).

[12] *Pearson*, 129 S Ct at 814.

[13] See, for example, *United States v Pollard*, 215 F3d 643, 648–49 (6th Cir 2000) (justifying police entry once the defendant "admitted [an] undercover agent and informant" who established probable cause); *United States v Bramble*, 103 F3d 1475, 1478–79 (9th Cir 1996) (invoking consent-once-removed "where an undercover agent is invited into a home, establishes the existence of probable cause to arrest or search, and immediately summons help from other officers"); *United States v Diaz*, 814 F2d 454, 459 (7th Cir 1987) (applying doctrine "where the agent (or informant) entered at the express invitation of someone with authority to consent, at that point established . . . probable cause . . . and immediately summoned help from other officers").

[14] 494 F3d 891 (10th Cir 2007).

[15] *Callahan*, 494 F3d at 898 ("[W]hile our case law would support a holding that the Fourth amendment allows an undercover officer to summon backup officers within a home after that officer has been invited with consent, neither the case law nor a rational extension of the case law would support including officers summoned by an informant within a home.").

officer or an informant; if he were, he would not sell drugs. The logic of the Tenth Circuit's distinction is therefore not apparent, either immediately or on reflection, and it contradicts the reasoning of other circuits, which treat undercover officers and confidential informants the same for this purpose.[16] Perhaps the best that can be said for the Tenth Circuit's position is that it limits (even if arbitrarily) the warrantless search and entry of private homes and might be thought on that broad ground desirable.

Whatever the merits of the Tenth Circuit's view of the Fourth Amendment, its approach to qualified immunity was, beyond per-adventure, wrong. Despite a respectable collection of cases endorsing consent-once-removed and the absence of any authority directly against it,[17] the Tenth Circuit found that reliance on that theory violated the clearly established "right to be free in one's home from unreasonable searches and arrests."[18] At this level of generality, the right is both clearly established and largely uninformative. The Supreme Court has inveighed against such abstraction and demanded that the right be established with greater specificity.[19] The Tenth Circuit's approach so plainly contradicted those instructions that it is hard to know whether the error sprang from misapprehension or noncompliance. *Pearson* should have been a textbook case for qualified immunity. Regardless of whether consent-once-removed is accepted or rejected (in whole or as applied to civilian informants), the claimed constitutional violation was not sufficiently well established to defeat qualified immunity.

Even if the Tenth Circuit had correctly applied qualified immunity, *Saucier* would have required that the merits be addressed nonetheless. The goal of this procedure is to clarify the law and to

---

[16] See *United States v Yoon*, 398 F3d 802, 806–08 (6th Cir 2005) ("extend[ing]" consent-once-removed from cases involving "an undercover agent and an informant . . . to cases in which a confidential informant enters a residence alone . . ."); *United States v Paul*, 808 F2d 645, 648 (7th Cir 1986) ("We think the principle extends to the case where the initial, consensual entry is by a confidential informant.").

[17] See *Pearson*, 129 S Ct at 822–23 (citing approval of consent-once-removed by three circuits and two state supreme courts and noting that the Tenth Circuit was the first to rule against the doctrine's application to confidential informants).

[18] *Callahan*, 494 F3d at 898.

[19] See, for example, *Brosseau*, 543 US at 198 ("It is important to emphasize that this inquiry 'must be undertaken in light of the specific context of the case, not as a broad general proposition.'"), quoting *Saucier*, 533 US at 201; *Saucier*, 533 US at 202 ("[T]he right allegedly violated must be defined at the appropriate level of specificity before a court can determine if it was clearly established."), quoting *Wilson v Layne*, 526 US 603, 615 (1999).

reduce the future scope of qualified immunity. When the lack of a clearly established right precludes recovery in one case, adjudication of the merits puts the next case on a different footing. Either the claim fails, or the right becomes clearly established and enforceable through money damages. Without merits adjudication, the legal rule would remain unclear, and development of the law would be forestalled by repeated applications of qualified immunity.[20]

The intended operation of *Saucier* can be illustrated on the facts of *Pearson*. If the Supreme Court had followed *Saucier*'s order of battle, a split in the circuits would have been resolved. "Consent-once-removed" would have been accepted or rejected, and the Tenth Circuit's distinction between officers and informants would have been adopted or reversed. The specific defendants sued in *Pearson* would have been protected by qualified immunity, but that defense would have become irrelevant to future cases. The asserted right against warrantless search, despite the undercover invitee's report of contraband in plain view, would have become either clearly established or clearly nonexistent. If the former, money damages would have become routinely available; if the latter, there would be no claim. One way or the other, qualified immunity would have been eliminated for consent-once-removed searches in the future.

The role of the merits-first order of battle in development of the law is thus easily seen. What may not be quite so obvious, but is in fact far more important, is the degradation of constitutional rights that may result when *Saucier* is not followed and constitutional tort claims are resolved solely on grounds of qualified immunity. For rights that depend on vindication through damage actions, the repeated invocation of qualified immunity will reduce the meaning of the Constitution to the lowest plausible conception of its content. Functionally, the Constitution will be defined not by what judges, in their wisdom, think it does or should mean, but by the most grudging conception that an executive officer could reasonably entertain. This effect will be ameliorated for rights that arise in settings

---

[20] See generally John C. Jeffries, Jr., *The Right-Remedy Gap in Constitutional Law*, 109 Yale L J 87 (1999); John M. M. Greabe, *Mirabule Dictum! The Case for "Unnecessary" Constitutional Ruling in Civil Rights Damages Actions*, 74 Notre Dame L Rev 403 (1999). Compare with Sam Kamin, *Harmless Error and the Rights/Remedies Split*, 88 Va L Rev 1, 49 (2002) ("It is only when the Court first looks at the substance of each constitutional claim brought before it and then looks to whether the plaintiff will be entitled to benefit that qualified immunity can have the progressive influence on the law that Jeffries and others ascribe to it.").

that do not trigger qualified immunity, but for rights that depend on vindication through money damages, abandoning merits adjudication will reduce constitutional protections to the least-common-denominator understanding of their meaning.

A

As *Pearson* explains, there are costs to *Saucier*'s regime, and these are discussed below. Preliminarily, however, we should pause to consider the surprising argument that the benefit of merits adjudication is in fact not a benefit—that the clarification of constitutional rights for future enforcement is not desirable. In a prominent criticism of merits-first adjudication, Thomas Healy points out that courts reaching the merits of constitutional tort claims "will not necessarily rule that the right exists."[21] This is certainly true, but it is also, as Healy sometimes recognizes, irrelevant: "a ruling that a right does not exist leaves future [damages] litigants no worse off than a ruling that the right is not clearly established; either way, they will be denied relief."[22] Nevertheless, Healy claims that merits rulings "do harm future criminal defendants and civil rights plaintiffs seeking equitable relief, since they are entitled to relief as long as the right exists, even if it is not clearly established."[23] So far as I can tell, this is simply confused. Criminal defendants and those seeking injunctive relief differ from constitutional tort plaintiffs in that they do not have to overcome qualified immunity. They do not differ from constitutional tort plaintiffs in having to show that a right exists. They cannot defeat criminal prosecution or secure injunctive relief by asserting claims that the courts do not accept. Courts might be liberal or conservative, generous or grudging, but whatever their predisposition, they have to confront the merits before granting relief.

For merits adjudication in constitutional tort cases to be undesirable, one would have to show, not that courts might rule against constitutional claims (which is obvious), but rather that courts are *more* likely to rule against constitutional claims in dam-

---

[21] Thomas Healy, *The Rise of Unnecessary Constitutional Rulings*, 83 NC L Rev 847, 857 (2005).

[22] Id.

[23] Id.

ages actions than those same courts would be to rule against those same claims if raised in other contexts.[24] The assumption is implausible, and Healy does not support it.

Of course, *if there were no qualified immunity*, there would be good reason to fear that constitutional tort cases would produce more cramped and restrictive determinations than would otherwise be reached. In a world without qualified immunity, the prospect of imposing damages liability for past violations of new pronouncements would inhibit courts from some rulings they might otherwise embrace.[25] But that is not the law. Indeed, a major rationale for qualified immunity is precisely to constrain the damages remedy in ways that do not constrain the definition of rights. In a world where money damages are limited by qualified immunity, there is no reason to think that merits adjudication in constitutional tort claims would be less expansive than constitutional adjudication elsewhere. All claims in all contexts may run up against judicial conservatism or the likelihood that most new claims fail, but these factors are not particular to constitutional torts. Given qualified immunity, there is nothing differentially inhospitable about adjudicating rights in constitutional tort cases.

Nancy Leong attempts to rehabilitate this argument by invoking cognitive dissonance.[26] This psychological concept takes center stage at the end of an article devoted mostly to an empirical assessment of the impact of the merits-first order of battle. Not surprisingly, Leong found that merits adjudications rose after *Saucier*, as that opinion required and directed. More interestingly, she also found that these adjudications were asymmetric: There was a "sharp increase in the percentage of cases in which courts explicitly held that no constitutional violation had occurred," but no "statistically significant increase in the recognition of new constitutional rights."[27] Thus, Leong concludes, "[s]equencing leads

---

[24] Logically, one would also have to show that the vindication of more claims would be normatively desirable. Not everyone will find that conclusion obvious, but for the purpose of untangling the debates about *Saucier*, it suffices to assume that vindication of additional constitutional claims is in principle desirable.

[25] See Jeffries, 109 Yale L J at 98–105 (cited in note 20) (explicating this argument).

[26] Nancy Leong, *The Saucier Qualified Immunity Experiment: An Empirical Analysis*, 36 Pepperdine L Rev 667, 671, 702–07 (2009).

[27] Id at 670.

to the articulation of more constitutional law, but not the expansion of constitutional rights."[28]

Leong's attempt to assess *Saucier* empirically is impressive. If
confirmed, her finding of sharp asymmetry in the results of merits
adjudications would be interesting, but perhaps not surprising.
One would predict that most expansionist claims would fail. Certainly, that will be true for claims that break substantial new
ground. Though it is crucial that the opportunity for constitutional
innovations be preserved, one would not expect to see them often.
Perhaps Leong has found nothing more than the influence of the
status quo on a system based on prior decision.[29]

In any event, Leong's results have not gone unchallenged. Indeed, they have been disconfirmed in the only other article to have
attempted a rigorous empirical evaluation of *Saucier*'s effects on
constitutional development.[30] Like Leong, Paul W. Hughes found
that *Saucier*'s order of battle produced more merits adjudication:
"The empirical data proves that mandatory *Wilson-Saucier* sequencing is necessary to ensure robust articulation of constitutional rights."[31] But unlike Leong, Hughes did not find radical

---

[28] Id.

[29] The influence of the status quo may or may not be particularly pronounced when the
Supreme Court is dominated by "conservatives" (depending on the kind of "conservatives"
they are). It would be possible, I suppose, to try to construct constitutional doctrine with
an eye to the supposed political proclivities of the particular individuals who are judges
at the time, but almost impossible to think that kind of gamesmanship could succeed.
Michael Wells has cautioned against trying to time doctrinal structures to the perceived
sympathies of the federal judiciary:

> The point . . . is not that obliging courts to decide more rather than fewer
> constitutional issues will result in a proliferation of newly-minted constitutional
> rights. On the contrary, the contemporary federal judiciary often finds against
> the claimed constitutional right rather than for it. Partisans of seeing to it that
> state officers are made accountable for their violations may prefer a regime in
> which rights remain undefined over one in which courts rule against the plaintiff's
> substantive argument on the merits [citing Healy].
>   In this author's view, this view is short-sighted. For one thing, if it is true that
> the current crop of federal judges are not especially sympathetic to expensive
> interpretations of the Bill of Rights, it is also true that the political composition
> of the federal judiciary changes over time. The partisan of expansive readings of
> constitutional rights, who prefers the avoidance doctrine today may find himself
> in an embarrassing position when a new President names a raft of new judges.

Michael Wells, *The "Order-of-Battle" in Constitutional Litigation*, 60 SMU L Rev 1539,
1563 (2007).

[30] Paul W. Hughes, *Not a Failed Experiment: Wilson-Saucier Sequencing and the Articulation
of Constitutional Rights*, 80 U Colo L Rev 401, 417 n 107 (2009).

[31] Id at 420.

asymmetry in the results of those merits adjudications. On the contrary, he found a substantial fraction of cases (just over 10 percent) where the court found a constitutional violation en route to granting qualified immunity because the right had not previously been clearly established.[32] Presumably, those rulings would render the underlying rights sufficiently clear to support money damages in future cases (if sufficiently similar), which is exactly what *Saucier* aimed to accomplish.[33]

Although the empirical dispute about *Saucier*'s effects is intriguing, more directly relevant for present purposes is Leong's argument for *why* merits adjudications in constitutional tort cases might be biased toward the negative. Her claim is grounded in the theory of cognitive dissonance.[34] "The existence of a dissonant state," she summarizes, "leads individuals to seek or accept information that reduces dissonance, while discounting evidence that increases dissonance by ignoring, discrediting, or denying it."[35] According to Leong, judges suffer cognitive dissonance when required by *Saucier* to rule in favor of the merits of the plaintiff's claim while denying the remedy of money damages. Rather than tolerate the psychological distress that (she assumes) accompanies adjudications of right without remedy, "judges may be subconsciously inclined to deny that a constitutional violation occurred at all."[36] Leong concludes that cognitive dissonance offers a "compelling explanation for the lopsidedness of constitutional articulation" that she (but not Hughes) found after *Saucier*.[37] If this were true, it would be a telling point, for it would suggest that constitutional tort cases might, after all, present a peculiarly inhos-

---

[32] Id at 423.

[33] The differences in the findings of Leong and Hughes may reflect differences in methodology, in the databases, and conceivably in the timing of the two studies. Hughes counts a maximum of two claims per case, while Leong imposes no such limit. Additionally, Leong includes published and unpublished district and circuit court opinions, whereas Hughes studies only circuit court opinions. Leong claims that the introduction of these cases did not affect her results, 36 Pepperdine L Rev at 688–90, 701 (cited in note 26), but the difference in data complicates comparison of the two studies. Finally, Hughes and Leong studied slightly different periods, so historical factors, such as the passage of the Prison Litigation Reform Act of 1996, possibly might have affected their results. Compare id at 686, 694–97, with Hughes, 80 Colo L Rev at 420 n 114 (cited in note 30).

[34] Leong, 36 Pepperdine L Rev at 702–08 (cited in note 26).

[35] Id at 703.

[36] Id at 704.

[37] Id.

pitable environment for the adjudication of rights. On this perception, clarification and development of constitutional law *in the context of constitutional tort actions* could plausibly be seen as undesirable.

The first thing to note about this argument is that it is not empirical. Although most of Leong's article reports an attempt at empirical assessment of the effects of *Saucier*, there is no study or data that purport to link cognitive dissonance with merits-first adjudication in constitutional tort cases. Leong's argument is, rather, an erudite speculation on the application of a psychological theory to a particular context of judicial decision making. And it is a most unlikely context. As Leong at one point recognizes, "the drive to reduce cognitive dissonance inheres in a decision only when that decision is made freely."[38] That is, only when an individual feels psychologically at liberty to decide as he or she pleases does the sense of personal responsibility trigger efforts to reduce cognitive dissonance. This seems to be Leong's view of judging. She describes trial judges as "exercis[ing] virtually unfettered choice," with "freedom to choose the outcome of a case."[39] But this description is apt only for judges wholly unconstrained by law. To the extent this condition exists, it is unfortunate. But to the extent that judicial decision making is constrained by the external authority of the law, cognitive dissonance theory is, in its own terms, inapposite.

In searching for cognitive dissonance, therefore, it is critical to recognize that *Saucier* did not set judges at liberty to do as they please, nor did it burden them with personal responsibility for reconciling right and remedy. On the contrary, the whole point of *Saucier* was to *require* that judges address right and remedy separately, in distinct inquiries, with different criteria leading (potentially) to different conclusions. The psychological anguish of "right without remedy" (if it exists) does not fall on the individual decision maker but on the superior authority that required that result. It is hard to imagine that judges would be psychologically disabled from answering separate questions separately when explicitly directed to do so by higher authority. In any event, cognitive dissonance theory does not so suggest.

---

[38] Id at 703, citing Darwyn E. Kinder et al, *Decision Freedom as a Determinant of the Role of Incentive Magnitude in Attitude Change*, 6 J Personality & Soc Psychol 245 (1967).

[39] Leong, 36 Pepperdine L Rev at 704 (cited in note 26).

More generally, speculation of this sort swims upstream against the broad current of legal reasoning. Lawyers are trained to distinguish categories of analysis and to think linearly, with questions coming in sequence. Nothing is more familiar than separate questions that must be answered separately. Thus, judges routinely distinguish among claims, allowing or approving some and rejecting others. They routinely resolve jurisdictional issues (both subject matter and personal) as distinct from the merits, and just as routinely consider defenses, such as statutes of limitation, that also operate independently of the merits. And they hold separate hearings on a variety of matters (voluntariness of confessions, the legality of searches and seizures, qualifications of purported experts, etc.) precisely so that such issues will be decided apart from the merits. This is not to say that litigation inquiries are completely isolated from one another. On the contrary, decision makers' views on one issue may well influence the resolution of others. Most obviously, judges may decide one question with conscious awareness of its effect on another, as in the case of a judge who stretches to find jurisdiction *in order to* reach the merits. This kind of purposeful adjudication has nothing to do with cognitive dissonance and in any event occurs across the spectrum of judicial decision making. With so much of the business of judging bound up with sequential analysis and issue categorization and in the absence of any direct evidence on this point, it is unreasonable to assume that cognitive dissonance plays a uniquely disabling role in the order of battle in constitutional torts.

B

Unlike some commentators, the Supreme Court does not doubt the desirability in principle of merits adjudication in constitutional tort cases. On the contrary, the *Pearson* Court endorsed and approved addressing the merits even when the defendant is protected by qualified immunity, concluding only that the procedure "should no longer be regarded as mandatory."[40] This conclusion reflects appreciation of the systemic advantages of merits adjudication. Most of the opinion, however, is taken up with a recitation of particular circumstances in which the benefits of merits-first adjudication are, or might be, outweighed by the costs. Thus, *Saucier*

---

[40] 129 S Ct at 818.

sometimes requires "a substantial expenditure of scarce judicial resources" on merits issues that do not affect the outcome, an expenditure of resources about which busy courts are "understandably unenthusiastic."[41] Sometimes, the merits are so "fact-bound" that addressing them "provides little guidance for future cases."[42] Occasionally, resolving the constitutional issue requires that the federal courts interpret state statutes and issue opinions about them that may not be authoritative.[43] Sometimes, the constitutional issue will depend on uncertain facts[44] (though this is also true of qualified immunity) or be poorly briefed and argued[45] (again, also true elsewhere).

The most serious problem concerns appealability. The defendant who loses on the merits but prevails on qualified immunity may face difficulty securing appellate review.[46] As Justice Scalia has noted, there are other examples of allowing appeals on collateral issues by parties who prevailed below,[47] but the situation is undeniably awkward. This problem was made fully visible, on unusual facts, in *Bunting v Mellen*,[48] when cadets at the Virginia Military Institute challenged a daily prayer as violative of the Establishment Clause. Presumably, the case could have been brought

---

[41] Id.

[42] Id at 819.

[43] Id (citing cases in which the First, Second, and Third Circuits "identified an 'exception' to the *Saucier* rule for cases in which resolution of the constitutional question requires clarification of an ambiguous state statute").

[44] Id ("When qualified immunity is asserted at the pleading stage, the precise factual basis for the plaintiff's claim or claims may be hard to identify. . . . Accordingly, several courts have recognized that the two-step inquiry 'is an uncomfortable exercise where . . . the answer [to] whether there was a violation may depend on a kaleidoscope of facts not yet fully developed.'") (citations omitted; quotation altered in original).

[45] Id at 820 ("There are circumstances in which the first step of the *Saucier* procedure may create a risk of bad decision-making. The lower courts sometimes encounter cases in which the briefing of the constitutional questions is woefully inadequate.").

[46] *Brosseau v Haugen*, 543 US at 202 (Breyer, J, with whom Scalia and Ginsburg, JJ, joined, concurring) (noting that *Saucier* may lead to "a constitutional decision that is sometimes insulated from review"). Accord, *Horne v Coughlin*, 191 F3d 244, 247 (2nd Cir 1999) (saying, of the situation described above, that "[t]he government defendants, as the prevailing parties, will have no opportunity to appeal for review of the newly declared constitutional right in the higher courts").

[47] See *Bunting v Mellen*, 541 US 1019, 1023 (Scalia, J, with whom Rehnquist, J, joined, dissenting from denial of certiorari) ("I think it plain that this general rule [against appealability] should not apply where a favorable judgment on qualified-immunity grounds would deprive a party of an opportunity to appeal the unfavorable (and often more significant) constitutional determination.").

[48] *Mellen v Bunting*, 327 F3d 355 (4th Cir 2003), cert denied, 541 US 1019 (2004).

as a class action but it was not, so the prayer for injunctive relief became moot when the plaintiffs graduated. That left only damages claims, which triggered qualified immunity. The Fourth Circuit ruled for the plaintiffs on the merits but for the defendants on qualified immunity, which left General Josiah Bunting, former Superintendent of VMI, in the awkward position of petitioning for Supreme Court review (on the merits) of a judgment he had won below (on qualified immunity). Justice Scalia's suggestion (joined by Chief Justice Rehnquist) that the merits should nevertheless be reviewable[49] was countered by Justice Stevens's suggestion (joined by Justices Ginsburg and Breyer) that the problem be solved by overruling *Saucier*,[50] as the full Court did in *Pearson*. At the very least, *Bunting* shows that in some, albeit infrequent, situations, following *Saucier* requires tinkering with appellate review.

Broader criticisms of *Saucier* have also been advanced. Most prominent is Pierre Leval's James Madison Lecture at New York University, "Judging Under the Constitution: Dicta About Dicta."[51] Judge Leval offers a wide-ranging attack on dicta, or, rather, on the failure to distinguish dicta from holdings.[52] Much of his argument is a plea for judicial modesty. He sees a decline in judicial restraint and the rise of a self-perception that leads to wide-ranging pronouncements: "[W]e have come to see ourselves as something considerably grander—as lawgivers, teachers, fonts of wisdom, even keepers of the national conscience."[53] Skepticism about judicial "grandeur" is well taken, but it does not pertain directly or especially to *Saucier*'s order of battle. Similarly, Judge Leval's criticism of seriously wrong-headed judicial pronouncements is also sound,[54]

---

[49] See note 47 above.

[50] *Bunting*, 541 US at 1019 (Stevens, J, with whom Ginsburg and Breyer, JJ, joined, opinion respecting denial of certiorari).

[51] Leval, 81 NYU L Rev 1249 (cited in note 5). See also Judge Jeffrey Sutton's thoughtful concurrence in *Lyons v City of Xenia*, 417 F3d 565, 580–84 (6th Cir 2005), and Healy, 83 NC L Rev 847 (cited in note 21).

[52] Id at 1253 ("What is problematic is not the utterance of dicta, but the failure to distinguish between holding and dictum.").

[53] Id at 1256. See also id at 1267 ("Another pernicious stimulus for making law through dictum lies in the desire of us judges to appear erudite [by engaging in] unnecessary, discursive, scholarly discussions . . . .").

[54] See, for example, id at 1266–67 (criticizing the Court's erroneous suggestion that "every commercial use of copyrighted material is presumptively an unfair exploitation of the [copyright] privilege"), quoting *Sony Corp. of America v Universal City Studios, Inc.*, 464

but again not particularly relevant. Indeed, some of Judge Leval's comments are specifically *in*applicable to this context. Thus, he notes that courts are poorly designed for lawmaking, as they lack the institutional capacity for "broad, integrated study" that could be done by a legislature.[55] This may be true, but it is not here relevant. However much a court may be hampered by its inability to hold legislative hearings, employ experts, commission studies, and the like, these limitations are endemic to all constitutional adjudication.

Despite these loose connections, Judge Leval singles out *Saucier*'s merits-first requirement as a prime example of objectionable "dicta." *Saucier*, he says, is "a blueprint for the creation of bad constitutional law."[56] The crux of the argument seems to be the conviction that "[w]hen law is made in dictum, the likelihood is high that it will be bad law."[57] Thus, because the merits rulings required by *Saucier*'s order of battle are (for the particular cases in which qualified immunity obtains) "unnecessary," they will therefore be ill-considered or erroneous, or at least substantially more likely to be so than merits rulings made by the same judges in other contexts. Conceivably this may be true, and the intuitions of distinguished observers should not be lightly set aside, but it is worth noting how unlike Judge Leval's image of judges "glibly announc[ing] new constitutional rights"[58] the merits-first adjudication in constitutional tort cases really is. First, and most important, *Saucier* does not call for the adjudication of hypotheticals. The facts on which merits adjudications are based are not the result of speculations about imagined situations; they are the actual facts of the case at hand. Thus, they do not lack the concreteness needed for sound adjudication.[59] Moreover, there is little reason to think that merits rulings *required* by the order of battle in constitutional tort cases receive

US 417, 451 (1984); Leval, 81 NYU L Rev at 1272–73 (cited in note 5) (describing the Court's opinion in *Boykin v Alabama*, 395 US 238 (1969), where the Court confusingly suggested not only that the knowing and voluntary character of a guilty plea had to be established when the plea was taken but also that specific constitutional rights waived by a plea had to be individually discussed).

[55] Leval, 81 NYU L Rev at 1260 (cited in note 5).

[56] Id at 1279.

[57] Id at 1260.

[58] Id at 1277 ("[T]he Supreme Court now *requires* that courts glibly announce new constitutional rights in dictum . . . .").

[59] Compare with id at 1262.

"scant attention."[60] Such rulings are not peripheral to the facts before the court, much less unrelated. On the contrary, they are an-
alytically central to resolving the case at hand. What *Saucier* requires
is that the courts go *further* in resolving merits issues that are fully
and fairly presented than would be necessary to dispose of the case
on qualified immunity, not that they indulge in uninformed speculation about what the law would be on other facts.

However sound they may be elsewhere, as applied to this particular issue, Judge Leval's criticisms seem to me overblown. That
said, there may be residual risk, as Judge Leval claims, that a defendant who knows he will win on qualified immunity may lack the
incentive to dig in on the merits.[61] This seems logically plausible,
but how likely may be doubted. For one thing, it would require
otherworldly confidence for a defense attorney to duck an opportunity to contest the merits of a constitutional claim on the ground
that her client was certain to win under qualified immunity, given
that qualified immunity depends on the uncertainty of *those same
merits*. Arguing that a claim lacks merit would be an obvious and
effective way of showing that, at a minimum, it is not clearly established. Indeed, it would be surprising for defense counsel ever
to concede, even tacitly, that a claim is meritorious, where success
depends on showing that the merits are in fact unclear. Put simply,
the analytic connection between the merits and qualified immunity
militates against taking a dive.

Moreover, the concern that defense lawyers in constitutional tort
cases might duck the merits ignores the extent to which they are
repeat players. Very rarely are defense lawyers paid by the individual
officers they defend. Almost always, officer defendants are represented by lawyers provided by their government employers, who
will bear the expense of representation and the burden of any adverse judgments.[62] Lawyers paid by governments have strong in-

---

[60] Compare with id ("There is a high likelihood that peripheral observations, alternative
explanations, and dicta will receive scant attention.").

[61] Id at 1278 (hypothesizing a defense lawyer who refuses to join issue on the merits
because of supposedly certain victory on other grounds).

[62] John C. Jeffries, Jr., *In Praise of the Eleventh Amendment and Section 1983*, 84 Va L
Rev 47, 49–50 (1998) ("Very generally, a suit against a state officer is functionally a suit
against the state, for the state defends the action and pays any adverse judgment. So far
as can be assessed, this is true not occasionally and haphazardly but pervasively and de-
pendably."); Cornelia T. L. Pillard, *Taking Fiction Seriously: The Strange Results of Public
Officials' Individual Liability Under Bivens*, 88 Georgetown L J 65, 67, 76–77 (1999) (reporting the same for *Bivens* actions).

centives to defend the actions of their employers, regardless of the qualified immunity claims of individual defendants, assuming (as would surely be true here) that there is no conflict of interest.

At a global level, the upshot of all this is an argument in standoff. There is more to be said for a requirement of merits-first adjudication than *Pearson* suggests, but there are also disadvantages. Many criticisms of *Saucier* are inapposite or exaggerated, but not entirely empty. The need to accommodate appellate review, in particular, is a legitimate problem, and other concerns cannot be dismissed.

My own view is that, considered as a general issue to be resolved across the board, the question of the order of battle in constitutional tort cases may have no right answer. If adjudication of the merits is mandatory, as *Saucier* contemplated, the occasional difficulty becomes a telling objection. But if the matter is left to judicial discretion, there will be too little judicial investment in resolving the merits of constitutional tort claims. The essential problem is that *Saucier*'s benefits are forward-looking and systemic, while its costs are felt here and now. Busy trial judges who see a short route to decision on qualified immunity will often be unwilling to come to grips with the merits, even though the failure to do so may be costly in the long run. And trial judges who rest on qualified immunity will usually preclude appellate courts from authoritatively adjudicating the merits, as it would be awkward for appellate judges to rule on grounds not considered below.

If *Saucier*'s rule of merits adjudication has costs, so does merits avoidance. These costs are not measured solely, or even chiefly, in the persistence of uncertainty in the law. The greater problem is the underenforcement of constitutional rights while such uncertainty continues. The perpetuation of qualified immunity dilutes the meaning of constitutional protections from whatever the legitimate authorities believe the Constitution requires to some lesser standard of reasonable misperception. For that, *Pearson* has no good answer.

II

The least satisfying passage in *Pearson* concerns alternative remedies. It comprises only two sentences:

> Moreover, the development of constitutional law is by no means entirely dependent on cases in which the defendant may seek

> qualified immunity. Most of the constitutional issues that are
> presented in § 1983 damages actions and *Bivens* cases also arise
> in cases in which that defense is not available, such as criminal
> cases and § 1983 cases against a municipality, as well as § 1983
> cases against individuals where injunctive relief is sought instead
> of or in addition to damages.[63]

This statement is not inaccurate, but it is extremely broad brush.
It is true that qualified immunity is unavailable when constitutional
tort claims are brought directly against local governments,[64] but it
is also true that direct governmental liability may be imposed only
for "official policy or custom."[65] As "official policy or custom" has
been narrowly construed,[66] the prospect of routine merits adjudication in direct damages actions against local governments is largely
illusory.

Even less likely to provide merits adjudications are suits for declaratory or injunctive relief. In most cases, victims are not fore-
warned of constitutional violations and thus have no opportunity
to seek prospective relief. Even when the problem is foreseen, limitations on standing (and allied doctrines of justiciability) often preclude anticipatory litigation. A plaintiff has to show not merely that
the defendant is engaged in unconstitutional conduct likely to cause
identifiable future harm, but rather that foreseeable future miscon-

---

[63] *Pearson*, 129 S Ct at 821–22.

[64] *Owen v City of Independence*, 445 US 622 (1980). States, of course, are treated differently. Indeed, they are not "persons" under § 1983 and are therefore absolutely immune
from damages liability. *Will v Michigan Dept of State Police*, 491 US 58 (1989). This disparity
mirrors the Eleventh Amendment but creates a functional anomaly for which no plausible
explanation has ever been offered.

[65] *Monell v New York City Dept of Social Services*, 436 US 658 (1978) ("[I]t is when execution
of a government's policy or custom, whether made by its lawmakers or those whose edicts
or acts may fairly be said to represent official policy, inflicts the injury that the government
as an entity is responsible under § 1983."). Ironically, the limitation on governmental
liability imposed by *Monell* is the same limitation rejected for individual officers, over
Justice Frankfurter's dissent, in *Monroe v Pape*, 365 US 167 (1961). The whole point of
Monroe was to provide an independent federal remedy against state officers who violated
federal rights, even when state law (and practice) condemned such conduct and provided
effective remedies for it.

[66] See, for example, *City of St. Louis v Praprotnik*, 485 US 112 (1988) (reversing a judgment of municipal liability on the ground that the managers who engaged in a retaliatory
employment action did not have policy-making authority with respect to that act); *City
of Canton v Harris*, 489 US 378 (1989) (holding that governmental liability for failure to
train requires "deliberate indifference" to the violation of constitutional right, a standard
that effectively reintroduces qualified immunity by the back door). See also Jeffries, 84
Va L Rev at 59 (cited in note 62) (concluding from these and other cases that direct
governmental liability for constitutional torts is only "a narrow deviation from the generally
applicable rule of liability based on fault").

duct will injure *this* plaintiff individually.[67] Of course, overbreadth doctrine facilitates prospective challenges to statutes that infringe on free speech, but facial review is the exception rather than the rule. Generally speaking, potential plaintiffs must wait for focused threats of immediate injury, by which time no practical opportunity for injunctive relief may exist.[68]

That leaves the defensive assertion of constitutional rights. For some criminal procedure rights, exclusion of evidence is the principal remedy. Exclusion is required for violations of the Fifth Amendment, including its implementation through *Miranda*,[69] and is the routine remedy for illegal search and seizure. Today, of course, the routine remedy for Fourth Amendment violations is considerably less than routine. Illegally seized evidence may be used in grand jury proceedings,[70] in impeaching testimony by the accused,[71] in prosecuting someone who had no protected interest in the premises searched,[72] in cases of "reasonable reliance on a search warrant issued by a detached and neutral magistrate but ultimately found to be unsupported by probable cause,"[73] and in cases of a reasonable belief in an outstanding arrest warrant based on search of a database that had been improperly maintained elsewhere.[74] These limitations on the exclusionary remedy have been accompanied by curtailment of enforcement. Since *Stone v Powell*, federal habeas review of Fourth Amendment exclusion has been restricted to ensuring that the defendant had an opportunity for "full and fair litigation" of her

---

[67] See, for example, *City of Los Angeles v Lyons*, 461 US 95 (1983) (holding that an individual who had been subject to an allegedly unconstitutional "chokehold" after a traffic stop could not challenge police policy on that subject absent showing of a "real and immediate" threat that it would happen *to him* again).

[68] For hopeful comments on the past and future of structural reform injunctions, see John C. Jeffries, Jr., and George A. Rutherglen, *Structural Reform Revisited*, 95 Cal L Rev 1387, 1408–22 (2007).

[69] *Miranda v Arizona*, 384 US 436 (1966).

[70] *United States v Calandra*, 414 US 330, 348 (1974) (authorizing limiting of suppression to "those areas where its remedial objectives are thought most efficaciously served").

[71] *Walder v United States*, 347 US 62, 65 (1954). Compare with *Harris v New York*, 401 US 222, 225–26 (1971) (same rule for statements made in violation of *Miranda*).

[72] *Rakas v Illinois*, 439 US 128, 139–40 (1978) (replacing the prior notion of "Fourth Amendment standing" with an inquiry into whether "the disputed search and seizure has infringed an interest of the defendant which the Fourth Amendment was designed to protect").

[73] *United States v Leon*, 468 US 897, 918–25 (1984).

[74] *Herring v United States*, 129 S Ct 695 (2009).

claim.[75] When state courts, unlike those in *Pearson*, are reluctant to suppress reliable evidence, borderline Fourth Amendment violations will go unremedied.

In light of these developments, one may wonder just how effective the remedial structure of the Fourth Amendment currently is.[76] Even for those with doubts on that issue, it is a different question whether the exclusionary rule provides adequate opportunities for the definition of Fourth Amendment rights. The answer to that question, in my view, is generally "yes." So long as exclusion is not predictably confined to certain kinds of violations, the imposition of that penalty—even if more occasional than routine—likely will trigger adequate opportunities for determining what constitutes a constitutional violation. Of course, the ability to use illegally seized evidence to secure an indictment or to impeach exculpatory testimony at trial will increase the expected return to law enforcement of illegal activity and to that extent vitiate the prohibitions against it. For adequacy of enforcement, these loopholes are undoubted liabilities, and perhaps significant ones. For rights definition—the process of articulating, specifying, and clarifying what conduct is allowed—the limitations on exclusion are far less costly. Exclusion in some substantial sampling of cases will likely provide sufficient opportunity for law definition, even if the systemic adequacy of the remedial structure remains in doubt.

On this analysis, the rule of *Pearson v Callahan* is, *in context*, defensible. Where exclusion is available for illegal search and seizure, the opportunity for merits adjudication of Fourth Amendment claims depends only secondarily on constitutional tort actions. Moving straight to qualified immunity will not devalue constitutional rights if those rights are adequately defined elsewhere. *Saucier*'s strongest justification is therefore missing. Given the availability of alternative remedies, the potential costs of *Saucier* may well be taken to outweigh the benefits of merits-first adjudication.

That is not to say that there are no such benefits. The Tenth Circuit's limitation of consent-once-removed searches clarified the law for the states in that circuit and in doing so provided a "clearly established" basis for future damage actions. This is an unqualified gain in the enforcement of constitutional rights. That the Tenth

---

[75] 428 US 465, 494 (1976).

[76] See generally Jeffries and Rutherglen, 95 Cal L Rev at 1406–08 (cited in note 68).

Circuit's ruling may be thought mistaken is beside the point. There is nothing in the history of the litigation to suggest that the same court confronting the same question in any other context would have reached a different answer. None of the difficulties cited by *Saucier*'s critics was encountered here. The adjudication was concrete, adversarial, and based on well-developed facts, which were tested by committed advocacy. Nor is there reason to think that the judges took their responsibilities lightly or were in any way casual in reaching their conclusions. From all that appears, the answer given by the Tenth Circuit in this litigation was the *best* answer that court could have given. For those who nevertheless think the ruling error—and I confess to being among that number—the problem is not too much *Saucier*, but too little. Had the Supreme Court followed its own procedure and resolved the merits before addressing qualified immunity, the constitutionality of consent-once-removed searches would have been authoritatively resolved, nationwide, in an appropriate case after full consideration. Of course, it is always possible to suppose that a different court at a different time might reach a "better decision"—usually meaning one more nearly aligned with one's own views—but that is no reason to disparage or deny the need for effective enforcement of constitutional rights, whatever those rights may currently be understood to be.

The real problem with *Pearson*, however, is not the abandonment of *Saucier* when constitutional tort actions are secondary avenues for vindicating constitutional rights. The trouble is that constitutional tort actions are sometimes primary. Even within the doctrinal ambit of the Fourth Amendment, for example, there are constitutional violations for which exclusion of evidence is irrelevant. They include what is arguably the greatest challenge in all the law of constitutional remedies—inhibiting the abusive and excessive use of force by law enforcement. Although such wrongs are analyzed under the Fourth Amendment,[77] illegal seizure is not the problem, and exclusion of evidence not a remedy. Under current law, the most (nearly) plausible redress for excessive force is the award of

---

[77] *Graham v Connor*, 490 US 386, 395 (1989) (holding that "all claims that law enforcement officers have used excessive force—deadly or not—in the course of an arrest, investigatory stop, or other 'seizure' of a free citizen should be analyzed under the Fourth Amendment").

money damages.[78] Thus, although constitutional tort actions are distinctly secondary as a means of remedying most Fourth Amendment violations, in this context, they are essential. The same is true of searches and arrests not aimed at successful prosecution, but rather at the assertion of police authority or (what may be perilously close to the same thing) police harassment. And of course there are other constitutional violations—procedural due process for example—that arise outside criminal prosecution and may present no opportunity for defensive enforcement.

It is in these contexts that the rule of *Saucier* is most needed and its abandonment most to be lamented. As a broad generalization, applicable indifferently to the vindication of all rights, *Pearson* may be defensible. But in specific contexts, it has the potential to work real harm.

III

Elsewhere I have called for "disaggregating" constitutional torts.[79] Specifically, I argued that thinking about constitutional torts entirely transubstantively "obscures important differences among rights and suppresses clear thinking about remedies."[80] Instead, I suggested a strategy in which the "availability of money damages would depend on an assessment of their role in enforcing particular rights—and especially on the availability of alternative remedies that make damages more or less needful."[81] I made this argument with specific reference to qualified immunity, where the Supreme Court has insisted that the law reflect a balance struck "across the board"[82] and not one that varies with particular rights.[83] Anyone who reads the cases knows that qualified immunity doctrine, although simple enough in the abstract, is notoriously unstable in application.[84] In

---

[78] For an endorsement of greater use of structural reform injunctions in this area, see Jeffries and Rutherglen, 95 Cal at 1416–21 (cited in note 68).

[79] See John C. Jeffries, Jr., *Disaggregating Constitutional Torts*, 110 Yale L J 259 (2000).

[80] Id at 259.

[81] Id.

[82] *Harlow v Fitzgerald*, 457 US 800, 821 (1982) (Brennan, J, concurring).

[83] *Anderson v Creighton*, 483 US 635, 643 (1987) ("[W]e have been unwilling to complicate qualified immunity analysis by making the scope or extent of immunity turn on the precise nature of various officials' duties or the precise character of the particular rights alleged to have been violated.").

[84] See Karen M. Blum, *The Qualified Immunity Defense: What's "Clearly Established" and What's Not*, 24 Touro L Rev 501 (2008) (surveying current issues in administering qualified

my view, both the substance and the administrability of qualified immunity could be improved if the law were allowed to develop with specific reference to particular rights rather than being imprisoned in an overarching generalization purportedly applicable to all.

I would make much the same argument with respect to the order of battle in constitutional torts. In my view, the desirability of merits-first adjudication should be resolved not categorically and across the board but with specific reference to particular rights. The crucial variable is whether money damages provide the chief or substantial vehicle for vindicating the right in question. When that is true, the rule of *Saucier* should be retained and merits-first adjudication required. When constitutional tort actions are not of primary importance in enforcing a particular right (as was true in *Pearson*), the order of battle can be relaxed. In my view, the choice between *Saucier* and *Pearson* can sensibly be made, as other remedial choices can sensibly be made, only by considering the alternatives.

---

immunity); Chaim Saiman, *Interpreting Immunity*, 7 J Const'l L 1155 (2005) (describing qualified immunity doctrine as "in a perpetual state of crisis").

JACK M. BEERMANN

QUALIFIED IMMUNITY AND
CONSTITUTIONAL AVOIDANCE

The Roberts Court is beginning to make its mark in the area of constitutional torts.[1] In the 2008 Term, the Court decided six cases involving remedies under section 1983[2] and *Bivens*,[3] the two main

Jack M. Beermann is Professor of Law and Harry Elwood Warren Scholar, Boston University School of Law.

AUTHOR'S NOTE: Thanks to Karen Blum, Ron Cass, and Bill Ryckman for their help with this article. For excellent research assistance, I thank Brian Maloney and David Rod, Boston University School of Law classes of 2009 and 2011, respectively.

[1] The term "constitutional torts" denotes civil rights cases brought to enforce federal constitutional provisions, and to a lesser extent federal statutes, against state and local officials primarily under statutes passed in the immediate aftermath of the Civil War and to enforce federal constitutional provisions against federal officials under *Bivens v Six Unknown Named Agents of Federal Bureau of Narcotics*, 403 US 388 (1971).

[2] Civil Rights Act of 1871, section 1, 42 USC § 1983. During the October 2008 Term, the Court decided five cases that presented issues arising under section 1983, including immunities, jurisdiction, and availability of the section 1983 action. See *Safford Unified School Dist. No. 1 v Redding*, 129 S Ct 2633 (2009) (school officials immune from damages for ordering and conducting strip search of student suspected of possession and distribution of ibuprofen); *Haywood v Drown*, 129 S Ct 2108 (2009) (New York may not limit jurisdiction over section 1983 claims to state court of claims where action is available against state, not individual defendants, and where complete remedies, including punitive damages, are not available); *Van de Kamp v Goldstein*, 129 S Ct 855 (2009) (supervisory prosecutors have absolute immunity from damages in case involving failure to inform prosecuting attorney of exculpatory evidence); *Fitzgerald v Barnstable School Committee*, 129 S Ct 788 (2009) (Title IX does not displace section 1983 remedy in case alleging lack of appropriate response to student-to-student sexual harassment); *Pearson v Callahan*, 129 S Ct 808 (2009) (officials are immune from damages in case involving warrantless search; rule requiring courts to address merits before reaching qualified immunity is overruled).

[3] The *Bivens* action against individual federal officials for damages resulting from constitutional violations was created by the Supreme Court in *Bivens*, 403 US 388. The Court decided only one *Bivens* case in the October 2008 Term. See *Ashcroft v Iqbal*, 129 S Ct

avenues for asserting constitutional tort claims in federal court. The Court found in favor of official immunity in all three cases in which that was an issue,[4] it invalidated a state's attempt to substitute the state court of claims (with limited remedies) for general state court jurisdiction over a class of federal constitutional tort claims,[5] and it rejected supervisory constitutional tort liability against high-level federal officials in a case related to the "war on terror."[6] These decisions follow familiar patterns and suggest that the Roberts Court is not likely to break with the general pattern of constitutional tort jurisprudence laid down by the Rehnquist Court. Perhaps the Term's most notable constitutional tort opinion was in one of the immunities cases, *Pearson v Callahan*,[7] in which the Court overruled *Saucier v Katz*[8] and held that federal courts are no longer required to decide the merits of constitutional claims before determining whether a defendant is entitled to qualified immunity.[9]

Pearson is another entry in the Court's struggle to resolve a serious

---

1937 (2009) (supervisory defendant in *Bivens* action not liable without state of mind required for violation of underlying constitutional standard).

[4] *Safford*, 129 S Ct 2633; *Pearson*, 129 S Ct 808; *Goldstein*, 129 S Ct 855. Although the Court has decided a fair share of cases rejecting immunity, overall the Court has made it difficult for constitutional tort plaintiffs to overcome official immunity.

[5] *Haywood v Drown*, 129 S Ct 2108 (2009). The Court had previously been wary of state attempts to disadvantage constitutional tort claims in state court. See *Felder v Casey*, 487 US 131 (1988) (rejecting application of state notice of claim statute in section 1983 case brought in state court).

[6] *Iqbal*, 129 S Ct 1937. The Court has rejected government agency and private entity liability under *Bivens*. See *FDIC v Meyer*, 510 US 471 (1994) (federal agency cannot be held liable under *Bivens*); *Correctional Services Corporation v Malesko*, 534 US 61 (2001) (private corporation cannot be held liable under *Bivens*). The *Iqbal* decision, by ruling that supervisory liability is available only when supervisors have the state of mind required for the underlying constitutional violation, went even further than a long line of Second Circuit decisions that rejects constitutional tort liability without the direct personal involvement of the supervisor/defendant. See, for example, *Black v United States*, 534 F2d 524, 527–28 (2d Cir 1976) (plaintiff in *Bivens* action must allege defendant's personal involvement in deprivation of rights); *Colon v Coughlin*, 58 F3d 865, 873 (2d Cir 1995) (same rule applies in section 1983 actions). Sheldon Nahmod points out that the Court adopted its more restrictive view of supervisory liability without briefing or argument on the issue and that the defendants had actually conceded that supervisory liability could be based on knowledge of or deliberate indifference to constitutional violations which is more lenient than the Court's requirement that supervisory defendants have the state of mind of the underlying constitutional violation. See Sheldon Nahmod, *Constitutional Torts, Over-Deterrence and Supervisory Liability after Iqbal*, 14 Lewis & Clark L Rev 279 (2010).

[7] 129 S Ct 808 (2009).

[8] 533 US 194 (2001).

[9] For convenience, in this article I refer to the practice of deciding the constitutional claim before reaching qualified immunity as the "*Saucier* procedure," and I refer to the Court's now repudiated requirement that the issues be addressed in that order as "mandatory *Saucier*."

problem created by the standard for determining whether qualified immunity protects an official from damages liability in a constitutional tort case. Under current law, the qualified immunity is overcome only if the defendant violated a clearly established constitutional right of which a reasonable official in the defendant's position should have known. In some circumstances, repeated immunity findings can cause the law to stagnate. With regard to constitutional claims that are likely to be litigated only in the constitutional tort context, officials might repeatedly engage in the same conduct and successfully defend damages suits with qualified immunity, leaving the scope of constitutional rights undetermined. Some lower courts recognized this and decided to address the merits of the constitutional claim before determining whether any right violated was clearly established at the time of the violation.[10] Not only did the Supreme Court approve of this practice, but in *Saucier* it held that federal courts were required to reach the constitutional merits before deciding on immunity.[11]

Although *Saucier* resolved the problem of constitutional stagnation, it created its own problems. Most notably, it flew in the face of the well-established doctrine of constitutional avoidance, under which courts avoid deciding constitutional issues unless necessary.[12] The *Saucier* procedure violates the doctrine of avoidance because courts can usually determine whether any right alleged is clearly established without defining the contours of the right itself

---

[10] *Egger v Phillips*, 710 F2d 292, 314 n 27 (7th Cir 1983) (en banc) ("Although the qualified immunity ground would constitute an adequate basis upon which to affirm the judgment below, we nevertheless consider it appropriate to address the merits of the First Amendment claim. Egger certainly has standing to raise that claim, and to dispose of the case solely on the ground that at the time of the alleged constitutional violation the right in question was not clearly established would leave the status of such a right in limbo.").

[11] Even prior to *Saucier* the Court had stated that in qualified immunity cases the court "*must* first determine whether the plaintiff has alleged the deprivation of an actual constitutional right at all." *Conn v Gabbert*, 526 US 286, 290 (1999) (emphasis supplied). However, it was not until *Saucier* that it became clear that the procedure was really mandatory.

[12] See generally Thomas Healy, *The Rise of Unnecessary Constitutional Rulings*, 83 NC L Rev 847 (2005). The Supreme Court has embraced a strong form of constitutional avoidance in which courts interpret statutes to avoid not only actual unconstitutionality but any serious constitutional question. For an application this Term of the avoidance canon in statutory interpretation, see *In Northwest Austin Municipal Utility District No. 1 (NAMUDNO) v Holder*, 129 S Ct 2504 (2009). As Richard Hasen writes, "In *NAMUDNO* . . . the Court—without objection from a single Justice—embraced a manifestly implausible statutory interpretation to avoid the constitutional question." Richard L. Hasen, *Constitutional Avoidance and Anti-Avoidance by the Roberts Court*, 2009 Supreme Court Review 182 (2010).

or even determining whether the alleged right exists.[13]

The decision to overrule *Saucier* was no great surprise. Members of the Court had expressed the view that *Saucier* should be revisited and had asked the litigants in *Pearson* to brief the subject.[14] Moreover, many federal judges had expressed unhappiness with mandatory *Saucier* and had created various exceptions to it.[15] Most fundamentally, the decisions that resulted from the *Saucier* procedure were tarred with the label "advisory opinion."

Justice Alito's opinion for the Court in *Pearson* summarized the costs and benefits of the *Saucier* procedure, with a much more extensive discussion of its costs than its benefits. Even after recognizing all the costs of the *Saucier* procedure, the Court did not mandate its abandonment. Rather, it left it to the lower courts to determine "whether that procedure is worthwhile in particular cases."[16]

By leaving the decision whether to reach the constitutional merits to the apparently standardless and unreviewable discretion of the lower courts, what *Pearson* put in place is deeply problematic. In *Pearson* itself, after announcing that the *Saucier* procedure was no longer mandatory, the Court jumped immediately to decide whether the right alleged in *Pearson* was clearly established, without discussing whether it should reach the constitutional merits. This appears to be the procedure the Court intended, because in *Safford Unified School Dist. No. 1 v Redding*,[17] decided a few months after *Pearson*, the Court followed the *Saucier* procedure without explaining why it reached the constitutional merits rather than deciding only whether the right violated in that case was clearly established.

---

[13] In addition to the straightforward avoidance canon under which courts interpret statutes to avoid constitutional issues, there are several doctrines in the justiciability family that are designed to avoid deciding constitutional issues. The best example is *Pullman* abstention under which federal courts stay proceedings when resolution of state law issues in state court might moot a federal constitutional controversy. See *Railroad Commission of Texas v Pullman*, 312 US 496 (1941).

[14] *Pearson v Callahan*, 128 S Ct 1702, 1702–03 (2008) (Mem) ("In addition to the questions presented by the petition, the parties are directed to brief and argue the following question: 'Whether the Court's decision in *Saucier v Katz*, 533 US 194 (2001) should be overruled?'").

[15] Respected Circuit Judge Pierre Leval even published a law review article attacking mandatory *Saucier*. See Pierre N. Leval, *Judging under the Constitution: Dicta about Dicta*, 81 NYU L Rev 1249 (2006).

[16] *Pearson v Callahan*, 129 S Ct 808, 821 (2009).

[17] 129 S Ct 2633 (2009) (finding search of student for drugs was unreasonable but holding that right was not clearly established).

Leaving to the standardless, unreviewable discretion of courts the decision whether to reach the constitutional merits before determining whether a right is clearly established is arguably worse than mandating that they do it every time or that they never do it. This new regime invites strategic behavior by courts and litigants who, in each case, are left to determine whether it would be beneficial to reach the merits or to try to influence whether the merits are reached. Judges who believe strongly in the doctrine of constitutional avoidance will be in a quandary as they watch their colleagues shape constitutional law through merits decisions in qualified immunity cases. While plaintiffs must always address the constitutional merits—because they can prevail only if a constitutional right exists and is clearly established—defendants have no way to know whether the court in any particular case is likely to reach the merits. Risk aversion may lead them to address the merits even when they are confident that the right was not clearly established, but the uncertainty may also give them the opposite incentive, especially if they think they would lose on the merits. Finally, it seems inconsistent with fundamental principles of judicial behavior to leave the determination of whether to make an "unnecessary" decision of constitutional law to the unconstrained discretion of individual judges.

This article proceeds as follows. Part I lays out the basics of constitutional tort immunities and the *Saucier* procedure. Part II describes and analyzes *Pearson* and concludes that the Court should have established standards to govern the decision of whether to reach the merits in qualified immunities cases or at least explained why it did not reach the merits in *Pearson*. Part III proposes considerations that should govern the decision of whether to reach the merits going forward. Part IV concludes.

I. CONSTITUTIONAL TORT IMMUNITIES AND THE SAUCIER RULE

As part of the Civil Rights Act of 1871, Congress provided that "[e]very person who, under color of" state law deprives "any citizen of the United States or other person within the jurisdiction thereof . . . of rights, privileges, or immunities secured by the Constitution and laws . . . shall be liable to the party injured in an action at law, suit in equity, or other proper proceeding for redress."[18] This statute, together with its jurisdictional counterpart,

---

[18] Civil Rights Act of 1871, section 1, codified at 42 USC § 1983.

provides an action in federal court against state and local officials who violate federal constitutional and statutory rights.

It was not until the 1950s that a significant volume of cases was brought under this and related provisions, and the Court ruled early on that the words "every person . . . shall be liable" were not intended by Congress to override the immunities that government officials had traditionally enjoyed under the common law.[19] The first decision recognizing immunity involved the absolute immunity of legislators;[20] the next recognized the absolute immunity of judicial officers and the qualified immunity of those exercising executive functions.[21] The Court later extended the immunities it recognized in section 1983 cases to *Bivens* cases, the judicially created damages action against federal officials for violating constitutional rights.

The importation of common law immunities into section 1983 and *Bivens* has necessitated a common law–like process of elaboration of the immunities, sometimes under the influence of the preexisting common law but often conducted exclusively in light of contemporary policy concerns.[22]

A. ABSOLUTE IMMUNITY

One issue that has been elaborated with attention to the common law roots of the immunities is the determination of whether a particular official is protected by an absolute, as opposed to qualified, immunity from damages suits. The Court has generally refused to extend absolute immunity beyond its common law

---

[19] *Tenny v Brandhove*, 341 US 367, 376 (1951). The basic principle under which the immunities were recognized is that the Court presumes that Congress intended the general language of this statute, 42 USC § 1983, to incorporate well-established common law doctrines including immunities, principles of causation, and similar doctrines. However, the Court has failed to apply this principle in a coherent fashion, and has only selectively honored instructions from Congress on the matter. See Jack M. Beermann, *A Critical Approach to Section 1983 with Special Attention to Sources of Law*, 42 Stan L Rev 51 (1989).

[20] *Tenny*, 341 US 367.

[21] *Pierson v Ray*, 386 US 547, 553–55 (1967).

[22] The policy bases underlying official immunities relate primarily to the public interest in allowing public officials to take official action free from concern over liability and potentially expensive and time-consuming litigation. A secondary consideration is fairness to public officials who, because of their official duties, must engage in conduct that is likely to provoke litigation. See generally Ronald A. Cass, *Damage Suits Against Public Officers*, 129 U Pa L Rev 1110 (1981). Relatedly, immunity means that public officials are not distracted from their official duties by the necessity of defending lawsuits based on their official conduct.

moorings,[23] but it has constructed a doctrine to adapt the common law scope of absolute immunity to the contemporary government structure. It has done so by adopting a functional approach to absolute immunity which, in two distinct respects, determines whether an official enjoys absolute, as opposed to qualified, immunity.

The first aspect of the Court's functional approach is that, regardless of title or position in government, officials exercising the functions that the common law protected with absolute immunity will receive absolute immunity from constitutional tort damages. This means that, for example, in addition to actual judges, executive branch officials such as administrative law judges receive absolute judicial immunity when they engage in the judicial function.[24] The second aspect of the functional approach strips officials of absolute immunity, again regardless of title or position in government, when they engage in a function not traditionally protected by absolute immunity. So, for example, a judge enjoys only qualified immunity when sued over administrative functions such as hiring and firing.[25]

This second aspect of the functional approach to absolute immunity has given rise to difficult cases and fine distinctions.[26] For example, due to its close association with the judicial process, the Court has extended absolute immunity to prosecutors, but it has made clear that not everything a prosecutor does in the course of her job is considered within that function for immunity purposes. Thus, when a prosecutor engages in an investigatory function, the prosecutor is protected only by qualified immunity. In principle

---

[23] *Sheuer v Rhodes*, 416 US 232 (1974) (finding no common law basis for extending absolute immunity to high-level state executive officials including governor).

[24] See *Butz v Economou*, 438 US 478 (1978).

[25] See *Forrester v White*, 484 US 219 (1988).

[26] The best example of how difficult it is to distinguish between functions that are protected by absolute immunity and those that receive only qualified immunity is *Bogan v Scott-Harris*, 523 US 44 (1998). In that case, a discharged city employee sued the mayor and members of the city council alleging race discrimination in her termination, which occurred after the plaintiff complained that another, well-connected, city employee had used racial slurs against her. She argued that firing her was an administrative function and thus the members of the city council and the mayor were not protected by absolute legislative immunity. Because the city council had accomplished the discharge by voting to abolish the plaintiff's position, the Court held that the firing was a legislative action. The Court was unwilling to look behind the legislative form of the decision.

this may appear simple, but it is not always so easy to distinguish prosecutorial from investigatory functions.[27]

This Term's decision in *Van de Kamp v Goldstein*[28] illustrates how difficult it can be to discern the boundary between a protected function and an administrative function to which absolute immunity does not apply. In *Goldstein*, an exonerated criminal defendant sued supervisory officials in the Los Angeles County district attorney's office, alleging that their failure to institute a system for sharing exculpatory information with lower-level prosecutors violated his well-established constitutional right to that information before trial.[29] The plaintiff also claimed that line prosecutors were inadequately trained concerning their obligation to turn over exculpatory evidence. To avoid absolute judicial immunity, the plaintiff argued that the construction and operation of an information-sharing system to ensure that line prosecutors are aware of exculpatory information was an administrative aspect of a supervisory prosecutor's job, more like administration and investigation than presentation of the case to the court. Although the District Court and Court of Appeals held that the defendants were not absolutely immune, the plaintiff's argument may have appeared to the Supreme Court to be nothing more than an ingenious attempt to avoid the line prosecutor's absolute immunity

---

[27] The following pair of Court decisions perhaps best tests and illustrates the limits of the prosecutorial function. In *Kalina v Fletcher*, 522 US 118 (1997), the Court held unanimously that prosecutors are not absolutely immune from damages for making false statements in a warrant application, on the ground that preparing the warrant application is an investigatory function not sufficiently connected with the judicial function to give rise to absolute immunity. In *Burns v Reed*, 500 US 478 (1991), the Court held that prosecutors are absolutely immune from damages claims arising from their presentation in court of the factual and legal bases in support of the issuance of a warrant. In *Burns*, the Court also decided that prosecutors are not absolutely immune from damages for giving unconstitutional advice to police regarding the investigation, in that case concerning whether to hypnotize the suspect in a criminal investigation and whether the police had probable cause to make an arrest. It would be perfectly understandable if, in light of these two decisions, prosecutors are somewhat confused about which of their activities are protected by absolute immunity.

[28] 129 S Ct 855 (2009).

[29] See *Giglio v United States*, 405 US 150 (1972). Goldstein was convicted of murder based largely on the false testimony of a jailhouse informant. The defense was not informed that the witness had received favorable treatment in exchange for his testimony. Goldstein alleged that the supervising officials in the prosecutor's office failed to provide this information to the prosecutor who actually prosecuted the case and failed to adequately train and supervise the lower-level prosecutors in the office. See *Goldstein*, 129 S Ct at 860.

from damages for failing to reveal the exculpatory information.[30] The Court assumed for the sake of argument that the plaintiff was challenging administrative aspects of the supervising prosecutor's duties, but held that the defendants were nonetheless entitled to absolute immunity:

> [P]rosecutors involved in such supervision or training or information-system management enjoy absolute immunity from the kind of legal claims at issue here. Those claims focus upon a certain kind of administrative obligation—a kind that itself is directly connected with the conduct of a trial.[31]

This refinement of the functional approach should be generalizable across the range of absolute immunity functions. Simply characterizing a function as administrative is no longer sufficient to strip an official of absolute immunity. For example, while judges do not receive absolute immunity from damages when sued over hiring and firing of court personnel, they now have an argument in favor of absolute immunity for administrative matters connected to the conduct of a trial, such as record keeping, production of trial transcripts, and the like. The *Goldstein* analysis may thus expand the range of cases understood as within a function that receives absolute immunity.

B. QUALIFIED IMMUNITY AND THE DEVELOPMENT OF SAUCIER

1. *Qualified immunity basics.* Officials whose functions are not within the scope of absolute immunity are protected by qualified immunity. The basis for this immunity is the same as that for

---

[30] The parties argued over whether prosecutors' offices are required to establish administrative systems to ensure that all prosecutors in the office are aware of exculpatory evidence. In *Giglio*, which also involved a failure to share information regarding promises made to a prosecution witness, the Court stated: "To the extent this places a burden on the large prosecution offices, procedures and regulations can be established to carry that burden and to insure communication of all relevant information on each case to every lawyer who deals with it." 405 US at 154. The plaintiff in *Goldstein* argued that the establishment of an information-sharing system was an independent constitutional obligation of an administrative nature. See Brief for Respondent in *Van de Kamp v Goldstein*, at 16–17. The defendants characterized this argument as "a guarantee of boot-strapped constitutional claims for all aspects of purported prosecutorial misconduct." See Reply Brief for Petitioners at 20. Their point, which ultimately prevailed at the Court, was that the information-management system argued for by the plaintiff was inseparably connected to decisions concerning the manner in which cases are tried, which is the very function protected by absolute immunity. Id.

[31] 129 S Ct at 861–62.

absolute immunity: At the time section 1983 was enacted, all executive branch officials exercising discretion were protected by a qualified immunity, known also as good faith immunity.[32] The earliest formulation of qualified immunity provided that police officers would be immune from damages liability for an unconstitutional arrest if they "reasonably believed in good faith that the arrest was constitutional."[33] Qualified immunity was crystallized in 1975 into a two-pronged standard: a government official not entitled to absolute immunity would nonetheless be immune unless "he knew or reasonably should have known that the action he took within his sphere of official responsibility would violate the constitutional rights of the [victim], or if he took the action with the malicious intention to cause a deprivation of constitutional rights[.]"[34] On the first prong, the Court explained that officials should know of "clearly established constitutional rights."[35]

This formulation lasted only seven years. It soon became apparent to the Court that the subjective element of the immunity allowed too many insubstantial claims to go to trial, because allegations of malicious intent were difficult to rebut on a motion to dismiss or summary judgment.[36] Thus, in 1982, the Court, in *Harlow v Fitzgerald*,[37] eliminated the "malicious intention" prong of the immunity, which meant that defendants[38] not protected by absolute immunity would be liable in damages only if they violate clearly established constitutional rights of which the official knew

---

[32] See *Pierson v Ray*, 386 US 547 (1967); Healy, 83 NC L Rev at 872–77 (cited in note 12).

[33] *Pierson*, 386 US at 557.

[34] *Wood v Strickland*, 420 US 308, 322 (1975).

[35] Id.

[36] This standard provided the civil rights plaintiff with two ways of overcoming the immunity—the defendant was liable if she acted with malicious intent to violate the plaintiff's rights or if she violated a clearly established constitutional right. Because immunity was an affirmative defense, the burden of pleading entitlement to immunity was on the defendant. See *Gomez v Toledo*, 446 US 635 (1980). However, once the defendant claimed immunity, the plaintiff would attempt to overcome the immunity by arguing that the defendant acted maliciously or violated clearly established rights or both.

[37] 457 US 800 (1982).

[38] *Harlow* was an action brought against federal officials under the Supreme Court's decision in *Bivens* which created a cause of action against federal officials parallel to the section 1983 claim against state and local officials. In *Harlow*, the Court specifically stated that the immunities in *Bivens* actions and section 1983 actions are the same. *Harlow*, 457 US at 818 n 30.

or reasonably should have known. This dramatically expanded the immunity defense[39] and made it more likely that defendants would prevail before trial, which was the express reason for the change.[40]

2. *Development of the Saucier procedure.* Soon after the elimination of the subjective element of the immunity, a serious side effect was recognized: Repeated successful interposition of the immunity defense in similar cases could stunt the development of the law and allow government officials to violate constitutional rights with impunity. This would happen when a damages suit was the only realistic way to raise a constitutional issue.[41] In such situations, the court would not reach the merits of the constitutional claim if the right alleged was not clearly established at the time of the challenged conduct.[42] As the Seventh Circuit put it soon after *Harlow*, the inability to reach the merits due to the immunity defense "would leave the status of . . . a right in limbo."[43] To address this problem, the Seventh Circuit[44] and other lower courts

---

[39] This policy-based expansion of the qualified immunity defense in section 1983 cases points up the lack of true connection to the common law of immunities. The touchstone of the common law qualified immunity was good faith. In fact, even now, more than 25 years after the elimination of the subjective element of the qualified immunity, it is still sometimes referred to as "good faith immunity." See, for example, *Harrison v Ash*, 539 F3d 510, 517 (6th Cir 2008). When the Court eliminated the good faith element of the qualified immunity in *Harlow*, it severed the connection between the immunity and its common law roots, leaving the legitimacy of applying the immunity in section 1983 cases open to serious question. See Beermann, 42 Stan L Rev at 66–69 (cited in note 19). Because the *Bivens* action was created by the Court, the application of official immunities in *Bivens* cases raises no legitimacy question.

[40] Since *Harlow*, the Court has characterized qualified immunity as immunity from suit, not just immunity from damages. See *Mitchell v Forsyth*, 472 US 511 (1985).

[41] For example, claims alleging excessive force in making arrests, like *Saucier*, are unlikely to arise anywhere but in a damages suit, while claims alleging illegal searches arise frequently in criminal proceedings at suppression hearings. Around the same time as it decided *Harlow*, the Court tightened the standard for injunctive relief in civil rights cases, making damages actions the only way some claims are likely to be litigated. See *Los Angeles v Lyons*, 461 US 95 (1983).

[42] The effects of the change were significant for the very reason that the Court was motivated to eliminate the subjective element of the immunity in *Harlow*. Before *Harlow*, plaintiffs were much more likely to get past a motion to dismiss based on qualified immunity by arguing that the defendant acted with malicious intent. The motion to dismiss would have also raised the constitutional issue, both directly on the merits and on whether the rights alleged were clearly established. The denial of the motion based on a live allegation of malicious intent would have included a determination that the plaintiff had alleged a constitutional violation. Otherwise, the motion to dismiss would have been granted on the merits, without regard to immunity. See Healy, 83 NC L Rev at 873–74 (cited in note 12).

[43] *Egger v Phillips*, 710 F2d 292, 314 n 27 (7th Cir 1983) (en banc).

[44] See id at 314 n 27. *Egger* appears to be the first case in which a Court of Appeals

took to deciding the merits of constitutional claims before considering whether the defendant was immune.[45] The Supreme Court ultimately agreed that it was appropriate for a court to address the constitutionality of government action before deciding the immunity question.[46]

This was, in my view, a surprising development given the traditional reluctance to make constitutional rulings that are unnecessary to the outcome of the case. But not only did the Court approve of this practice, ultimately it required it. In *Saucier*, the Court unanimously held that federal courts are required to address the constitutional issue before determining whether any rights recognized are clearly established.[47] The Court explained that this procedure was necessary in order to clarify constitutional law:

> In the course of determining whether a constitutional right was violated on the premises alleged, a court might find it necessary to set forth principles which will become the basis for a holding that a right is clearly established. This is the process for the law's elaboration from case to case, and it is one reason for our insisting upon turning to the existence or nonexistence of a constitutional right as the first inquiry. The law might be deprived of this explanation were a court simply to skip ahead to the question whether the law clearly established that the officer's conduct was unlawful in the circumstances of the case.[48]

3. *Criticisms of Saucier*. The unanimity in the Court for making

---

determined that after *Harlow* it was appropriate to reach the merits of a constitutional claim before deciding whether any rights found to exist were clearly established.

[45] See *Garcia v Miera*, 817 F2d 650, 657 n 8 (10th Cir 1987).

[46] The first time the Court applied this procedure, it did so as a matter of logic in decision making, stating that "[a] necessary concomitant to the determination of whether the constitutional right asserted by a plaintiff is 'clearly established' at the time the defendant acted is the determination of whether the plaintiff has asserted a violation of a constitutional right at all." *Siegert v Gilley*, 500 US 226, 232 (1991). There is language in *Siegert* implying that this order of decision is normatively desirable, but it is unclear if that is what the Court was really saying. In the next case, however, *County of Sacramento v Lewis*, 523 US 833, 841 n 5 (1998), the Court made clear that "to escape from uncertainty . . . the better approach is to determine the right before determining whether it was previously established with clarity." Justices Breyer and Stevens expressed misgivings about applying the procedure to "difficult and unresolved" constitutional questions. Id at 859 (Stevens, J, concurring in the judgment); id at 858–59 (Breyer, J, concurring). As noted, the Court first used mandatory language in *Conn v Gabbert*, 526 US 286, 290 (1999), but it was not until *Saucier* that it became clear that the Court intended that the procedure be mandatory.

[47] *Saucier v Katz*, 533 US at 201 (2001).

[48] Id.

Saucier mandatory did not end the controversy. Rather, *Saucier* came under attack from judges[49] and commentators on both principled and practical bases.[50] The attacks were aimed both at the practice of reaching the constitutional question before resolving the immunity issue and at the decision to make that sequencing mandatory.

The most obvious problem with the *Saucier* procedure is that it flies in the face of the general norm against dicta,[51] and the related, even stronger norm against the unnecessary decision of constitutional issues.[52] Critics went so far as to label decisions on the constitutional merits when the defendant's immunity defense prevailed as "advisory opinions,"[53] which federal courts are prohibited from rendering under Article III of the Constitution.

Whether merits decisions in cases in which the defendant is found to be immune are advisory opinions is debatable. On the one hand, these rulings are rendered in cases involving actual controversies in which a real plaintiff is seeking an actual remedy, damages, from a real defendant. They do not look like the classic advisory opinion in which a court is asked to make a ruling outside the context of an actual Article III case or controversy.[54] On the

---

[49] For example, in *Scott v Harris*, 550 US 372 (2007), Justice Breyer called for the Court to overrule *Saucier* and give courts discretion over whether to decide the constitutional merits in qualified immunity cases, stating that "lower courts should be free to decide the two questions in whatever order makes sense in the context of a particular case." He noted that the First Circuit had criticized the requirement in *Dirrane v Brookline Police Dept*, 315 F3d 65, 69–70 (1st Cir 2002), calling mandatory *Saucier* "an uncomfortable exercise" when the facts of the case are not fully developed.

[50] Thomas Healy's article describes lower court reactions to the *Saucier* procedure, both before and after the Court made it mandatory. See Healy, 83 NC L Rev at 850, 879–82 (cited in note 12) .

[51] See Leval, 81 NYU L Rev (cited in note 15). Judge Leval built his critique of the *Saucier* procedure around the notion that the determination of the constitutional merits is dicta when it does not affect the outcome of the case.

[52] The classic formulation of the doctrine of constitutional avoidance is contained in Justice Brandeis's concurring opinion in *Ashwander v Tennessee Valley Auth.*, 297 US 288, 347 (1936) (Brandeis, J, concurring). See Healy, 83 NC L Rev (cited in note 12). The doctrine of constitutional avoidance has many manifestations, one of which is the practice of construing a statute to avoid the possibility of unconstitutionality. See, for example, *Industrial Union Dept, AFL-CIO v American Petroleum Institute* (*The Benzene Case*), 448 US 607 (1980) (plurality opinion), Hasen, 2009 Supreme Court Review (cited in note 12).

[53] Healy, 83 NC L Rev (cited in note 12).

[54] As is well known, the Justices of the Supreme Court declined, early on, to render advice to the President, proclaiming that rendering advisory opinions would be inconsistent with separation of powers and outside the scope of the judicial power. See Henry P. Johnston, *Correspondence and Public Papers of John Jay* 486–89 (1981), reprinted in David Currie, *Federal Courts: Cases and Materials* 10 (3d ed 1982). See also Michael L. Wells,

other hand, when a court delineates the contours of a constitutional right and also finds that the right was not clearly established at the time the conduct occurred, the court is arguably giving advice about the legality of future actions without a case before it in which the decision is necessary. In sum, while rulings under the *Saucier* procedure might not technically be advisory, they may nonetheless transgress the spirit of Article III's limitations on judicial power.

Thomas Healy has argued that *Saucier* violates the rule against advisory opinions. He builds his argument on two bases, first that the decision on the constitutional merits can never affect the outcome of the case, and second, because of the posture of the immunities issue, the constitutional arguments will never be argued vigorously in these cases.[55] Although his argument is interesting and creative, it fails to establish that *Saucier* requires advisory opinions.[56]

Healy's argument rests on an erroneous premise, that arguing whether a right is clearly established involves analyzing only precedent, whereas establishing that a right exists involves additional sources such as "the text and structure of the document, the original understanding of the framers, and the ethos of American democracy."[57] In Healy's view, because the plaintiff has to show only that the right violated was clearly established, the plaintiff's case does not depend on the actual existence of the right.[58] This is puzzling. Healy ignores the simple fact that unless the defendant

---

The "Order-of-Battle" in Constitutional Litigation, 60 SMU L Rev 1539, 1541 n 22 (2007). Some state constitutions allow their courts to render advisory opinions, subject to limitations and under specified procedures. See generally Jonathan D. Persky, Note, *"Ghosts that Slay": A Contemporary Look at State Advisory Opinions*, 37 Conn L Rev 1155 (2005).

[55] See Healy, 83 NC L Rev at 902–03, 910–15 (cited in note 12).

[56] Because the Court intends rulings on the constitutional merits to be binding in future litigation, no one claims that the *Saucier* procedure violates the classic example of an advisory opinion, when another branch of government is free to ignore or revise a judicial pronouncement. See *Hayburn's Case*, 2 US (2 Dall) 408 (1792); *Muskrat v United States*, 219 US 346 (1911). *Muskrat* involved an Act of Congress which purported to affect property shares of American Indians. The statute granted the Court of Claims and the Supreme Court jurisdiction to determine the validity of the act. That judgment might, in turn, affect the outcome of other proceedings concerning the rights of claimants. The Court characterized this jurisdiction to determine the validity of the Act of Congress without an actual controversy between the parties as impermissible jurisdiction to render advisory opinions. See *Muskrat*, 219 US at 363. In *Muskrat*, the Court employed the canon of avoidance and construed the relevant statute not to grant the forbidden jurisdiction.

[57] Healy, 83 NC L Rev at 912 (cited in note 12).

[58] Id at 902–03.

has violated the Constitution, the plaintiff will lose. The plaintiff thus must establish both that the defendant violated the Constitution and that any right violated was clearly established. Healy may be correct that the plaintiff's argument in immunities cases may be more focused on precedent, but that is because the plaintiff is making a strong claim about the state of the law—that the right is clear enough to overcome qualified immunity. Healy does not show that arguments in immunities cases systematically ignore constitutional principles in favor of case analysis, and it is my sense that even in immunities cases parties argue the constitutional merits in traditional terms.[59]

Ironically, although it is often said that the defendant has less of an incentive to argue the merits of the constitutional issue because the defendant can prevail on immunity grounds without winning that argument, in Healy's terms the defendant is likely to be a better litigant than the plaintiff, because the argument that no right exists can be built on the sources Healy claims are irrelevant to the determination of whether any right that does exist is clearly established. A defendant could concede that precedent points in the direction of existence of a clearly established right, but still prevail by showing that any extension of the precedent in the direction sought by the plaintiff would be inconsistent with the text, framers' intent, or the "ethos of American democracy."

Sam Kamin responds to Healy by proposing that before deciding whether to reach the merits in an immunities case, federal courts should "peek" at the merits to determine whether the plaintiff has a colorable claim that the right exists and is clearly established.[60] Kamin argues that if the plaintiff's claim meets a minimal standard of plausibility, addressing it is not an advisory opinion because its resolution might be necessary to the outcome of the case. The problem with Kamin's solution, which on its face seems

---

[59] In both *Pearson* and *Safford*, the two cases this Term in which the Court found in favor of defendants on qualified immunity grounds, the parties fully briefed the constitutional merits in a manner that appears indistinguishable from how they would have argued the merits had the cases arisen in a non-immunities context. In both cases, the questions upon which the Court granted review clearly separated the merits issues from the immunities issues. The constitutional arguments may be abbreviated by the need to devote space in briefs to immunities arguments, but that can happen in many other situations in which the Court reviews multiple issues, constitutional and nonconstitutional, in the same case.

[60] See Sam Kamin, *An Article III Defense of Merits-First Decisionmaking*, 15 Geo Mason U L Rev 53, 92 (2008).

practical, is that the determination of whether the plaintiff has a colorable claim would be just as advisory in Healy's terms as a full-blown decision on the merits. For the reasons stated below, in my view even if the plaintiff has no colorable claim, the court's decision finding it so is not an advisory opinion.

The basic difference between an advisory opinion and a decision on the merits under the *Saucier* procedure is simple. In cases decided under *Saucier*, the plaintiff is arguing for a damages remedy. In order to receive that remedy, the plaintiff must establish that the defendant violated the Constitution and that the right violated was clearly established. If the plaintiff does not prevail on both claims, he loses. The decision of such a case is not advisory. It is the decision of an actual case or controversy within the meaning of Article III.[61] An advisory opinion involves the resolution of a legal issue outside the context of an actual Article III case or controversy. The argument that *Saucier* entails advisory opinions depends on equating all dicta with advisory opinions, which would call into question such well-established practices as the inclusion in opinions of alternative holdings, the resolution of the merits in harmless error cases, and the flexible mootness doctrine which allows courts to decide moot cases that are "capable of repetition yet evading review."[62]

The arguable violation of the more general norm against dicta is twofold. The first aspect of this norm is that courts should address only those issues necessary to the decision of the case.[63] The second is that dicta do not constitute binding precedent.[64] In

---

[61] If the plaintiff seeks an additional remedy such as an injunction or declaratory judgment, Article III standing principles may come into play.

[62] See Healy, 83 NC L Rev at 866–68, 891–95, 897–905, 915–20 (cited in note 12) (discussing mootness, alternative holdings, and harmless error).

[63] The dicta/holding distinction has been recently characterized as follows: "A holding consists of those propositions along the chosen decisional path or paths of reasoning that (1) are actually decided, (2) are based upon the facts of the case, and (3) lead to the judgment. If not a holding, a proposition stated in a case counts as dicta." Michael Abramowicz and Maxwell Stearns, *Defining Dicta*, 57 Stan L Rev 953, 961 (2005). Decisions on the constitutional merits when the defendant is found to be immune are arguably dicta under this definition because they do not "lead to the judgment."

[64] See generally Michael C. Dorf, *Dicta and Article III*, 142 U Pa L Rev 1997 (1994). The reasons against writing and following dicta are directly implicated by the *Saucier* procedure. The main reason against deciding issues that are not directly presented by the case is that the parties may not have addressed the issue at all, or with the same care as issues that are more likely to affect the outcome of the case. This can lead to erroneous and ill-considered opinions, which also is why dicta should not constitute binding precedent. In qualified immunity cases, the plaintiff must address the constitutional merits

cases in which the defendant is immune, the only reason for the *Saucier* procedure is to delineate the scope of constitutional rights to apply in future cases, that is, to specify the scope of clearly established rights. In *Saucier*, the Court instructed lower federal courts to both formulate *and follow* dicta, and government officials are presumably supposed to treat pronouncements on the scope of rights as authoritative.[65] This is a clear violation of the second aspect of the norm against dicta, that courts are bound only by the aspects of prior decisions that were necessary to the outcome.

While the *Saucier* procedure may thus appear to be inconsistent with general principles regarding dicta, it may not be inconsistent with the norms that have been established and applied by the Supreme Court.[66] It is not always clear what actually constitutes dicta and whether it is always improper to treat dicta as authoritative.[67] The Court appears willing to provide state and federal courts with guidance with what, on a strict view, would be considered dicta. This may be owing to the limited number of cases

because the plaintiff can prevail only if the right exists. The defendant, however, can prevail regardless of the constitutional merits, if it is determined that any right that may exist was not clearly established at the time of the conduct. However, as discussed below, defendants often have strong incentives to address the merits even when they expect to prevail on qualified immunity grounds.

[65] Justice Scalia has stated that these decisions are not dicta since they are intended to create clear law "and make unavailable repeated claims of qualified immunity." *Bunting v Mellen*, 541 US 1019, 1023–24 (2004) (Scalia, J, dissenting from denial of certiorari). He is obviously correct in terms of the intent of the courts issuing the opinions, but it is more accurate to state that this is an authorized violation of the traditional rules against dicta rather than a situation not involving "mere dictum." Judge Guido Calabresi has expressed disagreement with both aspects of Justice Scalia's analysis. In a pre-*Saucier* decision in which the Second Circuit reached the merits while finding the defendants immune, Judge Calabresi opined that the decision on the merits was nonbinding dicta, although it obviously indicates the direction the court is likely to take if the issue arises again. The function of a merits ruling in a qualified immunity case is, according to Judge Calabresi, "to place government officials on notice that they ignore such 'probable' rights at their peril." *Wilkinson ex rel Wilkinson v Russell*, 182 F3d 89, 112 (2d Cir 1999) (Calabresi concurring). He flatly denied that merits rulings in such cases create binding law.

[66] Dorf's examples illustrate how the Supreme Court often departs from traditional views on dicta. One of Dorf's best examples is *Myers v United States*, 272 US 52 (1926), in which the Court opined on the constitutionality of substantive statutory restrictions on presidential power to remove executive officials when the case presented only the question whether Congress might require the advice and consent of the Senate before removal. See Dorf, 142 U Pa L Rev at 2015–18 (cited in note 64). A further example of the Court's loose application of the principle against dicta, *Middlesex County Sewerage Authority v National Sea Clammers Assn*, 453 US 1 (1981), is discussed below.

[67] See Dorf, 142 U Pa L Rev at 2049 (cited in note 64). Dorf argues that "a coherent understanding of the rule of law requires that the holding/dictum distinction turn on whether a principle is essential to the rationale of a case, not just its result, and that such a distinction provides a workable framework for implementing the design of Article III."

the Court can review as compared with the thousands of state and federal judges that look to the Court for guidance on the requirements of federal law. Along these lines, the Court sometimes describes as holdings what traditionally would be viewed as dicta.[68] The Court has also justified reaching issues not raised by the parties when this makes sense in light of the need for rational development of the law.[69] And the Court often provides alternative holdings, which raises the question of which is a holding and which is dicta. All of these tendencies are related to a felt need for the Court to provide guidance. Thus, although under traditional understandings many of the Court's practices, including *Saucier*, may appear to violate norms against dicta, these practices are consistent with the Court's general practices.

In a concurring opinion in a 2007 case in which the Court followed *Saucier* and ruled against a claim on the constitutional merits, Justice Breyer offered some additional criticisms of *Saucier* and suggested that the procedure should not be mandatory.[70] He raised three familiar criticisms of *Saucier*, first that it "wastes judicial resources," second that when a court finds a right to exist but then holds that it was not clearly established at the time of the conduct it "may immunize an incorrect constitutional ruling from review," and third that "some areas of law are so fact dependent that the result will be confusion rather than clarity." He also noted that the *Saucier* procedure "frequently" violates the

---

[68] Lisa M. Durham Taylor, *Parsing Supreme Court Dicta to Adjudicate Non-Workplace Harms*, 57 Drake L Rev 75 (2008).

[69] In *Middlesex County Sewerage Authority v National Sea Clammers Assn*, 453 US 1, 19 (1981), the Court, on its own, raised and rejected section 1983 as a basis for finding a private right of action in that case even though the plaintiff had not raised it. The resolution of an issue not raised by the parties is arguably dicta since even if a party attempted to raise it at a late stage in the litigation, the Court could avoid addressing it on the ground that it was waived. Despite this curious lineage, *Sea Clammers*' resolution of this issue quickly became an important precedent for determining when section 1983 provides a basis for a private right of action against state and local violators of federal statutes. This illustrates both that the Court consciously writes what is traditionally thought of as dicta and treats it in some circumstances as authoritative.

[70] *Scott v Harris*, 550 US 372, 387 (2007) (Breyer, J, concurring). Justice Breyer also expressed reservations about the *Saucier* procedure in several other cases, including *Brosseau v Haugen*, 543 US 194, 201–02 (2004) (Breyer, J, concurring). Notably, he was joined in that brief concurrence by Justices Ginsburg and Scalia. After Scott, he made the argument against the mandatory *Saucier* procedure at greater length in *Morse v Frederick*, 551 US 393, 425–33 (2007) (Breyer, J, concurring). Much of the discussion in that opinion was about why the Court should not have reached the constitutional issue in the particular case, but it also contains general criticisms of the mandatory *Saucier* procedure. See id at 430–32.

doctrine of constitutional avoidance,[71] but he did not go so far as to attack opinions rendered under *Saucier* as advisory or as improper dicta. In fact, he did not advocate abandoning the *Saucier* procedure, rather he called for flexibility.

Although Justice Breyer focused on the mandatory aspect of the *Saucier* procedure, two of his criticisms apply whenever the Court reaches the constitutional issue before determining that the defendant is immune. In all these cases, judicial resources are wasted if waste is defined as reaching issues that do not affect the outcome of the case. Further, under current practice such rulings are immune from review—if the defendant prevails on immunity grounds, he cannot appeal the ruling on the constitutional merits.[72] And the doctrine not only "frequently" violates the doctrine of constitutional avoidance, it always does, at least whenever the court finds in favor of immunity. In short, the only criticism that Justice Breyer made that would allow a substantial portion of cases to continue to be decided under the *Saucier* procedure is the one raising the fact-dependent nature of some constitutional claims.

Related to the criticism that the *Saucier* procedure results in the unnecessary resolution of constitutional issues is the concern that the constitutional merits will not be fully litigated by the parties.[73] There are strong reasons to doubt, however, that this is a serious problem in the qualified immunity area. In most cases, both parties are likely to take seriously the constitutional merits, even in cases in which government official defendants are likely to be found immune.

Plaintiffs, of course, will always address the constitutional merits, because otherwise they cannot prevail. Defendants, on the other hand, can prevail by showing that the right asserted by the plaintiff was not clearly established at the time of the violation.

---

[71] *Scott*, 550 US at 387–88.

[72] Pam Karlan focused on this aspect in her critique of the *Saucier* procedure. See Pamela S. Karlan, *The Paradoxical Structure of Constitutional Litigation*, 75 Fordham L Rev 1913, 1922–27 (2007).

[73] The need to ensure adversary presentation of issues was the primary basis upon which modern standing doctrine was built. *Flast v Cohen*, 392 US 83, 101 (1968) ("[I]n terms of Article III limitations on federal court jurisdiction, the question of standing is related only to whether the dispute sought to be adjudicated will be presented in an adversary context and in a form historically viewed as capable of judicial resolution."). Later, the Court substituted separation of powers as the primary basis of standing doctrine. See *Allen v Wright*, 468 US 737, 752 (1984) ("More important, the law of Art. III standing is built on a single basic idea—the idea of separation of powers.").

But in most cases the defendant is likely to address the merits of the underlying rights. To show that the asserted right was not clearly established, the defendant must address the state of constitutional law in the subject area of the case. This will usually take the defendant fairly close to the constitutional merits, which means that the marginal cost of addressing the merits is not likely to be very high. Further, if the defendant is not certain that the court will find that the right was not clearly established, he must address the merits to avoid liability. The only cases in which the defendant has no incentive to address the merits are the rare instances in which the plaintiff is litigating a hopeless claim.

There are also a substantial number of cases in which constitutional merits will likely be litigated at some time anyway. These include cases with local government or private party defendants because they have no immunities.[74] The merits will also be reached in cases in which the plaintiff has a claim for injunctive relief, because qualified immunity does not govern injunctions. In these cases, in which the merits are eventually subject to litigation, perhaps there is less of a need to address the merits at the early stage of considering official immunities, but if the court postpones such consideration, the other defendants might settle, perhaps even to avoid a ruling on the merits, thus frustrating the purpose of the *Saucier* procedure.

Relatedly, in many cases, individual defendants are represented by government attorneys, and the government entity may be intimately involved in the litigation of the defense.[75] These entities

---

[74] *Owen v City of Independence*, 445 US 622 (1980); *Richardson v McKnight*, 521 US 399 (1997). Some courts have recognized a common law good faith defense for private defendants. Sheldon Nahmod, *The Emerging Section 1983 Private Party Defense*, 26 Cardozo L Rev 81 (2004) (discussing private parties' good faith defense in section 1983 cases). This defense seems inconsistent with the Supreme Court's rejection of immunities for private defendants under civil rights laws, but the Court in *Richardson* did leave open the possibility of a good faith defense. See *Richardson v McKnight*, 521 US at 413–14; Jack M. Beermann, *Why Do Plaintiffs Sue Private Parties under Section 1983?* 26 Cardozo L Rev 9, 25 n 55 (2004) (describing inconsistency between section 1983 immunities jurisprudence and recognition of good faith defense for private defendants).

[75] See George A. Bermann, *Integrating Governmental and Officer Tort Liability*, 77 Colum L Rev 1175, 1188–89 (1977) (discussing statutes requiring indemnification of officials and requiring government to provide officials with legal defense by government attorneys). For example, New York law specifically requires local governments to represent and indemnify New York City employees sued under federal civil rights laws. See McKinney's General Municipal Law § 50-k 2. See also David F. Hamilton, *The Importance and Overuse of Policy and Custom Claims: A View from One Trench*, 48 DePaul L Rev 723, 730–31 (1999) (discussing indemnification of city employees in civil rights cases). For an interesting discussion of government participation in civil rights litigation against both individual and

will often have an incentive to litigate the merits to establish that there was no constitutional violation.[76] This enables government entities to end the prospect of further damages actions in areas of unclear law.

While there may be an underlying feeling that the *Saucier* procedure is a liberal creation designed to facilitate the creation of new constitutional rights,[77] this is not necessarily true. *Saucier* is just as likely to enable a court to make a conservative ruling as a liberal ruling. In fact, the *Saucier* procedure has resulted, by and large, in a proliferation of findings that asserted constitutional

---

government-entity defendants, see Note, *When the Interests of Municipalities and Their Officials Diverge: Municipal Dual Representation and Conflicts of Interest in § 1983 Litigation*, 119 Yale L J 86 (2009).

[76] See Nancy Leong, *The Saucier Qualified Immunity Experiment: An Empirical Analysis*, 36 Pepperdine L Rev 667 (2009). Leong found that after *Siegert*, "the percentage of claims for which the court found no constitutional right existed increased dramatically, from 65.7% pre-*Siegert* to 89.1% in 2006–2007." Id at 689. Leong found that the percentage of rulings that a right existed decreased over time as the courts became more likely to reach the constitutional merits in immunities cases. See id at 689–93. Another study that looked at a narrower group of cases found a similar increase in constitutional rulings in favor of defendants, but it also found an increase in rulings favorable to plaintiffs, as compared with cases in which previously the constitutional merits would not have been reached at all. See Paul Hughes, *Not a Failed Experiment: Wilson-Saucier Sequencing and the Articulation of Constitutional Rights*, 80 U Colo L Rev 101 (2009). Hughes's data indicate that under mandatory *Saucier*, the articulation of a positive right went way up from 3 or 4 percent of the cases to 19 percent of the cases, while negative constitutional rulings went up also, to 78 percent of all cases from 35 percent in the pre-*Saucier* period. Given this high likelihood of success even under Hughes's data, it is surprising that state governments, in briefs amicus curiae, have overwhelmingly supported making *Saucier* optional. See *Scott v Harris*, 550 US 372 (2007), Brief Amicus Curiae for the States of Illinois, Alabama, Alaska, Arizona, Arkansas, California, Colorado, Georgia, Hawaii, Idaho, Indiana, Massachusetts, Michigan, Mississippi, Montana, New Hampshire, North Dakota, Oklahoma, Oregon, Pennsylvania, Rhode Island, South Carolina, Tennessee, Texas, Utah, Vermont, Virginia, and Wyoming, and The Commonwealth of Puerto Rico, as Amici Curiae in Support of Petitioner. See also Wells, 60 SMU L Rev at 1559–60 (cited in note 54).

[77] Thomas Healy argues that the *Saucier* procedure was designed to benefit civil rights plaintiffs and that is why "the more liberal members of the Court—and perhaps even Kennedy—have embraced the *Siegert/Saucier* approach." Healy, 83 NC L Rev at 881 (cited in note 12). Healy ignores the fact that two of the more liberal members of the Court, Justices Stevens and Breyer, were among the first who expressed misgivings about mandatory *Saucier* and were among its more vocal critics, while the more conservative members of the Court were largely silent about the procedure. After Healy wrote, even Justice Ginsburg expressed a willingness to reexamine mandatory *Saucier*. See *Scott*, 550 US at 386 (Ginsburg, J, concurring) ("were this case suitable for resolution on qualified immunity grounds, without reaching the constitutional question, Justice Breyer's discussion would be engaging"). Perhaps the liberal members of the Court recognized that the effect of mandatory *Saucier* was to deny the existence of rights rather than clearly establish them. This may be one of those areas in which the liberals and conservatives agreed initially on a doctrine due to differing views on how it would work out in the long run. In this case, the conservatives were largely correct.

rights do not in fact exist. As Nancy Leong has described the results of her study of the *Saucier* procedure:

> In the aggregate, these data indicate that the Supreme Court's move toward mandatory sequencing has had a lopsided influence on the articulation of new constitutional law. Courts now avoid fewer constitutional questions, and as a result, generate more constitutional law. But the new constitutional law—law that would not have been made before *Saucier*—uniformly denies the existence of plaintiffs' constitutional rights.[78]

For these reasons, it is likely that both parties will fully argue the constitutional merits in a very high proportion of cases, even when the defendant is likely to prevail on qualified immunity grounds.

Another criticism of the *Saucier* procedure is that when the defendant prevails on immunity grounds, the defendant cannot appeal an unfavorable ruling on the constitutional merits. This is not a serious problem if the case ends in the district court (with an unappealed immunity finding), because a district court ruling on the merits is insufficient to create clearly established rights.[79] But if the plaintiff appeals, the constitutional merits are subject to appellate review even if the defendant is found to be immune. It is here that the problem arises—the whole point of the *Saucier* procedure was to allow the Courts of Appeals and the Supreme Court to create clearly established law, even when the defendant is immune. Decisions on the constitutional merits against an immune defendant may be binding and subject to no further review.

For several reasons, this problem is more theoretical than real.

---

[78] See Leong, 36 Pepperdine L Rev at 692–93 (cited in note 76).

[79] See *Thomas v Roberts*, 323 F3d 950, 954 (11th Cir 2003) (only decisions by U.S. Supreme Court, state supreme court, and Court of Appeals for the Eleventh Circuit can create clearly established rights in the Eleventh Circuit); *Pabon v Wright*, 459 F3d 241, 255 (2d Cir 2006) ("When neither the Supreme Court nor this court has recognized a right, the law of our sister circuits and the holdings of district courts cannot act to render that right clearly established within the Second Circuit"); Ted Sampsell-Jones, *Reviving Saucier: Prospective Interpretations of Criminal Laws*, 14 Geo Mason U L Rev 725, 752 (2007) ("In general, when adjudicating the existence of 'clearly established law,' courts look only to published in-circuit precedent."). But see *Ohio Civil Service Employees Assn v Seiter*, 858 F2d 1171, 1177 (6th Cir 1988) (suggesting that District Court can create binding precedent for itself). Interestingly, courts look beyond their own circuits when they decide, under *Saucier*'s first step, whether the Constitution was violated. See *Vinyard v Wilson*, 311 F3d 1340, 1348 n 11 (11th Cir 2002) ("Although we cite and examine other circuits' and district courts' decisions under the first prong of *Saucier*, we point out that these decisions are immaterial to whether the law was 'clearly established' in this circuit for the second prong of *Saucier*.").

First, the likelihood that any particular case will be accepted for review by the Supreme Court is so low that as a practical matter this procedural quirk does not significantly change the situation. Second, procedural innovations could ameliorate the problem further to the extent it exists. Justice Scalia has proposed, for example, that defendants who prevail on immunity but lose on the constitutional merits be allowed to seek review in the Supreme Court.[80] Such review would likely be financed by government entities, because individual defendants have little incentive to seek review after they have prevailed on immunity grounds.[81]

In recognition of these and additional objections to the *Saucier* procedure, lower federal courts identified several situations in which they would not reach the constitutional merits when the case could be resolved in favor of the defendant on immunity. Many of these were presented as exceptions to *Saucier*'s requirement that the court reach the constitutional merits before addressing qualified immunity. These included cases in which the federal constitutional issue depended in some way on an uncertain issue of state law,[82] the constitutional issue depended on unsettled

---

[80] *Bunting v Mellen*, 541 US 1019, 1023–24 (2004) (Scalia, J, dissenting from denial of certiorari). Justice Scalia noted that in two prior cases the Court had "entertained . . . appeals on collateral issues by parties who won below." Id at 1024. Justice Scalia cites two examples of such appeals, only one of which is really analogous to allowing an immune defendant to appeal an unfavorable ruling on the constitutional merits. In the first example, *Deposit Guaranty Nat. Bank v Roper*, 445 US 326 (1980), the Court allowed plaintiffs to appeal the denial of class certification even after they had received complete relief on the merits of their claims, because class certification might allow them to shift litigation costs to other members of the class. Justice Scalia is correct that the class certification issue is collateral to the merits of the case, but the plaintiffs in *Roper* had a concrete interest in pursuing class certification, similar to the interest a victorious civil rights plaintiff has in appealing the denial of attorneys' fees. In the second example, *Electrical Fittings Corp. v Thomas & Betts Co.*, 307 US 241 (1939), the Court allowed a victorious defendant to appeal a decision on the validity of a patent. The defendant was sued for patent infringement and the Court held that although the patent was valid, the defendant had not infringed it. The defendant appealed, hoping to establish the invalidity of the patent. The Court of Appeals dismissed the appeal on the ground that the defendant had been victorious in the trial court. The Supreme Court reversed, holding that the interest in amending the decree was sufficient to allow the defendant to seek review. This is very similar to the interest defendants in immunity cases have in attacking an unfavorable decision on the constitutional merits, except that the government employers of the immune individual defendants in constitutional tort cases might be the real parties in interest.

[81] In a similar procedural innovation, government entities concerned with the potential liability of their employees could be allowed to intervene and even seek declaratory relief, which would allow them to appeal an adverse ruling on the constitutional merits. It would have to be made clear that by intervening, the government entity is not subjecting itself to damages awards as a nonimmune defendant.

[82] See *Ehrlich v Town of Glastonbury*, 348 F3d 48, 58 (2d Cir 2003); *Hatfield-Bermudez v Aldanondo-Rivera*, 496 F3d 51, 60 & n 6 (1st Cir 2007).

factual questions,[83] the constitutional issue was about to be decided in a setting in which its resolution would not violate the rule of constitutional avoidance,[84] and decision of the constitutional issue would be of little precedential value,[85] perhaps because it was about to be decided by a higher court.[86]

These exceptions to *Saucier* appear to be contrary to the Court's understanding. The Court had made it clear that the normal procedure in immunity cases was to decide the constitutional merits before determining whether any right violated was clearly established at the time of the violation.[87] The Court had gone so far as to characterize the determination of whether a right actually existed as a "necessary concomitant to the determination of whether the constitutional right asserted by a plaintiff [was] 'clearly established' at the time the defendant acted[.]"[88] Even in the period before *Saucier* explicitly made the procedure mandatory, the Court had come down strongly in favor of clarity in the law governing potential damages actions against government officials, and was apparently unconcerned with the costs of deciding "difficult" issues of constitutional law. In one pre-*Saucier* case, the Court rejected an argument by Justice Stevens that it should not reach the constitutional merits because the issue was "both difficult and unresolved."[89] The Court replied with the standard reason for reaching the merits—that because officials need guidance, the better course is to decide the constitutional merits when they are presented in a damages action, even though immunity might apply.[90]

---

[83] *Dirrane v Brookline Police Dept*, 315 F3d 65, 69 (1st Cir 2002).

[84] *Koch v Town of Brattleboro*, 287 F3d 162, 166 (2d Cir 2002).

[85] *Egolf v Witmer*, 526 F3d 104, 113 (2008) (Smith concurring).

[86] *Motley v Parks*, 432 F3d 1072, 1078 (2005).

[87] See, for example, *Siegert v Gilley*, 500 US 226 (1991); *County of Sacramento v Lewis*, 523 US 833 (1998).

[88] Siegert, 500 US at 232.

[89] See *County of Sacramento v Lewis*, 523 US at 859 (Stevens, J, concurring in the judgment). Justice Breyer expressed agreement with Justice Stevens's position in the case, but he also concurred in the majority opinion which reached the constitutional merits. See id at 858–60 (Breyer, J, concurring). Justice Stevens argued that the Court should reach the constitutional question in immunity cases only "when the answer to the constitutional question is clear." Id. The argument ignores the value of clarifying the law in order to prevent future use of the immunity defense.

[90] See *Lewis*, 523 US at 842 n 5:

> [I]f the policy of avoidance were always followed in favor of ruling on qualified immunity whenever there was no clearly settled constitutional rule of primary

II. Pearson v Callahan

A. THE MERITS: FOURTH AMENDMENT AND QUALIFIED IMMUNITY

Pearson v Callahan presented a relatively routine section 1983 case against police officers who conducted a warrantless search of Callahan's home. Callahan sold methamphetamines to an informant (not a police officer) whom Callahan had allowed into his home. After the sale was completed, the informant signaled police, who entered the home and conducted the search. Callahan was convicted of the sale of methamphetamines in a Utah state trial court after the court rejected Callahan's argument that the warrantless search violated the Fourth Amendment. The Utah Court of Appeals disagreed with the trial court, rejecting arguments based on exigent circumstances and inevitable discovery as bases for admitting the evidence obtained in the search.[91] It is unclear whether the prosecution argued in state court that Callahan, by inviting the informant into his home, had consented to the search by police. Whether or not this ground was argued, the state courts did not rule on it.

After the Utah appeals court vacated Callahan's conviction, Callahan sued the officers and entities involved for damages in federal court under section 1983. The District Court found that the search was illegal, but granted the officers summary judgment on qualified immunity grounds, concluding that the officers could reasonably have believed that the "consent-once-removed" doctrine validated the search.[92] The consent-once-removed doctrine holds that a person who invites an undercover officer or informant into his home

---

conduct, standards of official conduct would tend to remain uncertain, to the detriment both of officials and individuals. An immunity determination, with nothing more, provides no clear standard, constitutional or nonconstitutional. In practical terms, escape from uncertainty would require the issue to arise in a suit to enjoin future conduct, in an action against a municipality, or in litigating a suppression motion in a criminal proceeding; in none of these instances would qualified immunity be available to block a determination of law. . . . But these avenues would not necessarily be open, and therefore the better approach is to determine the right before determining whether it was previously established with clarity.

[91] *State v Callahan*, 93 P3d 103 (Ut Ct App 2004).

[92] The District Court rejected the argument that principles of issue preclusion applied to preclude the officers from relitigating the validity of the search since the officers were not parties to the prosecution. See *Callahan v Millard County*, 2006 WL 1409130 *5–6 (D Utah 2006). See generally Joshua M. D. Segal, Note, *Rebalancing Fairness and Efficiency: The Offensive Use of Collateral Estoppel in § 1983 Actions*, 89 BU L Rev 1305 (2009).

thereby consents to a police search of the premises.[93] This doctrine had been accepted by several Courts of Appeals but not by the Supreme Court, and the closest Supreme Court authority seems to go against it.[94] The Tenth Circuit agreed with the District Court that the "consent-once-removed" doctrine was inconsistent with Fourth Amendment principles, but disagreed with the trial court's view on immunity, holding that the law was clearly established at the time the office violated Callahan's Fourth Amendment rights:

> Here, the Supreme Court and the Tenth Circuit have clearly established that to allow police entry into a home, the only two exceptions to the warrant requirement are consent and exigent circumstances. The creation of an additional exception by another circuit would not make the right defined by our holdings any less clear. Moreover, at the time of these events only the

---

[93] Several circuits had accepted the consent-once-removed doctrine and, at the time of Callahan's arrest, apparently none had rejected it. See *Callahan v Millard County*, 2006 WL 1409130 *7–8 (D Utah 2006) (citing *United States v Pollard*, 215 F3d 643, 648 (6th Cir 2000); *United States v Bramble*, 103 F3d 1475 (9th Cir 1996); *United States v Akinsanya*, 53 F3d 852 (7th Cir 1995); *United States v Diaz*, 814 F2d 454 (7th Cir 1987); and *United States v Paul*, 808 F2d 645 (7th Cir 1986)). The Tenth Circuit, in *Callahan*, rejected application of the doctrine to an informant, holding that inviting a non-police officer informant into the home does not constitute consent to a police search. *Callahan v Millard County*, 494 F3d 891 (10th Cir 2007). This distinction seems consistent with the Supreme Court's decision in *Georgia v Randolph*, 547 US 103 (2006), which held that when two occupants of a residence are present, with one objecting to a search and one consenting, the consent of one occupant is insufficient to render a warrantless search consistent with the Fourth Amendment's warrant requirement. In *Randolph*, the Court explained its decision with language that seems inconsistent with allowing an informant's presence to constitute consent to a search by the occupant of a home: "This case invites a straightforward application of the rule that a physically present inhabitant's express refusal of consent to a police search is dispositive as to him, regardless of the consent of the fellow occupant." *Randolph*, 547 US at 122–23. A Court could approve the consent-once-removed doctrine and distinguish Randolph on the basis that the informant is an agent of the police, and thus the occupant had already consented to an entry by police when the informant was allowed into the home. In my view, this is a weak argument, but it is not beyond the realm of possibility.

[94] The District Court opined that the Supreme Court would ultimately reject the consent-once-removed doctrine, finding it to be in tension with *Georgia v Randolph*, 547 US 103 (2006). See *Callahan v Millard County*, 2006 WL 1409130 *7–8 (D Utah 2006). The District Court predicted that "if confronted with a case squarely presenting the 'consent-once-removed' doctrine, the Supreme Court might well conclude that the objections of an occupant might trump the further warrantless police entry that occurs from an undercover operative or confidential informant originally receiving consent to enter from that occupant." Id. The Court concluded, however, that with multiple Courts of Appeals adopting the doctrine, the officers were entitled to qualified immunity. The Court of Appeals rejected this reasoning, concluding that the decisions of other circuits could not trump the Tenth Circuit's clearly established rule against nonconsensual warrantless searches. *Callahan v Millard County*, 494 F3d 891, 899 (10th Cir 2007). However, given changes in membership on the Court since Randolph was decided, it is conceivable that the Court would distinguish that case and approve consent-once-removed.

Seventh Circuit had applied the "consent-once-removed" doctrine to a civilian informant. . . . The precedent of one circuit cannot rebut that the "clearly established weight of authority" is as the Tenth Circuit and the Supreme Court have addressed it.[95]

The Supreme Court granted the officers' petition for certiorari and asked the parties to brief the additional question of whether the Court should retain the mandatory *Saucier* procedure. The Court then rejected the Tenth Circuit's immunity analysis and held that the officers in this case could reasonably have believed that the consent-once-removed doctrine validated the search:

> When the entry at issue here occurred in 2002, the "consent-once-removed" doctrine had gained acceptance in the lower courts. This doctrine had been considered by three Federal Courts of Appeals and two State Supreme Courts starting in the early 1980's. . . . It had been accepted by every one of those courts. Moreover, the Seventh Circuit had approved the doctrine's application to cases involving consensual entries by private citizens acting as confidential informants.[96]

The Supreme Court's rejection of the Tenth Circuit's immunity analysis typifies the Court's solicitude for government officials sued for damages in constitutional tort cases. The Court has required a relatively high degree of certainty and specificity to find the law sufficiently clearly established to overcome the qualified immunity defense. As Justice Scalia has explained, "the operation of [the qualified immunity] standard depends substantially upon the level of generality at which the relevant 'legal rule' is to be identified. . . . It should not be surprising . . . that our cases establish that the right the official is alleged to have violated must have been 'clearly established' in a more particularized . . . sense: The contours of the right must be sufficiently clear that a reasonable official would understand that what he is doing violates that right."[97]

---

[95] *Callahan v Millard County*, 494 F3d 891, 899 (10th Cir 2007), citing *United States v Paul*, 808 F2d 645, 648 (7th Cir 1986).

[96] *Pearson*, 129 S Ct at 822–23, citing *United States v Diaz*, 814 F2d 454, 459 (7th Cir), cert denied, 484 US 857 (1987); *United States v Bramble*, 103 F3d 1475 (9th Cir 1996); *United States v Pollard*, 215 F3d 643, 648–49 (6th Cir), cert denied, 531 US 999 (2000); *State v Henry*, 133 NJ 104, 627 A2d 125 (1993); *State v Johnston*, 184 Wis 2d 794, 518 NW 2d 759 (1994); *United States v Paul*, 808 F2d 645, 648 (7th Cir 1986).

[97] *Anderson v Creighton*, 483 US 635, 639–40 (1987).

In light of this understanding of the degree of specificity necessary to find the law sufficiently clear to overcome qualified immunity, the Tenth Circuit's reliance on more general principles of Fourth Amendment law was insufficient to overcome the uncertainty over whether the consent-once-removed doctrine validated the search in *Pearson*. Because more than one circuit had accepted the consent-once-removed doctrine and the Tenth Circuit had not specifically rejected it, the Court's qualified immunities jurisprudence pointed strongly toward immunity in *Pearson*.

B. THE SAUCIER PROCEDURE IN PEARSON

Justice Alito's opinion in *Pearson* recognized that the *Saucier* procedure sometimes entails minimal costs and provides significant benefits, but he clearly was not enthusiastic about it. He noted that in some cases, deciding whether a right is clearly established involves analyzing whether the right exists at all, making a decision on the constitutional merits relatively costless. He also recognized that "the two-step procedure promotes the development of constitutional precedent and is especially valuable with respect to questions that do not frequently arise in cases in which a qualified immunity defense is unavailable."[98] Justice Alito's opinion therefore recognized two relatively narrow categories of cases in which the *Saucier* procedure might be desirable, namely, when the immunity question requires opining on the constitutional issue itself[99] and when the constitutional issue is unlikely to arise in a context in which immunity is not available.[100]

The opinion contains a much more extensive catalog of problems with the *Saucier* procedure, including (1) expenditure of scarce judicial resources unnecessarily to decide difficult constitutional questions, (2) expenditure of parties' resources to litigate

---

[98] *Pearson*, 129 S Ct at 818.

[99] For example, the Eleventh Circuit has stated that deciding the immunity issue in Eighth Amendment excessive force claims entails deciding the constitutional issue because the constitutional standard is clearly established and no reasonable official could violate it. See *Danley v Allen*, 540 F3d 1298, 1310 (11th Cir 2008), quoting *Johnson v Breeden*, 280 F3d 1308, 1321–22 (11th Cir 2002) ("'there is no room for qualified immunity' in Eighth . . . Amendment excessive force cases because they require a subjective element that is 'so extreme' that no reasonable person could believe that his actions were lawful.").

[100] There are several contexts in which the immunity defense is not available including claims for injunctive relief, claims against local (not state) governments, and claims that arise in motions to suppress evidence in criminal proceedings, such as the Fourth Amendment issue in *Pearson*.

issues that do not affect the outcome of the case,[101] (3) production of fact-bound constitutional decisions that are not useful as precedent, (4) constitutional decisions by lower courts that are likely to be displaced by a decision of a higher court, (5) difficulty deciding constitutional questions on the pleadings when the facts have not been developed, (6) doubts about the precedential value of constitutional decisions involving uncertain state law issues, (7) difficulty deciding constitutional issues when they have not been fully briefed by one of the parties,[102] (8) difficulty obtaining appellate review when a defendant loses on the constitutional merits but prevails on an immunity defense, and, most fundamentally, (9) violation of the "general rule of constitutional avoidance" which counsels strongly against deciding constitutional issues unnecessarily. Like Justice Breyer's earlier critique of the *Saucier* procedure, many of the problems identified by Justice Alito apply to every case in which the procedure is used.[103]

The most noteworthy aspect of Justice Alito's opinion is the absence of an explanation for not reaching the merits in *Pearson* before finding that the defendants were entitled to qualified immunity. The opinion leapt directly from the catalog of costs and benefits of the *Saucier* procedure to an analysis of whether the law was clearly established. Although the Court's analysis of those benefits and costs may contain hints concerning the types of cases in which the merits should or should not be reached, there is no explicit discussion of the issue. The opinion simply ignores the issue. It contains no standard for lower courts (or the Court itself) to apply in deciding whether to reach the merits. The Court did

---

[101] This affects only defendants since plaintiffs must litigate both the merits and whether any rights are clearly established. Only the defendant can prevail without addressing the constitutional merits.

[102] Again, this is because the defendant may lack the incentive to fully address constitutional issues when it is apparent that any right alleged is not clearly established. This line of argument rests on the premise that the defendant is confident that the rights are not clearly established so that the plaintiff is irrationally litigating a hopeless case. This may be true in cases involving pro se plaintiffs, most notably prisoners, who are thought to litigate frivolous claims. However, as discussed above in text, defendants may have an overriding concern over the development of the law that would lead them to argue the merits even in cases in which they are likely to prevail on qualified immunity grounds.

[103] Specifically, it can be argued that deciding the constitutional merits in a case in which the defendant's immunity defense prevails is often or always problematic for the reasons numbered 1, 2, 4, 5, 7, 8, and 9. Thus, Justice Alito's critique is less of a criticism of mandatory *Saucier* than a critique of ever deciding the merits without also rejecting the immunity defense.

not even state which if any of the costs of the *Saucier* procedure were present in *Pearson*. In short, the determination whether to reach the merits before deciding the immunity defense appears to be completely discretionary, up to the standardless and unreviewable discretion of the deciding court.[104]

In *Pearson*, we are not even told, as we once were,[105] whether deciding the constitutional merits is the preferred decision-making procedure, or is simply allowed, as the Court had stated in the early days following the elimination of the subjective prong of the qualified immunity defense. Based on *Pearson*'s extensive catalog of the costs of the *Saucier* procedure and its rather tepid statement of the benefits, there does not appear any longer to be much enthusiasm for the procedure on the Court. But we cannot be sure even of that, in the absence of a standard or list of factors that lower courts are supposed to consider in order to determine whether to reach the constitutional merits in any particular case.

There were good reasons to reach the merits in *Pearson*: The consent-once-removed doctrine had been used by the lower courts for more than twenty years with no definitive Supreme Court decision, thus leaving an important issue of Fourth Amendment law unclear. Conflict persists among lower courts over whether consent to admit an informant entails consent to admit the police. The issue is relatively uncomplicated and had been fully briefed by both parties. It is difficult to understand why the Court found it better to leave the issue unsettled when it was fully briefed and argued in *Pearson*.

---

[104] Lower courts appear to understand that they now have discretion and do not have to provide reasons for reaching or not reaching the constitutional issue. There is some language that indicates that the lower courts may believe that they still have to reach the constitutional merits and that *Pearson* only grants discretion over the order in which they reach the issues. See *Moldowan v City of Warren*, 570 F3d 698, 720 (6th Cir 2009) ("In light of *Pearson*, then, we still are required to address the same questions in conducting our qualified immunity analysis, but now we are free to consider those questions in whatever order is appropriate in light of the issues before us."). However, other courts appear to realize that if they address immunity first and find all defendants immune, they will not go on to decide the constitutional merits. See *Rivera v Reisch*, 2009 WL 3713674 (8th Cir 2009) (unpublished) ("Putting aside the question whether Rivera alleged a violation of a constitutional right, *see Pearson* . . . (courts are permitted to exercise their sound discretion in deciding which prong of qualified immunity analysis should be addressed first in light of circumstances of particular case), we conclude that any constitutional right she possessed to different treatment was not so clearly established that a reasonable person in defendants' position would have known that his actions violated her constitutional right in this case").

[105] See *Siegert v Gilley*, 500 US 226 (1991); *County of Sacramento v Lewis*, 523 US 833 (1998).

Deciding the issue in *Pearson* would have provided guidance to courts and police departments across the country. The continued lack of clarity affects both civil rights plaintiffs and police departments. A risk-averse police department, fearing exclusion of evidence, may choose not to employ the technique until the Supreme Court rules on it. Although the legality of searches is subject to litigation in a motion to suppress, and is thus likely at some point to be resolved in that context,[106] the fact that it has not definitively been determined after more than twenty years raises questions about the wisdom of the Court's failure to reach the merits.

Deciding the constitutional merits in *Pearson* would have incurred only one of the costs Justice Alito listed, violation of the general rule of constitutional avoidance. Given the decline in the Supreme Court's caseload, the resources necessary for it to decide the issue are not particularly scarce. The parties had fully briefed and argued the constitutional merits, the issue was not fact bound (any determination would apply to many if not all instances of alleged consent by inviting a (non-police officer) informant into the home), there was no higher court that could displace the Supreme Court's decision, the facts were fully litigated, there were no uncertain state law issues, and there is no appellate review after the Supreme Court. Deciding the issue would have been of significant benefit to law enforcement agencies across the country and to plaintiffs in constitutional tort cases. In short, if the costs and benefits identified by Justice Alito in *Pearson* are supposed to guide the decision of whether to reach the merits, the Court should have done so. The only reason not to was the principle of constitutional avoidance. If that reason was sufficient, then the Court should have prohibited the *Saucier* procedure altogether.

Interestingly, in last Term's only qualified immunity decision rendered after *Pearson*, the Court reached the constitutional merits before determining that the defendants were immune, without

---

[106] The legality of searches based on consent-once-removed has been litigated often in the context of motions to suppress the evidence seized as a result of an allegedly illegal search. In *Pearson*, the Tenth Circuit noted the following cases which accepted consent-once-removed, involving undercover police officers or private informants. *United States v Pollard*, 215 F3d 643 (6th Cir 2000); *United States v Diaz*, 814 F2d 454 (7th Cir 1987); *United States v Bramble*, 103 F3d 1475, 1478 (9th Cir 1996); *United States v Paul*, 808 F2d 645 (7th Cir 1986); and *United States v Yoon*, 398 F3d 802 (6th Cir 2005). See *Pearson*, 129 S Ct at 896.

explaining why it was doing so.[107] In *Safford Unified School Dist. No. 1 v Redding*,[108] school officials conducted a strip search of a student who was suspected of distributing ibuprofen, an over-the-counter pain reliever. The Court held that the search violated the student's Fourth Amendment rights but that the right was not clearly established, thus immunizing the school officials from damages liability. Justices Stevens,[109] Ginsburg,[110] and Thomas[111] each wrote separate opinions, with Stevens and Ginsburg disagreeing with the Court's immunity determination and Thomas disagreeing with the Court's determination on the constitutional merits. No Justice questioned, or even mentioned, the decision to reach the constitutional merits.

Because the Court did not address the issue, it is impossible to know why the Court chose to reach the merits in *Safford* but not in *Pearson*. If anything, *Pearson* was a better case for deciding the merits than *Safford*. In both cases, the constitutional merits were fully briefed by both parties, and both cases involved tricky issues of Fourth Amendment law. But the differences outweigh these similarities. *Pearson* involved a long-standing legal issue with a clear conflict in authority and was much less fact bound than the constitutional issue in *Safford*. In *Pearson*, the Court could have settled the consent-once-removed issue with regard to private citizen informants. By contrast, in *Safford* the nature of the issue is such that small differences in the type of the medication or the reliability of the information creating the suspicion reduce its precedential value. If it was sensible for the Court to reach the merits in *Safford*, it was even more sensible to do so in *Pearson*.

Perhaps the Court decided not to construct any governing criteria because it would be well nigh impossible to supervise lower courts in their decisions on whether to reach the constitutional merits in particular cases. Without alteration of accepted legal practices, no party can force a court to reach the merits or seek review of the decision whether to reach the constitutional merits in an immunity case. The Court is unlikely to accept a case for review to instruct the lower court to reach the merits in a case in

---

[107] See *Safford Unified School Dist. No. 1 v Redding*, 129 S Ct 2633 (2009).

[108] Id.

[109] Id at 2644 (Stevens, J, concurring in part and dissenting in part).

[110] Id at 2645 (Ginsburg, J, concurring in part and dissenting in part).

[111] Id at 2646 (Thomas, J, concurring in the judgment and dissenting in part).

which it agrees that the defendant is entitled to immunity even if a constitutional violation occurred. For whatever reason, the Court in *Pearson* not only moved the law to the pre-*Saucier* situation of not mandating that the constitutional merits be determined before making the immunity determination, but did so without providing any guidance on when the merits should be reached. In what follows, I discuss the wisdom of purely discretionary *Saucier*, concluding that the current version leaves a great deal to be desired.

C. PURELY DISCRETIONARY SAUCIER

The purely discretionary *Saucier* procedure is an anomaly in the law. It is not common for judges to have complete discretion over whether to decide unsettled constitutional issues, with no standard governing when the judges should reach the issue, and in circumstances in which the decision will not affect the outcome of the case before the court. Perhaps only the Court's certiorari procedure (and similar procedures in state supreme courts) comes close to having this range of discretion, but even there, a set of traditional criteria guide the determination of whether the Court should review a particular case, and the Court's decision is likely to affect the outcome of the case. Flexibility and discretion can be a virtue in procedural regimes, but there are reasons to be highly suspicious of purely discretionary *Saucier*. For reasons elaborated below, the purely discretionary *Saucier* procedure may represent the worst possible regime.

Writing in 2007, Michael Wells criticized Justice Breyer's suggestion that the *Saucier* procedure be made discretionary.[112] Wells was concerned that when the immunity determination is much easier, judges with discretion will clear their dockets by not deciding difficult constitutional issues, which would lead to stagnation in constitutional law. As Wells suggests, the hard constitutional cases may be the ones that need to be decided in order to provide guidance in areas of uncertainty, but with discretion, the harder the issue, the less likely the court will decide it. Wells suggests following Justice Scalia's lead and allowing defendants who prevail on immunity grounds to seek review of any adverse ruling on the constitutional merits. Wells disputes the argument

---

[112] Wells, 60 SMU L Rev at 1565 (cited in note 54) (discussing Justice Breyer's opinion in *Scott v Harris*).

that defendants will not devote sufficient resources to arguing constitutional merits issues. He points out that cases that are clear on immunities are unlikely to be litigated, and thus defendants are not likely, in a substantial portion of cases, to be so confident of winning on immunity grounds that they would not fully argue the constitutional merits.[113]

Except in his first argument, Wells is responding to criticisms of *Saucier* generally, not merely discretionary *Saucier*. But there are strong arguments against discretionary *Saucier* that are distinct from arguments against the procedure in general.

The first problem with *Pearson* is that it did not relieve defendants of the burden of addressing the merits in qualified immunity cases. With no governing standard, defendants cannot safely predict whether the court will reach the merits in any particular case and thus may find it necessary to expend resources addressing the constitutional merits even when they expect to prevail on immunity grounds. If the Court had stated a standard for determining when a court should reach the merits, then at least defendants could make an educated determination of whether it was necessary to argue the merits in a particular case. Even worse, a defendant who wants the court to clarify the law may expend substantial resources arguing the merits, only to be disappointed when the court, without even an explanation, does not reach them. Moreover, future litigants on the same or similar issues will be left in the dark as to whether they should address the merits. Even a defendant who previously prevailed on qualified immunity grounds without a ruling on the merits may not know in the next case whether to argue the merits. In short, *Pearson* may satisfy judges who would rather not decide the merits, but it ignores the substantial costs to defendants of uncertainty.

Discretionary *Saucier* may, however, empower defendants to try to influence whether a court will reach the merits. Defendants may behave strategically, pressing the constitutional merits only when they perceive a strong likelihood of prevailing, which may depend on such variables as the state of authority in the circuit or whether the plaintiff's case presents particularly sympathetic or unsympathetic facts.[114] This will make it even more likely that

---

[113] See id at 1558–68.

[114] Plaintiffs, of course, must always press the constitutional merits, because a plaintiff

when the court decides the constitutional merits, it will decide in favor of government interests.

If the defendant is willing to risk a decision on the merits without much input, a strategic choice not to press the constitutional merits might influence the court's decision whether to decide them. In a difficult case with only one side presenting a comprehensive argument on the merits, a court might be inclined to decide the immunities issue only, thereby saving resources and avoiding decisions that should be considered with fuller briefing. The plaintiff, on the other hand, always has to argue the constitutional merits, and is therefore virtually helpless to influence the court's decision in this regard.

Judges may also find that *Pearson* puts them in a difficult bind. While many may be relieved that they no longer have to reach the merits, views on the wisdom of reaching the merits will vary. Some may be committed to principles of restraint that disfavor reaching the merits, whereas others may place a higher value on ensuring that the law develops despite qualified immunity. Some judges may reach out to decide constitutional issues to further a policy agenda and decline to decide the constitutional merits when the law leads in a direction contrary to their preferences. Judges committed to the avoidance canon might then feel disadvantaged because they will be on the sidelines watching their colleagues create clearly established law with which they may disagree.

By deciding whether to reach the constitutional merits at the trial stage, district judges may also be able to influence the decision at the Court of Appeals level over whether to address the merits, because the higher court may be more likely to reach the merits if the lower court has already done so. This could happen for three related reasons. First, the Court of Appeals may feel more confident in its judgment if it has the analysis of the District Court to review. Second, the Court of Appeals may find a greater need to reach the merits to clarify whether the District Court's view was correct, especially if the Court of Appeals disagrees with the trial court's conclusion. Finally, a decision on the merits at the trial level might inspire the parties to pay more attention to the constitutional merits on appeal, thus providing fuller briefing which may make the Court of Appeals more likely to reach the merits.

---

cannot prevail without winning on both the immunity issue and the constitutional merits. Defendants, by contrast, need prevail on only one of the two issues.

Had *Pearson* created a standard for determining when to reach the merits, the disparity in behavior among judges would not be eliminated, because the standard would likely be at least somewhat discretionary, but it would be reduced. There are certainly marked disparities in how judges apply standards such as standing, mootness, ripeness, abstention, and other jurisdiction-limiting doctrines. It is well known, for example, that some Supreme Court Justices are stricter than others in reaching the merits in the face of standing concerns.[115] But each of these doctrines is governed by a set of rules and standards that cabin the exercise of judicial discretion and allow the Court to oversee their application in the lower courts.

Although reaching the merits in qualified immunity cases implicates the rule against advisory opinions, purely discretionary *Saucier* may be even worse. In jurisdictions that allow advisory opinions, established limitations on the practice avoid excessive judicial action in the absence of a live controversy.[116] One common limitation is that only specified officials or bodies are allowed to submit requests for advisory opinions.[117] Other limitations restrict advisory opinions to important matters involving public rights concerning the immediate exercise of the executive or legislative function.[118] And some courts will not render an advisory opinion on a matter already in litigation.[119] Some of the limitations on rendering advisory opinions are best characterized as rules, while others constitute more flexible standards. What most jurisdictions have in common is the rejection of a free-for-all in which courts exercise unguided discretion over the decision whether to issue an advisory opinion.[120]

---

[115] Most famously, Justice Scalia has developed a narrow standing doctrine in line with his views on separation of powers and the unitary executive theory. See Cass R. Sunstein, *What's Standing After Lujan? Of Citizen Suits, Injuries, and Article III*, 91 Mich L Rev 163, 215–20 (1992) (discussing Justice Scalia's conception of standing).

[116] See Persky, 37 Conn L Rev (cited in note 54).

[117] For example, in Rhode Island only the governor and each house of the state legislature have the power to request an advisory opinion. Id at 1156. In Florida, which represents the extreme case, only the governor can request an advisory opinion. See id at 1168, citing Florida Const, Art 4, § 1.

[118] See id at 1185.

[119] See id at 1187.

[120] In three jurisdictions, Alabama, Florida, and Michigan, advisory opinions are discretionary with the courts, and the courts operate under no external constraints concerning whether to answer any particular question. Even so, the courts in those jurisdictions appear to operate under self-imposed guidelines. In Florida and Alabama, the courts appear to answer every question posed, unless there is a jurisdictional problem, while in Michigan

Discretionary *Saucier* is worse than existing advisory opinion regimes for another reason. The *Saucier* procedure allows nearly 700 federal district judges[121] to choose, with no guidance, whether to decide constitutional questions. If discretionary *Saucier* were limited to the Supreme Court, or perhaps even to the Courts of Appeals, standards would likely evolve that would guide the decision of whether to reach the constitutional merits. Now, however, hundreds of district judges have unfettered discretion to choose whether to decide constitutional questions in qualified immunity cases, even though their decisions ordinarily will not provide the one benefit they are designed to provide, that is, clearly establishing the law for future guidance and litigation.[122]

III. Less Discretionary Saucier

It may be appropriate for courts to exercise some discretion over whether to reach the merits in qualified immunities cases, but this discretion should be exercised within established guidelines. The question then becomes what guidelines should replace mandatory *Saucier*. Assuming that the Court is not likely either to prohibit or mandate the procedure, the Court, or perhaps initially the Courts of Appeals, should construct principles to guide the determination of whether to reach the constitutional merits in cases in which the defendant prevails on qualified immunity grounds.

At a minimum, in light of the strong reasons for reaching the constitutional merits, courts should be required to give reasons for not doing so. Even if no standard is created immediately to guide the decision of whether to reach the merits, a requirement that courts give reasons could foster the development, in a common law manner, of a set of practices that could ultimately crystallize into governing standards. Moreover, the parties should be able to argue to the Court of Appeals that it should reach the constitutional merits even if the District Court did not do so. Further, even if the Court of Appeals affirms the District Court's decision, it should either reach the constitutional merits or state reasons for not doing so.

---

the courts have ceased issuing advisory opinions, at least for the last 20 years or so. See id at 1194–95. None of these jurisdictions picks and chooses among advisory opinion requests with no standard.

[121] For a table on the number of authorized District Judgeships, see http://www.uscourts.gov/history/tableh.pdf.

[122] See cases cited in note 9 (decisions of Supreme Court and Court of Appeals establish clear law for circuits).

As far as the substance of the standard that should apply, there should be a presumption in favor of deciding the merits.[123] The principles guiding the decision of whether to reach the merits should be derived from the advantages and disadvantages of the *Saucier* procedure. The reason for reaching the merits in qualified immunities cases is to prevent stagnation of constitutional law and to prevent defendants from escaping liability through repeated rulings that rights are not clearly established. There are numerous situations in which it is desirable to reach the constitutional merits.[124] The cases in which there would be a strong argument against deciding the constitutional merits are those in which resolving the federal constitutional issue would not provide clearly established law to guide future constitutional tort litigation.[125] In deciding whether to reach the merits, courts should also consider whether the conduct is likely to be repeated.

In light of these principles, courts may decide not to reach the merits in the following types of cases: fact-bound situations in which a ruling will not provide useful precedent, cases in which the constitutional decision is tied to an uncertain issue of state law with a substantial likelihood that a determination of the state law issue would render the federal constitutional ruling irrelevant, cases that present issues that will soon be decided by a higher court so that the lower court's ruling will lack precedential value, and cases in which the facts needed to identify a constitutional violation are not

---

[123] This presumption is not a presumption in favor of expanding constitutional rights. It would work in favor of both plaintiffs and defendants who would benefit from clarity in the law, and, in light of the history of rulings favorable to defendants under the *Saucier* procedure, may actually be more favorable to defendants than plaintiffs.

[124] These include cases in which guidance over permissible actions is needed, *Pearson v Ramos*, 237 F3d 881, 884 (7th Cir 2001) ("The issue on the merits is important and should be resolved without further delay."); cases in which the issue is unlikely to arise in a context other than a constitutional tort action for damages; cases in which the questions of whether the right is clearly established and whether there is a constitutional violation are bound up so that deciding both is either necessary or relatively costless; and cases that may not otherwise arise in a federal court. See also John M. M. Graebe, *Mirabile Dictum!: The Case for "Unnecessary" Constitutional Rulings in Civil Rights Damages Actions*, 74 Notre Dame L Rev 403, 407 (1999) ("[M]y primary point is that, because novel constitutional claims brought in civil rights damages actions often involve the use of new technologies and procedures by executive actors who are not constitutional experts and who therefore are not themselves well-equipped to judge the constitutionality of their conduct, the merits rulings I advocate have important notice-giving aspects that should not be overlooked.").

[125] Even though District Court decisions do not create clearly established law, they should reach the merits whenever the Court of Appeals would reach the merits, if for no other reasons than to encourage the defendant to address the merits and to frame the issues for decision by the Court of Appeals.

fully developed, so that the precedential value of ruling is highly uncertain. In all of these situations, the value of the ruling on the constitutional merits is likely to be small.

Note that these cases identified as appropriate candidates for not reaching the constitutional merits are not based on the principle of constitutional avoidance. In all cases in which the defendant ultimately prevails on qualified immunity grounds, deciding the merits is in tension with this principle. If the principle of constitutional avoidance were sufficient to rebut the presumption in favor of deciding the constitutional merits, there would be few, if any, cases in which courts would reach the merits. Thus, the principle of avoidance alone should be insufficient to rebut the presumption in favor of deciding the constitutional merits.

The principle of constitutional avoidance does provide an argument, albeit a weak one, against deciding the constitutional merits when the issue is subject to litigation in a non-immunities context. In this case, the law is likely to be clarified elsewhere without implicating the principle of avoidance. This argument is weak because it is usually speculative as to whether the law on any particular issue is likely to be clarified outside the constitutional tort context. Take the experience discussed above with the rule at issue in *Pearson*— we still do not know when the law concerning consent-once-removed with regard to informants and undercover officers will be resolved. Thus, in my view, the better practice would be to reject this as a reason for not reaching the merits. Of course, courts may not agree with this analysis, and may go beyond the parameters I have outlined. Even under *Saucier*, some courts declined to reach the merits in cases in which it was obvious that the rights were not clearly established, especially when the cases presented complex, difficult, unsettled issues of constitutional law.

But the fact that the issue in any given case may be complex and unsettled points in favor of deciding it, not avoiding it, in order to provide guidance for future conduct and create clearly established constitutional law. If, however, courts decide that the complexity of the issue is a valid reason for not reaching the merits, this consideration should be weighed against the value of providing guidance for future behavior and preventing repeated claims of immunity in the face of potential constitutional violations. Courts should be more likely to reach the merits in recurring situations and less likely in unusual situations. And in all cases in which a court decides not to reach the merits, the court should state its reasons for not doing so.

A remaining question is whether courts should have the discretion to reach the constitutional merits even in those situations in which the decision is unlikely to have precedential value. For two reasons, the answer is no. First, if a decision on the merits of a constitutional issue is unlikely to aid in the establishment of clear law and if it is unnecessary to the outcome of the case at hand, there is no reason to decide it and a host of reasons not to. Second, this would rein-stitute the extreme discretion that, in my view, is the primary failing of *Pearson*, presenting all of the problems with the current doctrine, discussed above. In sum, if the Supreme Court or the Courts of Appeals create standards for determining whether the constitutional merits should be reached, those standards should be mandatory.

IV. Conclusion

The Supreme Court's elimination of the subjective element of the qualified immunity defense in constitutional tort cases had the unanticipated effect of creating the potential for constitutional stagnation. The Supreme Court has not yet successfully dealt with this problem. The Court's most recent effort to address the problem is itself highly problematic because it stated no standard that federal courts should apply in deciding whether to reach the constitutional merits in any particular case. In *Pearson* itself, the Court did not reach the merits and did not explain why. In *Safford*, a qualified immunity case decided this Term after *Pearson*, the Court did reach the merits, again without explaining why.[126] The decision whether to reach the constitutional merits in constitutional tort cases in which all defendants are immune has apparently been left to com-plete judicial discretion, with no governing standard. This is a se-rious failing.

While it may be appropriate for courts to exercise discretion over whether to reach the constitutional merits in qualified immunity cases, this discretion should be guided by clear standards that pro-vide guidance to the parties and prevent strategic behavior designed to influence whether the merits are reached in a particular case. The primary factor that should guide the discretion is whether a

---

[126] In both *Safford* and *Pearson*, the Court held that the defendants were immune, thus rendering the decision on the merits unnecessary to the outcome in both cases.

decision on the merits is likely to have precedential value in future constitutional tort cases, that is, whether deciding the merits will create, or deny the existence of, clearly established rights. If courts find that other factors should also influence whether the merits should be reached, such as the complexity or difficulty of the constitutional issue and the simplicity of determining that no rights are yet clearly established, they should balance those factors against the need for clarity in the law. While it may be surprising that the Court has authorized, and even required, courts to decide constitutional issues when not necessary to the outcome of the case, it should be even more surprising that the Court has now made the determination of when to do so completely discretionary, with no standard to guide the exercise of that discretion.

RICHARD L. HASEN

CONSTITUTIONAL AVOIDANCE AND ANTI-AVOIDANCE BY THE ROBERTS COURT

I. Introduction

At the (apparent but not real) end of the October 2008 Supreme Court Term, the Court took diametrically opposing positions in a pair of sensitive election law cases. In *Northwest Austin Municipal Utility District No. 1 v Holder* (*NAMUDNO*),[1] the Court avoided deciding a thorny question about the constitutionality of a provision of the Voting Rights Act. The Court did so through a questionable application of the doctrine of "constitutional avoidance." That doctrine (also known as the "avoidance canon") encourages a court to adopt one of several plausible interpretations

Richard L. Hasen is William H. Hannon Distinguished Professor of Law, Loyola Law School, Los Angeles.

Author's note: Thanks to Neal Devins, Ned Foley, Beth Garrett, Hal Krent, Nate Persily, Rick Pildes, and Mark Tushnet for useful comments and suggestions. As this article went to press, the Supreme Court decided *Citizens United v FEC*, 130 S Ct 876 (2010). The Court, in a 5–4 opinion written by Justice Kennedy, overruled the *Austin* case and part of the *McConnell v FEC* case discussed in this article. The majority opinion spent considerable time explaining why it could not apply the doctrine of constitutional avoidance, and why it felt compelled to reach the constitutional questions. 130 S Ct at 888-96. Chief Justice Roberts's concurrence explicitly sought to distinguish the use of constitutional avoidance in *NAMUDNO*. See id at 918. Justice Stevens, in dissent for four Justices, set forth many means to avoid the constitutional issue and remarked, "Each of the [avoidance] arguments . . . is surely at least as strong as the statutory argument the Court accepted in last year's Voting Rights Act case [*NAMUDNO*]." Id at 938 n 16.

[1] 129 S Ct 2504 (2009).

of a statute in order to avoid deciding a tough constitutional question.[2] In *NAMUDNO*, however, the Court—without objection from a single Justice—embraced a manifestly implausible statutory interpretation to avoid the constitutional question.[3]

A week after *NAMUDNO* was issued, the Court announced it would not be deciding a campaign finance case, *Citizens United v Federal Election Commission*,[4] by the Court's summer break as scheduled. Instead, the Court set the case for reargument in September (before the start of the new Court Term), expressly asking the parties to brief the question whether the Court should overturn two of its precedents upholding the constitutionality of corporate spending limits in candidate elections.[5] The constitutional issue had been abandoned by the law's challengers in the court below and was not even mentioned in the challengers' jurisdictional statement.[6] Moreover, the constitutional question could easily be avoided through a plausible interpretation of the applicable campaign finance statute. Thus, in *Citizens United*, the Court gave itself an opportunity to apply a little-noticed (and rarely used) tool of *anti*-avoidance: the Court will eschew a plausible statutory interpretation in order to decide a difficult constitutional question.[7] It remains to be seen whether the Court will actually decide the constitutional question when it issues its decision. But the reargument order itself was a use of the anti-avoidance tool: the Court went out of its way to make a thorny constitutional question more prominent by scheduling briefing and argument on it despite a plausible statutory escape hatch.

In both cases the Court failed to follow the usual understanding of the avoidance canon: in *NAMUDNO*, the Court applied the canon to adopt an implausible reading of a statute that appeared

---

[2] See Part II.A (describing doctrine).

[3] See Part III.A.

[4] 129 S Ct 2893 (2009).

[5] Id. ("This case is restored to the calendar for reargument. The parties are directed to file supplemental briefs addressing the following question: For the proper disposition of this case, should the Court overrule either or both *Austin v Michigan Chamber of Commerce*, 494 U.S. 652 (1990), and the part of *McConnell v Federal Election Comm'n*, 540 U.S. 93 (2003), which addresses the facial validity of Section 203 of the Bipartisan Campaign Reform Act of 2002, 2 U.S.C. § 441b?").

[6] See Part III.B.

[7] The discovery of the anti-avoidance tool lends some credence to Llewellyn's complaint that every canon of construction has a contrary "counter-canon." Karl Llewellyn, *Remarks on the Theory of Appellate Decision and the Rules or Canons About How Statutes Are to Be Construed*, 3 Vand L Rev (1950).

contrary to textual analysis, congressional intent, and administrative interpretation. In *Citizens United*, the Court failed to dispose of the case initially through a plausible reading of a statute, setting itself up to address a constitutional question head-on that was not properly presented to the Court. What explains the divergent approaches in the two cases, and what does the divergence tell us about the Roberts Court? In this article, I describe the divergent approaches the Court took in these cases in detail and identify the evidence supporting three competing explanations for the Court's actions, ranging from the most charitable to least charitable reading of the Court's motives.

First, the *fruitful dialogue* explanation posits that the Court will use constitutional avoidance only when doing so would further a dialogue with Congress that has a realistic chance of actually avoiding constitutional problems through redrafting. On this reading, the Voting Rights Act got "remanded" to Congress because Congress may fix it in ways that do not violate the Constitution, but the corporate spending limits provision of federal campaign finance law perhaps does not deserve remand because the campaign finance laws are not constitutionally fixable.

Second, the *political legitimacy* explanation posits that the Court uses the constitutional avoidance doctrine when it fears that a full-blown constitutional pronouncement would harm its legitimacy. Some evidence supports this understanding. In the same Term that the Court avoided the constitutional question in *NAMUDNO*, it used the same avoidance canon to narrowly construe a different provision of the Voting Rights Act in *Bartlett v Strickland*,[8] and it applied constitutional avoidance (in deed if not in name) to narrowly construe Title VII of the 1964 Civil Rights Act in *Ricci v DeStefano*,[9] the controversial New Haven firefighters case. Each of these cases involved tough questions of race relations whose resolution could harm the Court's legitimacy. In contrast, campaign finance issues are much lower salience to the public, and are less likely to arouse the passion of interest groups and perhaps the ire of Congress.

Third, the *political calculus* explanation posits that the Court uses constitutional avoidance to soften public and Congressional resistance to the Court's movement of the law in a direction that the

[8] 129 S Ct 1231 (2009).
[9] 129 S Ct 2658 (2009).

Court prefers as a matter of policy. Under this positive political theory explanation of the Court's actions, the difference between *NAMUDNO* and *Citizens United* is simply one of timing, and the cases are not so different after all. The Court had already laid the groundwork for a deregulatory campaign finance regime through its earlier campaign finance rulings: it may now be ready to put a stake in the heart of the corporate spending limits. Under that reading, the Voting Rights Act's time of demise will come, and the public will come to expect it once the Court first raised constitutional doubts in *NAMUDNO*. The avoidance canon is just another doctrinal tool in the Court's arsenal to move constitutional law and policy in the Court's direction and at the Court's chosen speed. Like the political legitimacy argument, the political calculus argument is one about the Court's legitimacy, but it is one that views the Court as strategic in pursuing an agenda rather than as fearful.

While it is impossible to know which of these explanations is correct (and more than one may be in play for at least some of the Justices), the developments of the October 2008 Term suggest that the constitutional avoidance doctrine offers broad clues about the Roberts Court and its willingness to make major changes to American constitutional law. In Part II, I briefly review justifications for and criticisms of the constitutional avoidance doctrine and survey the few decisions of the Roberts Court thus far applying the doctrine. Part III describes in greater detail the use of avoidance and anti-avoidance in *NAMUDNO* and *Citizens United*. Part IV explores the competing explanations for the Roberts Court's selective use of constitutional avoidance doctrine. Whether intended or not, the use of constitutional avoidance and anti-avoidance allows the Court to control the speed and intensity of constitutional and policy change.

II. A Brief Survey of the Constitutional Avoidance Doctrine and Its Use by the Roberts Court

A. JUSTIFICATIONS FOR, AND CRITICISMS OF, THE AVOIDANCE CANON[10]

Roughly speaking, "canons" are rules of thumb or presumptions that courts use to interpret the meaning of statutes. Constitutional

---

[10] I do not intend here to give a full-blown examination to the avoidance canon. I rather sketch the main arguments to provide relevant context for the remainder of this article. This section appears in similar form in Richard L. Hasen, *The Democracy Canon*, 62 Stan L Rev 69 (2009).

avoidance (or the "avoidance canon") is a substantive canon of statutory interpretation. Substantive canons "are generally meant to reflect a judicially preferred policy position. [They] reflect judicially-based concerns, grounded in the courts' understanding of how to treat statutory text with reference to judicially perceived constitutional priorities, pre-enactment common law practices, or specific statutorily based policies."[11] Besides the avoidance canon, among the most important substantive canons are the rule of lenity (a "rule against applying punitive sanctions if there is ambiguity as to underlying criminal liability or criminal penalty"[12]) and a host of "federalism" canons protecting state sovereignty against congressional intrusion.[13]

Substantive canons stand in contrast to language canons, which "consist of predictive guidelines as to what the legislature likely meant based on its choice of certain words rather than others, or its grammatical configuration of those words in a given sentence, or the relationship between those words and text found in other parts of the same statute or in similar statutes."[14]

Substantive canons are controversial.[15] Eskridge and Frickey have defended them as part of an "interpretive regime" serving rule-of-law and coordination functions.[16] That is, substantive canons can act as gap-filling devices that provide clarity for the law and allow courts to signal policy preferences to legislatures, which may draft around such preferences when desired.[17] Eskridge further defends

[11] James J. Brudney and Corey Ditslear, *Canons of Construction and the Elusive Quest for Neutral Reasoning*, 58 Vand L Rev 1, 13 (2005).

[12] William N. Eskridge, Jr., Philip P. Frickey, and Elizabeth Garrett, *Cases and Materials on Legislation: Statutes and the Creation of Public Policy* app. B32 (West, 4th ed 2007).

[13] Id at app. B30–32; see also below Parts III and IV.

[14] Brudney and Ditslear, 58 Vand L Rev at 12 (cited in note 11). One of the most important language canons is the *expressio unius* canon, "the expression of one thing suggests the exclusion of others." Eskridge, Frickey, and Garrett, *Cases and Materials on Legislation* at app. B19 (cited in note 12) ("expressio unius est exclusio alterius"). Justice Scalia gives this example, "What [the *expressio unius* canon] means is this: If you see a sign that says children under twelve may enter free, you should have no need to ask whether your thirteen-year-old must pay. The inclusion of the one class is an implicit exclusion of the other." Antonin Scalia, *A Matter of Interpretation: Federal Courts and the Law* 25 (Princeton, 1997).

[15] Eskridge, Frickey, and Garrett, *Cases and Materials on Legislation* at 945 (cited in note 12) (describing "intellectual warfare" over the canons).

[16] William N. Eskridge, Jr., and Philip P. Frickey, *The Supreme Court, 1993 Term Foreword: Law as Equilibrium*, 108 Harv L Rev 26, 66 (1994).

[17] Id at 66–69.

them as "a way for 'public values' drawn from the Constitution, federal statutes, and the common law to play an important role in statutory interpretation."[18]

In contrast, Justice Scalia argues against substantive canons, which he characterizes as "the use of certain presumptions and rules of construction that load the dice for or against a particular result."[19] Calling substantive canons "a lot of trouble" to "the honest textualist,"[20] Justice Scalia describes them as indeterminate,[21] leading to "unpredictability, if not arbitrariness" of judicial decisions. He also questions "where courts get the authority to impose them,"[22] doubting whether courts can "really just decree we will interpret the laws that Congress passes to mean more or less than they fairly say."[23]

Despite these statements, Justice Scalia has approved of and repeatedly applied the avoidance canon,[24] as have all other current members of the Supreme Court. The avoidance canon provides that courts in appropriate circumstances should "avoid [statutory] interpretations that would render a statute unconstitutional *or* that would raise serious constitutional difficulties."[25] Traditional supporters of the canon's use raise three justifications.

"First, [the avoidance canon] may be a rule of thumb for ascertaining legislative intent."[26] The underlying assumption is that Congress either prefers not to press the limits of the Constitution in its statutes, or it prefers a narrowed (and constitutional) version of its statutes to a statute completely stricken by Congress. This is the rationale often raised by the Supreme Court in applying the canon.[27]

---

[18] Eskridge, Frickey, and Garrett, *Cases and Materials on Legislation* at 48 (cited in note 12).

[19] Scalia, *A Matter of Interpretation* at 27 (cited in note 14).

[20] Id at 28.

[21] Id ("it is virtually impossible to expect uniformity and objectivity when there is added, on one side or the other, a thumb of indeterminate weight").

[22] Id at 29.

[23] Id.

[24] Id at 20 n 22. See also Part II.B (discussing Justice Scalia's opinions concerning the avoidance canon).

[25] Eskridge, Frickey, and Garrett, *Cases and Materials on Legislation* at app. B29 (cited in note 12). The next section describes the mechanics of the canon in greater detail.

[26] Id at 918.

[27] See, for example, *Rust v Sullivan*, 500 US 173, 191 (1991) ("This canon is followed out of respect for Congress, which we assume legislates in the light of constitutional limitations."); *Clark v Martinez*, 543 US 371, 382 (2005) ("The canon is thus a means of giving effect to congressional intent, not of subverting it.").

Second, the canon may provide "a low salience mechanism for giving effect to what Larry Sager calls 'underenforced constitutional norms.'"[28] As Eskridge explains: "While a Court that seeks to avoid judicial activism will be reluctant to invalidate federal statutes in close cases, it might seek other ways to protect constitutional norms. One way is through canons of statutory construction."[29] Avoidance in effect remands the statute to Congress. The canon "makes it harder for Congress to enact constitutionally questionable statutes and forces legislatures to reflect and deliberate before plunging into constitutionally sensitive issues."[30]

Third, the canon may help "courts conserve their institutional capital,"[31] what I term the "political legitimacy" rationale. Phil Frickey has defended the early Warren Court avoidance decisions (many involving government action against Communists[32]) on legitimacy grounds, seeing avoidance as allowing "the [Warren] Court to slow down a political process that is moving too hastily and overriding human rights, but without incurring the full wrath of a political process that doesn't like to be thwarted."[33]

Much other recent scholarship has expressed skepticism about the avoidance canon, at least as traditionally defended. Fred Schauer rejects the assumption that the avoidance canon furthers congressional intent, in the absence of any evidence that Congress would prefer a narrow interpretation of its statute to a Court actually confronting whether the statute passes constitutional muster.[34]

---

[28] Eskridge, Frickey, and Garrett, *Cases and Materials on Legislation* at 918 (cited in note 12).

[29] William G. Eskridge, Jr., *Dynamic Statutory Interpretation* 286 (Harvard, 1994).

[30] Id.

[31] Eskridge, Frickey, and Garrett, *Cases and Materials on Legislation* at 918 (cited in note 12).

[32] See Neal Devins, *Constitutional Avoidance and the Roberts Court*, 32 U Dayton L Rev 339, 340 (2007) ("During the 1956–1957 term of the Warren Court, twelve cases were decided involving Communists. The Court ruled against the government in every case, though never on constitutional grounds.").

[33] Id, citing Philip P. Frickey, *Getting from Joe to Gene (McCarthy): The Avoidance Canon, Legal Process Theory, and Narrowing Statutory Interpretation in the Early Warren Court*, 93 Cal L Rev 397 (2005).

[34] Frederick Schauer, *Ashwander Revisited*, 1995 Supreme Court Review 71, 74; see also id at 92–93 ("there is no evidence whatsoever that members of Congress are risk-averse about the possibility that legislation they believe to be wise policy will be invalidated by the courts. On the contrary, given the essentially political nature of the job of legislating, and given that the American political system does not penalize legislators for voting for good (in the eyes of the voters) policies that are determined by the courts to be unconstitutional, one would expect members of Congress to be anything but risk-averse. One

Judge Friendly worried that the canon would be applied selectively, making it "have almost as many dangers as advantages."[35] Indeed, even Frickey rejects a view of the avoidance canon as a tool of judicial modesty: "the avoidance canon is not so much a maxim of statutory interpretation as a tool of constitutional law . . . it involves judicial lawmaking not judicial restraint; the outcomes it produces are at least sometimes inconsistent with current congressional preferences; and it will not always foster a deliberative congressional response."[36]

Still other scholars, like Frickey, seek to rehabilitate the avoidance canon through a realist view of the Court's power of judicial lawmaking. Ernest Young, like Frickey, believes that the avoidance canon is a tool of constitutional adjudication, not statutory construction. Young views the avoidance canon as a "resistance norm," an intermediate constitutional rule "that raises obstacles to particular governmental actions without barring those actions entirely."[37] Finally, Trevor Morrison adopts what might be called a "fence around the Torah"[38] defense of the canon: "the avoidance canon . . . guards the [constitutional] boundaries by making it more difficult for Congress even to approach them."[39]

In sum, though modern legislation scholars see the avoidance

would expect them to err on the side of assuming constitutionality under conditions of uncertainty about what the courts are likely to do."); Ernest A. Young, *Constitutional Avoidance, Resistance Norms, and the Preservation of Judicial Review*, 78 Tex L Rev 1549, 1581 (2000) (arguing that the canon might actually *undermine* congressional intent: "a holding that constitutional doubts compel a narrow statutory construction has a 'go ahead, make my day' quality to it, and Congress might reasonably conclude that enactment of the broader reading would only result in invalidation on the merits").

[35] Henry Friendly, *Benchmarks* 211 (Chicago, 1967). Judge Friendly remarked that challenging the avoidance canon "is rather like challenging the Holy Writ," id, but he worried that wide use of the rule would become one of "evisceration and tergiversation." Id at 212; see also Lisa Kloppenberg, *Avoiding Constitutional Questions*, 35 BC L Rev 1003 (1994).

[36] Frickey, 93 Cal L Rev at 402 (cited in note 33).

[37] Young, 78 Tex L Rev at 1585 (cited in note 34).

[38] In Jewish religious tradition, the oral law provided additional rules to supplement the written rules in the Torah and to make sure that those written rules were not violated. "The rabbis used the metaphor of a fence around the Torah as a means of protecting the essence of Torah in the midst of the proliferation of new demands." Leonard Kravitz and Kerry M. Olitzky, eds and trans, *Perke Avot: A Modern Commentary on Jewish Ethics* 2 (URJ Press, 1993).

[39] Trevor W. Morrison, *Constitutional Avoidance in the Executive Branch*, 106 Colum L Rev 1189, 1217 (2006); see also *United States v Marshall*, 908 F2d 1312, 1318 (7th Cir 1990) (Easterbrook) ("The canon about avoiding constitutional decisions, in particular, must be used with care, for it is closer cousin to invalidation than to interpretation. It is a way to enforce the constitutional penumbra, and therefore an aspect of constitutional law proper.").

canon as sometimes playing an important role in Supreme Court adjudication and its relation with Congress, there seems to be consensus that the canon's use signals a Court that is actively engaged in shaping law and policy, not acting modestly.

B. THE SCOPE OF THE MODERN AVOIDANCE DOCTRINE

I turn now away from the rationale for the avoidance canon and to its mechanics. There are two main mechanical questions about when the canon should be invoked: first, how much constitutional doubt must there be before the canon comes into play? Second, must the statute in question be truly ambiguous before the canon comes into play?

On the first point, Adrian Vermeule has traced the transformation of the doctrine from "classical avoidance" to "modern avoidance."[40] Under classical avoidance, a court would have to conclude that one interpretation of a statute would render the statute unconstitutional before the canon may be applied. Under modern avoidance doctrine, in contrast, the canon may be applied once the court concludes that one interpretation of the statute would raise *serious doubts* as to the constitutionality of the statute. As Morrison explains, "modern avoidance departs from classical avoidance by allowing serious but potentially unavailing constitutional objections to dictate statutory meanings."[41]

On the second question, the stated rule of the modern Court is that the avoidance canon comes into play only when the statutory interpretation that avoids constitutional doubt is in fact *reasonable or plausible*:

> The doctrine of constitutional doubt does not require that the problem-avoiding construction be the preferable one—the one the Court would adopt in any event. Such a standard would deprive the doctrine of all function. "Adopt the interpretation that avoids the constitutional doubt if it is the right one" produces precisely the same result as "adopt the right interpretation." Rather, the doctrine of constitutional doubt comes into play when the statute is "susceptible of" the problem-avoiding

---

[40] Adrian Vermeule, *Saving Constructions*, 85 Georgetown L J 1945, 1949 (1997).

[41] Morrison, 106 Colum L Rev at 1203 (cited in note 39); see also John Nagle, *Delaware & Hudson Revisited*, 72 Notre Dame L Rev 1495 (1997) (tracing history of "doubts" canon in detail).

interpretation—when *that interpretation is reasonable, though not necessarily the best.*[42]

As Justice Scalia put it for a majority of the Court in 2005, the canon "is a tool for choosing *between competing plausible interpretations* of a statutory text, resting on the reasonable presumption that Congress did not intend the alternative which raises serious constitutional doubts."[43]

Despite the formal requirement of some kind of textual ambiguity to allow for the Court to adopt one of two reasonable interpretations, Frickey explains that "for the [Warren] Court. . . . statutory textual ambiguity is not a necessary condition for invoking the canon. Instead, what is needed is a judicial conclusion that Congress had not actively considered—and ideally, deliberated on—a matter of 'grave importance,' especially when that involves underenforced constitutional norms."[44]

The most recent extended Supreme Court debate over the scope of the avoidance canon occurred in 2005, during the last few months of the Rehnquist Court, in the case of *Clark v Martinez.*[45] An alien who has been found to be inadmissible into the United States ordinarily must be removed from the country within ninety days.[46] *Clark* concerned an immigration statute providing the Secretary of Homeland Security may detain an alien who has been found to be removable beyond this statutory ninety-day removal period.[47] Detained aliens who had never legally been admitted into the United States challenged "the Secretary [of Homeland Security]'s authority to continue to [indefinitely] detain an inadmissible alien subject to a removal order *after* the 90-day removal

---

[42] *Almendarez-Torres v United States*, 523 US 224, 270 (1998) (Scalia, J, dissenting) (emphasis added and citations omitted). Though Justice Scalia wrote this as part of his dissenting opinion, on this point, the majority agreed: "[For the canon to apply, t]he statute must be genuinely susceptible to two constructions after, and not before, its complexities are unraveled. Only then is the statutory construction that avoids the constitutional question a 'fair' one." Id at 238. The majority and dissent disagreed in the *Almendarez-Torres* case over whether the statutory language at issue pointed "significantly in one direction," id, and over whether there was "grave[] doubt" about the constitutionality of the statute under one of the interpretations. Id at 239.

[43] *Clark v Martinez*, 543 US 371, 382 (2005) (emphasis added).

[44] *Frickey*, 93 Cal L Rev at 460–61 (cited in note 33).

[45] 543 US 371 (2005).

[46] 8 USC § 1231(a)(1)(A).

[47] 8 USC § 1231(a)(6).

period has elapsed."[48] The *Clark* Court followed an earlier Supreme Court opinion construing the same statute to hold that aliens who had initially gained lawful entry into the United States presumptively could not be detained under the statute for more than six months after the ninety-day removal period.[49] In *Clark*, the Court held that the same rule applied to aliens who had never gained lawful entry into the country—even though the Secretary would not necessarily violate the Constitution by holding such aliens for a period exceeding six months.

In reaching the conclusion that the six-month presumptive period applied to aliens who had never gained lawful entry into the country, the *Clark* Court applied the avoidance canon. The Court noted that the contrary interpretation of the statute urged by the government—allowing detention for more than six months—would raise serious constitutional concerns for aliens who had lawfully been admitted into the country. "If [one of two plausible statutory constructions] would raise a multitude of constitutional problems, the other should prevail—whether or not those constitutional problems pertain to the particular litigant before the Court."[50]

The dissenters viewed this aspect of the Court's ruling as an "end run around black-letter constitutional doctrine governing facial and as-applied challenges."[51] To the dissenters "an ambiguous statute should be read to avoid a constitutional doubt only if the statute is constitutionally doubtful as applied to the litigant before the court."[52] The dissenters argued that because the aliens before the Court in *Clark* could be held longer than six months without raising constitutional concerns, these aliens should not be able to rely upon the avoidance canon.

The majority rejected the dissent's argument, holding that application of the avoidance canon furthered congressional intent: "when a litigant invokes the canon of avoidance, he is not attempting to vindicate the constitutional rights of others, as the dissent believes; he seeks to vindicate his own *statutory* rights."[53]

---

[48] *Clark*, 543 US at 372.

[49] *Zadvydas v Davis*, 533 US 678 (2001).

[50] *Clark*, 543 US at 380–81.

[51] Id at 394 (Thomas, J, dissenting).

[52] Id.

[53] Id at 382.

To the majority, the Court should presume Congress did not write a statute that would be unconstitutional in some of its applications. The majority also pointed to an administrative concern with the dissent's contrary rule, stating that the dissent's rule would "render every statute a chameleon, its meaning subject to change depending on the presence or absence of constitutional concerns in each individual case."[54]

The Court's interesting disagreement in *Clark* over the relationship between the avoidance canon and as-applied challenges should not obscure the Court's unanimity on basic points related to the avoidance canon. All the Justices on the *Clark* Court accepted the avoidance canon as a legitimate tool of statutory interpretation and all believed it applied in cases where there were two "plausible" interpretations of a statute, one of which raises serious constitutional doubts. (They differed only in whether those doubts had to involve the litigants before the Court.) Given this agreement on the fundamental contours of the avoidance canon, the Roberts Court has repeatedly cited to *Clark* for the blackletter of the avoidance canon.

C. CONSTITUTIONAL AVOIDANCE AND THE ROBERTS COURT

The Roberts Court has not yet had the occasion to engage in any great debates about the meaning of the avoidance canon, but the canon was mentioned in thirteen cases from January 2006 to June 2009.[55] The most important discussions of the canon thus

---

[54] Id.

[55] *Gonzales v Oregon*, 546 US 243, 291–92 (2006) (Scalia, J, dissenting) (arguing that the canon did not apply to Attorney General directive on assisted suicide); *Kansas v Marsh*, 548 US 163, 169 (2006) (describing Kansas Supreme Court's use of the doctrine); *Hamdan v Rumsfeld*, 548 US 557, 584 n 15 (2006) (declining to decide "the manner in which the canon of constitutional avoidance should affect subsequent interpretation of the" Detainee Treatment Act); *Rita v United States*, 551 US 338 (2007) (Scalia, J, dissenting) (criticizing majority for failure to follow *Clark v Martinez* rule); *Office of Senator Mark Dayton v Hanson*, 550 US 511, 514 (2007) (Court unanimously following *Clark* for "our established practice of interpreting statutes to avoid constitutional difficulties"); *Gonzales v Carhart*, 550 US 124, 153–54 (2007) (relying on avoidance canon to interpret federal abortion statute so as not to apply to certain abortion procedures); *Gonzalez v United States*, 128 S Ct 1765, 1771 (2008) (declining to apply avoidance canon because there was no serious constitutional doubt raised by one of the interpretations); *Boumediene v Bush*, 128 S Ct 2229, 2271–72 (2008) (declining to apply canon when the text and purpose require a contrary interpretation); *Pearson v Callahan*, 129 S Ct 808 821 (2008) (unanimous Court endorsing Justice Brandeis's statement in *Ashwander v TVA*, 297 US 288, 347 (1936), that "The Court will not pass upon a constitutional question although properly presented by the record, if there is also present some other ground upon which the case may be disposed

far in the Roberts Court have come in controversial cases involving abortion, the detainment of unlawful enemy combatants at Guantánamo Bay, Cuba, and race.

In *Gonzales v Carhart*, the Court relied on the avoidance canon to interpret a federal abortion statute not to apply to certain abortion procedures. Justice Kennedy, for the majority, first quoted an earlier Court case for the proposition that it is an "elementary rule . . . . that every reasonable construction must be resorted to, in order to save a statute from unconstitutionality."[56] He added that the avoidance canon "in the past has fallen by the wayside when the Court confronted a statute regulating abortion. The Court at times employed an antagonistic canon of construction under which in cases involving abortion, a permissible reading of a statute [was] to be avoided at all costs."[57] Here, as described more in Part IV below, Justice Kennedy recognized the occasional Court use of the anti-avoidance tool in the abortion context.

In *Boumediene v Bush*, the Court held that it could not construe the Detainee Treatment Act (DTA) of 2005, applicable to enemy combatants being held by the United States in Guantánamo Bay, Cuba, to give detainees at the Court of Appeals the "right to present relevant exculpatory evidence that was not presented" at an early military tribunal.[58] The Court held that in applying the avoidance canon to the DTA, "[w]e cannot ignore the text and purpose of the statute in order to save it."[59] The majority concluded that "[t]he language of the statute, read in light of Congress's reasons for enacting it" cannot bear the interpretation that allowed the presentation of such evidence.[60] Accordingly the Court reached the constitutional question and held the procedure in the

---

of"); *Bartlett v Strickland*, 129 S Ct 1231, 1247–48 (2008) (relying on avoidance canon in declining to read section 2 of the Voting Rights Act to allow influence district claims); *Hawaii v Office of Hawaiian Affairs*, 129 S Ct 1436, 1445 (2008) (applying *Clark*'s avoidance statement to congressional resolution concerning apology to Hawaii); *Federal Communications Comm'n v Fox Television Stations, Inc.*, 129 S Ct 1800, 1811–12 (2009) (holding that avoidance canon does not apply to "limit the scope of authorized executive action"); *Northwest Austin Municipal Utility District Number One v Holder*, 129 S Ct 2504 (2009) (applying avoidance canon to section 5 of the Voting Rights Act).

[56] 550 US 124, 153 (2007).

[57] Id at 153–54 (internal quotations omitted).

[58] 128 S Ct 2229, 2271–72 (2008).

[59] Id at 2271.

[60] Id at 2274.

DTA that barred detainees from presenting exculpatory evidence to the Court of Appeals was unconstitutional.

In *Bartlett v Strickland*,[61] the Court applied the avoidance canon to conclude that section 2 of the Voting Rights Act did not allow plaintiffs to raise "crossover district claims," which would have had the effect of creating more electoral districts in which members of minority groups could elect candidates of their choice.[62] "If § 2 were interpreted to require crossover districts throughout the nation, it would unnecessarily infuse race into virtually every redistricting, raising serious constitutional questions."[63] Such an interpretation "would reverse the canon of avoidance. It invites the divisive constitutional questions that are both unnecessary and contrary to the purposes of our precedents under the Voting Rights Act."[64] Similarly, in *NAMUDNO*, described fully in Part III below, the Court relied heavily upon the avoidance canon to reach its surprising interpretation of section 5 of the Voting Rights Act.

Finally, though the word "avoidance" does not appear in the opinions, the avoidance canon was in play in the Supreme Court's most prominent race case of the October 2008 Term, *Ricci v DeStefano*.[65] In the so-called "New Haven firefighters case," the Court held that Title VII of the Civil Rights Act of 1964 did not allow the city to throw out the result of a test used to identify firefighters for promotion, after the test showed white candidates outperformed minority candidates. Plaintiffs claimed that throwing out the test results violated both Title VII and the Equal Protection Clause of the Fourteenth Amendment of the Constitution. The Supreme Court declined to reach the constitutional question, citing a 1984 voting rights case, *Escambia County*, stating

---

[61] 129 S Ct 1231 (2009) (plurality).

[62] The Court set forth the statutory question this way: "In a district that is not a majority-minority district, if a racial minority could elect its candidate of choice with support from crossover majority voters, can § 2 require the district to be drawn to accommodate this potential?" Id at 1238.

[63] Id at 1247 (internal quotations omitted).

[64] Id at 1248. Though not phrased in explicit avoidance terms, the issue arose in Justice Kennedy's opinion involving a controversial Texas re-redistricting plan. *LULAC v Perry*, 548 US 399, 446 (2006) (Kennedy) (plurality) ("Accordingly, the ability to aid in Frost's election does not make the old District 24 an African-American opportunity district for purposes of § 2. If § 2 were interpreted to protect this kind of influence, it would unnecessarily infuse race into virtually every redistricting, raising serious constitutional questions.").

[65] 129 S Ct 2658 (2009).

that "normally the Court will not decide a constitutional question if there is some other ground upon which to dispose of the case."[66] The Court then applied a new test for judging Title VII claims,[67] thereby avoiding the constitutional question. The *Ricci* opinion noted two more times that "we need not decide" the constitutional question in this case.[68]

In his *Ricci* concurrence, Justice Scalia noted the tension between Title VII's requirements for race-conscious employment decisions and his view of the Equal Protection Clause. "The Court's resolution of these cases makes it unnecessary to resolve these matters today. But the war between disparate impact and equal protection will be waged sooner or later, and it behooves us to begin thinking about how—and on what terms—to make peace between them."[69]

III. NAMUDNO AND CITIZENS UNITED: AVOIDANCE AND ANTI-AVOIDANCE

Against the backdrop set forth in Part II, I now consider in detail how unusual the Court's actions in *NAMUDNO* and *Citizens United* actually were, compared to the Supreme Court's usual constitutional avoidance cases.

A. NAMUDNO

In 1965, Congress enacted the Voting Rights Act (VRA).[70] Section 5 of the VRA requires that "covered jurisdictions" obtain preclearance from the federal government before making any changes in voting practices or procedures,[71] for changes as major as a ten-year redistricting plan or as minor as moving a polling place across the street. For each one, the covered jurisdiction must demonstrate that the change was made without a discriminatory

---

[66] Id, citing *Escambia County v McMillan*, 466 US 48, 52 (1984) (per curiam). *Escambia County* was an interesting case because "the parties did not brief or argue the statutory question on appeal. The Supreme Court vacated the decision and remanded the matter to the appellate court, instructing the court to consider first whether it could affirm the district court based solely on the Voting Rights Act." Kloppenberg, 35 BC L Rev at 1029 (cited in note 35).

[67] Linda Greenhouse, *Who Called Off the Charge?*, "The Breakfast Table," *Slate* (June 29, 2009), online at http://www.slate.com/id/2220927/entry/2221819/.

[68] *Ricci*, 129 S Ct at 2664, 2676.

[69] Id at 2683 (Scalia, J, concurring).

[70] 42 USC §§ 1973–1973p (2004).

[71] Id at § 1973c.

purpose and that it will not make the affected minority groups worse off. Section 5's aim was to prevent state and local governments with a history of discrimination against racial minorities from changing their voting rules without first proving that such changes would have neither a discriminatory purpose nor effect.

Some southern states immediately challenged parts of the VRA as exceeding congressional power. In the first of these cases, *South Carolina v Katzenbach*, South Carolina challenged core provisions of the Act, including the preclearance provision.[72] The Court rejected South Carolina's argument that the challenged provisions "exceed[ed] the powers of Congress and encroach[ed] on an area reserved to the States by the Constitution."[73] It held that Congress had acted appropriately under its powers granted in Section 2 of the Fifteenth Amendment.[74] In so holding, the Court gave considerable deference to congressional determinations about the means necessary to "enforce" the Fifteenth Amendment.

Over the years, Congress continued to renew section 5, adding in additional coverage areas. In 1982, Congress renewed the provision for a twenty-five-year period, expiring in 2007. The City of Rome, Georgia, challenged the renewed preclearance provision and the Court again rejected the challenge.[75] Then-Justice Rehnquist dissented, raising federalism concerns.[76]

In the years after *City of Rome*, the Supreme Court underwent a federalism revolution, narrowing Congressional power over the states. Beginning with *City of Boerne v Flores*,[77] the Court has limited Congress to passing "remedial" statutes. It has rejected congressional attempts to expand the scope of constitutional rights through legislation beyond that which is "congruen[t] and proportional[]"[78] to remedy intentional unconstitutional discrimination by the states. In *Board of Trustees v Garrett*,[79] the Court indicated that it will search for an adequate *evidentiary record* to support a congressional determination that states are engaging in

---

[72] *South Carolina v Katzenbach*, 383 US 301, 307 (1966).

[73] Id at 323.

[74] Id at 337.

[75] *City of Rome v United States*, 446 US 156, 187 (1980).

[76] Id at 210–15 (Rehnquist, J, dissenting).

[77] 521 US 507, 519 (1997).

[78] Id at 520.

[79] 531 US 356, 373 n 8 (2001).

sufficient intentionally unconstitutional conduct so as to justify congressional regulation.

Because of these new standards, many election law scholars worried that unless Congress made changes to the existing section 5 regime, a renewed section 5 could be struck down as unconstitutional.[80] Though Congress did make some changes to section 5 when it renewed the Act in 2006, such as rejecting an earlier Supreme Court interpretation of the applicable section 5 standard in *Georgia v Ashcroft*,[81] it did not make changes to two key provisions of the Act which would have updated the Act to account for changed political realties. First, Congress did not change the coverage formula that determines which jurisdictions must engage in preclearance. That formula used data from the 1964, 1968, or 1972 elections.[82] Second, Congress did not consider ways to make it easier for jurisdictions that have been covered to "bail out" from coverage under the Act, such as by putting the onus on the federal government to prepare a list of jurisdictions presumptively entitled to bail out because of their good record on voting and race.[83] These were politically sensitive subjects, and it appears that Congress did not have any political incentive to take a close look at these difficult race and politics questions[84] before reauthorizing section 5 for another twenty-five years by a wide margin.[85]

---

[80] Richard L. Hasen, *Congressional Power to Renew the Preclearance Provisions of the Voting Rights Act after Tennessee v. Lane*, 66 Ohio St L J 177 (2005); Samuel Issacharoff, *Is Section 5 of the Voting Rights Act a Victim of Its Own Success?* 104 Colum L Rev 1710 (2005); The Continuing Need for Section 5 Pre-Clearance: Hearing before the Senate Committee on the Judiciary, 109th Cong, 2d Sess 10 (2006) (statement of Richard H. Pildes). See generally David Epstein et al, eds, *The Future of the Voting Rights Act* (Russell Sage, 2008).

[81] *Georgia v Ashcroft*, 549 US 461 (2003). See 42 USCA § 1973c(b) (West Supp 2007). For an exhaustive look at how the renewed section 5 deals with the *Georgia v Ashcroft* precedent, see Nathaniel Persily, *The Promise and Pitfalls of the New Voting Rights Act*, 117 Yale L J 174 (2007).

[82] 42 USCA § 1973c(a).

[83] See Richard Hasen, *Pass the VRA Bailout Amendment*, Roll Call (July 11, 2006), online at http://electionlawblog.org/archives/bailout.pdf.

[84] Persily, 117 Yale L J 174 (cited in note 81); Richard H. Pildes, *Political Avoidance, Constitutional Theory, and the VRA*, 117 Yale L J Pocket Pt 148 (2007), online at http://thepocketpart.org/2007/12/10/pildes.html.

[85] *Northwest Austin Municipal Utility District Number One v Mukasey*, 573 F Supp 2d 221, 229 (DDC 2008) (three-judge court) ("in July 2006 Congress extended section 5 for an additional twenty-five years. Entitled the Fannie Lou Hamer, Rosa Parks, and Coretta Scott King Voting Rights Act Reauthorization and Amendments Act of 2006, the statute, which passed overwhelmingly in both chambers (unanimously in the Senate and by 390–33 in the House), overruled several Supreme Court decisions interpreting section 5's substantive test, but otherwise left the law virtually unchanged. 2006 Amendments, 120 Stat. at 577. President George W. Bush signed the bill into law on July 27, 2006.").

Soon after Congress passed the renewed section 5, the Project on Fair Representation, a group ideologically opposed to section 5 as impermissible race-based legislation, backed litigation to challenge section 5 as exceeding congressional power under the Fifteenth Amendment.[86] An obscure Austin utility district, the Northwest Austin Municipal Utility District Number One, brought the challenge, which was initially heard by a three-judge federal district court in Washington, D.C. Though its main argument was against the continued constitutionality of the preclearance provision of section 5, the utility district also argued it should be entitled to bail out from coverage under the Act as a "political subdivision" covered by section 5.

The three-judge court in *NAMUDNO v Mukasey*, in an exhaustive and unanimous opinion, rejected both arguments.[87] The court spent five pages addressing the bailout question, and then forty-eight pages addressing the thorny constitutional question (with the remainder of the opinion consisting of maps and appendices). For purposes of this article, I examine only the bailout analysis.

In addressing the argument of the utility district that it should be allowed to bail out, the court began by noting that until 1982, section 4(a) of the Act "limited bailout to two types of entities (1) covered states, and (2) political subdivisions covered 'as a separate unit.'"[88] Section 14(c)(2) of the VRA defines "political subdivision" to "mean any county or parish, except that where registration for voting is not conducted under the supervision of a county or parish, the term shall include any other subdivision of the state which conducts registration for voting." "As a result, [under the pre-1982 version of section 4(a) of the VRA] only political subdivisions separately designated for coverage could seek bailout. So, for example, Texas could seek bailout as a covered state. . . . But po-

---

[86] See Chuck Lindell, *Star Lawyer Makes Supreme Court Splash*, Austin-American Statesman (July 5, 2009), online at http://www.statesman.com/news/content/news/stories/local/2009/07/05/0705coleman.html ("When he has a choice of cases, [utility district lawyer Greg] Coleman said he looks for pro bono work that fits his philosophy. He took the Voting Rights Act case largely for free, with only a 'five-figure' contribution for expenses from the Project on Fair Representation, an advocacy group that challenges race-based government policies, Coleman said.").

[87] *Northwest Austin Municipal Utility District Number One v Mukasey*, 573 F Supp 2d 221 (DDC 2008) (three-judge court).

[88] Id at 230. Some covered jurisdictions include only parts of states, explaining the second type of entity.

litical subdivisions within covered states—such as Travis County, in which the District is located—could not apply for bailout despite meeting the section 14(c)(2) definition because they had never been separately designated for coverage."[89] The court confirmed this understanding of the section 4(a) bailout provision by citing to the Supreme Court's *City of Rome* case, in which the Court held that the city of Rome, Georgia, "was ineligible to seek bailout because the coverage formula of § 4(b) ha[d] never been applied to it."[90]

"In 1982, however, Congress expanded bailout eligibility to include section 14(c)(2) political subdivisions within covered states"[91] by adding language to section 4(a) allowing bailout by "any political subdivision of such State . . . , though such determinations were not made with respect to such subdivision as a separate unit."[92] As the court explained, "[b]y including political subdivisions within covered states even though they had not been designated for coverage 'as a separate unit,' Congress made jurisdictions like Travis County eligible to seek bailout."[93]

The utility district in *NAMUDNO* conceded it did not qualify, like Travis County, as a "political subdivision" under section 14(c)(2) because it was not a county and it never conducted registration for voting. The utility district nonetheless argued that it constituted a "political subdivision" in the ordinary meaning of that term and therefore could bail out.[94] In support of the argument, the utility district cited to a 1978 Supreme Court case, *United States v Board of Commissioners of Sheffield, Alabama*,[95] a case in which the Supreme Court held that "once a state has been designated for coverage, section 5's preclearance requirement applies to all political units within it regardless of whether the units qualify as section 14(c)(2) political subdivisions."[96] The utility district focused on dictum in *Sheffield* stating that "section 14(c)(2)'s

[89] Id at 231.
[90] Id (citing *City of Rome*, 446 US at 167).
[91] Id.
[92] 1982 Amendments § 2(b)(2), 96 Stat at 131 (codified at 42 USC § 1973b(a)(1)).
[93] *Northwest Austin Municipal Utility District Number One v Mukasey*, 573 F Supp 2d at 231.
[94] Id.
[95] 435 US 110 (1978).
[96] *Northwest Austin*, 573 F Supp 2d at 232.

definition 'was intended to operate only for purposes of determining which political units in nondesignated states may be separately designated for coverage under § 4(b).'"[97] The utility district
argued that when Congress amended the bailout provisions of the
VRA, it did so "in light of *Sheffield*'s dictum that the only purpose
of section 14(c)(2)'s definition is to identify which political subunits qualify for coverage,"[98] and therefore section 14(c)(2) was
no bar to the court holding it should be considered a "political
subdivision" entitled to seek bailout under section 4(a).

The district court rejected this argument on numerous grounds.
First, the court offered a textual analysis, stating that the utility
district's definition would render the phrase in the amended statute
"though [the coverage] determinations were not made with respect
to such subdivision as a separate unit" as impermissible surplus-
age.[99] In other words, if Congress intended to allow *all* political
subdivisions (and not just section 14(c)(2) subdivisions) to be eligible for bailout, it did not need to include that extra clause.
"This language demonstrates that Congress intended 'political
subdivision' to refer only to section 14(c)(2) subdivisions—that is,
counties, parishes, and voter-registering subunits—since only
'such subdivisions' can be separately designated for coverage."[100]

The court also pointed to unambiguous statements in House
and Senate Reports accompanying the 1982 amendments which
"clarify that Congress intended the expanded bailout mechanism
to encompass only section 14(c)(2) political subdivisions."[101] For
example, the Senate Report states that:

> Towns and cities within counties may not bailout separately.
> This is a logistical limit. As a practical matter, if every political
> subdivision were eligible to seek separate bailout, we could not
> expect that the Justice Department or private groups could re-
> motely hope to monitor and to defend the bailout suits. It would
> be one thing for the Department and outside civil rights liti-
> gators to appear in hundreds of bailout suits. It would be quite
> another for them to have to face many thousands of such actions
> because each of the smallest political subunits could separately

---

[97] Id at 232.

[98] Id.

[99] Id.

[100] Id.

[101] Id at 232–33.

bail out. Few questioned the reasonableness and fairness of this cutoff in the House.[102]

The district court concluded its discussion by noting that the Attorney General issued a regulation confirming that only section 14(c)(2) jurisdictions may seek bailout, and that the Supreme Court has traditionally afforded substantial deference to the Attorney General's interpretation of section 5.[103] The court also noted that Congress was silent in 2006 when it reauthorized the Voting Rights Act in light of the practice of bailout by eleven Virginia political subdivisions that relied upon the Attorney General's interpretation.[104] Congress did so despite the fact that two witnesses unsuccessfully urged Congress "to expand bailout eligibility to encompass governmental units smaller than counties and parishes."[105]

"Given this extensive evidence of clear legislative intent—both textual and historical—we need say little about *Sheffield*."[106] The court dismissed the *Sheffield* statement as dicta, and concluded that "[i]n any event, even if, as *Sheffield*'s dictum suggests, section 14(c)(2)'s definition originally operated only to identify entities eligible for coverage, the amended section 4(a)'s text and legislative history make clear that Congress used that definition in 1982 for an additional purpose: to identify those entitles eligible to seek bailout."[107]

In light of the statutory tour de force of the district court, voting rights experts believed that the statutory bailout argument had no chance when *NAMUDNO* was appealed to the Supreme Court.[108]

---

[102] Id at 233 (citing S Rep No 97-417 at 57 n 192, US Code Cong & Admin News 1982, p 235, no 192).

[103] Id.

[104] Id at 233–34.

[105] Id at 234.

[106] Id.

[107] Id. The court also rejected the utility district's arguments that it should rely on Texas law's definition of political subdivision, and that accepting the government's definition of political subdivision for section 5 purposes would interfere with application of section 2 of the Act.

[108] See Heather Gerken, *The Supreme Court Punts on Section 5*, Balkinization (June 22, 2009), online at http://balkin.blogspot.com/2009/06/supreme-court-punts-on-section-5 .html ("the statutory argument is one that almost no one (save Greg Coleman, the lawyer who argued the case and who is now entitled to be described as a mad genius) thought was particularly tenable because of prior Court opinions."); Richard L. Hasen, *Sordid Business: Will the Supreme Court Kill the Voting Rights Act?* Slate (Apr 27, 2009), online at

Instead, it seemed unavoidable that the Court would address the constitutionality of the renewed section 5.

At oral argument, Justice Souter pushed the bailout argument,[109] but the conservative members of the Court, led by the Chief Justice, focused instead on the constitutional questions and severely criticized section 5.[110] In addition to asking Debo Agebile, counsel for the NAACP, whether "it is your position that today southerners are more likely to discriminate than northerners,"[111] the Chief Justice remarked: "Counsel, . . . our decision in City of Boerne said that action under section 5 has to be congruent and proportional to what it's trying to remedy. Here, as I understand it, one-twentieth of 1 percent of the submissions are not precleared. That, to me, suggests that they are sweeping far more broadly than they need to, to address the intentional discrimination under the Fifteenth Amendment."[112] Once Justice Kennedy weighed in repeatedly with questions about whether preclearance undermined the sovereignty and dignity of the covered states,[113] most Court watchers predicted a 5–4 decision striking down section 5 of the Act on constitutional grounds.[114]

---

http://www.slate.com/id/2216888/ ("Since there's no good statutory loophole, the larger constitutional question seems unavoidable.").

[109] *Northwest Austin Municipal Utility District Number One v Holder*, Oral Argument Transcript, Apr 29, 2009, at 14, online at http://www.supremecourtus.gov/oral_arguments/argument_transcripts/08-322.pdf ("Well Mr. Coleman, this is important to me. Do you—do you acknowledge that if we find on your favor on the bailout point we need not reach the constitutional point?").

[110] Justice Ginsburg also offered some cogent criticisms of the statutory bailout argument, along the lines of the district court's analysis of the issue. See, e.g., id at 4 ("And what do you do with a statute that has three categories—the State, political subdivision, and then there's 'governmental unit'? The district qualifies as a governmental unit. Why would Congress add that third category if the district came within 'political subdivision'?"); id at 4–5 ("the statute does use the term 'governmental unit' to encompass districts. And if they were also subdivisions, why would Congress need to add an additional category?"); id at 8 ("There was a proposal [in 2006], was there not, to allow governmental units to bail out—to allow anyone who was required to preclear to bail out?"); id at 9 ("The Department of Justice has—does it—does it not have a regulation that contradicts your reading? And hasn't that been out there wasn't it out there before the 2006 extension?"). Justice Ginsburg must have swallowed hard before signing the opinion of the Court.

[111] Id at 48.

[112] Id at 27.

[113] See, e.g., id at 34 (statement of Justice Kennedy) ("Congress has made a finding that the sovereignty of Georgia is less than the sovereign dignity of Ohio.").

[114] Adam Liptak, *Skepticism at Court on Validity of Vote Law*, NY Times (Apr 29, 2009), online at http://www.nytimes.com/2009/04/30/us/30voting.html ("A central provision of the Voting Rights Act of 1965, designed to protect minorities in states with a history of discrimination, is at substantial risk of being struck down as unconstitutional, judging from the questioning on Wednesday at the Supreme Court.").

In a surprising and relatively short opinion, however, the Court on an 8–1 vote decided *NAMUDNO* on statutory grounds, ruling that the utility district was entitled to bail out.[115] Justice Thomas, speaking only for himself, would have held section 5 unconstitutional.[116]

The Court's opinion, written by Chief Justice Roberts, begins by stating the avoidance canon in an interesting way that fails to mention the need for a *plausible* interpretation of a statute to avoid deciding constitutional questions.[117] "Our usual practice is to avoid the unnecessary resolution of constitutional questions."[118] After five pages of background, the Court turned to give a detailed explanation of the serious constitutional questions raised by the case. The court noted that the "Act . . . differentiates between the States, despite our historic tradition that all the States enjoy 'equal sovereignty.'"[119] It said a departure from this principle "requires a showing that a statute's disparate geographic coverage is sufficiently related to the problem that it targets."[120] It flagged the federalism concerns and noted the danger that "[t]he evil that § 5 is meant to address may no longer be concentrated in the jurisdictions singled out for preclearance."[121] After noting that the coverage formula is thirty-five years old and possibly outdated, the Court noted that "Congress heard warnings from supporters of extending § 5 that evidence in the record did not address" differences between covered and noncovered states.[122]

Following this discussion raising serious doubts about section 5's constitutionality, the opinion stated that "we are keenly mindful of our institutional role. We fully appreciate that judging the Constitutionality of an Act of Congress is the 'gravest and most delicate duty that this Court is called upon to perform.'"[123] Then, as in

---

[115] *Northwest Austin Municipal Utility District Number One v Holder*, 129 S Ct 2504 (2009).

[116] Id at 2517 (Thomas, J, concurring in part and dissenting in part).

[117] See above Part II.B.

[118] *NAMUDNO*, 129 S Ct at 2508.

[119] Id at 2512.

[120] Id.

[121] Id.

[122] Id. The Court then noted that it was an open question whether the congruence and proportionality standard or an easier rational basis review might apply to the constitutional question. Id.

[123] Id at 2512–13 (quoting *Blodgett v Holden*, 275 US 142, 147–48 (1927) (Holmes, J, concurring)).

Ricci,[124] the Court cited *Escambia County* for the proposition that the Court will not decide a constitutional question if there is some other ground to dispose of the case.[125] Again, there was no mention of the need for a plausible interpretation of the statute.

The Court then offered a superficial textual analysis of the bail-out question. The Court did not discuss the textual analysis offered by the district court. Nor did it quote from and examine the legislative history showing Congress's unambiguous intent to limit bailout to states and political subdivisions that register voters. The Court also ignored the Department of Justice's regulations stating that only jurisdictions that register voters may bail out, and refused to afford any deference to such regulations.

Instead, the Court began by conceding that if section 4(a) were considered in isolation, "the District Court's approach might well be correct. But here, specific precedent, the structure of the Voting Rights Act, and the underlying constitutional concerns compel a broader reading of the statute."[126] The Court then relied upon the dicta in *Sheffield*,[127] and stated that the Court confirmed that dicta in another 1978 case.[128] The Court then appeared to concede that these dicta went against the Court's later *City of Rome* holding,[129] which seemed to foreclose the utility district's argument that it

---

[124] See note 65 above.

[125] The majority and Justice Thomas then debated whether a finding on bailout for the utility district would dispose of the case. Citing a concession by the utility district, the majority concluded it would do so. See *NAMUDNO*, 129 S Ct at 2513; see also id at 2517–18 (Thomas, J, concurring in part and dissenting in part).

[126] Id at 2513. The Court began the section with the statement that "'Statutory definitions control the meaning of statutory words, of course, in the usual case. But this is an unusual case.' *Lawson v. Suwannee Fruit & S.S. Co.*, 336 U.S. 198, 201, 69 S.Ct. 503, 93 L.Ed. 611 (1949); see also *Farmers Reservoir & Irrigation Co. v. McComb*, 337 U.S. 755, 764, 69 S.Ct. 1274, 93 L.Ed. 1672 (1949); *Philko Aviation, Inc. v. Shacket*, 462 U.S. 406, 412, 103 S.Ct. 2476, 76 L.Ed.2d 678 (1983)." But those cases involved statutory readings that went against the main purposes of the statute, in a way that the interpretation of the bailout provision did not. In *Lawson*, the Court refused to construe a provision in a statute governing disability payments in a way that would "create obvious incongruities in the language, and would destroy one of the major purposes of the second injury provision: the prevention of employer discrimination against handicapped workers. We have concluded that Congress would not have intended such a result." In *McComb*, the Court looked to legislative history to confirm the meaning of the statute. In *Shacket*, the Court refused to construe a statute to "defeat the purpose of the legislation."

[127] See notes 95–106 above.

[128] *NAMUDNO*, 129 S Ct at 2514 (citing *Dougherty County Bd of Ed. v White*, 439 US 32 (1978)).

[129] Id at 2515 ("Even if that is what *City of Rome* held . . .").

could bail out as a "political subdivision." But the Court then came up with this *deus ex machina*:[130]

> In 1982, however, Congress expressly repudiated *City of Rome* and instead embraced "piecemeal" bailout. As part of an overhaul of the bailout provision, Congress amended the Voting Rights Act to expressly provide that bailout was also available to "political subdivisions" in a covered State, "though [coverage] determinations were *not* made with respect to such subdivision as a separate unit." Voting Rights Act Amendments of 1982, 96 Stat. 131, codified at 42 U.S.C. § 1973b(a)(1) (emphasis added). In other words, Congress decided that a jurisdiction covered because it was within a covered State need not remain covered for as long as the State did. If the subdivision met the bailout requirements, it could bail out, even if the State could not. In light of these amendments, our logic for denying bailout in *City of Rome* is no longer applicable to the Voting Rights Act—if anything, that logic compels the opposite conclusion.

This paragraph is not at all supportable by the text of the statute or the legislative history.[131] There was no "express repudiation" of *City of Rome* in the text of the 1982 renewal. Indeed, *City of Rome* is not mentioned in the Senate Report as being repudiated.[132] Congress is not shy about mentioning statutory Supreme Court precedent it is overturning: The 1982 Senate Report is full of references to overturning *City of Mobile v Bolden*,[133] and the 2006 text of the VRA renewal itself (not to mention the legislative history) is full of references to overturning *Georgia v Ashcroft*.[134]

---

[130] Id at 2515–16.

[131] The Court ended its brief analysis by setting up a strawman argument: "The Government contends that this reading of *Sheffield* is mistaken, and that the district is subject to § 5 under our decision in *Sheffield* not because it is a 'political subdivision' but because it is a 'State.' That would mean it could bail out only if the whole State could bail out." Id at 2516. But that is not what the government argued. Instead, the government offered the following reading of *Sheffield*: "*Sheffield* held that, in light of the statutory structure and purposes, '§ 5's preclearance requirement for electoral changes by a covered 'State' reached all such changes made by political units in that State. *Ibid.*; see *Sheffield*, 435 U.S. at 127 ('The reference to 'State' in § 5 includes political units within it.')." Brief for Appellees at 13, online at http://www.abanet.org/publiced/preview/briefs/pdfs/07-08/08-322_AppelleeFederal.pdf. In other words, the government argued that *Sheffield* itself read the term "State" to include political units within it; it did not argue that the utility district *is* a state.

[132] Rick Hasen, *The Scalia Enigma in NAMUDNO*, Election Law Blog (June 23, 2009), online at http://electionlawblog.org/archives/013921.html.

[133] See *Thornburg v Gingles*, 478 US 30 (1986) (recounting in detail Congress's amendment of section 2 of the VRA to account for the Supreme Court's *City of Mobile* holding).

[134] See note 32 above (discussing *Georgia v Ashcroft* "fix").

The Court pointed to no evidence in the legislative materials of an express repudiation of *City of Rome*.

Nor was there any implicit repudiation of *City of Rome*. As illustrated by the district court opinion, all of the legislative history—ignored by the Court—points in the exact contrary direction to the analysis of the Court. Both the House and Senate Reports accompanying the 1982 VRA say that the "standard for bail-out is broadened to permit political subdivisions, *as defined in Section 14(c)(2)*, in covered states to seek bailout although the state itself may remain covered."[135] The Supreme Court's interpretation also went against the accepted understanding of the Act, as codified in the Attorney General's regulations.

Perhaps what is most remarkable about this statutory interpretation is the conspiracy of silence on the Court. No Justice, not even Justice Thomas in his partial dissent, objected to this analysis, which mangled Congress's statutory intent. Justice Thomas's only comment on the bailout point was to take the position that granting the utility district the chance to apply for bailout did not grant it the relief it sought in its complaint.[136]

B. CITIZENS UNITED[137]

In 2002, Congress passed the Bipartisan Campaign Reform Act of 2002 (BCRA, more commonly referred to as "McCain-Feingold").[138] This was the most significant federal campaign finance law since the 1974 amendments to the Federal Election Campaign Act (FECA), whose constitutionality the Supreme Court considered in *Buckley v Valeo*.[139] Although BCRA made many changes in the law, the changes most relevant for purposes of understanding this case concern BCRA's "electioneering communications" provisions.

FECA (continuing a law predating FECA) bars corporations

---

[135] *Northwest Austin Municipal Utility District Number One v Mukasey*, 573 F Supp 2d at 232–33 (citing House and Senate Reports).

[136] *NAMUDNO*, 129 S Ct at 2517–18 (Thomas, J, concurring in part and dissenting in part).

[137] The next few paragraphs are drawn from Richard L. Hasen, *Beyond Incoherence: The Roberts Court's Deregulatory Turn in FEC v Wisconsin Right to Life*, 94 Minn L Rev 1064 (2008).

[138] Bipartisan Campaign Reform Act of 2002 § 101, 2 USC § 441i(a) (Supp V 2007).

[139] 424 US 1 (1976).

and unions from spending general treasury funds on certain election-related activities.[140] FECA allowed corporations and unions instead to set up separate political committees (commonly referred to as PACs) to spend money on these campaigns, but it limited both the amount that could be contributed and who could be solicited to contribute to these PACs.

By the 1990s, many people viewed the FECA as ineffective, thanks to an interpretation of the statute by the Court in *Buckley*.[141] The *Buckley* Court held that, to avoid vagueness and overbreadth problems within FECA, its provisions should be interpreted to reach only election-related activity containing "express advocacy," such as "Vote for Smith."[142] Individuals, corporations, and unions began running "issue ads" that appeared aimed at influencing federal elections but that escaped FECA regulation through an avoidance of words of express advocacy. Thus, individuals and entities that spent money on "Vote against Jones" ads had to disclose the sources of payment, and those ads could not be paid for with corporate or union treasury funds. In contrast, there were no such limitations on ads that appeared intended to influence federal elections but that avoided the magic words of "express advocacy," such as an ad which said "Call Senator Jones and tell her what you think of her lousy vote on the stimulus bill." Spending on such ads increased dramatically in the 1990s.[143]

BCRA sought to close this issue advocacy "loophole" by creating new "electioneering communications" provisions. Electioneering communications are television or radio (not print or Internet) advertisements that feature a candidate for federal election and are capable of reaching 50,000 people in the relevant electorate thirty days before a primary or sixty days before a general election. Anyone making electioneering communications over a certain dollar threshold must disclose contributions funding the ads and spending related to the ads to the FEC (BCRA § 201).[144] Corporations and unions cannot spend general treasury funds on such ads

---

[140] 2 USC § 441b.

[141] See *McConnell v FEC*, 540 US 93, 126 (2003).

[142] *Buckley*, 424 US at 44 n 51.

[143] See *McConnell v FEC*, 540 US at 126–27.

[144] See Bipartisan Campaign Reform Act of 2002 § 201, 2 USC § 434(f)(1) (Supp V 2007).

(but could pay for the ads through their PACs) (BCRA § 203).[145] In addition, anyone broadcasting an electioneering communication must state in the ad the person or committee funding the ad and whether it is authorized by any candidate (BCRA § 311).[146]

The section 203 spending limit does not apply to nonprofit corporations that meet certain requirements, including that the nonprofit has a policy not to take for-profit corporate or union funding.[147] These groups are referred to as *MCFL* groups (named after a 1986 Supreme Court case, *FEC v Massachusetts Citizens for Life*[148]), and they still must comply with the disclosure provisions in BCRA § 201 and § 311.

A broad coalition of plaintiffs challenged each of these BCRA provisions (along with a number of others) in *McConnell v FEC*.[149] By a 5–4 vote, the Supreme Court upheld BCRA section 203 against facial challenge. It reaffirmed the Court's controversial holding in *Austin v Michigan Chamber of Commerce*.[150] *Austin* held that corporate spending on elections could be limited because of what the Court termed the "distorting and corrosive effects" of immense aggregations of wealth accomplished with the corporate form, which could be spent on elections despite the corporation's ideas having little or no public support.[151] Relying on *Austin*'s upholding of corporate limits on "express advocacy," the *McConnell* Court held that the "issue ads" regulated by the electioneering communications provisions of BCRA could constitutionally be limited because most of them were the "functional equivalent of express advocacy."[152]

The Court in *Wisconsin Right to Life v Federal Election Commission* (*WRTL I*)[153] held that *McConnell* did not preclude an "as applied" challenge to BCRA section 203 by a corporation or union whose ads were not the "functional equivalent of express advocacy." *WRTL I* involved a corporate-funded broadcast advertisement that men-

---

[145] See Bipartisan Campaign Reform Act of 2002 § 203, 2 USC § 441b(b)(2) (2000 & Supp V 2007).

[146] See Bipartisan Campaign Reform Act of 2002 § 311.

[147] *McConnell*, 540 US at 210–11.

[148] 479 US 238 (1986).

[149] 540 US 93 (2003).

[150] 494 US 652 (1990).

[151] Id at 660.

[152] *McConnell*, 540 US at 206. By an 8–1 vote, the Court also upheld BCRA § 201 and § 311 against facial challenge.

[153] 546 US 410 (2006).

tioned Senator Feingold's and Senator Kohl's positions on judicial filibusters and was to be broadcast in Wisconsin during the period of Senator Feingold's reelection campaign. After remand, in which the lower court found the ads were not entitled to an exemption because they were the functional equivalent of express advocacy, the case returned to the Supreme Court.[154]

The Court in *Wisconsin Right to Life v Federal Election Commission (WRTL II)*[155] held, on a 5–4 vote, that BCRA section 203 could not be constitutionally applied to such ads. Three Justices in the majority (Justices Kennedy, Scalia, and Thomas) held, consistent with their dissenting opinions in *McConnell*, that BCRA section 203 was unconstitutional as applied to *any* corporate advertising, stating that *McConnell* and *Austin* should be overruled.[156] Chief Justice Roberts and Justice Alito, in a narrower controlling opinion, did not reach the question whether *McConnell* and *Austin* should be overruled. They held instead that the only corporate-funded advertisements that BCRA could bar constitutionally were those that were the "functional equivalent of express advocacy."[157]

The controlling opinion held that in making the "functional equivalent" determination, the question the FEC or a court must consider is whether, without regard to context (such as the fact that the filibuster issue was one that conservatives were using to attack liberal Democrats) and without detailed discovery of the intentions of the advertisers, the advertisement was susceptible of no reasonable interpretation other than as an advertisement supporting or opposing a candidate for office.[158] Unless the ad was susceptible to "no reasonable interpretation" other than as an advertisement supporting or opposing the candidate, it would be unconstitutional to apply BCRA section 203 to bar corporate funding for it. The controlling opinion then held that the ad at issue in *WRTL II* was susceptible to an interpretation as something other than an ad against Senator Feingold: it did not mention Senator Feingold's character or fitness for office, and had no other clear indicia of the functional equivalent of express advocacy. Accordingly, WRTL was

---

[154] See Hasen, 94 Minn L Rev at 1076–77 (cited in note 137).

[155] 127 S Ct 2652 (2007).

[156] See id at 2674–87 (Scalia, J, concurring).

[157] Id at 2658–74 (principal opinion).

[158] Id.

entitled to an as-applied exemption and could pay for the ads with corporate funds.[159]

Citizens United is a follow-on case to *WRTL II*.[160] Citizens United, a nonprofit ideological corporation (but one that took some for-profit corporate funding), produced a feature-length documentary entitled *Hillary: The Movie*. The documentary appeared in theaters and was available to order via DVD during the 2008 primary season. Citizens United wished to distribute the movie as well through a cable television "video-on-demand" service. In exchange for a $1.2 million fee, a cable television operator consortium would have made the documentary available to be downloaded by cable subscribers for free "on demand" as part of an "Election 08" series. The documentary contained no express advocacy, but it did contain many negative statements about Hillary Clinton, including statements that she was a "European socialist" and not fit to be Commander-in-Chief. The FEC took the position that the documentary was the functional equivalent of express advocacy and therefore subject to BCRA section 203, meaning it was an electioneering communication that could not be paid for with corporate funds.[161]

Pursuant to a special jurisdictional provision of BCRA,[162] Citizens United filed suit against the FEC before a three-judge United States District Court for the District of Columbia (with direct appeal to the Supreme Court). Citizens United moved for a preliminary injunction barring enforcement of BCRA section 203 for its broadcast of the documentary through "video-on-demand."[163]

The three-judge court unanimously rejected Citizens United's arguments.[164] The court held that under *WRTL II* the documentary

---

[159] Id.

[160] The facts appear in *Citizens United v FEC*, 530 F Supp 2d 274 (DDC 2008).

[161] Citizens United also wished to broadcast some 10-second and 30-second advertisements promoting the documentary. The corporation wished to do so without complying with BCRA § 201 (requiring disclosure of funders) or § 311 (requiring the "disclaimer" stating who paid for the advertisement and that it was not approved by any candidate or committee). The FEC conceded that the advertisements (as opposed to the documentary itself) were not the "functional equivalent of express advocacy," but it took the position that the rules of BCRA § 201 and § 203 still applied. According to the FEC, the disclosure rules were not eligible for the "as-applied" exemption that the Court created for corporate *spending* in *WRTL II*. *Citizens United*, 530 F Supp 2d 274.

[162] Bipartisan Campaign Reform Act of 2002 § 403, 2 USC § 437(h) (2000 & Supp V 2007); 28 USC § 2284 (2000).

[163] It also sought to bar enforcement of BCRA § 201 and § 311 disclosure requirements as to the advertisements.

[164] *Citizens United v FEC*, 530 F Supp 2d 274 (DDC 2008) (three-judge court).

was the functional equivalent of express advocacy and was therefore not entitled to an as-applied exemption: the movie could not be paid for with for-profit corporate funds.[165] Citizens United appealed from the denial of the preliminary injunction to the Supreme Court, which dismissed the appeal.[166] The case returned to the district court, which then granted summary judgment, relying on its earlier opinion on the preliminary injunction.[167]

The Supreme Court noted probable jurisdiction and set the case for argument.[168] On appeal, Citizens United raised a number of arguments against the government's position that this documentary could not be broadcast over cable television's "video-on-demand" service because it constituted a corporate-funded "electioneering communication." Some of the arguments were statutory; others were constitutional.[169] Its narrowest argument is that the FEC regulations should not be construed to apply to "video-on-demand" cable broadcasts.[170] Simply put, the Court can hold that video-on-demand, which requires a cable subscriber to choose to download video for viewing, is not a *broadcast, cable or satellite communication* that refers to a candidate for federal office"[171] as defined by BCRA.

Citizens United concedes that it did not make this argument below, but it notes that the district court passed on it and that the canon of constitutional avoidance gives the Court a reason to address this statutory question.[172] Citizens United's broadest argument

---

[165] As to the advertisements, the district court held that the *WRTL II* exemption did not apply to the disclosure rules, relying on language in *McConnell* broadly upholding these requirements. Id.

[166] 128 S Ct 1732 (2008).

[167] 2008 WL 2788753 (DDC July 18, 2008).

[168] 129 S Ct 594 (2008)

[169] Among the arguments raised is that the Court should expand the *MCFL* exemption for nonprofit corporations that take some for-profit funds, and that its documentary was not the functional equivalent of express advocacy.

[170] *Citizens United v FEC*, Brief for Appellants at 27 n 2, online at http://www.abanet .org/publiced/preview/briefs/pdfs/07-08/08-205_Appellant.pdf.

[171] 2 USC § 434(f)(3)(A) (Supp V 2007).

[172] Id. The government disagrees that the Court should reach the question, Brief for Appellee at 24 n 7, online at http://www.abanet.org/publiced/preview/briefs/pdfs/07-08/ 08-205_Appellee.pdf, but the BCRA legislative sponsors (Senators McCain and Feingold, and former Representatives Shays and Meehan) filed an amicus brief suggesting that if the Court is otherwise inclined to find for Citizens United in this case, it should do it on grounds that the FEC's implementing regulations did not clearly apply to "video-on-demand" broadcasts. Brief Amici Curiae of Senators McCain and Feingold, and Former Representatives Shays and Meehan, online at http://www.abanet.org/publiced/preview/ briefs/pdfs/07-08/08-205_AppelleAmCuMcCain.pdf at 18–19 ("To the extent that there

in its merits brief is that *Austin* was wrongly decided and should be overruled; then even express advocacy by corporations in federal elections could be paid for with corporate treasury funds.[173] But as to the *Austin* argument, the FEC notes that Citizens United did not raise this point below, either, and that Citizens United expressly abandoned any facial challenges in the district court.[174] The issue also was not raised in Citizen United's jurisdictional statement, and the usual Court rule is that the Court will not consider issues not fairly raised therein.[175]

The case was argued in March 2009, and media accounts suggest that the government's case seemed threatened when the Deputy Solicitor General had trouble answering a hypothetical question about the regulation of books containing "the functional equivalent of express advocacy."[176] Still, it was somewhat of a surprise when, on the last regular day of the Court's Term in June 2009, the Court announced it would rehear the case in September. More surprising, the Court asked for supplemental briefing on the following question: "For the proper disposition of this case, should the Court overrule either or both *Austin* v. *Michigan Chamber of Commerce*, 494 U.S. 652 (1990), and the part of *McConnell* v. *Federal Election Comm'n*, 540 U.S. 93 (2003), which addresses the facial validity of Section 203 of the Bipartisan Campaign Reform Act of 2002, 2 U.S.C. §441b?"[177] If the Court were going to decide the case on narrow statutory grounds, such as a ruling that video-on-demand is not properly classified as an electioneering communication, rear-

---

may be some ambiguity in the applicability of the regulations, the Court could possibly conclude that it is sufficiently doubtful that on-demand viewing of *Hillary: The Movie* would have been within the scope of the FEC's current regulations that the Court should withhold judgment on the constitutional issue until such time as the FEC made a more specific regulatory determination to include such transmissions within the regulatory definition of electioneering communications. In no event, however, should the Court accept Citizens United's broad constitutional arguments that would place even express advocacy beyond the bounds of regulation if it is accessed at the choice of the viewer.").

[173] *Citizens United v FEC*, Brief for Appellants, at 30 (cited in note 170) ("*Austin* was wrongly decided and should be overruled").

[174] *Citizens United v FEC*, transcript of oral argument (March 24, 2009) at 27–28, online at http://www.supremecourtus.gov/oral_arguments/argument_transcripts/08-205.pdf.

[175] *Citizens United v FEC*, Brief for Appellee, at 33–34 (cited in note 170).

[176] Adam Liptak, *Justices Consider Interplay Between First Amendment and Campaign Finance Laws*, NY Times (March 24, 2009), online at http://www.nytimes.com/2009/03/25/washington/25scotus.html; Dahlia Lithwick, *The Supreme Court Reviews Hillary: The Movie*, Slate (March 24, 2009), online at http://www.slate.com/id/2214514/.

[177] *Citizens United v FEC*, Order, 129 S Ct 2893 (2009).

gument on the constitutional question would be unnecessary.[178] The order indicates a Court that is at least seriously considering that question.

C. NAMUDNO, CITIZENS UNITED, AND THE SUPREME COURT'S USUAL APPROACH TO CONSTITUTIONAL AVOIDANCE

Neither *NAMUDNO* nor *Citizens United* fits comfortably in the Supreme Court's usual approach to the constitutional avoidance doctrine. *NAMUDNO* does not fit because the Court adopted an implausible interpretation of the statute. Indeed, the Court's statutory interpretation analysis was so weak that the Court failed even to respond to the contrary statutory points raised by the government and offered in detail by the district court. It is probably no surprise that in stating the avoidance principle in *NA-MUDNO*, the Court did not cite the usual formulation of the rule requiring a *plausible* statutory interpretation. Instead, the Court stated more flatly that "[o]ur usual practice is to avoid the unnecessary resolution of constitutional questions."[179] The Court then stated that "judging the Constitutionality of an Act of Congress is the 'gravest and most delicate duty that this Court is called upon to perform.'"[180] Finally, the Court cited *Escambia County* for the proposition that the Court will not decide a constitutional question if there is some other ground to dispose of the case.[181] In practice, the Court jettisoned the requirement of a plausible statutory interpretation in *NAMUDNO* to avoid a sensitive and difficult constitutional question.

But the Court's approach was even starker when viewed against the *Citizens United* order the Court issued just one week later. The Court undoubtedly could avoid deciding whether to overrule *Austin* and *McConnell*'s upholding of spending limits on corporations and unions through a plausible interpretation of the electioneering communication statute so as not to apply to video-on-demand. But regardless of how it ultimately decides the case, it ratcheted

---

[178] See Richard L. Hasen, *The Supreme Court Gets Ready to Turn on the Fundraising Spigot*, Slate (June 29, 2009), online at http://www.slate.com/id/2221753/.

[179] *NAMUDNO*, 129 S Ct at 2508.

[180] Id at 2513.

[181] See id.

up the importance of the case and the rhetoric through the re-argument order.

Thus, the operative question here is not simply how plausible a statutory construction must be before the avoidance canon kicks in,[182] but why the Court adopted such an inconsistent approach. If it is true that the "usual practice" is to "avoid the unnecessary resolution of constitutional questions" and that it is the "gravest and most delicate duty" to review the constitutionality of an Act of Congress, why did the Court in *Citizens United* not conclude, as in *NAMUDNO*, *Ricci*, and *Escambia County*, that the Court will not decide the constitutional question because there is some other ground to dispose of the case? Is not avoidance especially war-ranted in a case in which the constitutional issue was abandoned in the trial court and not presented in the jurisdictional statement? Why did the Court not follow its usual practice in *Clark v Martinez*, to the effect that "[i]f [one of two plausible statutory con-structions] would raise a multitude of constitutional problems, the other should prevail. . . ."?[183] Why did the Court instead set up an in-your-face, high-stakes constitutional showdown on the ques-tion—whether or not it ultimately issues a constitutional ruling on the merits?

IV. Understanding Avoidance and Anti-Avoidance at the Roberts Court

The contrast between the Court's treatment of *NA-MUDNO* and *Citizens United* is the latest (and especially high-profile) illustration of Judge Friendly's observation that the doc-trine of constitutional avoidance will be selectively employed.[184] In the final part of this article, I explore three potential theories to explain the differing treatment of the two cases. With a data set of just these cases (plus the few other significant constitutional avoidance decisions of the Roberts Court), and with no inside information about the Justices' thought processes, at this point it

---

[182] Schauer, 1995 Supreme Court Review at 85 (cited in note 34) ("In reality, 'fairly possible' is a matter of degree, even assuming some interpretations are not fairly possible. Extending 'no vehicles in the park' to bicycles is more possible—less of a reach—than extending it to sleds, even though neither extension is compelled and neither is prohibited.").

[183] *Clark*, 543 US at 380–81.

[184] See note 35 above.

is impossible to say which of the three theories best explains the action of the Court in these two cases. But I set out these potential theories to test against future use of the avoidance canon and the anti-avoidance canon by the Roberts Court.

Fruitful dialogue. The *fruitful dialogue* explanation posits that the Court will use constitutional avoidance only when doing so would further a dialogue with Congress that has a realistic chance of actually avoiding constitutional problems through redrafting. On this reading, the Voting Rights Act got remanded to Congress because Congress may fix the VRA in ways that do not violate the Constitution, but the corporate spending limits provision of federal campaign finance law perhaps does not deserve remand because the provisions are not constitutionally fixable.

This is the most charitable reading of the Court's contrasting orders in *NAMUDNO* and *Citizens United*. In this view, the Court would not tolerate the political avoidance that Congress exhibited during the 2006 amendment process,[185] but the Voting Rights Act is just too important to throw away without giving Congress a chance to face the problems head on. In other words, the statute is so important that the Court was willing to jettison its usual rules of statutory interpretation despite the strong negative views of some members of the Court on the underlying constitutional question to give Congress one more chance to save the statute. This at least may have been the view of Justice Kennedy, and without his vote the Court would have spoken in a fractured way in this important case.

Campaign finance, in contrast, stands on different footing. The Court is already well on its way to striking down corporate spending limits as a violation of the First Amendment.[186] Giving Congress a chance to fix BCRA section 203 to clarify whether or not video-on-demand counts as an electioneering communication is not going to solve the Court's fundamental problem with the *Austin* rationale for limiting corporate spending. If Congress cannot limit corporate spending even on express advocacy, then it matters little whether Congress intended to cover the "functional equivalent of express advocacy" contained in a video-on-demand documentary.

---

[185] See note 84 above.

[186] See generally Hasen, 94 Minn L Rev at 1064 (cited in note 137).

Understood this way, the Court's decision to make the issue front and center at a second oral argument makes sense. This anti-avoidance device—pushing the constitutional question front and center—can serve the penumbral "fence around the Torah" function of keeping Congress away from even *thinking* of legislating further in a protected area.

Furthermore, some members of the Court may have thought the constitutional issue needed to be addressed given that *Citizens United* came to the Court under its rare mandatory appellate jurisdiction.[187] The Court had been facing a flurry of mandatory appeals under BCRA, and perhaps it saw that the only way to lessen the volume of cases was through a constitutional knockdown of BCRA's foundations.

Indeed, even Justices unsure of their constitutional views going into *Citizens United* might have seen a judicial administration benefit to deciding the constitutional questions straightforwardly. Addressing constitutional questions squarely in the campaign finance area might be especially important given the incoherence and fractured nature of the Supreme Court's existing campaign finance jurisprudence.[188] Lower courts would certainly benefit from more guidance.

Such use of the anti-avoidance tool is not unprecedented. Perhaps the Court's refusal to apply the avoidance canon to save the Detainee Treatment Act of 2005 in *Boumendine*[189] was a way for the Court to warn Congress off further attempts to deny basic

---

[187] As I detail in Richard L. Hasen, *The Supreme Court and Election Law: Judging Equality from Baker v. Carr to Bush v. Gore* 36–38 (NYU Press, 2003), *Harper v Virginia State Board of Elections*, 383 US 663 (1966), the Supreme Court case striking down the use of poll taxes in state elections, came to the Supreme Court under a statute mandating Supreme Court appellate jurisdiction. Internally, the case appeared headed for a 6–3 summary affirmance of the lower court's upholding of the poll tax. Justice Goldberg wrote a draft dissent for three Justices, reprinted in Appendix 2 of my book. In that draft dissent, Justice Goldberg wrote in the first footnote of the differences between considering a case brought up on appeal compared to a case coming up on a writ of certiorari, whose denial says nothing about the Court's view of the merits. "However, this is an appeal, which by statute we must and do determine on the merits. Whatever[] may have been my decision as to whether or not certiorari should be granted on this issue, since his case is an appeal, I am compelled to face up to the substantial constitutional issue presented." (Citation omitted.) Similarly, it may be that some Justices considering the *Citizens United* case on mandatory appeal feel compelled to face the constitutional questions, even if the questions were not raised in the jurisdictional statement and were abandoned in the court below. Of course, *NAMUDNO* too reached the Court through mandatory appellate jurisdiction, yet only Justice Thomas reached the constitutional question.

[188] See generally Hasen, 94 Minn L Rev 1064 (cited in note 137).

[189] See note 58 above and accompanying text.

trial rights to Guantanamo detainees. Conservative Justices skeptical of the Court's abortion rights jurisprudence see anti-avoidance there too: construing ambiguous abortion statutes to raise constitutional problems chills new abortion-related legislation. Justice Kennedy made the point in *Gonzales v Carhart*,[190] but he was not the first. The idea seems to have originated with Justice White's dissent in *Thornburgh v American College of Obstetricians and Gynecologists*.[191] There, Justice White argued that "[t]he Court's rejection of a perfectly plausible reading of [an abortion] statute flies in the face of the principle—which until today I had thought applicable to abortion statutes as well as to other legislative enactments—that '[w]here fairly possible, courts should construe a statute to avoid a danger of unconstitutionality.' The Court's reading is obviously based on an entirely different principle: that in cases involving abortion, a permissible reading of a statute is to be avoided at all costs."[192]

Though the fruitful dialogue theory sounds plausible, it is not clear that it explains the actual thinking of the Justices. The explanation views the Court as bending over backwards in *NAMUDNO* to spur Congressional dialogue on the constitutionality of race-based remedies in voting, dialogue which the Congress showed in 2006 it had no interest in undertaking. From oral argument, it did not sound like members of the Court had much interest in dialogue either. Justice Scalia pointedly noted that the 2006 renewal passed 98–0 in the Senate, and on a similarly lopsided vote in the House, asking: "You know, the—the Israeli Supreme Court, the Sanhedrin, used to have a rule that if the death penalty was pronounced unanimously, it was invalid, because there must be something wrong there. Do you ever expect—do you ever seriously expect Congress to vote against a reextension of the Voting Rights Act? Do you really think that any incumbent would—would vote to do that?"[193]

It seems more accurate to say that the liberals, led by Justice

---

[190] 550 US at 153.

[191] 476 US 757 (1986).

[192] Id at 812 (White, J, dissenting) (internal citation omitted); see also id at 829 (O'Connor, J, dissenting) (same); *Stenberg v Carhart*, 530 US 914, 977 (2000) (same).

[193] *Northwest Austin Municipal Utility District Number One v Holder*, transcript of oral argument (Apr 29, 2009) at 51, online at http://www.supremecourtus.gov/oral_arguments/argument_transcripts/08-322.pdf.

Souter, were looking for some way to avoid an adverse ruling striking down section 5 as unconstitutional, and that the conservatives were ready to strike down section 5. Why everyone but Justice Thomas agreed to go along with a very weak avoidance interpretation seems driven less by a desire for dialogue with Congress than from fear[194] or strategic calculation. It is to these alternatives that I now turn.

Political legitimacy. The *political legitimacy* explanation posits that the Court uses the constitutional avoidance doctrine when it fears that full-blown constitutional pronouncement would harm its legitimacy.[195] Some evidence supports this understanding of *NAMUDNO* and the reargument order in *Citizens United.* During the same Term that the Court avoided the constitutional issue in *NAMUDNO*, it used the same avoidance canon to narrowly construe a different provision of the Voting Rights Act in *Bartlett v Strickland*,[196] and it applied constitutional avoidance (in deed if not in name) to narrowly construe Title VII of the 1964 Civil Rights Act in *Ricci v DeStefano*,[197] the controversial New Haven firefighters case. Each of these cases involved tough questions of race

---

[194] As Heather Gerken observed: "The real worry for supporters of Section 5 is the possibility that the Court's liberals thought that sending a crystal clear, united message to Congress was Section 5's best hope. That is, the four Justices on the Court may have been as convinced as many commentators are that Section 5 will fall when the case returns, and they were hoping that a unanimous opinion would light a fire under Congress." *Gerken: Can Congress Take a Hint?*, Election Law Blog (June 23, 2009), online at http://electionlawblog.org/archives/013911.html. On the message the Court conservatives might have been sending to Congress, see Ellen Katz, *Ellen Katz: Roberts Didn't Blink*, Election Law Blog (June 24, 2009), online at http://electionlawblog.org/archives/013926.html, and Richard H. Pildes, *A Warning to Congress*, NY Times Room for Debate Blog (June 22, 2009), online at http://roomfordebate.blogs.nytimes.com/2009/06/22/the-battle-not-the-war-on-voting-rights/?scp = 1 &sq = Pildes&st = cse#richard.

[195] For some early expressions of these ideas, see Bruce Ackerman, *Section Five and the On-going Canonization of the Civil Rights Movement*, Balkinization Blog (June 22, 2009), online at http://balkin.blogspot.com/2009/06/section-five-and-on-going-canonization.html; Jack Balkin, *Why Has the Roberts Court Suddenly Gone Minimalist?* Balkinization Blog (June 29, 2009), online at http://balkin.blogspot.com/2009/06/why-has-roberts-court-gone-minimalist.html; *Guest Post: Behind the Scenes in NAMUDNO*, Election Law Blog (June 24, 2009), online at http://electionlawblog.org/archives/013932.html. On the debate over whether the Roberts Court's decision in *NAMUDNO* was an act of "statesmanship," see Sam Issacharoff, *Issacharoff: On Statesmanship*, Election Law Blog (June 24, 2009), online at http://electionlawblog.org/archives/013927.html, and Dahlia Lithwick, *Our Judges with Attitude*, Slate (June 26, 2009), online at http://www.slate.com/id/2220927/entry/2221700/.

[196] 129 S Ct 1231 (2009).

[197] 129 S Ct 2658 (2009).

relations whose resolution could harm the Court's legitimacy.[198] A Court fearful of Congressional or public reaction, especially with the other two branches dominated by the more liberal Democrats, just might have blinked.[199]

In contrast, campaign finance issues are much lower salience to the public[200] and are less likely to arouse the passion of interest groups and perhaps the ire of Congress. A court concerned about political legitimacy might think it has a great deal more latitude in how it deals with questions of money in politics than with fundamental questions of race relations. Under this reading, the Court can afford anti-avoidance when it comes to lower salience questions such as campaign finance, but it needs avoidance to quell the racial waters.

While that explanation seems to make sense viewing these two cases alone, it is harder to square with the use of anti-avoidance in the abortion context, which is much higher salience. Perhaps another factor is at work: how convinced the Court is that the government action is unconstitutional. This would tie together elements of legitimacy and fixability.

Political calculus. The *political calculus* explanation is that the Court uses constitutional avoidance and similar doctrines (such as the use of "as-applied" constitutional challenges[201]) to soften public and Congressional resistance to the Court's efforts to move the law in the Justices' preferred policy direction.[202] Like the political legitimacy argument, the political calculus argument too is one about the Court's legitimacy, but it is one that views the Court as strategically pursuing an agenda, rather than as fearfully anticipating a backlash. It advances a view of the Court, and of the

---

[198] The *Ricci* case in particular dominated the news in the days after the opinion, especially as one of the judges on the Second Circuit panel, reversed by the Supreme Court, was then-nominee Judge Sotomayor.

[199] Rick Hasen, *Initial Thoughts on NAMUDNO: Chief Justice Roberts Blinked*, Election Law Blog (June 22, 2009), online at http://electionlawblog.org/archives/013903.html.

[200] Glenn H. Utter and Ruth Ann Strickland, *Campaign and Election Reform* 192 (2d ed, ABC-CLIO, 2008) ("Americans typically have not viewed campaign finance reform as a top priority for the federal government to address").

[201] See Nathaniel Persily and Jennifer S. Rosenberg, *Defacing Democracy? The Changing Nature and Rising Importance of As-Applied Challenges in the Supreme Court's Recent Election Law Decisions*, 93 Minn L Rev 1644 (2009), and Joshua A. Douglas, *The Significance of the Shift Toward As-Applied Challenges in Election Law*, 37 Hofstra L Rev 635 (2009).

[202] Mark Tushnet, *How the Supreme Court's Ruling on Ricci v. DeStefano Hints at Trouble Ahead*, Dissent (July 12, 2009), online at http://dissentmagazine.org/online.php?id=270.

Chief Justice in particular, as sophisticated and calculating. A recent portrayal of Chief Justice Roberts in a critical *New Yorker* article by Jeffrey Toobin referred to the Chief as a "stealth hard liner."[203] The view also has echoes in Justice Scalia's lament in the *WRTL II* case that the Roberts-Alito "as applied" decision on BCRA section 203 was "faux judicial restraint."[204]

Under this positive political theory explanation[205] of the Court's actions, the difference between *NAMUDNO* and *Citizens United* is simply one of timing. The Court had already laid the groundwork for a deregulatory campaign finance regime through its earlier campaign finance rulings which exhibited some of that faux judicial restraint: it is now ready to put a stake in the heart of the corporate spending limits, if not in *Citizens United*, then in another challenge soon to come. If that reading is correct, the Voting Rights Act's time of demise will come, and the public will come to expect it once the Court first raised constitutional doubts in *NAMUDNO*. The avoidance canon is just another doctrinal tool in the Court's arsenal to move constitutional law and policy in the Court's direction and at the Court's chosen speed.

Tom Goldstein seems to take this view of the Court, seeing the conservative majority using the avoidance doctrine and similar doctrines as laying the groundwork for subsequent overruling.

> I am struck in particular by the opinions of the Chief Justice that seem to lay down markers that will be followed in later generations of cases. *NAMUDNO* details constitutional objections to Section 5 of the Voting Rights Act that seem ready-made for a later decision invalidating the statute if it is not amended. . . .
> If I'm right about the direction of the case law, the Court's methodology is striking. It is reinforcing its own legitimacy with

---

[203] Jeffrey Toobin, *Annals of Law: No More Mr. Nice Guy: The Supreme Court's Stealth Hard Liner*, New Yorker (May 25, 2009), online at http://www.newyorker.com/reporting/2009/05/25/090525fa_fact_toobin.

[204] *WRTL II*, 127 S Ct at 2683–84 n 7 (Scalia, J, concurring).

[205] Positive political theory views political actors seeking to maximize their preferences within institutional constraints. For an introduction to the concept as applied to statutory interpretation and interactions between the Supreme Court and Congress (and within each institution), see Eskridge, Frickey, and Garrett, *Cases and Materials on Legislation* at 75–76 (cited in note 12). More technically sophisticated versions of PPT use game theory to model these interactions, and consider as well the role of the executive. The basic idea of PPT in the Supreme Court–Congress game is that a majority of Court Justices seeks to move statutory law in its preferred policy direction without facing overruling by the Congress through amended legislation.

opinions that later can be cited to demonstrate that it is not rapidly or radically changing the law. This approach may be in the starkest relief if next Term the Court cites its recent decision in *Wisconsin Right to Life* as precedent for concluding that *McConnell v. FEC* and *Austin v. Michigan* have been significantly undermined and should be overruled. The plurality and concurrence in *Wisconsin Right to Life* famously debated how aggressively the Court should go in overruling prior campaign finance precedent. The Chief Justice urged patience—not moving more quickly than required—and the wait may not have been long.[206]

The political calculus explanation meshes particularly well with the peculiar nature of the *NAMUDNO* statutory decision. Ordinarily when Congress considers overriding a statutory interpretation decision of the Supreme Court, doing so will restore a popular law enacted by Congress (leaving open the possibility that the Court will later strike the law down on constitutional grounds).[207] Here, the situation is different: Congress is not going to consider overriding the Court's interpretation of the bailout provision in the Voting Rights Act; there is not much to gain by doing so (we do not know how many jurisdictions will now seek bailout that could not before) and an override could goad the Court into striking down section 5. Either Congress will do nothing—in which case the Court has laid the groundwork for invalidating section 5 in a future case—or the Congress will pass legislation watering down section 5's key provisions to please the conservatives on the Court. It is a win-win situation for a Court making strategic calculations to move the law toward its policy preferences.

As I noted, we do not have enough data from the cases to know which of these three explanations for alternating avoidance and anti-avoidance best represents reality. Likely one's views on which explanation coheres best correlates with one's views on the general motivations and sincerity of the Justices on the Supreme Court. But it is simply too early to tell, and always hazardous to generalize

---

[206] Tom Goldstein, *Thoughts on This Term and the Next*, SCOTUSblog (June 29, 2009), online at http://www.scotusblog.com/wp/thoughts-on-this-term-and-the-next/.

[207] On the nature and frequency of statutory overrides from a positive political theory perspective, see William N. Eskridge, *Overriding Supreme Court Statutory Interpretation Decisions*, 101 Yale L J 331 (1991); Pablo T. Spiller and Emerson H. Tiller, *Invitations to Override: Congressional Reversals of Supreme Court Decisions*, 16 Int'l Rev L & Econ 503 (1996).

about the actions of a multimember body.[208] Some members of the Court may be concerned about its legitimacy; others may wish to engage in a dialogue; others may be acting more strategically. Perhaps the simplest explanation of the divergence in the cases is Justice Kennedy's different position in the two cases.

One test of the theories may come if Congress does nothing to amend the VRA or it amends the Voting Rights Act but not in any way that meaningfully addresses the Court's concerns in *NA-MUDNO*. A Court that does not act then to strike down the Act looks more like one motivated by fear;[209] a Court that strikes down section 5, citing the earlier warnings in *NAMUDNO*, may fit more into the political calculus explanation. Then again, at that point a Court that seeks to encourage fruitful dialogue with Congress might simply give up on the Congress in this particular area.

V. CONCLUSION

The Supreme Court can choose at will to use the avoidance canon or anti-avoidance for myriad purposes.[210] Looking at the Warren Court, Phil Frickey viewed the canon as being used to further civil liberties in a time of irrational fear of communists.[211] He suggested avoidance could come in handy for the Roberts Court too as a way of furthering civil liberties, by cutting back on Congress's overreaching in the terrorist cases.[212] Writing at the beginning of the Roberts Court's Term, Neal Devins disagreed with Frickey on this point, stating a belief that the Roberts Court would not likely rely much on the doctrine of constitutional avoidance.[213] First, Devins said, Congress is less engaged in constitu-

---

[208] For a classic PPT criticism of the concept of collective congressional intent, see Kenneth Shepsle, *Congress Is a "We," Not an "It": Congressional Intent as an Oxymoron*, 12 Int'l Rev L & Econ 239 (1992). As applied to courts, see Adrian Vermeule, *The Judiciary Is a They Not an It: Interpretive Theory and the Fallacy of Division*, 14 J Contemp Legal Issues 549 (2005).

[209] See Ackerman, Balkinization Blog (cited in note 195) ("If Roberts and Kennedy don't have the courage of their convictions now, will they really lead the charge when the Obama justices are forcefully resisting, and legal momentum is on their side?").

[210] See Harold J. Krent, *Avoidance and Its Costs: Application of the Clear Statement Rule to Supreme Court Review of NLRB Cases*, 15 Conn L Rev 1, 1 (1983) (noting the "great latitude" avoidance-like doctrines give to the Supreme Court and the ad hoc nature of some Court decisions to invoke the avoidance canon).

[211] Frickey, 93 Cal L Rev 397 (cited in note 33).

[212] Id at 463–64.

[213] Devins, 32 U Dayton L Rev at 345 (cited in note 32).

tional matters and less interested in dialogue than during the Warren Court era. Second, Congress does not seem poised to strike back at the Court. And third, Congress did not significantly respond during the Rehnquist Court era when the Court struck down all or part of thirty-one statutes on federalist grounds, so there is no reason for the Court to fear Congress.[214]

Devins may have been wrong about the Court's interest in dialogue with Congress, at least as to those statutes, like the VRA, which might be constitutionally saved. The Court may be embarking on a new era of dialogue with Congress, at least for "fixable" statutes.

Then again, even if the Roberts Court has no interest in dialogue, or in protecting civil liberties at a time of national peril, the Court still may find good reason for selective use of avoidance and anti-avoidance. The rare use of anti-avoidance lays down constitutional markers and builds a fence around the majority's view of proper constitutional boundaries. The avoidance canon gives the public appearance of a Court moving moderately and slowly. Notably, the headlines after *NAMUDNO* were about the Court "upholding" and "preserving" though "narrowing" the VRA,[215] not about it taking the next step toward striking the VRA down. If the agenda of the Roberts Court is major change in constitutional law, the calculation may be that medicine usually goes down more palatably when in small doses.

---

[214] Id.

[215] See the headlines collected by Howard Bashman at his "How Appealing" blog on June 23, 2009, online at http://howappealing.law.com/062309.html#034476.

AZIZ Z. HUQ

AGAINST NATIONAL SECURITY EXCEPTIONALISM

Terrorist attacks trigger novel policy responses. New policies selected by the federal executive after the 9/11 attacks strained against
constitutionally permissible margins. Affected individuals lodged
legal challenges to the new policies in federal court. Judges' responses ranged from self-abnegating denials of jurisdiction to un-
equivocal repudiations of the executive's initiatives. The diversity
of judicial responses prompted debate and analysis. The resulting
scholarly literature is largely normative. Sustained attention to
"what courts actually do" has been "sparse."[1] Nevertheless, the normative accounts of courts' role in national security emergencies that
now dominate the legal scholarship include not only evaluative "justification[s]" but also efforts at descriptive "fit."[2] That is, the dominant accounts of judicial responses to national security crises each
offer, with varying degrees of conviction, a descriptive account of

Aziz Z. Huq is assistant professor of law, University of Chicago Law School.

AUTHOR'S NOTE: Many thanks to participants at a University of Chicago Law School
faculty workshop for helpful and insightful criticism. I am grateful for comments from
Daniel Abebe, Emily Berman, Adam Cox, Rosalind Dixon, Bernard Harcourt, Alison
LaCroix, Saul Levmore, Jonathan Masur, Richard McAdams, Martha Nussbaum, Eric
Posner, Adam Samaha, Stephen Schulhofer, Geoffrey Stone, and especially David Strauss.
All errors, of course, are mine alone.

[1] Cass R. Sunstein, *Judging National Security Post-9/11: An Empirical Investigation* *2
(unpublished manuscript, 2008), online at http://papers.ssrn.com/sol3/papers.cfm?abstract_id
=1297287.

[2] The distinction is adapted from Ronald Dworkin, *Law's Empire* 254–58 (Harvard,
1986).

225

what courts in fact do in national security emergencies. Each account further claims that courts do something *distinctive* in these
cases. This descriptive claim—that what courts do in national security crises is somehow different from what they do elsewhere—
in turn underwrites theories of what courts should do differently
in security emergencies. I call the threshold descriptive claim "national security exceptionalism."[3]

This essay examines the descriptive claim that judicial responses
to national security emergencies are in some fashion distinctive and
hence warrant special, separate justification or criticism. I argue that
"national security exceptionalism" finds no empirical support in at
least one important class of post-9/11 cases: challenges to emergency detention policies.[4] In the litigation trenches, judicial responses to national security emergencies do not match up with the
responses predicted by any of the dominant theories found in the
literature. Rather, they align more closely with transubstantive
trends in public law and with judicial responses to nonsecurity emergencies. This suggests there is nothing *sui generis* about the behavior
of courts in instances of national security exigency, or at least that
the thesis of exceptionalism is overstated.

One case from the October 2008 Term places in clear relief the
close and largely unexamined relationship between national security
jurisprudence and the larger domain of public law doctrine and
practice. In *Ashcroft v Iqbal*, a five-Justice majority of the Court
dismissed as inadequately pleaded a civil damages suit filed by a
Pakistani national detained in the immediate aftermath of the 9/11
attacks.[5] On the one hand, *Iqbal* can be viewed (and indeed has been
understood) as the most recent in a run of cases in which the Court

---

[3] I use this term to describe only judicial responses to national security emergencies.
None of the accounts address—and I am not concerned with—each and every case that
might conceivably be subsumed under a "national security" label, from servicemen's religious liberty claims, see *Goldman v Weinberger*, 475 US 503 (1986) (holding that First
Amendment does not prevent Air Force from prohibiting yarmulkes), to clashes between
environmental rules and military training needs, see *Winter v Natural Resource Defense
Council, Inc.*, 129 S Ct 365 (2008) (overturning a preliminary injunction against the Navy
that was based on threat to marine wildlife).

[4] The kind of case study approach here raises problems of sample bias and selection
effects. In my view, the noncriminal detention cases are the most consequential in terms
of both security and liberty; they are also the most contentious. If this analysis simply
throws light in a nonquantitative way on the direction and general motivating factors
behind judicial intervention, I believe it contributes to the literature.

[5] 129 S Ct 1937 (2009) (dismissing for failure to state a claim a damages action by
former immigration detainee against two high-level federal officials).

has grappled with the granularity of the threshold pleading rule in federal civil actions.[6] On the other hand, Justice Kennedy's majority opinion in *Iqbal* transformed dramatically the basic pleading rule largely by dint of emphasizing the national security context of the case at bar. *Iqbal* illustrates one side of the relationship between national security case law and the larger domain of public law: Emergencies are opportunities for sweeping doctrinal and functional changes affecting many subject matters. The other side of the coin is the pervasive influence of familiar remedial and doctrinal strategies in what has been characterized as a unique body of national security jurisprudence.

Rejecting the descriptive claim of national security exceptionalism has consequences for understanding and evaluating federal courts' work in the face of national security exigency. Analyzing judicial responses to national security emergencies in tandem with the larger body of public law draws attention to transubstantive trends in judicial behavior, and also to the role that emergencies can play in catalyzing larger changes across public law. The analysis may have a further bearing on the emergent "national security" discipline in the legal academy.

The argument proceeds in three parts. Part I explores the disjunction between the outcomes predicted by the dominant accounts of national security jurisprudence and litigated outcomes. Part II compares national security cases first to a larger domain of public law and, second, to a recent nonsecurity emergency in which the federal courts played a minor role. Part III concludes by offering some tentative hypotheses about the consequences of rejecting the descriptive claim of national security exceptionalism.

I

The literature on judicial responses to national security emergencies is diverse but largely normative. In one corner are celebrations of judges' countermajoritarian role as a "corrective" to the popular democratic tendency "to give inadequate weight to civil liberties in wartime" or crisis, when panic and other emotions distort

---

[6] See, for example, *Bell Atlantic Corp. v Twombly*, 550 US 544, 556 (2007); *Erickson v Pardus*, 551 US 89, 93–94 (2007) (per curiam). Even before it was decided, *Iqbal* was viewed as the continuance of this line of cases. See Robert G. Bone, *Twombly, Pleading Rules, and the Regulation of Court Access*, 94 Iowa L Rev 873, 877 (2009).

policy outcomes.[7] In another are prescriptions of broad judicial deference on the ground that "there is no general reason to think that judges can do better than government at balancing security and liberty during emergencies."[8] Intermediate positions posit judges as agents of social learning,[9] or praise their fidelity to separation-of-power ideals.[10] Seemingly disparate, these accounts are alike in two important ways. First, each makes some descriptive claim, relatively strong or weak, about what federal courts do in cases touching on national security emergencies.[11] Such descriptive claims of "fit" are made in support of normative arguments. Second, all the descriptive claims share a common assumption: Each asserts there is something distinctive about the pattern of judicial supervision of emergency national security policies. Because each theory aspires to justify a normative account of the judicial role distinct to national security, it paints judicial behavior in the exigent national

---

[7] Geoffrey R. Stone, *Perilous Times: Free Speech in Wartime from the Sedition Act of 1798 to the War on Terrorism* 544 (W. W. Norton, 2004). Accord Stephen Holmes, *The Matador's Cape: America's Reckless Response to Terror* 233 (Oxford, 2007) ("Wartime leaders . . . need some form of adversarial process to protect them from cognitive bias and false certainties.").

[8] Eric A. Posner and Adrian Vermeule, *Terror in the Balance: Security, Liberty, and the Courts* 31 (Oxford, 2007).

[9] Mark Tushnet, *Defending Korematsu: Reflections on Civil Liberties in Wartime*, 2003 Wis L Rev 274.

[10] Samuel Issacharoff and Richard H. Pildes, *Between Civil Libertarianism and Executive Unilateralism: An Institutional Process Approach to Rights during Wartime*, 5 Theoretical Inq L 1 (2004).

[11] All of the accounts discussed here trade in descriptive claims even if they are largely normative. The descriptive claims can be isolated from the larger prescriptive frameworks. First, the "social learning" thesis looks to "historical examples" and "identifies a pattern in those examples." Tushnet, 2003 Wis L Rev at 274 (cited in note 9). Second, the "heroic" countermajoritarian model is the most cautious of the five in advancing descriptive claims. See generally Stone, *Perilous Times* at 542–50 (cited in note 7). But some of its advocates propose that "the Court [has] imposed essential checks on executive power." Erwin Chemerinsky, *The Assault on the Constitution: Executive Power and the War on Terrorism*, 40 UC Davis L Rev 1, 17 (2006). Third, the executive accommodation view purportedly "describes the law as it has actually operated in the courts." Posner and Vermeule, *Terror in the Balance* at 16 (cited in note 8). Fourth, national security minimalists say that "an identifiable form of minimalism captures the practices of the American courts when national security is threatened." Cass Sunstein, *Minimalism at War*, 2004 Supreme Court Review 47, 50; see also Cass R. Sunstein, *Clear Statement Principles and National Security: Hamdan and Beyond*, 2006 Supreme Court Review 1, 1 ("Liberty-promoting minimalism can be found at diverse stages of American history."). Finally, bilateralism institutional endorsement is offered as the "framework for analysis that American courts have used in earlier eras of exigent circumstances." Issacharoff and Pildes, 5 Theoretical Inq L at 5 (cited in note 10). Whatever the larger normative projects of these accounts, in each case there is a descriptive element that plausibly can be isolated. In each case, the descriptive claim implies that judicial behavior in national security cases is distinctive.

security context as different from judicial behavior at other times. Implicitly or explicitly, the theories assume that some factor unique to national security emergencies—for example, the tendency of democratic governments to echo public panics, the breakdown of multibranch deliberation, or the executive's informational advantage and agility—already shapes what courts do. National security exceptionalism is thus underwritten implicitly by the sense that judicial behavior changes in response to the unique dynamics of a security emergency.[12]

This part begins by sketching briefly the five dominant theoretical accounts in the literature that identify regularities in judicial responses to national security policies on the way to making normative claims about what courts should do. It then describes the observed consequences of federal court litigation in one particular area of law—noncriminal detention on national security grounds. Specifically, I gauge consequences by looking at judges' selection between different remedies. This focus on remedies is central to my analytical method. Remedies provide a more fine-grained tool for assessing the consequences of judicial action than dichotomous metrics such as win/loss rates or tendencies to deference that are used in other studies. Finally, I consider whether any of the five dominant theoretical accounts generate good predictions of observed outcomes.

Three caveats are in order. First, this part isolates descriptive elements from accounts that are largely normative. To the extent they include description, the theories of the judicial role in national security on offer generally do not try to predict *every* case outcome in the way that a theory in the physical sciences might. Instead, a theory will "set an agenda" or "prescribe a direction" that fits a majority or large plurality of cases.[13] It will also provide a baseline to identify and to criticize outlying results.[14] A perfect hit rate is neither demanded nor ever found.

---

[12] National security exceptionalism could take strong and weak forms. The strong form suggests that a unique dynamic directs outcomes in all cases touched by national security concerns. The weak version of national security exceptionalism suggests that *exigent* responses to national security threats elicit different judicial responses from exigent policies in other policy domains. This weak version of national security exceptionalism, which seems more plausible, is the one principally examined here.

[13] David A. Strauss, *The Intellectual Crisis of Judicial Conservatism* *9 (unpublished manuscript, July 2009) (on file with author).

[14] See, for example, Posner and Vermeule, *Terror in the Balance* at 271 (cited in note 8) (describing the result in *Hamdan* as "lawless").

Second, theoretical accounts of the role of courts in regard to national security tend to operate at a high level of generality. None of the accounts examined in this part identifies which judicial remedies it would prescribe or predict in particular cases, nor even discusses the question of remedial selection at all. This is a failing of each account. It is not clear that the cost to analytic parsimony from closer attention to the question of remedies would be great. But the absence of discussion of remedies also means that none of the theoretical accounts can be criticized directly for failing to predict particular outcomes.[15] As a result, the analysis in this part must proceed by trying as best as possible to identify the distribution of remedies implied by a given theoretical account, and then by comparing that inferred set of outcomes to the observed outcomes.

Third, one counterargument to my analytic project would point out that some of the theoretical accounts considered here are not limited to national security. Hence, it might be argued, they make no claim to identify a unique pattern of judicial responses in national security cases. Minimalism, to pick the most obvious candidate, took shape first as a general account of the judicial role.[16] The object of criticism here, the claim of descriptive "uniqueness," is thus chimerical. But this counterargument is overstated. Even theories with broader normative ambitions are presented as especially attractive in the national security domain because the latter is one area of law in which courts follow the normative prescription. Consider minimalism, the most generalizable of the five theoretical accounts considered. Minimalism is presented as especially successful in the national security arena even though, its proponents concede, in other areas of the law it is only aspirational.[17] Minimalism may have broad ambitions, but its narrow claim to descriptive success is articulated most powerfully with respect to national security jurisprudence. Hence it is properly classified as a kind of national security exceptionalism.

---

[15] It seems to me unsatisfying, though, to defend a theory against the allegation of inaccuracy with the assertion that the theory operates only on a higher level of generality. Why bother with a general theory of judicial review in a given policy space if it bears no relation to judicial outcomes on the ground?

[16] See generally Cass Sunstein, *One Case at a Time: Judicial Minimalism on the Supreme Court* (Harvard, 1999).

[17] See Cass R. Sunstein, *Problems with Minimalism*, 58 Stan L Rev 1899, 1910–15 (2006) (describing challenges to minimalism).

A

Scholarly attention to the judicial role respecting national security has produced five accounts of the federal courts' function: (i) the "social learning" thesis, (ii) heroic countermajoritarianism, (iii) the executive accommodation account, (iv) national security minimalism, and (v) bilateral institutional endorsement. Each theory is "a set of interrelated causal propositions" that "hol[d] out the . . . promise of a successful explanation."[18] The five theories also each leverage a descriptive account of what courts do to support a normative prescription about what courts should do.[19] The descriptive and the normative converge. Exceptions are cause for condemnation and criticism.

The first account of the judicial role in national security is the "social learning" model. This model offers an explanation of judicial outcomes within a larger framework of historical change. Social learning views judicial intervention as a cog in "a process of social learning in which past examples of what come to be understood as incursions on civil liberties progressively reduce the scope of civil liberties violations in wartime."[20] The government acts; the courts endorse; but then "society" concludes that the threat was exaggerated and the response excessive.[21] *Korematsu v United States*[22] furnishes the archetypal example. Both democratic branches of the national government adopted a sweeping detention policy later endorsed by the federal courts. Subsequently, "society reache[d] a judgment that the action was unjustified and courts mistaken."[23] Rather than providing affirmative guidance for subsequent decisions, the ensuing precedent exerts a negative gravity by instantiating the Court's moral nadir.[24]

---

[18] Jon Elster, *Explaining Social Behavior: More Nuts and Bolts for the Social Sciences* 17 (Cambridge, 2007).

[19] See note 11 (collecting citations and quotations of descriptive claims for each account).

[20] Tushnet, 2003 Wis L Rev at 275 (cited in note 9).

[21] Id at 287.

[22] 323 US 214 (1944).

[23] Tushnet, 2003 Wis L Rev at 287 (cited in note 9); Stone, *Perilous Times* at 537 (cited in note 7).

[24] See, for example, *Stenberg v Carhart*, 530 US 915, 953 (2000) (Scalia, J, dissenting) (invoking *Korematsu* and *Dred Scott*, as negative examples of Court at its worst); *Reno v Flores*, 507 US 292, 344 n 30 (1993) (Stevens, J, dissenting) (urging that any attempt to follow *Korematsu* must proceed with "extreme caution"); *Skinner v Railway Labor Executives' Ass'n*, 489 US 602, 635 (1989) (Marshall, J, dissenting) (same); see also *City of Richmond*

Second, the "heroic" model views the federal judiciary as a coun-termajoritarian check on the political branches' tendency to trade away constitutional entitlements in moments of crisis. Like the social learning model, it starts from the view that at times when "the nation faced extraordinary pressures—and temptations" to suppress dissent and to target vulnerable minorities, politicians have succumbed to those pressures and have gone "too far" de-taining and punishing individuals for their views or because of their ethnic, racial, or religious identity.[25] On this account, the constituent pressure on government to engage in animus-based measures lacking sound justification increases in wartime. For ad-vocates of the heroic model, the "countermajoritarian difficulty" then becomes a "striking" advantage for the federal courts.[26] In-sulated by life tenure, judges will resist the momentary heat wave of invidious motives better than elected officials.[27] It is predictable and "appropriate," on this account, that "the judiciary gives greater protection to civil liberties than the legislature or the executive."[28]

Third, the "executive accommodation" model insists on the dex-terity and informational advantages of the executive over both other branches, and argues on this basis that judicial interventions will in the aggregate do more harm than good. This model is based on the observation that the executive has an institutional advantage in responding to emergencies because of its ability to aggregate and process information, to respond quickly, and to do so in secret.[29] Judicial action will be characterized by high error rates because courts lack information and suffer from the same distorting influences as the democratic branches. At the same time, "erroneous judicial invalidation of new security policies can pro-duce large harms."[30]

---

v *J. A. Croson Co.*, 488 US 469, 501 (1989) (invoking *Korematsu* as a reason not to defer to official justifications for the use of race in government decision making).

[25] Stone, *Perilous Times* at 12–13 (cited in note 7); id at 528–30; see generally David Cole, *Enemy Aliens: Double Standards and Constitutional Freedoms in the War on Terrorism* (New Press, 2003); Erwin Chemerinsky, *Civil Liberties and the War on Terrorism*, 45 Wash-burn L J 1, 14 (2005).

[26] Stone, *Perilous Times* at 543 (cited in note 7); cf. Alexander Bickel, *The Least Dangerous Branch: The Supreme Court at the Bar of Politics* 16 (Bobbs-Merrill, 1986).

[27] See, for example, Chemerinsky, 40 UC Davis L Rev at 17 (cited in note 11).

[28] Stone, *Perilous Times* at 544 (cited in note 7).

[29] See generally Posner and Vermeule, *Terror in the Balance* at 15–129, 161–81 (cited in note 8) (canvassing other checking devices).

[30] Id at 45.

The fourth model is national security minimalism.[31] Minimalism in general is characterized by a preference for "shallowness"—incompletely reasoned decisions that eschew theorization of divisive fundamental issues—and "narrowness"—resolution of as few legal or factual disputes as feasible per decision.[32] Standing alone, minimalism is "a strictly procedural instruction" that generates no guidance as to the choice between government and a private litigant.[33] In the national security context, minimalism has three traits: a demand for clear congressional authorization, the requirement of individual "hearing rights," and a preference for "narrow, incompletely theorized decisions."[34]

The final account of courts' role in national security, "bilateral institutional endorsement," endows the judiciary with a democratic deliberation-forcing function. It suggests courts are not well placed to make first-order decisions about the allocation of substantive liberties. Judges' comparative advantage instead lies in identifying the appropriate institutional arrangement to generate optimal policy decisions.[35] In war and emergency, as power ebbs to the executive, judges insist on a sharing of decisional power between the two elected branches "with different democratic pedigrees, different incentives, and different interests."[36] On this account, better decisions emerge from the judicially mandated participation of multiple democratic actors.[37] The courts' goal, therefore, is the forcing of multibranch democratic deliberation at a time when such deliberation has been short-circuited by exigency.

B

What have federal courts in fact done? Do any of these theories

---

[31] The model is developed in Sunstein, 2006 Supreme Court Review at 1 (cited in note 11); see also Sunstein, 2004 Supreme Court Review at 47 (cited in note 11).

[32] Sunstein, 2004 Supreme Court Review at 48–49 (cited in note 11); see generally Cass R. Sunstein, *Burkean Minimalism*, 105 Mich L Rev 353, 362–66 (2006).

[33] Posner and Vermeule, *Terror in the Balance* at 19 (cited in note 8).

[34] Sunstein, 2004 Supreme Court Review at 53–54 (cited in note 11).

[35] Issacharoff and Pildes, 5 Theoretical Inq L at 5 (cited in note 10) (stressing "process-based, institutionally-focused approach"); Samuel Issacharoff, *Political Safeguards in Democracies at War*, 29 Oxford J Legal Stud 189, 190 (2009).

[36] Issacharoff and Pildes, 5 Theoretical Inq L at 5 (cited in note 10).

[37] See also Bruce Ackerman, *Before the Next Attack: Preserving Civil Liberties in a Time of Terror* 139 (Yale, 2006) (arguing that courts should preserve the political equilibrium between the political branches).

successfully predict the responses of courts in actual cases? The purely descriptive literature is "sparse."[38] Studies to date have examined invalidation rates, panel effects, and the longitudinal interaction between wartime and changes to aggregate judicial protection of rights.[39] Previous empirical analyses have looked in the main at win/loss rates but elide important questions of what *form* judicial intervention takes.

To take stock of the effect of judicial interventions into exigent national security policy-making, I look instead at what remedies courts have issued. A focus on remedies is instrumentally useful as a means of getting at the consequences of judicial intervention for three reasons. First, remedial selection is more varied and more consequential in practical terms than metrics such as win/loss rates or decisions to defer or not. Judges have within reach a range of remedial strategies, including injunctions and damages actions. Injunctive relief can also be tailored by being granted ex ante or ex post. Or it can be issued in retail or wholesale form. When courts toggle between damages and various injunctive forms, costs and gains to security or liberty may vary. Inattention to remedies thus elides significant differences.

Second, attention to remedies and their effects illuminates important timing questions and downstream consequences. It invites particular scrutiny of the question whether an individual judgment's effect rippled out to change larger institutional practices.

Third, a focus on remedies is more informative than separate treatment of substantive and procedural rules. For one thing, substantive rulings have been few and far between in the post-9/11 context. Little has turned on whether substantive constitutional rules are weakened in crisis times.[40] By contrast, procedural rulings have been consequential. The cash value of judicial intervention is a function of both interlocutory and final jurisdictional and procedural rulings that have little directly to do with the relative

---

[38] Sunstein, *Judging National Security Post-9/11* at 2 (cited in note 1).

[39] Id; Lee Epstein et al, *The Supreme Court During Crisis*, 80 NYU L Rev 1 (2005).

[40] See generally Jenny Martinez, *Process and Substance in the "War on Terror,"* 108 Colum L Rev 1013 (2008). One way of explaining this result is by noticing the relative absence of criminal cases. Courts thus have few opportunities for what might be called offensive remediation—dealing with government overreach by, say, dismissing an indictment. Rather, they have instead engaged in defensive remediation by denying motions to dismiss on jurisdictional grounds and by demanding do-overs with more or different procedure. Hence, there have been fewer opportunities for merits rulings and more scope for policy arbitrage through procedural manipulation.

strength of substantive rules in times of crisis.[41] At least in the set of cases under examination here, there is thus "no room for a distinction between the abstract, analytic definitions of constitutional rights and remedial concerns that prevent courts from enforcing those rights to their 'true' limits."[42]

I attend here to one especially active area of national security law in which courts are relatively unbounded by statutory limits or channels: new noncriminal detention policies that emerged in response to the September 2001 al Qaeda attacks. National security concerns, of course, impinge also on the criminal law, surveillance regulation, federal disclosure law, immigration law, and financial regulation of charitable giving. But noncriminal detention is a useful object of isolated attention. It too presents novel legal issues, complex implementation challenges, and a rich body of case law. Unlike criminal cases or litigation under the Freedom of Information Act,[43] noncriminal detention litigation does not channel courts into a statutorily determined menu of responses. It thereby enables a study of courts' remedial selections largely undistorted by most exogenous constraints.[44]

Requests for judicial supervision in noncriminal detention cases after September 2001 have taken four forms: injunctive relief granted before the government acts against an individual; injunctive relief granted to an individual after government has acted coercively; relief that restructures ongoing government operations (even if it is not in the technical form of a structural injunction); and damages remedies secured after a constitutional, statutory, or treaty right is violated. These four kinds of judicial relief diverge along several metrics. In opting between injunctions and damages,

---

[41] There is a large literature on whether courts should adjust substantive rules or remedies. See, for example, Mark V. Tushnet, *Weak Courts, Strong Rights: Judicial Review and Social Welfare Rights in Comparative Constitutional Law* (Princeton, 2006). Whatever use the distinction has in the social rights context, it is insufficiently granular (or largely irrelevant) as a tool for parsing what happens in contemporary national security cases.

[42] Daryl Levinson, *Rights Essentialism and Remedial Equilibrium*, 99 Colum L Rev 857, 924 (1999).

[43] 5 USC §§ 552 et seq.

[44] Remedies in national security detention cases will, however, be distorted by a selection effect because the executive will choose ex ante between legal forms of detention based on its estimation of the expected judicial response. To the extent that almost all forms of detention—criminal, administrative, and military—were tried in somewhat haphazard fashion after 9/11, this selection effect does not appear to preclude the comparative analysis proposed here.

courts select between property rules and liability rules.[45] Judges also toggle along a temporal scale between more or less ex ante or ex post action. They can allow either retail or wholesale interventions. Remedial choice is thus multifaceted and complex.

A synoptic view of the consequences of federal courts' intervention suggests that judicial selection of remedies in national security cases is asymmetrical. It is biased away from the granular toward the molar. Courts grant injunctive relief that disrupts and reorders the structure of entire government programs. They generally do not grant retail preliminary injunctive relief or individualized final injunctive remedies. Nor have litigants typically prevailed in suits for money damages pursuant to federal statutes, international law, or the Constitution. The post-9/11 remedial distribution is thus tilted toward broad remediation and away from individually tailored equitable relief or remedies at law. To illustrate this, I survey first individualized injunctive relief and damages, and then turn to what might be termed the more "structural" forms of intervention.

1. *Individual injunctive relief.* Injunctive relief can be sought before coercive government action happens. The warrant requirement for surveillance is a well-known example of ex ante regulation. Warrant requirements in the Fourth Amendment and the Foreign Intelligence Surveillance Act (FISA), as amended in July 2008, impel some limited prior judicial supervision of electronic surveillance in the national security context.[46] Although a warrant rule may alter the pool of surveillance requests, evidence of recent changes to eavesdropping policy is hard to discern. Even under the pre-2001, more stringent iteration of FISA, few warrants were denied.[47] Federal courts also have rejected efforts to impose more rigorous ex ante regulation on electronic surveillance.[48]

In noncriminal detention cases, ex ante remedies are vanishingly rare. No court has ever granted a remedy to an individual to

---

[45] Eugene Kontorovich, *Liability Rules for Constitutional Rights: The Case of Mass Detentions*, 56 Stan L Rev 755, 757–62 (2004). The canonical delineation of the property/liability rule distinction is Guido Calabresi and A. Douglas Melamed, *Property Rules, Liability Rules, and Inalienability Rules: One View of the Cathedral*, 85 Harv L Rev 1089 (1972).

[46] See, for example, FISA Amendments Act of 2008, § 702 (b)(1)-(5), Pub L No 110-261, 122 Stat 2436 (2008).

[47] Note, *Shifting the FISA Paradigm: Protecting Civil Liberties by Eliminating Ex Ante Judicial Approval*, 121 Harv L Rev 2200, 2205–06 (2008).

[48] *American Civil Liberties Union v National Security Agency*, 493 F3d 644 (6th Cir 2007).

prevent seizure or detention. Logistical difficulties obviously limit such remediation. Lawyers are scarce on the battlefield outside of law-school hypotheticals. In practical terms, government actors control and often can delay access to the courts for days or weeks. Despite the infrequency of ex ante intervention, the Supreme Court has in dicta disapproved of such relief. In *Hamdi v Rumsfeld*, a plurality singled out "initial captures," which "need not receive . . . process," as distinct from the judicially regulated subsequent "determination[s] . . . to *continue* to hold those who have been seized."[49] Four years later, the Court underscored that same message to lower federal courts.[50] As a practical and as a legal matter, federal courts are not now nor have they ever been in the business of regulating the direct application of coercion.

By contrast, litigants who have been detained for some time do seek—and at one point fleetingly enjoyed—some ex ante relief from changes to the circumstances of ongoing confinement. But the availability of such relief is diminishing. Litigants detained at Guantánamo have sought relief from certain aspects of their confinement and from anticipated transfers to third countries. Citing fears of torture, some Guantánamo detainees from 2005 onward sought and sometimes secured judicial orders requiring the government to provide them with thirty days' notice of any transfer from the base.[51] However, more recent requests for notice have been denied on jurisdictional grounds.[52] Similarly, requests for preliminary injunctive relief related to conditions of confinement and medical treatment have failed.[53]

---

[49] *Hamdi v Rumsfeld*, 542 US 507, 534 (2004) (plurality) (emphasis in original). *Hamdi*'s presumption is undertheorized. One of the challenges of regulating detention policy is the ample space for government circumvention and evasion. The more one locus or form of detention is regulated, that is, the more the regulated activity will shift to policy spaces with lower transaction costs. Allowing habeas jurisdiction to attach at the moment of capture is one way of mitigating the circumvention problem, whatever its other costs.

[50] *Boumediene v Bush*, 553 US 723, 128 S Ct 2229, 2275–76 (2008).

[51] See, for example, *al-Shareef v Bush*, No 05-2458, 2006 WL 3544736 (DDC, Dec 8, 2006); *Kurnaz v Bush*, No 04-1135, 2005 WL 839542 (DDC, Apr 12, 2005); *Al-Marri v Bush*, No 04-2035, 2005 WL 774843 (DDC, Apr 4, 2005). Cf. *Almurabi v Bush*, 366 F Supp 2d 72 (DDC 2005) (denying preliminary injunction but requiring notice). But see *O.K. v Bush*, 377 F Supp 2d 102 (DDC 2005) (denying preliminary injunction). As of March 2006, one commentator identified twenty-seven pro-detainee decisions and six progovernment decisions. Robert Chesney, *Leaving Guantanamo: The Law of International Detainee Transfers*, 40 U Richmond L Rev 657, 667 (2006).

[52] See, for example, *Zalita v Bush*, 2007 WL 1183910 (DDC, Apr 19, 2007).

[53] See *Al-Adahi v Obama*, 596 F Supp 2d 111 (DDC 2009) (force-feeding); *In re Guan-*

The Supreme Court's 2008 decision in *Munaf v Geren* minimizes the likely availability of ex ante injunctions against transfers.[54] In *Munaf*, the Court consolidated review of habeas petitions from two U.S. citizens seized and detained in Iraq. In one case, the detainee successfully sought injunctive relief from lower courts against transfer to Iraqi criminal custody based on fears of torture.[55] A unanimous Supreme Court not only chastised the lower court for granting preliminary injunctive relief but found it "appropriate to proceed further" to the merits issues not adjudicated below to hold that "the Constitution [does not] preclude[e] the Executive from transferring a prisoner to a foreign country for prosecution in an allegedly unconstitutional trial."[56] While *Munaf* does not directly concern transfers from Guantánamo Bay, its foreign-policy-based deference to the executive's third-country dealings sounds in general terms. As applied by the D.C. Circuit, it renders extensive ex ante judicial supervision of transfers from Guantánamo or elsewhere nugatory.[57] Injunctive relief to prevent a harmful action, even long after an initial seizure, will thus likely remain a rarity.

A second variety of injunctive remedy is sought after the government has taken coercive action against an individual in circumstances where that coercive action persists in time. Detention, most obviously, endures over time and is remedied by an injunction. Detainees typically seek injunctive relief in the form of a writ of habeas corpus to dissolve ongoing detention and to secure release.

Despite the volume and rancor of political and legal debate over the availability of habeas corpus for detainees situated outside the territorial United States, individualized habeas relief as a direct result of a federal court order remains elusive. As of January 2010, federal courts had issued final judgments finding no lawful detention authority in thirty-two cases. But, only eleven detainees had

---

tanamo Bay Detainee Litigation, 570 F Supp 2d 13 (DDC 2008) (intrabase transfers); *Al-Ghizzawi v Bush*, No 05-2378, 2008 WL 948337 (DDC, Apr 8, 2008) (medical treatment).

[54] 128 S Ct 2207 (2008). Caveat lector: I was counsel for habeas petitioners in this case.

[55] *Omar v Harvey*, 416 F Supp 2d 19 (DDC 2006).

[56] *Munaf*, 128 S Ct at 2220.

[57] Accord *Kiyemba v Obama*, 561 F3d 509 (DC Cir 2009) (denying injunctive relief against transfers of Guantánamo detainees to possible torture based on *Munaf*).

been released.[58] A formal release order in a habeas case, therefore, is an uncertain predictor of de facto relief. Overall, 575 prisoners have been released from Guantánamo between 2002 and January 2010.[59] Final judgments in habeas cases were thus directly and proximately linked to relief in less than two percent of actual releases from Guantánamo. Implicitly recognizing this reality, district courts no longer direct release as a remedy but instead order "all necessary and appropriate diplomatic steps to facilitate . . . release."[60]

Habeas's individualized efficacy is unlikely to grow with the transition from the Bush to the Obama Administration. One of the central policy puzzles related to the closure of the Guantánamo detention operation is how to release detainees who are unable to return to their home countries due to a substantial risk of torture. After *Boumediene v Bush*'s[61] ruling on habeas's availability at Guantánamo, both Congress and the federal courts imposed new impediments to individual injunctive remediation via habeas involving release into the United States. In Congress, for example, riders attached to 2009 appropriations legislation bar certain transfers from Guantánamo to the United States, and impose fifteen-day notice rules for transfers to third countries.[62] Complicating the picture further, the Court of Appeals for the D.C. Circuit has also rejected release into the United States as a habeas remedy for detainees who cannot be transferred to third countries for fear of torture.[63] That D.C. Circuit judgment was slated for review by the Supreme Court in 2010 until superseding events prompted

---

[58] For data and further analysis, see Aziz Z. Huq, *What Good Is Habeas?* Const Comm (forthcoming 2010) (manuscript at 15). See also Chisun Lee, *An Examination of 31 Gitmo Detainee Lawsuits*, Propublica (Sept 29, 2009), online at http://www.propublica.org/special/an-examination-of-31-gitmo-detainee-lawsuits-722.

[59] *Transferred—The Guantanamo Docket*, NY Times, online at http://projects.nytimes.com/guantanamo/detainees/transferred.

[60] See, for example, Order, *Al Rabiah v Gates*, No 1:02-cv-00828-CKK (DDC, Sept 17, 2009), online at http://media.miamiherald.com/smedia/2009/09/17/22/rabia.source.prod_affiliate.56.pdf.

[61] 128 S Ct 2229 (2008).

[62] See, for example, Supplemental Appropriations Act 2009, Pub L No 111-32, HR 2346, § 14104(a) (2009) ("None of the funds made available in this or any prior Act may be used to release an individual who is detained as of the date of enactment of this Act, at Naval Station, Guantanamo Bay, Cuba, into the continental United States, Alaska, Hawaii, or the District of Columbia.").

[63] *Kiyemba v Obama*, 555 F3d 1022 (DC Cir 2009).

the Court to decline jurisdiction.[64] In short, doctrinal and legislative hurdles mean that, even in cases where a district court finds
no lawful basis for detention and orders release, the habeas judgment as an individual remedy will remain underrealized.

2. *"Structural" rulings.* There is a class of habeas cases in which
federal courts have granted relief that has had the expected and
realized consequence of transforming the institutional structure
of a national security program in dramatic and wide-ranging ways.
Individual petitioners do not, however, always benefit. The causal
vector is largely indirect. Three cases in particular have intervened
in ongoing security operations and wrought significant changes in
the constraints to which the government is subject. The relief in
these cases is somewhat akin to that achieved by a structural injunction.

The first of these cases is *Rasul v Bush,*[65] where the Court ruled
that detainees seized at extraterritorial sites can challenge the legality of their detention in civilian courts and are not limited to
the procedures that the military affords. (*Boumediene v Bush* merely
reaffirmed the institutional rewiring achieved by *Rasul* and provided further specification of its geographic ambit.[66]) In the same
Term as *Rasul,* the Court in *Hamdi* displaced the then-existing
procedural mechanism used to sort detainees and ordered the use
of a vaguely defined but presumably more robust alternative.[67]
Whereas *Rasul* altered the institutional site of detainee screening,
Hamdi prescribed details about the content of such screening. The
net effect of these two rulings was institutional transformation.
Nine days after judgment in those cases, the Department of Defense announced a new, two-tier procedural apparatus at Guantánamo for the processing and designation of all detainees
therein.[68] This procedural apparatus aimed to conform to *Hamdi's*
direction by supplying internal process. The perceived price of
institutional autonomy from judicial scrutiny was internal pro-

---

[64] *Kiyemba v Obama,* 130 S Ct 458 (Oct 20, 2009) (granting writ of certiorari), vacated
and remanded 130 S Ct 1235 (Mar 1, 2010).

[65] 542 US 466 (2004).

[66] 128 S Ct 2229, 2259–63 (2008). See also *Al Maqaleh v Gates,* 604 F Supp 2d 205
(DDC 2009) (allowing some detainees at Bagram, Afghanistan, to seek habeas relief).

[67] 542 US 507, 527–34 (2004) (plurality).

[68] Memorandum from Paul Wolfowitz, Deputy Sec'y of Defense, to Gordon R. England,
Sec'y of the Navy (July 7, 2004), online at http://www.defenselink.mil/news/Jul2004/
d20040707review.pdf.

cedural reform and the attendant risk of further releases.

In the third case, *Hamdan v Rumsfeld*,[69] the Court again used an individual habeas petition as a vehicle for institutional transformation. *Hamdan* extinguished a November 2001 executive initiative to establish military commissions for persons captured in overseas counterterrorism operations. In so doing, it set benchmarks for any new commission system. A pointed concurrence lingered on perceived democratic flaws in the commission's original creation.[70] The Court's critique of military commissions further "depend[ed] explicitly on substantive concerns" about fairness and accuracy.[71] The *Hamdan* decision set in motion another institutional transformation. Less than four months after the judgment, Congress enacted the Military Commission Act of 2006, in part responding to the Court's critique with a rewired system of military tribunals.[72] As with *Rasul* and *Hamdi*, an individual habeas action netted a significant institutional shake-up. But the *Hamdan* Court also went out of its way to stress the absence of individualized habeas relief.[73]

The *Hamdan* Court's structural reform ambitions went further than mere reorganization of military commissions. The decision also addressed questions of detainee treatment that had been a focus of public and legislative debate since 2004. Its effects thus rippled beyond the military. In a holding collateral to its main result, the *Hamdan* Court decreed that Common Article 3 of the 1949 Geneva Conventions[74] extended to detainees at Guantánamo and beyond.[75] The majority likely knew that Common Article 3's prohibition on "outrages upon personal dignity, in particular hu-

---

[69] 548 US 557 (2006).

[70] Id at 613–35. See also id at 637 (Breyer, J, with Kennedy, Souter, and Ginsburg, JJ, concurring).

[71] Martinez, 108 Colum L Rev at 1056 (cited in note 40).

[72] Pub L No 109-366, 120 Stat 2600 (2006) (codified in scattered sections of 10, 18, and 28 USC). New military commissions are authorized in § 3(a)(1) of the act, codified at 10 USC § 948b(b).

[73] *Hamdan*, 548 US at 635 (noting "the Government's continued power to detain [Hamdan] for the duration of active hostilities").

[74] Geneva Convention (III) Relative to the Treatment of Prisoners of War, Aug 12, 1949, Art 3, 75 UNTS 135, 136. Each of the four 1949 Geneva Conventions uses common language to articulate a baseline set of norms for "conflicts not of an international character occurring in the territory of one of the High Contracting Parties." Id.

[75] *Hamdan*, 548 US at 632. The Court had already held that the military commissions at issue violated Articles 21 and 36 of the Uniform Code of Military Justice. Id at 624–25.

miliating and degrading treatment" had a direct bearing on interrogation and detention practices separate from the procedural issues at stake in *Hamdan*. As President Bush explained, the Court's reorientation of the benchmarks for interrogation "put in question" operations by diverse agencies, including the CIA, which had not been party to the *Hamdan* litigation.[76]

Hamdan's Common Article 3 holding catalyzed further institutional transformation. Eight days after the judgment, the Deputy Secretary of Defense issued a memorandum directing all services to conform to Common Article 3.[77] A year later, this instruction was superseded by a presidential directive setting forth a more reticulated and arguably weaker understanding of Common Article 3.[78] *Hamdan*, therefore, began an extended sequence of changes to the terms and conditions of detainee treatment and interrogation not only by the armed services at Guantánamo, but more broadly by all federal agencies at diverse geographic locations. An unexpected collateral effect has been to push interrogation operations into the hands of allied countries, such as Pakistan and Egypt, with fewer restraints on torture or illegal treatment.[79] This globalized displacement effect has been little analyzed.[80]

3. *Damages*. Numerous suits for money damages have been lodged against the government in respect to noncriminal detentions after the 9/11 attacks. Several of these proceeded under the *Bivens* right of action.[81] Others rested on statutory rights of action,

---

[76] President George W. Bush, President Discusses Creation of Military Commissions to Try Suspected Terrorists (Sept 6, 2006), online at http://www.whitehouse.gov/news/releases/2006/09/print/20060906-3.html (on file with author). The ambit of Common Article 3 had long been of concern to the Administration. See David J. Barron and Martin S. Lederman, *The Commander-in-Chief at the Lowest Ebb—Framing the Problem, Doctrine, and Original Understanding*, 121 Harv L Rev 689, 707 n 48 (2008) (describing 2002 Justice Department suggestion that application of Common Article 3 to counterterrorism operations might infringe Article II powers of the President).

[77] Memorandum from Gordon England, Deputy Sec'y of Defense, on the Application of Common Article 3 of the Geneva Conventions to the Treatment of Detainees in the Department of Defense to Department of Defense Officials (July 7, 2006), online at http://www.fas.org/sgp/othergov/dod/geneva070606.pdf. Deputy Secretary England claimed that this involved no change in policy, which is a stretch.

[78] Interpretation of the Geneva Conventions Common Article 3 as Applied to a Program of Detention and Interrogation Operated by the Central Intelligence Agency, Exec Order No 13340, 72 Fed Reg 40707 (2007).

[79] See Eric Schmitt and Mark Mazzetti, *U.S. Relies More on Aid of Allies in Terrorism Cases*, NY Times (May 23, 2009).

[80] See Huq, Const Comm (cited in note 58) (discussing displacement effects).

[81] See *Bivens v Six Unknown Named Agents of the Federal Bureau of Narcotics*, 403 US 388

including the Religious Freedom Restoration Act[82] and the Torture Victim Protection Act.[83] No case to date has advanced under the generally available vehicle for federal tort liability, the Federal Tort Claims Act.[84] Almost all damages suits challenging extraterritorial detention operations failed. In the domestic arena, challenges to policies and patterns of detention and arrest also have failed, but some actions seeking damages for ambient abuse or discrimination by low-level officials have proceeded to discovery, or, in a couple of instances, have settled. At best, damages actions provide a means to challenge isolated acts of abuse, but no avenue for effecting larger programmatic change. The Supreme Court's judgment in *Iqbal* will have little effect on this basic picture.

Before *Iqbal*, damages actions arose in response to five different kinds of detention decisions. First, federal law enforcement authorities used the "material witness" statute to detain at least seventy suspects in relation to terrorism investigations across the United States.[85] Two sued. One, Brandon Mayfield, a Portland, Oregon, lawyer erroneously detained in relation to the March 2004 Madrid bombings, secured a $2 million settlement after it emerged that forensic evidence upon which his arrest had been made was grossly flawed.[86] Another sought damages for his detention from federal and state officials, overcoming motions to

---

(1971). *Bivens* established a private right of action for damages under the Fourth Amendment.

[82] 42 USC §§ 2000bb et seq. See, for example, *Rasul v Myers*, 563 F3d 527, 532–33 (DC Cir 2009), cert denied 130 S Ct 1013 (Dec 14, 2009).

[83] 28 USC § 1350 note; see, for example, *Arar v Ashcroft*, 532 F3d 157, 162 (2d Cir 2008).

[84] The absence of claims under the Federal Tort Claims Act (FTCA), 28 USC §§ 1346(b), 2671–80, is a result of statutory exceptions that encompass most national-security-related torts, including "[a]ny claim arising out of the combatant activities of the military or naval forces during time of war," § 2680(j); many claims arising out of "assault, battery, false imprisonment [or] false arrest," § 2680(h); "any claim arising in a foreign country," § 2680(k); and any claim based on "the exercise or performance or the failure to exercise or perform a discretionary function," § 2680(a), which shields most discretionary policy judgments. Individual suits are no substitute for actions against the United States because of the Federal Employees Liability Reform and Compensation Act, or Westfall Act, see Pub L No 100-694, 102 Stat 4563 (1988), which allows the United States to be substituted for individual officer defendants sued for actions taken within the scope of their employment, and thereafter channels suit into the FTCA.

[85] 18 USC § 3144; Human Rights Watch, *Witness to Abuse: Human Rights Abuses under the Material Witness Law Since September 11* at 16 (June 2005).

[86] Eric Lichtblau, *U.S. Will Pay $2 Million to Lawyer Wrongly Jailed*, NY Times (Nov 30, 2006).

dismiss by defendant former Attorney General John Ashcroft.[87] This result is arguably in some tension with the new and more stringent pleading rules specified in *Iqbal* and discussed below.

The second kind of domestic detention—in military custody via "enemy combatant" designation—was rare, even among the wave of first responses to 9/11. Among the three "enemy combatants" detained in the United States, one waived his right to sue as a condition of release.[88] The only one to sue for damages, Jose Padilla, aimed at a former government lawyer in one law suit based on allegations that the lawyer played an instrumental role in designing torturous interrogation protocols.[89] The action survived a post-*Iqbal* motion to dismiss based on the alleged insufficiency of the allegations.[90] The ensuing decision is a possibly vulnerable outlier. While citing *Iqbal*, the district court did not analyze extensively the effect of that case on pleading rules.

Third, the government used immigration powers in its post-9/11 investigation to detain at least 750 noncitizen suspects pending inquiry by the FBI. Immigrants detained in that period, whether clearly linked to the attacks or not, were ranked by varying degrees of "interest." To enable continuing FBI investigations, some were subject to continued detention even after being cleared of immigration-related charges. Conditions of confinement were significantly harsher than those in routine immigration custody. During the ensuing detentions, some noncitizens endured physical or verbal abuse, as well as denials of access to legal counsel or medical care.[91] Suits arising from this program of immigration detention challenged both policy decisions and discrete, dispersed, and individualized acts of discrimination and abuse. *Iqbal*, dis-

---

[87] See *Al-Kidd v Ashcroft*, 580 F3d 949 (9th Cir 2009) (denying qualified immunity). See also *Al-Kidd v Gonzales*, No CV 05-093-EJL-MHW, 2006 WL 5429570 (D Id, Sept 27, 2006); *Al-Kidd v Gonzales*, No CV 05-093-EJL-MHW, 2008 WL 2795137 (D Id, July 17, 2008) (dismissing conditions claims).

[88] Motion of Defendant to Stay Proceedings, *Hamdi v Rumsfeld*, No 2:02CV439 ¶ 13 (ED Va, Sept 24, 2004), online at http://www.humanrightsfirst.org/us_law/inthecourts/hamdi_briefs/Hamdi_Agreement.pdf.

[89] See Complaint, *Padilla v Yoo*, No 08-CV-0035 (ND Cal, Jan 4, 2008), online at http://jurist.law.pitt.edu/pdf/YooComplaint.pdf.

[90] *Padilla v Yoo*, 633 F Supp 2d 1005 (ND Cal 2009).

[91] See generally U.S. Department of Justice, Office of the Inspector General, *The September 11 Detainees: A Review of the Treatment of Aliens Held on Immigration Charges in Connection with the Investigation of the September 11 Attacks* 2–5 (April 2003), online at http://www.usdoj.gov/oig/special/0306/index.htm.

cussed further below, barred suits against policy-makers, but left open the possibility of suits against rank-and-file officials.[92] A companion case concerning similarly unsanctioned abuse during confinement settled in part for $300,000.[93] In another action, the federal courts dismissed challenges to the lawfulness of arrests—an issue going to investigative strategies—while allowing conditions claims to proceed to discovery.[94]

Fourth, military operations outside the United States have generated a significant volume of long-term detainees. The latter are either held by the U.S. government (e.g., in Guantánamo) or transferred to cooperating foreign governments. Detention operations at Guantánamo, in Iraq, and in Afghanistan have led to damages litigation. Unlike domestic actions, where challenges to conditions have gained some traction, these suits uniformly fail. Federal courts dismiss the complaints on the theory that plaintiff-detainees held overseas lack constitutional rights that can be vindicated via a damages action or because defendants benefit from qualified immunity.[95] The final and related category of suits involves detention that is outsourced to foreign sovereign proxies or moved to CIA "black sites." Two actions against government officials based on detention in a CIA "black site" and in the proxy custody of another sovereign (Syria) have been rejected based, respectively, on the "state secrets" doctrine and the "special factors" exception to *Bivens* liability.[96] By contrast, a suit against private companies allegedly involved in the same program survived dismissal efforts

[92] *Ashcroft v Iqbal*, 129 S Ct 1937, 1952 (2009) ("Respondent's account of his prison ordeal alleges serious official misconduct that we need not address here.").

[93] *Iqbal v Hasty*, 490 F3d 143, 147 (2d Cir 2007), rev'd sub nom *Ashcroft v Iqbal*, 129 S Ct 1937 (2009).

[94] *Turkmen v Ashcroft*, No 02-CV-2307, 2006 WL 1662663 *1 (EDNY, June 14, 2006), aff'd in part and rev'd in part, 589 F3d 542 (2d Cir 2009) (per curiam). Under the Second Circuit's ruling, the plaintiffs in the *Turkmen* case can pursue conditions challenges but not challenges to the duration of their confinement.

[95] See *Rasul v Myers*, 563 F3d 527 (DC Cir 2009), cert denied 130 S Ct 1013 (Dec 14, 2009) (after vacatur of an earlier judgment by the Supreme Court in light of *Boumediene*, reinstalling dismissal of constitutional, international law, and statutory causes of actions lodged by former Guantánamo detainees); *In re: Iraq and Afghanistan Detainees Litigation*, 479 F Supp 2d 85 (DDC 2007) (same for military detainees in Iraq and Afghanistan). Suits against private contractors not operating under exclusive military control have prevailed against motions for summary judgment. See *Ibrahim v Titan Corp.*, 556 F Supp 2d 1, 10 (DDC 2007) (distinguishing claims based on degree of military control).

[96] *El-Masri v Tenet*, 479 F3d 296, 308–11 (4th Cir 2007) (dismissal based on "state secrets" doctrine); *Arar v Ashcroft*, 585 F3d 559 (2d Cir 2009) (en banc) (dismissing suit based on insufficiency of allegations and absence of *Bivens* remedy).

grounded on the state secrets doctrine but will be subject to vigorous attack via appellate review.[97]

The Supreme Court's ruling in *Iqbal* will do little to change the daunting obstacles facing plaintiffs in these cases. *Iqbal* emerges from the third category: immigration detention. Javaid Iqbal, a Pakistani national, was arrested by FBI and immigration agents in November 2001 and detained in the Metropolitan Detention Center in Manhattan. In January 2002, he was transferred to a high-security unit called the Administrative Maximum Special Housing Unit (the "ADMAX SHU"), where he remained until July 2002. In April 2002, Iqbal pleaded guilty to federal criminal charges of conspiracy to defraud the United States and fraud in relation to identification documents. He was released in January 2003 and deported to Pakistan.[98] In May 2004, Iqbal filed damages actions against thirty-four current and former government officials. He did not challenge the legality of his initial arrest. His complaint instead alleged discriminatory assignment to the ADMAX SHU and unconstitutional beatings and denial of medical care. By the time his case reached the Supreme Court, the district court had rejected statutory claims of religious discrimination and conspiracy,[99] while the court of appeals had knocked out Iqbal's due process claims.[100] The Supreme Court granted plenary review to former Attorney General John Ashcroft and FBI director Robert Muller.[101]

Writing for a five-Justice majority, Justice Kennedy reversed the Second Circuit to hold that Iqbal had failed to plead sufficient facts to meet the pleading standard of Federal Rule of Civil Procedure 8(a)(2).[102] Some background is necessary to understand this procedural ruling. Rule 8(a)(2) was long understood to establish

---

[97] *Mohamed v Jeppeson Dataplan, Inc.*, 563 F3d 992, 997, en banc review granted 586 F3d 1108 (9th Cir 2009).

[98] See *Iqbal v Hasty*, 490 F3d 143, 147–49 (2d Cir 2007).

[99] *Elmaghraby v Ashcroft*, 04-CV-1409, 2005 US Dist LEXIS 21434 *95–*109 (EDNY, Sept 27, 2005).

[100] *Iqbal*, 490 F3d at 160–68.

[101] Compare *Ashcroft v Iqbal*, 128 S Ct 2931 (2008) (granting certiorari), with *Hasty v Iqbal*, 129 S Ct 2430 (2009) (granting and remanding in light of the Court's opinion in *Iqbal*).

[102] Rule 8(a)(2) requires "a short and plain statement of the claim showing that the pleader is entitled to relief."

notice pleading in federal civil practice.[103] Its drafters intended to "escape the complexities of fact pleading" under common law rules by opening wide the federal courthouse door and relying on post-discovery sorting to eliminate low-value suits.[104] The Court previously had rejected lower-court attempts to impose heightened pleading standards or new burdens of proof.[105] But in a 2007 anti-trust action, the Court changed course. It held that district courts must ascertain whether a complaint supports a "plausible" inference of liability in antitrust actions.[106] Muddying the waters further, another decision weeks later flipped back to the familiar notice pleading formulation.[107] Summarizing the resulting guidance to lower courts, Judge Cabranes of the Second Circuit Court of Appeals decried the law of pleading as "less than crystal clear and fully deserv[ing] reconsideration by the Supreme Court at the earliest opportunity."[108]

In response, the *Iqbal* Court held that the "plausibility" standard first suggested in 2007 was not confined to antitrust but applied generally to federal civil litigation. It established a two-stage test for "plausibility" presumptively applicable to all federal civil suits. First, a court should discard all "legal conclusions" and "mere conclusory statements" in a complaint. Second, it should ascertain if what remains "states a plausible claim of relief" in "context" by drawing on "judicial experience and common sense."[109] Applying this test, the Court reversed the court of appeals' judgment and remanded for a determination whether Iqbal should be allowed to replead.[110]

---

[103] See *Conley v Gibson*, 355 US 41 (1957) ("[A] complaint should not be dismissed for failure to state a claim unless it appears beyond doubt that the plaintiff can prove no set of facts in support of his claim which would entitle him to relief.").

[104] Richard L. Marcus, *The Revival of Fact Pleading Under the Federal Rules of Civil Procedure*, 86 Colum L Rev 433, 433, 437–40 (1986).

[105] See, for example, *Crawford-El v Miller*, 523 US 574, 593–95 (1998).

[106] *Bell Atlantic Corp. v Twombly*, 550 US 544, 556 (2007).

[107] *Erickson v Pardus*, 551 US 89, 93–94 (2007) (per curiam).

[108] *Iqbal v Hasty*, 490 F3d 143, 178 (2d Cir 2007) (Cabranes concurring).

[109] *Ashcroft v Iqbal*, 129 S Ct 1937, 1949–50 (2009).

[110] Before reaching the pleading question, the Court also confirmed the availability of interlocutory jurisdiction. *Ashcroft v Iqbal*, 129 S Ct 1937, 1945–49 (2009). It then held that supervisory liability based on a defendant's "knowledge and acquiescence" was not available, at least for intentional government torts, an argument that prompted a lengthy reply by Justice Souter, who argued that the majority had overlooked the defendants' concession on this point. Compare id at 1948 with id at 1955–58 (Souter, J, dissenting).

Putatively a case about an emergency national security policy, *Iqbal* will not change any trend in national security damages litigation. Plaintiffs in such cases already face a thicket of procedural hurdles from categorical exceptions to *Bivens* liability to the "state secrets" privilege to qualified and absolute immunity. These threshold doctrines already direct dismissal before discovery. By raising pleading standards, *Iqbal* does not change even the timing of likely dismissal. It just endorses a new legal theory on which dismissal may be grounded.[111] The basic pattern will remain the same: Challenges against discrete, isolated, and unauthorized acts of abuse sometimes prevail, but suits targeting allegedly unconstitutional policies will be turned away at the courthouse door. As discussed in more detail below, *Iqbal*'s effect on general civil litigation, however, was immediate and dramatic, in striking contrast to its consequences for the local domain of national security cases.[112]

4. *Conclusion.* A pattern emerges from this survey of post-9/11 case law about detention programs. Private litigants prevail in actions for what are de facto structural injunctions (although they do not have that technical legal form), which catalyze significant change in national security programs but yield few proximate benefits for the named petitioners. But private litigants meet limited or no success in seeking more tailored ex ante or ex post retail injunctions. Damages actions also are generally unavailing, except in a scattering of cases challenging discrete, isolated, and unauthorized acts of abuse or discrimination. *Iqbal* may render damages actions incrementally less likely to prevail. It is hard to see, though,

---

[111] Seemingly contrary to this view are the results in both *Al-Kidd* and *Padilla*. But these cases do not alter the basic fact of *Iqbal*'s inconsequentiality for national security. As an initial matter, it is unclear how to count decisions, such as *Al-Kidd* and *Padilla*, which do not grapple seriously with *Iqbal*'s reformulation of the pleading standard. Even if these cases are indicative of future trends—which seems doubtful—they are evidence that *Iqbal* is opaque and that its two-stage doctrinal rule is easy to circumvent. Just as some lower courts for years resisted the Supreme Court's direction to hew to notice pleading, see Christopher M. Fairman, *Heightened Pleading*, 81 Tex L Rev 551, 552 (2002), so now that the Court has pivoted to fact pleading other lower courts will resist that transition. It is not only that the judiciary is "a they, not an it," but that the "they" is saddled with imperfect mechanisms of internal doctrinal discipline. Cf. Adrian Vermeule, *The Judiciary Is a They, Not an It: Interpretive Theory and the Fallacy of Division*, 14 J Contemp L Issues 549, 554 (2005) ("Empirically, it is often costly or simply infeasible for the judiciary to coordinate upon a particular course of action, and to sustain that coordination to the degree necessary to affect the behavior of other institutions and actors.").

[112] See text accompanying notes 189–96.

this difference having much practical significance in the national security domain.

C

What can be learned from a comparison of the observed consequences of judicial intervention in exigent noncriminal detention policies with the patterns of judicial action described in or extrapolated from the five, largely normative theories above? A faithful explanation of the federal courts' role in national security must explain both judicial parsimony in ex ante injunctions and damages actions and also the more ample role of courts in issuing de facto "structural" injunctions that affect whole national security programs. If one of the five descriptive accounts outlined in Part I.A captured the observed distribution of results, this would be evidence it had isolated a distinctive dynamic motivating judicial outcomes in these particular national security cases. But none of the theories achieves this goal.

1. *The social learning thesis.* The social learning thesis does not easily cash out into any expected pattern of remedial outcomes. It operates across history and does not select between contemporary remedial options. It predicts though that synchronic variance between judicial and elite consensus will be small. Courts, therefore, will generally accord deference to claims of necessity but resist claims of government power that track or echo historically discredited models. Taking social learning seriously, courts after 9/11 would resist measures that resembled past discredited security efforts, while accepting innovations. Dissents from today's decisions that endorse novel security responses would one day be celebrated as prescient when new information emerges about the flaws in current security programs.

But this account does not describe well the actual outcomes, and it casts little light on the differential treatment of narrow versus broad-gauge remedies. As the basis for the claim that national security jurisprudence is exceptional, that is, the social learning thesis provides scant support. To the contrary, the Supreme Court has done little to cabin the use of race-based or ethnicity-based criteria as proxies for dangerousness, despite the aversive precedent of *Korematsu*. To be sure, the absence of a post-9/11 mass internment of Muslim-Americans might be credited to the "social learning" of *Korematsu*. Another explanation would focus on differences in political economy. In the World War II internment, rival agricultural interests eager for land were an important motivating force for a roundup of ethnic Japanese living on the west coast.[113] The absence of similar interest group pressure on the east coast explains the absence of German or Italian internment later in World War II, and may also better explain the absence of Muslim-American internment today.

Nor does *Iqbal* fit the social learning thesis. In hindsight, *Korematsu* at a minimum suggests that governments, after a security crisis, often act on the basis of invidious or inaccurate generalizations about disfavored minorities. Yet the *Iqbal* decision not only makes bias significantly harder to police, it also rests on carelessly racialized reasoning that even the government as litigator eschewed. As an initial matter, the *Iqbal* majority was cavalier about the risk of ambient animus distorting discrete outcomes in a national crisis. Leaning on his "experience and common sense," Justice Kennedy rejected out of hand circumstantial evidence of discriminatory intent in Iqbal's case. Noting that the 9/11 attacks were "perpetrated by 19 Arab Muslim hijackers . . . members in good standing of al Qaeda, an Islamic fundamentalist group . . . headed by another Arab Muslim," he asserted that it therefore came as "no surprise" that responsive policies had "a disparate, incidental impact on Arab Muslims."[114] "Common sense and experience" here served to deny Iqbal even the opportunity to identify bias through discovery.

Further, Justice Kennedy's logic is itself based on dubious premises about ethnicity and religion. As Judge Jon O. Newman explained in his opinion for the Second Circuit, "Iqbal is a Muslim and a Pakistani but not an Arab. . . . [H]is claim is fairly to be understood as alleging unlawful treatment . . . because officials believed, perhaps because of his appearance and his ethnicity, that he was an Arab."[115] Categorizing a Pakistani as an Arab, as Justice Kennedy does, is about as accurate as calling an American "European" based on a perception of shared ethnic heritage.[116] The

---

[113] Stone, *Perilous Times* at 292–93 (cited in note 7).

[114] *Ashcroft v Iqbal*, 129 S Ct 1937, 1951 (2009).

[115] *Iqbal v Hasty*, 490 F3d 143, 148 n 2 (2d Cir 2007).

[116] Justice Kennedy may be implying that possession of a religious identity—Muslim—suffices to warrant suspicion when it comes to terrorism today. But even the government's brief is careful to reject so sweeping a claim about religious identity. See Brief for Peti-

Court's opinion thus rests on the very act of plainly erroneous racial miscategorization that Iqbal attacked as invidious. In short, it is not only that the "social learning" thesis provides little basis for predicting or understanding observed results in the case law, but that *Iqbal* in particular casts doubt on whether the Court has learned much from its less noble history.

2. *The heroic model.* The heroic model is typically more aspirational than descriptive. If the heroic model is understood to rest on the assumption that democratic decision making under emergency pressure will tilt toward animus-inflected error, either along racial or ideological lines, then federal courts should police resulting policies vigorously, applying searching scrutiny to check their rationality. Recognizing that money damages fall short as a substitute for incommensurable constitutional entitlements,[117] at a minimum because of valuation difficulties, advocates of the heroic model might tilt toward ex ante solutions without abandoning residual judicial review via damages actions. The most insightful advocates of the heroic model, of course, are not Pollyannaish. They recognize that political constraints bind judges and that emergencies raise hard policy questions.[118] As a result, they may endorse some judicial hesitation to intervene by ex ante or even in media res injunctions.

But the result and reasoning of *Iqbal*, alongside the larger vacuum in damages actions, are difficult to square with a countermajoritarian thesis. Reliance on structural injunctions alone seems radically underinclusive of the heroic model's goals. That model also struggles with the absence of individualized injunctive relief. It thus may well be that the heroic model identifies one important feature of judicial thinking and strategy, but it also underplays the complex influence and interaction of other factors. The heroic model therefore cannot underwrite a descriptive claim of national security exceptionalism.

3. *The executive accommodation model.* Executive accommoda-

---

tioners in *Ashcroft v Iqbal*, No 07-1015, 129 S Ct 1937 (2009), at 31 (carefully refusing to contend that religious identity is a trait legitimately useful in investigations).

[117] Cf. *Carey v Piphus*, 435 US 247 (1978) (allowing award of nominal damages for procedural due process violation); see also *Memphis Community School District v Stachura*, 477 US 299 (1986) (rejecting valuation of abstract value of constitutional right).

[118] See Stone, *Perilous Times* at 544 (cited in note 7); David Cole, *"Strategies of the Weak": Thinking Globally and Acting Locally Toward a Progressive Constitutional Vision*, in J. M. Balkin and R. B. Siegel, eds, *The Constitution in 2020* at 297, 299–300, 306 (Oxford, 2009).

tionists favor roughly the opposite distribution of remedial out-comes from the heroic model. They will reject out of hand ex ante or in media res judicial interventions. They also will be leery of constitutional tort litigation to the extent it limits future options by articulating new constitutional norms to constrain subsequent executives. Emergencies are unpredictable along multiple axes; it is impossible ex ante to determine what rules will be bent in the next one.[119] Yet accommodationists may also see utility in com-pensation if it can be separated from the norm-enunciation func-tion of constitutional tort. They "fully agree" that "decisionmakers should at minimum take pains to commemorate the values or rights or interests that [were] overridden in the service of other commitments."[120] Indeed, if courts adjudicate damages actions af-ter some lapse of time—which is inevitable given the glacial pace of civil litigation in federal courts[121]—then information asym-metries and the comparative cost of judicial examination and cor-rection may have waned in the interim. The emergency itself is also more likely to have expired.[122]

The outcomes of cases decided since 9/11 do not converge on this pattern. To be sure, the observed distribution of remedies and their consequences illustrates federal courts' identification and in-sulation of a zone of discretion at the point of first contact between government and a threat. This explains the absence of ex ante remedies and the federal courts' reluctance, so manifest in *Iqbal*, to chill front-end discretionary decision making.[123] To the extent that the executive accommodation theory suggests that the role of courts trends stronger as time elapses after an emergency, how-ever, that theory finds little support in the judicial treatment of damages liability. Also, judicial remediation to date has clustered around the most invasive form of intervention—structural in-junctions—while more tailored options have been slighted. That

---

[119] Cf. Posner and Vermeule, *Terror in the Balance* at 18, 169 (cited in note 8) (noting that Congress may have "little information about the nature of future emergencies").

[120] Id at 296 n 9.

[121] See *Nken v Holder*, 129 S Ct 1749, 1754 (2009).

[122] See Adrian Vermeule, *Holmes on Emergencies*, 61 Stan L Rev 163, 191 (2008). Since damages actions look back to past actions temporally proximate to the emergency, rather than examining continuing policies, they are not a form of "ex post sunsetting" whereby judges rescind emergency powers once they determine that as a matter of fact the emer-gency has elapsed. Id.

[123] *Ashcroft v Iqbal*, 129 S Ct 1937, 1953 (2009).

result obviously cannot be accounted for by a thesis of deference.

4. *National security minimalism.* In its tripartite form of clear statement rule, hearing rights, and decisional thinness, minimalism is offered as a template that "to a remarkable degree, captures the practices of the American courts when national security is threatened."[124] National security minimalism does not, however, predict well the overall pattern of remedies in national security cases. Courts have forgone tailored individual remedies, whether ex ante or ex post, in favor of quasi-structural injunctions in *Hamdi*, *Hamdan*, *Rasul*, and *Boumediene*. Rather than just changing conditions for one litigant, these decisions have each prompted institutional transformation in large national security programs. *Hamdan*'s Common Article 3 holding in particular rewired not only military commission policy but also interrogation policy. The Court thus opted for wide-bore remedial strategies over a narrow approach. Its interventions disrupted government operations beyond the case at hand. Judicial responses in the national security context, that is, have been maximalist in important ways.

The ruling in *Iqbal* is also hard to square with minimalism along several dimensions. First, the Court's grant of certiorari was unusual[125] insofar as there was no clear conflict among the circuits on either question presented,[126] and the second question challenged a theory of government tort liability—supervisory liability by constructive notice—that had not been raised by the plaintiffs or decided below.[127] A truly minimalist Court would rather incline against review where legal issues do not cleanly fit Supreme Court Rule 10's criteria for review.[128] The votes for certiorari review in *Iqbal*, indeed, seemed driven less by the legal issues presented than

---

[124] Sunstein, 2004 Supreme Court Review at 50–51 (cited in note 11).

[125] A grant of certiorari is always unusual: In the 2007 Term, only 1.1 percent of the 8,374 petitions filed led to review. *The Statistics*, 122 Harv L Rev 522, 523 (2008).

[126] Compare Pet for Cert No 01-1015, *Ashcroft v Iqbal*, 129 S Ct 1937 (2009) at i (listing questions presented), with Sup Ct R 10 (listing grounds for review by certiorari). The petition strained to identify a conflict in the circuits on the pleading standard and did not assert that the conflict was the primary ground for granting review. See Petition for Certiorari at 18–21.

[127] See Brief in Opposition in No 01-1015, *Ashcroft v Iqbal*, 129 S Ct 1937 (2009) at 28–29.

[128] Rule 10(a) and 10(b) refer to divisions of opinion between courts the Supreme Court supervises respecting federal law; 10(c) covers "important question[s] of federal law."

by the identity of the petitioners.[129] Second, the majority opinion cannot be described as minimalist. It swept broadly by possibly eliminating supervisory liability in damages actions against government officials for violations of constitutional rights.[130] Even more significantly, it reordered pleading rules for federal civil actions in a manner that likely will generate future uncertainty and disparities between district courts. Third, the *Iqbal* Court resolved the pleading dispute on broader factual and legal grounds than those suggested by defendant-petitioners. The Court could have sidestepped the problem of racial or religious bias in law enforcement by picking up on the uncontested fact, raised by defendants' brief, that 578 of the 762 detainees targeted by the investigation were not identified as being of "high interest" or placed in the ADMAX SHU.[131] That is, it could have looked to uncontested facts as a means to respond to Iqbal's claim of bias. Despite its claims to descriptive success in the national security domain, minimalism thus fails to provide an accurate characterization of either the overall pattern of outcomes or specific results such as *Iqbal*.

5. *Bilateral institutional endorsement.* Like other accounts, bilateral institutional endorsement is presented as both descriptively accurate and normatively appealing.[132] Indeed, in his separate *Hamdan* concurrence, Justice Breyer invited renewed democratic deliberation in terms that echo this theory's logic.[133] Yet, as with the other dominant theoretical accounts, bilateral institutional endorsement does not generate sound predictions for two reasons. First, democratic deliberation has not been the touchstone that the theory suggests. Second, the theory itself lacks predictive force because it contains no account of when or why courts should find democratic deliberation inadequate.

The first problem is that bilateral institutional endorsement

---

[129] The petition is larded with references to the petitioners' ranks and the importance of being "a cabinet-level official or other high-ranking official." Petition for Certiorari in *Ashcroft v Iqbal*, No 07-1015, 129 S Ct 1937 (2009), at i.

[130] See note 110. Justice Kennedy's opinion is not wholly clear on this. But see *Ashcroft v Iqbal*, 129 S Ct 1937, 1957 (2009) (Souter, J, dissenting) ("Lest there be any mistake . . . the majority is not narrowing the scope of supervisory liability; it is eliminating *Bivens* supervisory liability entirely.").

[131] Brief for Petitioners in *Ashcroft v Iqbal*, No 07-1015, 129 S Ct 1937 (2009) at 33 n 4.

[132] Issacharoff and Pildes, 5 Theoretical Inq L at 5 (cited in note 10).

[133] *Hamdan v Rumsfeld*, 548 US 557, 636 (2006) (Breyer, J, concurring).

does not well explain constitutional rulings in cases such as *Hamdi* and *Boumediene*. The theory's proponents claim that *Boumediene* can be assimilated into this model as "an explication of the structural mechanisms that preserve" rights.[134] Yet the *Boumediene* Court rejected the twice-considered judgment of Congress that plenary habeas jurisdiction over Guantánamo was neither wise nor necessary. The Court not only found inadequate the jurisdictional scheme designed by the political branches but did so without even allowing that scheme to be tested and found wanting. Extending rights under the Suspension Clause and the Due Process Clause to detainees, the Court materially reduced the policy space of the political branches in the teeth of considered and repeated deliberative exercises of the democratic will.

The second, more serious concern with bilateral institutional endorsement's descriptive claim is its indeterminacy. Many cases in the national security domain, including *Hamdi*, *Hamdan*, and *Rasul*, hinge on whether a long-standing statute authorizes the executive branch to establish a novel policy that could not have been anticipated by the enacting Congress. The Court on occasion finds bilateral endorsement in statutory ambiguity.[135] Other times, it rejects innovation based on the absence of sufficient endorsement. Bilateral institutional endorsement supplies no theory to explain when and how the Court should read ambiguous statutes to support an innovative policy. Without this baseline, it cannot generate predictions in the large number of cases in which the Court is confronted by a claim of bilateral action grounded in legislative language of uncertain relevance.[136] Nor does the theory well explain what the Court has in fact done in the face of an ambiguous statute. In *Hamdi*, the relevant baseline seemed to be built of "fundamental and accepted . . . incident[s] of war."[137] But this term is far more opaque than district courts or commentators have recognized.[138] In *Hamdan*, the Court looked to a complex,

---

[134] Issacharoff, 29 Oxford J Legal Stud at 211 (cited in note 35).

[135] See, for example, *Hamdi v Rumsfeld*, 542 US 507, 518 (2004) (plurality).

[136] Issacharoff and Pildes do not miss this problem; they implicitly recognize it when they discuss whether to treat an ambiguous statute as authorization for a contentious executive action. See Issacharoff and Pildes, 5 Theoretical Inq L at 38–39 (cited in note 10).

[137] *Hamdi*, 542 US at 518 (plurality).

[138] The baseline is explored in Curtis A. Bradley and Jack L. Goldsmith, *Congressional Authorization and the War on Terrorism*, 118 Harv L Rev 2047 (2005).

and not entirely pellucid, blend of historical practice and statutory authorization. The Court may have a baseline in mind, in other words, but it may be a mutable and only partially conceptualized one that bilateral institutional endorsement does little to illuminate.

Analysis of *Iqbal* and the damages cases through the lens of bilateral institutional endorsement suffers from the same drawback: It is impossible to determine what the baseline is against which the Court should view the availability of a *Bivens* damages remedy. On the one hand, the Court might believe that Congress has acquiesced to the availability of a *Bivens* remedy because "'where federally protected rights have been invaded it has been the rule from the beginning that courts will be alert to adjust their remedies.'"[139] On the other hand, Congress might be presumed to recognize that today "the Court is reluctant to extend *Bivens* liability."[140] Absent some account of what the appropriate baseline is in damages actions, bilateral institutional endorsement cannot generate a meaningful prediction of results in damages cases any more than it yields forecasts of judicial responses to executive action resting on other marginal claims to statutory authority.

D

To summarize, five accounts of judicial responses to new national security policies can be identified in the current literature. Each makes a claim of descriptive fit as well as normative persuasion. Each singles out a unique judicial response to national security emergencies based on its understanding of what makes the policy environment after such an emergency distinct. But a review of the federal courts' remedial decisions in post-9/11 noncriminal detention cases suggests that none of these accounts yields a fully satisfying explanation of what courts are doing. This result provides a first reason for doubting the descriptive power of national security exceptionalism.[141]

---

[139] *Bivens v Six Unknown Named Agents of the Federal Bureau of Narcotics*, 403 US 388, 392 (1971) (quoting *Bell v Hood*, 327 US 678, 684 (1946)).

[140] *Ashcroft v Iqbal*, 129 S Ct 1937, 1948 (2009). This was as true of the Rehnquist Court as the Roberts Court.

[141] One possible response to this argument might go as follows. Even if taken individually none of these theories has explanatory power alone; in the *aggregate* they encompass all the reasons courts have to act. Hence, their cumulative force is explanatory. I am not convinced. In the absence of some algorithm to assign weights to and then aggregate these

II

This part develops a second reason for skepticism about national security exceptionalism. I argue first that the gap between judicial responses to national security emergencies and other problems of constitutional compliance within complex institutions and policies has been overstated. To a surprising degree, remedies in national security cases correspond to remedies in other areas of public law where federal courts have grappled with complex state institutions. I then examine one set of judicial responses to the financial crisis of 2008–09 to see whether courts behave differently in security and nonsecurity emergencies.

A

Federal courts have developed a distinctive set of rules and remedies in enforcing constitutional entitlements in policing, prisons, mental institutions, and education. While generalized accounts of this particular body of public law are sparse, some regularities are evident. In the larger corpus of public law, it is possible to discern trends in ex ante injunctions, ex post release via habeas, damages liability, and structural remedies. Examination of each of these four areas suggests that the judicial approach to national security cases is not as distinct as is generally believed from other public law domains. In both national security and general public law, there is an asymmetry between scarce-on-the-ground individual remedies and structural judicial orders that effectively reorganize government institutions. Benefiting a discrete litigant at bar is of secondary concern in both domains. Thus, common explanations may underlie judicial responses to exigent government programs in both national security and other public law contexts.

Why are there such strong similarities between the remedies in national security cases and those in other public law cases? There are several possible explanations. It may be that judges model, either consciously or instinctively, their remedial strategies on familiar approaches in public law (an effect amplified perhaps via

competing and irreconcilable accounts, the argument from aggregation is question-begging. I do not doubt that different judges are responding in different ways to the concerns raised by the five theories, or that collegial decision making might be characterized by cycling or unstable outcomes. I am merely suggesting here that the five theories alone do not help us while bracketing the more intractable question of how best to explain how judges behave.

precedential learning). Or it may be that screening devices at the courthouse door select for similar kinds of cases in the two domains. Alternatively, and more promisingly in my view, the correlation may be explained by reputational or other judicial motivations that reach across substantive doctrinal boundaries. But construction of a larger model of judicial motivation and behavior is beyond my aims here. My goal rather is solely to show that national security cases are not sharply different from other lines of public law jurisprudence.

Consider first the absence of ex ante injunctive relief in national security case law, identified in Part I.B. Ex ante prevention of potentially unconstitutional government action, especially involving coercion, is almost always the exception in other areas of public law. Doctrinal barriers from abstention rules to "political question" constraints to standing doctrine generally push judicial intervention away from the front end of government action. Plaintiffs cannot seek preemptive relief against anticipated government coercion without evidence that they specifically will be targeted.[142] In one area of police-citizenry contact frequently litigated in the Supreme Court—automotive stops—the Justices have stayed on the margins. "Officer safety" is the dominant concern of Fourth Amendment cases elaborating rules for encounters between police and drivers.[143] Even at the apogee of the Warren Court's criminal procedure jurisprudence, the "more immediate interest" that the Court recognized, documented, and protected was the protection of police against "unnecessary risk."[144] In its recent narrowing of the scope of permissible car searches incident to arrest, the Court still followed officer safety as its lodestar.[145] Current regulation of the use of police deadly force is also weak and ex post.[146] The regulatory vacuum at the sharp edge of national security policy,

---

[142] *City of Los Angeles v Lyons*, 471 US 95 (1983); *Laird v Tatum*, 408 US 1 (1972); cf. *United States v Richardson*, 418 US 166 (1974).

[143] See, for example, *Thornton v United States*, 541 US 615, 621 (2004). Even last Term's narrowing of auto stop search authority was careful to endorse officer safety as a trumping concern. *Arizona v Gant*, 129 S Ct 1710, 1716 (2009).

[144] *Terry v Ohio*, 392 US 1, 23 (1968). Chief Justice Warren included a detailed footnote documenting the risk to officers in police stops. Id at 24 n 21.

[145] See *Arizona v Gant*, 129 S Ct 1710, 1716 (2009).

[146] See Barbara Armacost, *Organizational Culture and Police Misconduct*, 72 Geo Wash L Rev 453, 466–78 (2004) (describing absence of criminal or civil remedies against officers or institutional for police use of excessive force).

in other words, is not distinct from the situation in analogous areas of social control. Rather, the national security case law is close to the norm rather than exceptional.

Second, the absence of individual release via habeas corpus in national security cases is in line with trends in relief when habeas is used as a postconviction remedy under 28 USC § 2254. In the national security context, even named habeas petitions in landmark cases win minimal individualized relief and do not secure release. For the habeas petitioner, victory on procedural grounds instead generally leads to more process, more delay, and thus more detention. Winning in the Supreme Court, for example, meant Hamdan risked at worst indefinite detention and at best protracted delay until the reconstitution of new military tribunals. Hamdi and the *Rasul* petitioners also won Pyrrhic remands and the prospect of extended future litigation. Like petitioners under the Administrative Procedure Act seeking reconsideration of a feeble agency rule, detainees often found that success had the practical result of deferring their desired goal.[147] Although *Rasul, Hamdi,* and *Boumediene* did lead to releases, these followed indirectly from changes in policy and not directly from compliance with specific judgments. Detainees acquitted in new military commission proceedings also do not thereby gain freedom. To the contrary, in July 2009 the general counsel of the Department of Defense emphasized that the government reserved the right to continue to hold terrorism-related detainees after an acquittal under a claim of wartime detention authority.[148]

The situation is strikingly similar to quotidian federal habeas review of state court criminal convictions. Federal postconviction review of state criminal judgments today yields vanishingly small returns. A 2007 study found that of 2,384 noncapital habeas cases sampled, only *eight* resulted in a grant of habeas relief, and one of those was reversed on appeal.[149] One account of the 2007 study

---

[147] For the asymmetry in the administrative law context, see Richard L. Revesz and Michael A. Livermore, *Retaking Rationality: How Cost-Benefit Analysis Can Better Protect the Environment and Our Health* 159–61 (Oxford, 2008).

[148] See Spencer Ackerman, *Obama Military Commissions Vision Takes Shape*, Wash Indep (July 7, 2009), online at http://washingtonindependent.com/49966/obama-military-commissions-vision-takes-shape. See also Testimony of Jeh Johnson, General Counsel, Department of Defense to United States Senate Committee on the Judiciary, July 28, 2009, online at http://judiciary.senate.gov/hearings/testimony.cfm?id=4002&wit_id=8157.

[149] Nancy J. King et al, *Final Technical Report: Habeas Litigation in U.S. District Courts: An Empirical Study of Habeas Corpus Cases Filed by State Prisoners Under the Antiterrorism*

concluded that "as a means of correcting or deterring routine case-specific constitutional errors, habeas is completely ineffective."[150] The parallel remedial lacuna in two very different contests does not necessarily prove that the underlying frequency of meritorious claims is similar in the two areas. Such a claim would be hard to sustain not least because the notion of a "meritorious" claim is endogenous to evolving procedural standards under the different sections of the federal habeas statute implicated by collateral review and executive detention cases.[151] Rather, the parallel shows simply that federal courts are equally unwilling or unable in two disparate applications of habeas to indulge in the individualized remedy of release.

Third, the difficulty of recovering money damages under *Iqbal* and its ilk is familiar from *Bivens* and constitutional tort jurisprudence more generally.[152] Reformers have long advocated a transition from individual to government liability,[153] even as other scholars evince skepticism about constitutional tort's deterrence value.[154] *Iqbal* adds little novel to the familiar moves in constitu-

---

and Effective Death Penalty 52, 58, 116 (2007), online at http://www.ncjrs.gov/pdffiles1/nij/grants/219558.pdf. Success rates are slightly higher in state court habeas actions. See Anup Malani, *Habeas Settlements*, 92 Va L Rev 1, 64–65 (2006).

[150] Joseph L. Hoffman and Nancy J. King, *Rethinking the Federal Role in State Criminal Justice*, 84 NYU L Rev 791, 793 (2009).

[151] See, for example, *Brecht v Abrahamson*, 507 US 619, 623 (1993) (announcing "substantial and injurious effect" test for certain constitutional errors in habeas).

[152] More recent empirical research suggests that prospects for *Bivens* plaintiffs are more sanguine. One study sampled cases from five federal district courts. It suggested that *Bivens* litigants prevail in roughly the same proportion of cases (16 percent) as other civil rights claimants, without controlling for clearly frivolous cases that are dismissed *sua sponte*. Alexander A. Reinert, *Measuring the Success of Bivens Litigation and Its Consequences for the Individual Liability Model*, 62 Stan L Rev (forthcoming 2010), online at http://papers.ssrn.com/sol3/papers.cfm?abstract_id=1475356. This is not inconsistent with the pattern of limited success observed in national security cases. Rather, the Supreme Court's disapproving view of *Bivens* claims persists across both national security and non-national-security cases. See, for example, *Wilkie v Robbins*, 127 S Ct 2588 (2007); *Correctional Servs Corp. v Malesko*, 534 US 61 (2001).

[153] Peter H. Schuck, *Suing Our Servants: The Courts, Congress, and the Liability of Public Officials for Damages*, 1980 Supreme Court Review 281, 307–10, 345–51 (making deterrence argument and commending entity liability). See also Larry Kramer and Alan O. Styles, *Municipal Liability under § 1983: A Legal and Economic Analysis*, 1988 Supreme Court Review 249, 290–94 (positing a negligence rule for municipal liability, as not eliminating personal liability where doing so would insulate potential tortfeasors, while isolating cases in which entities have cost-effective tools for minimizing malfeasance).

[154] See Daryl Levinson, *Making Government Pay: Markets, Politics, and the Allocation of Constitutional Costs*, 67 U Chi L Rev 345, 370–71 (2000). But see David Rudovsky, *Running in Place: The Paradox of Expanding Rights and Restricting Remedies*, 2005 U Ill L Rev 1119, 1125 (2005) (arguing that damages do deter).

tional tort law. Rather, *Iqbal* merely replays the Court's long-standing efforts to find some equilibrium between compensatory and expressive aims on the one hand, and the mitigation of disfavored deterrence effects on the other.[155] But the Court is not trading off between these two goals in any coherent way. The Court in *Iqbal* demoted tort's compensatory function. In another case the same Term, a unanimous Court marginalized constitutional tort's expressive function.[156] The net result is entrenchment of a regime of *de minimis* liability with no correlative expansion of the expressive or norm-clarification function. This regime is stable only because an elusive residual possibility of remediation suffices to deflate interest-group mobilization for congressional modifications.[157] Outright judicial repudiation of constitutional tort—so far a move the Court has not intimated—would probably be needed now to reset policy in any meaningful way.[158]

Further, it is not clear that the magnitude of deterrence effects from government tort liability would differ between the national security context and the larger public law context, and in which direction any variance from the mean would be.[159] The scale of any overdeterrence from damages awards (under *Bivens* but also under 42 USC § 1983) is not known. In part this is because the government often (but not always) provides defendants in individual liability suits with representation and pays settlements or judgments.[160] It is also not clear whether the risk of overdeterrence

---

[155] Compensation awards depend on a finding of liability, and hence have an asymmetrical deterrence effect on officials, who are focused to internalize the cost of mistakes even though they do not internalize the full benefit of their actions.

[156] See *Pearson v Callahan*, 129 S Ct 808 (2009) (rejecting the rule of *Saucier v Katz*, 533 US 194 (2001), that courts adjudicating qualified immunity defenses must ascertain whether a constitutional rule was violated before determining whether it was clearly established at the time of the alleged tort). *Pearson* saps the justification of qualified immunity as a means of reducing the transaction costs of innovation in constitutional norms. John C. Jeffries, Jr., *The Right-Remedy Gap in Constitutional Law*, 109 Yale L J 87, 92 (1999).

[157] See Cornelia T. L. Pillard, *Taking Fiction Seriously: The Strange Results of Public Officials' Individual Liability under Bivens*, 88 Geo L J 65, 68 (1999) (observing status quo in mid-1990s legislative efforts). In any case, it is hardly clear how the diffuse class of possible constitutional tort plaintiffs could overcome evident transaction costs to collective actions to seek legislated change.

[158] Cf. Eric A. Posner and Adrian Vermeule, *Reparations for Slavery and Other Historical Injustices*, 103 Colum L Rev 689, 693 (2003).

[159] Daryl Levinson has questioned both deterrence effects and deterrence-based rationales. See Levinson, 67 U Chi L Rev at 370–71 (cited in note 154).

[160] See 28 CFR § 50.15(a), (b) (indemnification regulations for Department of Justice employees); see Pillard, 88 Geo L J at 77 n 54 (cited in note 157) (listing indemnification

is greater or less in national security cases. It may be more because "[f]ear compels people"—including government officials—"to devote resources to solving a problem that for a dispassionate and uninvolved person may be interesting but not compelling."[161] Under this logic, there is simply more to deter. Alternatively, the prospect of compensation for errors may ease conscientious officials' discomfort, making more stringent exigent responses less costly and hence more frequent. Absent empirical evidence about the motivations of government officials, it is impossible to know whether or how deterrence operates differently in national security and in general constitutional tort law. Functionally as well as doctrinally, it is therefore hard to segregate national security from the larger domain of public law when it comes to damages.

The final trend that demands explanation is the surprising incidence of de facto "structural" injunctions in national security law. Here again, there is a correlation with trends in general public law. Federal courts have grappled now for decades with allegations of pervasive constitutional violations within "large-scale organizations, particularly government bureaucracies [that] define to a substantial degree our social existence."[162] In these contexts, just as in national security, there is a persistent "large gap between executive discretion and judicial capacities."[163] Individual remediation, from the judiciary's perspective, is a suboptimal strategy because it has little dampening effect on the rate of future violations. The close link between right and remedy typifying private-law adjudication breaks down in complex environments, precipitating judicial experiments with broader, process-based remedies.[164] In a range of areas of social policy, from prisons to policing and from psychiatric institutions to education, courts instead select interventions that ramify beyond an individual case "to unsettle and open up public institutions that have chronically failed to meet their obligations and that are substantially insulated from the normal

---

regulations for other agencies and departments). Pillard suggests that generally "indemnification is a virtual certainty." Id at 76–77.

[161] Posner and Vermeule, *Terror in the Balance* at 63 (cited in note 8).

[162] Susan P. Sturm, *A Normative Theory of Public Law Remedies*, 79 Geo L J 1355, 1386 (1991).

[163] Eric Posner and Adrian Vermeule, *The Credible Executive*, 74 U Chi L Rev 893 (2007); id at 890–93 (cataloging reasons why judicial oversight may fall short, even if not "a total failure").

[164] Sturm, 79 Geo L J at 1377, 1388 (cited in note 162) (listing distinctive features of public law remedies).

processes of political accountability."[165] Although structural injunctions common in the 1960s and 1970s are no longer frequent, similar remedial forms obtain today. These do not always take the form *sensu stricto* of structural injunctions celebrated by previous generations of legal scholars, but they are nonetheless orders that "see[k] to effectuate the reorganization of a social institution."[166] In a recent survey of de facto structural public law remedies, numerous judicial actions were identified in several areas of public policy that tended to "disentrench or unsettle a public institution when, first, it is failing to satisfy minimum standards of adequate performance and, second, it is substantially immune from conventional political mechanisms of correction."[167]

Interventions with structural consequences in the post-9/11 national security detention domain are analogous to these public law remedies. General public law remediation of defective institutions aims to include previously excluded voices, force systemic reform by imposing new standards of conduct drawn from other fields, and generate transparency mandates to "induc[e] the institution to reform itself."[168] Analogously, rulings adverse to the executive in national security detention have opened the policy-making field not only to the federal courts and Congress, but also to detainees via counsel. Against the executive's urgings, the Court imposes exogenous standards derived from international humanitarian law "to define minimum performance."[169] Merely by allowing cases to move forward, the federal courts additionally force transparency via attorney access and the availability of discovery. Repeated resort to orders with structural repercussions in national security case law is thus of a piece with federal courts' strategies in other areas of public law.

One especially intriguing parallel turns on the federal courts' use of the habeas remedy as part of a strategy of structural change in two quite distinct contexts. Federal court remediation of errors in state criminal adjudications is a relatively recent phenomenon.[170]

---

[165] Charles F. Sabel and William H. Simon, *Destabilization Rights: How Public Law Litigation Succeeds*, 117 Harv L Rev 1015, 1020 (2004).

[166] Owen Fiss, *The Civil Rights Injunction* 7 (Indiana, 1978).

[167] Sabel and Simon, 117 Harv L Rev at 1062 (cited in note 165).

[168] Id at 1056, 1062–73.

[169] Id at 1063.

[170] See Joseph L. Hoffman and William J. Stuntz, *Habeas after the Revolution*, 1993 Supreme Court Review 65, 73–76.

Only after the 1953 judgment in *Brown v Allen*[171] did habeas review of state criminal adjudication systems become a tool in the restructuring of state criminal justice processes. Habeas's shift was not an isolated event. It occurred at a time that the Court was simultaneously "radically transform[ing] the role of federal constitutional law in state criminal cases."[172] Habeas was a means "to retry new cases applying the newly created rules,"[173] one tool in the larger due process revolution that swept state criminal procedure during the Warren Court. Hence, whereas *Hamdan, Hamdi,* and *Boumediene* aim to bring military detention into procedural conformity with the Justices' ideal of due process, the post-*Brown* incarnation of habeas (which did not endure long past the Warren Court) was a way of bringing state criminal justice systems into conformity with another due process ideal. Far from being a tool of individual liberation one case at a time, perhaps the central purpose of twentieth-century and early twenty-first-century habeas has been justice at a systemic, aggregated level.[174]

One way of explaining the Court's willingness to grant sweeping structural remedies may be as a response to public and elite expectations of judges fostered by a heroic countermajoritarian narrative of the judicial role that was born in the second half of the twentieth century. On this account, Justices inherit and apply a heroic model of the federal courts exemplified best by *Brown v Board of Education*.[175] If Justices' role-conception and sense of prestige entails a commitment to a heroic model, they may prefer to channel interventions into high-profile cases in which their stance will be observed more widely and celebrated, further enhancing their prestige.[176] Individual remediation, notwithstanding periodic judicial

---

[171] 344 US 443 (1953) (holding that federal habeas courts were not precluded by state rulings on matters of constitutional right). Also significant was *Fay v Noia*, 372 US 391 (1963), which limited for a time the effect of state court procedural defaults.

[172] Hoffman and Stuntz, 1993 Supreme Court Review at 77 (cited in note 170). Even Gerald Rosenberg, who is otherwise skeptical of the efficacy of judicial action, attributes significance to decisions about the right to counsel. See Gerald D. Rosenberg, *The Hollow Hope: Can Courts Bring About Social Change?* 330–31 (Chicago, 1991).

[173] Lucas A. Powe, Jr., *The Warren Court and American Politics* 424 (Harvard, 2000). Powe properly cautions that many new rights were not retroactively applied. Id at 425–29.

[174] I do not mean to suggest, however, any conclusion about *how* effective quasi-structural injunctive litigation has been. This seems to me a hard, and properly contested, question.

[175] 347 US 483 (1954).

[176] Cf. Richard A. Posner, *What Do Judges and Justices Maximize? (The same thing everyone else does)*, 3 Sup Ct Econ Rev 1, 13–14, 31–32 (1993) (suggesting prestige and reputation, as part of judges' utility function).

verbiage about the value of individual rights,[177] secures the courts little political or reputational capital. It is thus slighted. More cynically, this account might be supplemented by the suggestion that the Justices' reputational motivations are constrained by the possibility, however remote, of the public backlash that would ensue if an individual who gains individual relief later goes on to participate in a terrorist conspiracy. Here, the Justices' beliefs about the public reception of decisions play a large role. A less cynical account would posit that the Justices are allocating scarce judicial time and public support to maximize their constitutional goals. On this account, the emphasis on structural interventions is simply a way to secure maximal policy change with limited tools under conditions of constraining political opposition.

There is, in sum, a correlation between courts' remedial strategies in national security law and in public law. Plausible accounts of the causal mechanisms behind this correlation can be imagined. Exploration of these causal accounts would demand further scrutiny beyond the scope of this article. The important point here is that the similarity between national security cases and the general public law is a second source of evidence that the national security exceptionalism hypothesis is flawed.

B

The mine run of public law cases is not the only body of jurisprudence against which judicial responses to national security emergencies might be compared. A second way of testing the exceptionalism thesis may be to look at judicial responses to crises that lack a national security dimension. By way of example, the financial crisis of 2008–09 precipitated numerous extraordinary legislative and executive initiatives designed to stave off an economic depression.[178] Despite claims that government responses

---

[177] See, for example, *Lujan v Defenders of Wildlife*, 504 US 555, 576–77 (1992) (justifying denial of standing on the principle, drawn from *Marbury v Madison*, 5 US (1 Cranch) 137, 170 (1803), that the role of the federal courts "is, solely, to decide on the rights of individuals").

[178] See, for example, Edmund L. Andrews, *Fed in an $85 Billion Rescue of an Insurer Near Failure*, NY Times (Sept 17, 2008) at A1 (calling AIG bailout "the most radical intervention in private business in the central bank's history"); Stephen Labaton, *Agency's '04 Rule Let Banks Pile Up New Debt, and Risk*, NY Times (Oct 3, 2008) at A1 (describing investment bank bailout as "the most serious financial crisis since the 1930s"); see also Andrew Ross Sorkin, *Too Big to Fail* 292–408 (Viking, 2009) (describing AIG bailout).

overstepped constitutional bounds,[179] judicial challenges to the diverse regulatory reactions to the financial sector's failure[180] have been few and far between. The one exception to this pattern— the challenge to the bankruptcy sale of the auto maker Chrysler's assets from Indiana-based pension and retirement funds—does not support the proposition that federal courts behave differently in national security emergencies than in nonnational security crises.

In April 2009, Chrysler filed a prepackaged Chapter 11 bankruptcy petition in the Southern District of New York with the support and involvement of the federal government. The petition proposed the transfer of substantially all of Chrysler's operating assets to a new entity to be part owned by the Italian firm Fiat.[181] Indiana pension and retirement funds attacked the sale as, among other things, a sub rosa reorganization.[182] After the bankruptcy judge and the Second Circuit signed off on the proposed bidding procedures and sale, the Second Circuit nevertheless temporarily stayed the sale so as to allow Supreme Court review.[183] Despite urgent pleas to enjoin the sale, and even though a sale would have been very hard subsequently to unwind, the Supreme Court declined to intervene via its emergency stay power.[184]

Two aspects of this complex litigation are salient here. First, as in the national security context, the federal courts identified "consequential and vexed"[185] constitutional issues in the asset sale but nonetheless declined an invitation to ex ante intervention. The Roberts Court resisted any temptation to follow the example of the Chase Court's short-lived and ill-fated effort, one hundred and fifty years previously, to regulate the Lincoln Administration's

---

[179] John Schwartz, *Some Ask if Bailout Is Unconstitutional*, NY Times (Jan 15, 2009) at A8 (describing some potential separation-of-powers concerns related to the government's response to the financial crisis).

[180] See Mark Zandi, *Financial Shock: Global Panic and Government Bailouts—How We Got Here and What Must Be Done to Fix It* 201–09 (Financial Times Press, 2009) (listing measures taken before stimulus legislation enacted).

[181] See *In re Chrysler*, 576 F3d 108, 111–12 (2d Cir 2009), vacated as moot 130 S Ct 1015 (Dec 14, 2009).

[182] See Douglas G. Baird, *Car Trouble* *12–17 (unpublished manuscript, December 2009) (on file with author) (discussing challenges to the sale of Chrysler's assets under 11 USC § 363). Cf. Todd Zywicki, *Chrysler and the Rule of Law*, Wall St J (May 13, 2009) (challenging Chrysler sale under Contracts Clause).

[183] *Chrysler*, 576 F3d at 112.

[184] *Indiana State Police Pension Trust v Chrysler LLC*, 129 S Ct 2275 (2009) (per curiam) (vacating temporary stay granted by Justice Ginsburg and denying stay).

[185] *Chrysler*, 576 F3d at 122.

emergency resort to paper money in response to the fiscal crisis created by the Civil War.[186] The absence of ex ante judicial regulation in this case echoes the pattern observed in public law more generally. Second, the mechanism of an asset sale used to reconstitute Chrysler in its "basic structure" is "increasingly . . . the norm."[187] That is, in its details as well as in the overall shape of judicial supervision, the federal courts' response to this part of the financial crisis did not break new ground but mimicked a pattern emerging under nonemergent conditions.[188] In sum, while this snapshot of judicial responses to the financial crisis is no doubt incomplete, it does provide an additional datum in support of the thesis of commonality between judicial responses across policy areas.

III

What is the significance of this continuity between remedial strategies in national security cases on the one hand and in public law generally on the other? If national security exceptionalism is either overstated or untenable, what follows for our accounts of judicial behavior in the national security domain? In the balance of this essay, I identify two possible lines of further exploration. One is analytic, the other normative.

The first possible lesson is analytic: To understand judicial responses in the national security domain, it is necessary to look at interactions between that area and transubstantive bodies of rules concerning procedures and remedies. This interaction can have implications both for substantive bodies of law—for example, the direction of national security law—and for transubstantive procedural and remedial rules. At the moment, however, interaction

---

[186] In *Hepburn v Griswold*, 5 US (8 Wall) 603 (1870), the Court invalidated the Legal Tender Act of 1862. *Hepburn* was overruled the following year by *Knox v Lee*, 79 US (12 Wall) 457 (1871); accord *Juilliard v Greenman*, 110 US 421 (1884).

[187] Baird, *Car Trouble* at *18–19 (cited in note 182).

[188] But will courts intervene with restructuring aspirations somewhere down the road, as they have done in other areas of public law? Consider an intriguing parallel: The 2002 Sarbanes Oxley Act, 15 USC §§ 7211–19, was another response to a (milder) financial crisis. Only in 2009, long after the accounting scandals of Enron and Worldcom had faded from the news cycle and the policy debate, was a systemic challenge to the institutional architecture subsequently put in place in the Supreme Court. See *Free Enterprise Fund v Public Co. Accounting Oversight Bd*, 537 F3d 667 (DC Cir 2008), cert granted 129 S Ct 2378 (2009). The *Free Enterprise Fund* suit is in effect a request for modification of government structure, just like the remedies sought and obtained in other areas of public law.

effects between substantive law and procedural rules are insufficiently studied.

Iqbal furnishes an example of this interaction. Consider the result in *Iqbal* from two different points of view: the decision's effect
on national security law and its impact on general civil litigation.
As national security litigation goes, *Iqbal* was a damp squib. It will
not have a significant effect on damages litigation in the area
because few claims prevail anyway.[189] But *Iqbal* works a sea change
in the general federal civil litigation landscape.[190] *Iqbal* "has ex-
ponentially expanded the reach of fact pleading" and repudiated
the notice pleading rule applied for more than fifty years.[191] In
even the first two months after it was handed down, *Iqbal* was cited
in 603 district court and court of appeals decisions;[192] it also triggered a movement for legislative reform.[193] Anecdotal data suggest
that the elevated citation rate reflects new decision costs that flow
from heightened uncertainty about an elemental pleading rule.[194]

This odd combination of local inconsequentiality and global
significance is the result of an interaction between a substantive
field of policy and transubstantive rules. The opinion manages this
feat because it muddies the distinction between national security
concerns and transubstantive procedural questions. Justice Kennedy warned of the "heavy costs" exacted when government officials are sued, costs present whenever the government is re-
strained[195] but "magnified" in the national security context.[196]
Justice Kennedy then implicitly reasoned from this local diagnosis
to a transubstantive result.

---

[189] See Part I.B above.

[190] Note that this is consistent with the claim in Part II that transubstantive law *correlates*
with the law of national security.

[191] Arthur R. Miller, *Access v. Efficiency: Reflections on the Consequences of Twombly and Iqbal*,
GCP (July 2009), Release Two at 2.

[192] Based on a search of the "ALLFEDS" database in Westlaw for "Iqbal /3 Ashcroft"
between May 19, 2009 and July 19, 2009.

[193] Tony Mauro, *Plaintiff Groups Mount Effort to Undo "Iqbal,"* Nat'l L J (Sept 21, 2009).

[194] See Adam Liptak, *9/11 Case Could Bring Broad Shift on Civil Cases*, NY Times (July
20, 2009).

[195] To the contrary, the same theme sounds in similar terms in other decisions insulating
prosecutorial decisions in criminal and immigration law from judicial inquiry. *Reno v
American-Arab Anti-Discrimination Comm.*, 525 US 471, 488 (1999) (rejecting judicial inquiry into selective enforcement in immigration law); *United States v Armstrong*, 517 US
456, 463–65 (1996); see also *McCleskey v Kemp*, 481 US 279 (1987).

[196] *Ashcroft v Iqbal*, 129 S Ct 1937, 1953 (2009).

Iqbal is not unique in this regard. In 1949, Judge Learned Hand wrote a path-marking opinion on official immunity in *Gregoire v Biddle*, which concerned the arrest and prolonged detention of a French national erroneously believed to be an enemy alien during the Cold War.[197] *Gregoire* provided the basis for the Supreme Court's twentieth-century resurrection of immunity doctrines based on concern about the possible chilling of official action in all areas, not just national security.[198] As in *Iqbal*, analysis of an issue apparently local to the national security context motivated a larger transubstantive change. Both *Gregoire* and *Iqbal* illustrate a mechanism beneath the oft-overlooked truism that "each dispute . . . affects others and reshapes the political landscape, inhibiting some behaviors and enabling others."[199] While some consequences of the efflorescence of a federal common law of official immunity are reasonably clear, it remains to be seen how *Iqbal*'s change in pleading rules will alter the pool of civil cases filed, especially in the national security domain, and how this change will in turn stimulate further shifts in the federal civil pleading regime or other transubstantive rules.

This kind of interaction may be frequent, even if not pervasive, in legal doctrine. Consider the interaction between the Court's changing attitude to the death penalty on the one hand and its adjustment of habeas rules on the other, or the interaction of standing doctrine with environmental law.[200] There is no reason national security law would be free of it. This dynamic also raises important institutional design questions. Consider, for example, the optimal approach to changing transubstantive procedural rules. On one account, *Iqbal* achieved this with low initial decision costs: Reliance on national-security-specific reasons eased the adoption of the new transubstantive rule. From a wider perspective, though, the wisdom of changing transubstantive rules through reasoning rooted in one substantive area of law may be doubted. Even if a more robust pleading rule were needed—a

---

[197] *Gregoire v Biddle*, 177 F2d 579, 579 (2d Cir 1949).

[198] See *Barr v Mateo*, 360 US 564, 572 (1959) (citing *Gregoire*, 177 F2d at 579); Jerry L. Mashaw, *Civil Liability of Government Officer: Property Rights and Official Accountability*, 42 L & Contemp Probs 8, 15 (1978).

[199] Robert Jervis, *System Effects: Complexity in Political and Social Life* 50 (Princeton, 1997).

[200] For one analysis linking changes in procedural rules to substantive norms, see Jody Freeman and Adrian Vermeule, *Massachusetts v EPA: From Politics to Expertise*, 2007 Supreme Court Review 51.

matter about which I express no view here[201]—it is difficult to defend the manner in which the *Iqbal* Court chose to rewrite that rule. There is a statutorily designated avenue for reconsideration of procedural rules: a multistage rule-making procedure set forth in the Rules Enabling Act. Rule-making under the act likely would have generated information and clarity,[202] but it was not used. As a result, the scope of *Iqbal* is unclear.[203] Moreover, the resulting rule is costly to apply. For fifty years, Rule 8 had been applied in a clear, if arguably generous,[204] manner. Displacing a well-known and fully explored rule, *Iqbal* propounds a vague, open-textured, and subjective standard. The stability benefits of fifty years' precedent were, at a stroke, eviscerated.[205] Justice Kennedy's opinion leaves tantalizing clues as to how it should be applied without attaining precision or clarity. The Court's emphasis on "context," for example, hints that the Justices have in mind some taxonomy of issue-specific pleading rules.[206] But *Iqbal* gives no guidance as to how to classify and organize complaints by "context."[207] Instead,

---

[201] Is the pleading standard in *Iqbal* too harsh? This question concerns the economy of federal civil litigation and is beyond the scope of this article. But it is plausible to view *Iqbal* as the Justices' overreaction to periodic problems that can be dealt with by district court control of discovery. The Justices, after all, are far removed from the realities of district court litigation and may be biased by the sample of cases that come before them. Even this judgment, though, depends on a contestable normative claim about the optimal constraints on access to federal court. It also rests on an empirical question about how significant an effect *Iqbal* has had, and in which areas of law. It would seem that the latter is a question ripe for empirical testing.

[202] Amendments to the rules are proposed by an Advisory Committee on Civil Rules, and reviewed by a Standing Committee, the Judicial Conference, and the Supreme Court. See 28 USC §§ 2072–73. Note that the Court plays a significant catalytic role in this process. So it cannot be said that reform by case law was necessitated by the failure of congressional action.

[203] The precise mischief to which *Iqbal* responds is also murky. The 2007 case on pleading rules, *Bell Atlantic v Twombly*, cited two (nonempirical) law review articles, one critical of notice pleading, and one supportive. See *Bell Atlantic Corp. v Twombly*, 550 US 544, 562 (2007). *Iqbal* itself adduced no evidence about pleading's dysfunction.

[204] The Federal Rules of Civil Procedure were adopted in 1938, an era when the mix of federal-court litigation was significantly different. See Richard A. Epstein, *Bell Atlantic v. Twombly: How Motions to Dismiss Became (Disguised) Summary Judgments*, 25 Wash U J L & Policy 61, 62 (2007).

[205] It is impossible not to observe the striking contrast between this fluid and unpredictable standard and the concern expressed by four of the Justices who comprised the *Iqbal* majority about open-ended standards in other areas of litigation management. See *Caperton v AT Massey Coal Co. Inc.*, 129 S Ct 2252, 2268–72 (2009) (Roberts, J, dissenting).

[206] *Leatherman v Tarrant County Narcotics Intelligence & Coordination Unit*, 507 US 163, 164–69 (1993) (rejecting a heightened pleading rule for municipal liability); see also *Swierkiewicz v Sorema, N.A.*, 534 US 506 (2002).

[207] Courts could, for example, divide the litigation universe by policy area, by type of

the decision invites 680-plus district judges to conjure rules on the fly by applying 680-plus distinct bodies of "judicial experience and common sense" to assess "plausibility."

To summarize, interactions between substantive bodies of law and transubstantive rules change the way that judicial decision rules are adopted and amended. These interactions are thus important independent objects of study. Future longitudinal studies of the development of national security programs via the interplay of courts, legislative institutions, public opinion, and the executive may reveal other causal mechanisms, such as feedback loops,[208] and variables with predictive value that until now have been overlooked.

Rejection of the descriptive claim of national security exceptionalism has a second consequence, one related to normative theorizing about the judicial role in emergencies. Specifically, the rejection of national security exceptionalism may be welcomed or condemned depending on its net effects, which have until now not been carefully considered. Begin with the implications of my argument for a civil libertarian who views the federal courts as a bulwark for individual rights. On the one hand, a finding of invariance between judicial responses to national security and larger dynamics in public law may be troubling. Spillover effects that result from the convergence of national security with general public law, such as in *Iqbal*, may create an incrementalist avenue to across-the-board abrogation of the federal courts' liberty-protecting function.[209] Routinized emergencies, or even a persistent flow of cases arising from one emergency, may therefore have broadly corrosive effects. On the other hand, continuity between national security law and other domains may strengthen the prophylactic effect of the federal judiciary's presence. The belief that judges have a stable disposition or follow constant rules may induce beliefs on the part of other governmental actors that minimize

---

defendant (government vs. private), by the kind of claim (constitutional or statutory), or by the particular evidentiary problems raised by certain causes of action. See Epstein, 25 Wash U J L & Policy at 67–68 (cited in note 204) (noting difficulties of drawing inferences from parallel context in the antitrust context).

[208] For a general specification of feedback mechanisms, see Paul Pierson, *Increasing Returns, Path Dependence, and the Study of Politics*, 94 Am Pol Sci Rev 251, 260–62 (2000).

[209] See Jervis, *System Effects* at 287 (cited in note 199) ("Understanding feedbacks . . . may allow actors to follow indirect routes to their goals, especially when information and beliefs are not fully shared."). *Iqbal*, by making civil suits more difficult to file, is a significant step on such a road.

rights violation.[210] The net effect of the analysis, in short, is uncertain from a civil libertarian perspective.

Another normative consequence of the rejection of national security exceptionalism for civil libertarians may be the need to
rethink the role of democratic politics in setting emergency responses. The trajectory of national security programs is thought
to be wholly fixed in the "red hot" furnace of emergency.[211] This
emphasis on emergency can be generalized into a model of sovereignty as "unitary and decisive, committed to its own invulner-
ability" and insulated from democratically determined legal
rules.[212] But, the rejection of national security exceptionalism turns
attention away from a narrow focus upon how best to respond to
specific emergencies, and toward the matter of how a democracy
"surviv[es] the emergency situation with integrity as a democracy."[213] That is, it raises the question of how doctrinal and judicial
incentives should be structured to ensure the continuity of rules,
procedures, and remedies across emergencies and other times. If
this kind of integrity is valued—and, of course, many reject its
significance—courts might be institutional mechanisms for the
preservation of a larger public "*culture* of civil liberties."[214] Alternatively, it may be that emergencies are moments at which such
a culture is abandoned or incrementally sapped. From an alternative normative perspective more concerned with security, similar
questions arise about the judicial role in national security and its
effect on the broader operation of the federal judiciary.

One final consequence is worth noting. "National security law"
is fast becoming a subdiscipline within the legal academy with a
paraphernalia of case books, specialists, central questions, and
well-defined camps. In the early stages of this development, there
may be an understandable tendency to make claims on behalf of

---

[210] Id at 23. For a related argument urging courts to look to administrative law rules as
constraints on national security actions, see Jonathan Masur, *A Hard Look or a Blind Eye?
Administrative Law and Military Deference*, 56 Hastings L J 441, 501–19 (2005) (examining
and rejecting arguments for a distinction between the two fields of law).

[211] Posner and Vermeule, *Terror in the Balance* at 44 (cited in note 8).

[212] Bonnie Honig, *Emergency Politics: Paradox, Law, Democracy* 2 (Princeton, 2009). This
model has been extended from the emergency context to general administrative law in
Adrian Vermeule, *Our Schmittian Administrative Law*, 122 Harv L Rev 1095, 1103–04
(2009).

[213] Honig, *Emergency Politics* at 9 (cited at note 212).

[214] Stone, *Perilous Times* at 537 (cited in note 7) (emphasis in original).

the subdiscipline's insulation from other legal debates. My analysis of national security exceptionalism suggests this would be an error. Scholars of national security law will learn more by comparative glances across disciplinary lines than by the construction of distinguishing walls or isolating moats.

CONCLUSION

National security exceptionalism does not find substantial support in the behavior of courts in post-9/11 noncriminal detention cases. The remedies that courts provide in these cases are surprisingly consistent, however, with the approach taken in other domains of public law. Taken together, these results provide some reason to view judicial responses to exigent national security policies not as exceptional but as thoroughly imbricated in the larger texture of American public law.

BARBARA E. ARMACOST

ARIZONA v GANT: DOES IT MATTER?

Prior to the Supreme Court's recent opinion in *Arizona v Gant*,[1] it was standard practice under *New York v Belton*[2] for police to conduct a search incident to arrest (SITA) of the passenger compartment of an automobile whenever they arrested the driver or a recent occupant of the vehicle.[3] The traditional justifications for the search incident to arrest, as articulated in *Chimel v California*,[4] are to allow police to secure any weapons that the arrestee might seek to use to resist arrest or escape *and* to preserve evidence the arrestee might attempt to conceal or destroy.[5] *Belton* purported to apply *Chimel*'s rationale to arrests in automobiles. Searches of passenger compartments of automobiles, however, were routinely deemed lawful even if the arrestee was handcuffed and nowhere near where he could access weapons or contraband inside the vehicle.[6]

Barbara E. Armacost is Professor of Law, University of Virginia School of Law.

AUTHOR'S NOTE: I am grateful to Anne Coughlin, Mike Seidman, and David Strauss for many helpful comments and to Andrea Lucas and the librarians at the University of Virginia School of Law for excellent research assistance. I am also grateful to my students whose comments and questions make me a better scholar.

[1] 129 S Ct 1710 (2009).

[2] 453 US 454 (1981).

[3] *Gant*, 129 S Ct at 1722 (noting that the broad reading of *Belton* "has been widely taught in police academies and that law enforcement officers have relied on the rule in conducting vehicle searches during the past 28 years").

[4] 395 US 752 (1969).

[5] Id at 763.

[6] See *Thornton v United States*, 541 US 615, 628 (2004) (listing reported cases). Some courts even permitted a search incident to arrest of an automobile after the arrestee had already left the scene. See, for example, *United States v McLaughlin*, 170 F3d 889, 890–91

After *Belton*, lower courts (and police officers themselves) began to treat the search incident to arrest of a vehicle as a "police entitlement rather than as an exception justified by the twin rationales" underlying post-arrest searches.[7] Moreover, police came to view the search incident to arrest as a powerful investigative tool because they could stop and arrest motorists for minor traffic offenses in order to get a free search for evidence of more serious crimes.[8]

At least as a formal matter, *Arizona v Gant* changed all this. In *Gant* the Arizona Supreme Court reviewed a Fourth Amendment challenge to an automobile search incident to arrest conducted after the driver had been arrested, handcuffed, and secured in the police car.[9] While lower courts had routinely upheld searches incident to arrest under similar circumstances, the Arizona Supreme Court struck down the search on the ground that neither of the *Chimel* rationales—police safety and preservation of evidence—justified a search incident to arrest under these circumstances.[10] The U.S. Supreme Court agreed. In a 5–4 decision written by Justice Stevens, the Court held that "[t]he safety and evidentiary justifications" underlying *Chimel*'s rule that police may search the space within the arrestee's immediate control "determine *Belton*'s scope."[11] The Court held, specifically, that police may not do a SITA of an automobile once the arrestee "has been secured and cannot access the interior of the vehicle" *unless* it is "reasonable to believe evidence relevant to the crime of arrest might be found in the vehicle."[12]

For all practical purposes this holding means the end of *Belton*

(9th Cir 1999). In *Belton* itself the search occurred after the arrestees were outside of the vehicle, but the Court nowhere explained why this fact did not make the search impermissible.

[7] *Thornton*, 541 US at 624 (O'Connor, J, concurring). See also id at 627 (Scalia, J, concurring in the judgment) ("Conducting a [search incident to arrest] is not the Government's right; it is an exception—justified by necessity—to a rule that would otherwise render the search unlawful.").

[8] See notes 77–85 and accompanying text. The SITA is justified only if police actually take the suspect into custody. For purposes of this article, I will use the word "arrest" to mean "custodial arrest." See *Knowles v Iowa*, 525 US 113 (1998) (holding that police may not do a search incident to a citation).

[9] *Arizona v Gant*, 162 P3d 640 (2007).

[10] Id at 643 (noting that all the arrestees were handcuffed and secured in patrol cars, there were no unsecured civilians in the vicinity, four officers were on the scene, and there was no reason to believe that anyone on the scene could have gained access to Gant's car).

[11] *Gant*, 129 S Ct at 1714.

[12] Id at 1714, 1719, quoting *Thornton*, 541 US at 632. By *Gant*'s second holding I mean the Court's rule permitting a search of the vehicle for evidence of the crime of arrest.

searches incident to arrest, as the majority acknowledged in a foot-note.[13] No police officer worth her salt will execute an arrest while the arrestee is still sitting inside the automobile. Nor will she arrest and then leave the suspect unsecured within grabbing distance of the automobile. As every officer knows well, a significant percentage of police officer shootings occur at traffic stops.[14] Thus, it is standard arrest protocol to order the suspect and any other occupants out of the automobile and then arrest, handcuff, and secure the arrestee in the officer's vehicle.[15] At that point, however, the justification for the SITA has ceased under *Arizona v Gant* because the arrestee can no longer access weapons or destroy evidence. As the prosecution had argued in *Thornton v United States*,[16] an earlier vehicle SITA case, "The practice of restraining an arrestee on the scene before searching a car that he just occupied is so prevalent that holding that *Belton* does not apply in that setting would . . . largely render *Belton* a dead letter."[17]

When *Arizona v Gant* came before the Supreme Court, law en-forcement officials viewed it as a big deal. A coalition of prosecutors, police organizations, police chiefs, and state attorneys general crit-icized the Arizona Supreme Court's opinion as seriously compro-mising officer safety and hamstringing police investigators. In a series of amicus briefs, they pointed to statistics demonstrating that a disproportionately large number of felonious shootings and as-saults of police officers occur during arrests, including traffic ar-

---

[13] *Gant*, 129 S Ct at 1719 n 4 ("Because officers have many means of ensuring the safe arrest of vehicle occupants, it will be the rare case in which an officer is unable to fully effectuate an arrest so that the real possibility of access to the arrestee's vehicle remains.").

[14] See, for example, *Maryland v Wilson*, 519 US 408, 414 (1997); Federal Bureau of Investigation, *Uniform Crime Reports: Law Enforcement Officers Killed and Assaulted* 71, 33 (1994) (noting that in 1994 alone there were 5,762 officer assaults and 11 officers killed during traffic pursuits and stops).

[15] For empirical evidence of police protocol of securing arrestees before searching, see Myron Moskovitz, *A Rule in Search of a Reason: An Empirical Reexamination of Chimel and Belton*, 2002 Wis L Rev 657, 674–76. See *Pennsylvania v Mimms*, 434 US 106, 110 (1997) (ordering the suspect out of the automobile and "[e]stablishing a face to face confrontation diminishes the possibility . . . that the driver can make unobserved movements . . . [which] reduces the likelihood that the officer will be the victim of an assault."). The Supreme Court has held that police officers who execute a traffic stop may—with no additional justification—order the driver and any passengers out of the automobile. See id at 111; *Maryland v Wilson*, 519 US 408, 414–15 (1997).

[16] 541 US 615 (2004).

[17] Id at 628 (Scalia, J, concurring in the judgment).

rests.[18] They argued that overturning *Belton*'s bright-line search rule would put arresting officers in danger by requiring them to make difficult fact-specific judgments during the rapidly changing and dangerous circumstances of a street arrest.[19] In addition, they predicted that the new rule would seriously hamper law enforcement officers who rely on the search incident to arrest in vehicles to investigate drug and weapons offenses and other serious crimes.[20]

The defense and civil liberties bars also viewed *Arizona v Gant* as a very important case. They urged the Supreme Court to use *Gant* as an opportunity to curb the widespread police practice of using traffic arrests as pretexts for conducting "purely exploratory searches."[21] Given the broad range of arrestable offenses, then-current Fourth Amendment law permitted police officers to stop, arrest, and search virtually any motorist without evidence that the motorist was guilty of the crime the police were actually interested in investigating. It also enabled officers to stop and arrest motorists on the basis of racial or other stereotypes they deemed related to criminal activity[22] and made it impossible to challenge such stops

---

[18] See, for example, Petitioner's Brief on the Merits, *Arizona v Gant*, No 07-542, *24–27, 29–37 (S Ct filed May 12, 2008) (citing statistics of officer assaults and shootings during arrests, including traffic arrests) ("Petitioner's Merits Brief").

[19] See, for example, Brief of Florida, Alabama, Alaska, California, Colorado, Hawaii, Idaho, Illinois, Indiana, Kansas, Maryland, Michigan, Minnesota, Missouri, New Hampshire, New Mexico, North Dakota, Oklahoma, Oregon, Pennsylvania, South Dakota, Tennessee, Washington, Wisconsin, and Wyoming, as Amici Curiae in Support of Petitioner, *Arizona v Gant*, 129 S Ct 1710, *24–33 (S Ct filed May 19, 2008) (arguing that police need a clear rule in the dangerous and uncertain circumstances surrounding arrests of potentially dangerous individuals); Motion for Leave to File and Brief of Amicus Curiae National Association of Police Organizations, Inc. in Support of Petitioner, *Arizona v Gant*, 129 S Ct 1710, *2–4 (S Ct filed April 2008) (citing evidence from FBI Uniform Crime Report that 42 percent of officer killings and assaults occurred while officers were conducting traffic stops or making arrests and arguing for a clear rule); Motion to File Brief and Brief Amici Curiae of Americans for Effective Law Enforcement, Inc., the International Association of Chiefs of Police, the National Sheriff's Association, the Arizona Law Enforcement Legal Advisors' Association, and the Arizona Association of the Chiefs of Police, *Arizona v Gant*, No 07-542, *11–16 (S Ct filed Mar 25, 2008) (describing dangers inherent in traffic stops and arguing for clear rule to protect officer safety).

[20] See, for example, Petitioner's Merits Brief at 27 (arguing that government's interest in preserving evidence argues against overruling *Belton*).

[21] See, for example, Brief for Amicus Curiae National Association of Criminal Defense Lawyers in Support of Respondent, *Arizona v Gant*, No 07-542, *8–11 (filed July 25, 2008) (arguing that "the current search-incident-to-arrest doctrine encourages officers to arrest people whom they would not otherwise arrest, in order to conduct exploratory searches they would not ordinarily be allowed to conduct").

[22] See, for example, David A. Harris, *"Driving While Black" and All Other Traffic Offenses: The Supreme Court and Pretext Stops*, 87 J Crim L & Criminol 544 (1997) ("Driving While Black"); David A. Harris, *Car Wars: The Fourth Amendment's Death on the Highway*, 66 Geo Wash L Rev 556 (1988) ("Car Wars").

under the Fourth Amendment.[23] Civil rights proponents urged the
Supreme Court to eliminate the automatic search incident to arrest,
which was widely viewed as the culprit that created incentives for
pretextual stops. They were joined by a long list of scholars who
routinely criticized *Belton* as incoherent and misguided.[24]

When the Supreme Court's opinion in *Gant* was handed down,
defense attorneys and civil rights activists were cautiously optimistic.
As one defense attorney colorfully explained, "the Fourth Amendment is not dead, it's just been in a 28-year coma."[25] The reaction
from the law enforcement community, however, has been remarkably muted. While there is widespread agreement that officers will
have to learn new, more nuanced rules for conducting traffic stop
searches, most police experts are predicting that, in the end, *Gant*
won't make much difference. On the one hand, they concede, police
officers will no longer be able to rely on the automobile SITA as
a "free" search. Police who rely on a SITA will be required to
articulate facts that justify the need for the search based on the twin
rationales of officer safety and preservation of evidence. On the
other hand, said one criminal justice educator, *Gant* "took a tool
we've had for 25 years and removed it from our toolbox . . . but
we still have other tools available to us."[26] For example, if police
cannot do a search incident to arrest, they will forgo the immediate
arrest and ask for consent to search, which suspects—even guilty
ones—often grant.[27] Alternatively, they can look for evidence in
plain view or pursuant to the SITA of the arrestee's person that
might justify a *Terry* frisk or warrantless search of the automobile.
If all else fails, police can arrest the driver, impound the vehicle,
and then do an inventory of the contents of the vehicle hoping to
find evidence of crime.[28] Finally, *Gant* itself permits police officers

---

[23] See *Whren v United States*, 517 US 806, 813–16 (1996).

[24] See *Gant*, 129 S Ct at 1720–21 (noting the widespread observation that a broad reading
of *Belton* gives police limitless discretion to conduct exploratory searches and citing
sources).

[25] John Wesley Hall, *Column from the President: A Great Awakening*, 33 Champion 5
(June 2009). Hall is the President of the National Association of Criminal Defense Lawyers,
Inc.

[26] Brian Smith, *Local Opinions Mixed on Vehicle Search Decisions*, Richmond Register (May
2, 2009), available online at http://www.richmondregister.com/archivesearch/local_story
_122215814.html (quoting Gerald Ross, staff attorney advisor for the legal training section
of the Department of Criminal Justice Training at Eastern Kentucky University).

[27] See note 108 (discussing state and national statistics on consent searches).

[28] See *South Dakota v Opperman*, 428 US 364 (1976).

to search an arrestee's vehicle if they have reason to believe that evidence of the crime of arrest will be found in the vehicle.

In my view, the reality is somewhere between these two perspectives. *Gant* will certainly make some difference. The *Belton* regime permitted police to search nearly any automobile by waiting to catch the driver in a minor traffic violation, arresting the driver, and searching incident to that arrest. While police do have other ways to justify a post-arrest vehicle search, the switch to these alternative strategies is not without cost. After *Gant*, police must either obtain consent, which may not be forthcoming and may be limited in scope, or they must articulate some justification for the vehicle search, either probable cause or reasonable suspicion. While the impoundment and inventory option requires no criminal justification, it is costly and time consuming. On the other hand, that these alternatives exist means that *Gant* will have less effect than its supporters had hoped. Exactly how much less depends upon a detailed analysis of the alleged alternative search "tools" that remain in the toolbox and the extent to which they are, in fact, equivalent to the old search incident to arrest.[29] Moreover, as police officers employ these alternatives more frequently, they too will be litigated, which will undoubtedly change the legal landscape again.

This article seeks to forecast the possible implications of the Court's holdings and analysis in *Gant*. Part I briefly describes the judicial landscape that gave rise to the reconsideration of *Belton* and analyzes the *Gant* opinions themselves. Part II explores the conflicting claims by police officers and the defense bar about the likely effect of *Gant* on police practices. I conclude that *Gant*'s first holding—effectively eliminating the vehicle SITA for traffic arrests— will make exploratory searches more costly but will not eliminate them. As to *Gant*'s second holding—that police may conduct a SITA if it is reasonable to believe evidence of the crime of arrest might be found in the vehicle—I fault the Court for using language that tracks neither probable cause nor reasonable suspicion. The Court's Delphic language is sure to leave the lower courts in disarray. Part III considers the broader implications of *Gant*. I argue first that *Gant* represents another step in the march toward a Fourth Amend-

---

[29] For further discussion of the costs and limitations of these alleged alternatives, see notes 108–13 and accompanying text.

ment jurisprudence of interest balancing rather than a regime in which a warrant plus probable cause is the sine qua non of Fourth Amendment law. Second, while *Gant* articulated a coherent rationale for the search incident to arrest in a vehicle, the same rationale may have destabilized search incident law applicable to arrests in the home under *Chimel*. Finally, I challenge the familiar claim—made by those who argued against overruling *Belton*—that "bright-line" rules are necessary in contexts that implicate police officer safety concerns.

I. The Case and Its Context

A. THE ROAD TO GANT

The majority in *Gant* began its analysis with an extensive reference to *Chimel v California*,[30] the case that outlines modern search incident to arrest doctrine. Prior to *Chimel*, the Supreme Court had held that a police officer who makes a lawful arrest may search the *person* of the arrestee and the *place* where the arrest occurred "in order to find and seize the things used to carry on the criminal enterprise."[31] Under the Court's early holdings, the SITA of the place of arrest was quite narrow, applying only if the arrestee was actively engaged in criminal activity at the site of the arrest.[32] In *United States v Rabinowitz*[33] and *Harris v United States*,[34] however, the Supreme Court adopted a broader SITA rule, holding that the search incident to arrest included all areas that were deemed to be in the "possession" or under the "control" of the person arrested.[35]

Chimel was the Court's attempt to rein in the *Harris-Rabinowitz* doctrine, which had led to decisions upholding searches of entire residences incident to arrest.[36] In *Chimel* the Supreme Court struck

---

[30] 395 US 752 (1969).

[31] *Marron v United States*, 275 US 192, 199 (1927) (cited in *Chimel*).

[32] See *Go-Bart Importing Co. v United States*, 282 US 344 (1931), and *United States v Lefkowitz*, 285 US 452 (1932).

[33] 339 US 56 (1950).

[34] 331 US 145 (1947).

[35] *Rabinowitz*, 339 US at 62–63.

[36] See *Chimel*, 395 US at 760 n 4, citing *Ker v California*, 374 US 23, 42 (1963); *Abel v United States*, 362 US 217 (1960); *Draper v United States*, 358 US 307 (1959); *Kremen v United States*, 353 US 346 (1957) (per curiam); *Chapman v United States*, 365 US 610

down as unlawful a search incident to arrest of a burglary suspect in which the arresting officers looked through an entire three-bedroom house, including the attic, the garage, and a small workshop.[37] Any search that is conducted without a warrant, the Court reasoned, must be constrained by its justification. Applying that analysis, the Court held that the scope of a search incident to arrest must be limited by the two rationales that justify it: the need for police to protect themselves by removing any weapons that the arrestee might use to resist arrest or effect his escape and the need to preserve evidence that the arrestee might try to destroy or conceal. These rationales justified a search incident to arrest of the arrestee's person and the "area 'within his immediate control,'"—construing that phrase to mean the area from within which he might gain possession of a weapon or destructible evidence. "There is no comparable justification," the Court said, "for routinely searching any room other than that in which an arrest occurs—or for that matter, for searching through all the desk drawers or other closed or concealed areas in that room itself."[38] Thus, while *Chimel* appeared to affirm a bright-line rule for the "when" of the search incident to arrest, it left the question of "where" to a case-by-case analysis. In other words, every arrest triggered a SITA,[39] but the permissible scope of that search depended upon an under-all-the-circumstances determination of what parts of the premises were in "the area from within which [the arrestee] might gain possession of a weapon or destructible evidence."[40] While *Chimel*'s case-by-case analysis remained the background rule for determining the scope of a search incident to arrest in a home,[41] the Court went on to adopt "bright-line" rules in two contexts:

(1961); *Jones v United States*, 357 US 493 (1958); *Chimel*, 395 US at 767–68, citing *United States v Kirschenblatt*, 16 F2d 202 (2d Cir 1926) (concluding that the search incident to arrest doctrine had come to resemble the general warrants against which the Fourth Amendment was adopted).

[37] *Chimel*, 395 US at 754.

[38] Id at 763.

[39] This point was implicit in *Chimel* but not completely clear until the Court's opinion in *United States v Robinson*, 414 US 218 (1973).

[40] *Chimel*, 395 US at 763.

[41] Some lower courts began to treat *Chimel* as permitting a search of the grabbing area even when the arrestee had been moved to a different location. See notes 135–37 and accompanying text.

searches of the person of the arrestee in *United States v Robinson*[42] and searches of automobiles in *New York v Belton*.[43]

In *Belton*, the Supreme Court granted certiorari in order to address what it deemed "disarray"[44] in the lower courts as they attempted to apply the case-by-case *Chimel* rule to post-arrest searches of automobiles. In *Belton*, a police officer who had stopped an automobile for speeding saw in plain view a distinctive package he believed to contain marijuana. The officer ordered the four occupants out of the car and placed them under arrest for drug possession. Having only one set of handcuffs, the officer patted the four men down and placed them in separate areas along the highway. He then reached into the automobile, grabbed the package, and opened it, finding marijuana. This was followed by a full search of the men and the passenger compartment of the car, revealing a black leather jacket in the back seat with cocaine in a zippered pocket. The officer then took the men into custody.

The New York Court of Appeals held that the search of a jacket in the vehicle was not a legitimate search incident to arrest because there was no longer any danger that the arrestees—who were then outside the automobile—might gain access to it.[45] Two dissenting justices disagreed, pointing out that the officer was acting alone to retain control of four arrestees who had been in a speeding car that none of them owned and that contained an uncertain quantity of drugs.[46] The Supreme Court used this disagreement in the New York Court of Appeals about whether the SITA was justified as a reason to conclude that police need a bright-line rule to guide their conduct in the rapidly unfolding and dangerous circumstances of an arrest in an automobile.[47] The Court reasoned that

---

[42] In *United States v Robinson*, 414 US 218 (1973), the Supreme Court held that an arrest triggers a full search of the person of the arrestee (including pockets and containers) without the case-by-case analysis ordinarily required by *Chimel*. In *Robinson*, the defendant was stopped and arrested for driving on a revoked license. Id at 220. When the officer conducted a search incident to arrest of the arrestee, he found a crumpled cigarette package, opened it, and found gelatin capsules that were later determined to contain heroine. Id at 222–23. The Supreme Court held that if the custodial arrest is lawful, a full search of the person of the arrestee—including pockets and containers—"requires no additional justification." Id at 235.

[43] 453 US 454 (1981).

[44] Id at 459 n 1.

[45] Id at 456.

[46] Id at 456–57.

[47] Id at 458.

the passenger compartment of a car is "generally, even if not in-evitably" within the grabbing distance of an individual who is arrested in that vehicle.[48] Hence the Court held that a police officer who makes a custodial arrest of the occupant of a car "may, as a contemporaneous incident of that arrest, search the passenger compartment of that automobile."[49] For reasons that are not en-tirely clear, the Court thought this bright-line rule was needed even in a case like *Belton* itself, where all of the suspects were already outside the vehicle when the search occurred.

In the years following *Belton*, the lower courts upheld searches incident to arrest as long as the search was reasonably contem-poraneous with the arrest[50] and regardless of whether the arrestee had been secured and was no longer within grabbing distance of the automobile at the time of the search. In addition, while in *Belton* there was probable cause to believe that there would be evidence of the crime of arrest—possession of marijuana—in the automobile, the Supreme Court had already held that the search incident to arrest of the *person* was not limited to evidence of the crime of arrest.[51] In other words, police could conduct a search incident to arrest of the person regardless of whether the arrest was for a traffic offense or some other crime. As nothing in the *Belton* opinion suggested otherwise, lower courts freely applied the *Belton* rule even if there was no reason to believe that evidence of the crime of arrest would be found in the vehicle. This ultimately led to the practice decried by the defendant in *Gant*: Police officers routinely used minor traffic offenses as a way to obtain exploratory searches of vehicles. There is also evidence that law enforcement officers use this strategy disproportionately to stop and search minority motorists.[52]

Despite these criticisms, in the 2004 case of *Thornton v United States*,[53] the Supreme Court affirmed the continuing vitality of *Belton*. The narrow issue in *Thornton* was whether the *Belton* rule is "limited to situations where the officer makes contact with the

[48] Id at 460.

[49] Id.

[50] See Wayne R. LaFave, 3 *Search and Seizure: A Treatise on the Fourth Amendment* § 7.1(c) at 515–16 (West, 4th ed 2004).

[51] See *Robinson*, 414 US at 235–36 (1973).

[52] See notes 82–85 and accompanying text (discussing racial profiling).

[53] 541 US 615 (2004).

occupant while the occupant is inside the vehicle, or whether it
applies as well when the officer first makes contact with the arrestee after the latter has stepped out of the vehicle."[54] Chief Justice Rehnquist, writing for the majority, concluded that *Belton*
applied to the latter situation as well as the former. The Court
declined to reach the argument that *Belton* searches incident to
arrest should be limited to "recent occupants" who are within
"reaching distance" of the automobile.[55] This is the issue that was
left open when the Court granted certiorari in *Gant*.

B. THE GANT OPINIONS

The facts of *Arizona v Gant*[56] presented the Court with a consummate example of an exploratory search. In *Gant* the officers
received an anonymous tip that drugs were being sold from a
residence on N. Walnut Ave. They proceeded to that address and
knocked on the door. Rodney Gant opened the door. He told the
officers he did not own the home but he expected the homeowner
to return later. Using the well-known strategy of investigating
traffic violations in hopes of getting a free search for evidence of
other crimes, police officers conducted a license check and found
that Gant's license had been suspended. When Gant returned to
the residence that evening in his automobile, police officers arrested him for driving on a suspended license, handcuffed him,
and placed him into the back of a patrol car. They then conducted
a search of Gant's automobile, finding a gun and a bag of cocaine
in the pocket of a jacket on the back seat. Gant argued that the
search of his automobile was not justified as a search incident to
arrest because he was handcuffed and not within reaching distance
of the automobile and because he had been arrested for a traffic
offense for which no evidence could be found in the vehicle.

The Arizona Supreme Court read *Belton* as addressing only the
allowed *scope* of the search incident to arrest of the recent occupant
of an automobile, but not addressing the prior, threshold question
of whether police may conduct a search incident to arrest *at all*
once the scene is secure. The court held that when an arrestee is
secure in a patrol car, the threshold requirements for a warrantless

---

[54] Id at 617.

[55] Id at 622.

[56] 128 S Ct 1710 (2009).

search incident to arrest—danger to the arresting officers or the risk that evidence might be destroyed—are not met. Justice Stevens's opinion for a 5–4 majority of the U.S. Supreme Court agreed. The Court rejected a reading of *Belton* that would have permitted an automatic search of the passenger compartment incident to every arrest of a recent occupant. The Court held that "the *Chimel* rationale authorizes police to search a vehicle incident to a recent occupant's arrest only when the arrestee is unsecured and within reaching distance of the passenger compartment at the time of the search" *or* "it is reasonable to believe the vehicle contains evidence of the offense of arrest."[57]

Belton itself is ambiguous on the scope/threshold distinction, and the Supreme Court opinions in *Arizona v Gant* exploited this ambiguity. All of the Justices agreed that *Belton* was a bright-line version of the *Chimel* standard for determining the scope of a SITA in the "particular and problematic" circumstances of an arrest in an automobile.[58] *Chimel* had held that police officers are entitled to search the area immediately surrounding the arrestee and from which he might be able to grab a weapon or evidentiary item. In *Belton*, the Court asserted that the passenger compartment of an automobile is "generally, even if not inevitably" within the area into which a suspect arrested in a car might reach. From this generalization, the Court adopted the bright-line rule that when an individual is arrested in an automobile, the arresting officer may search the entire passenger compartment. In other words, the officer (and reviewing court) need not ask the question whether under the particular facts at hand, the entire passenger compartment was *actually* within grabbing distance of the particular arrestee. On this reading of *Belton*, all members of the *Gant* Court agreed.

The Justices joined issue, however, on the question identified by the Arizona Supreme Court: whether *Belton* established a bright-line rule only for determining the *scope* of the automobile SITA or also for determining the threshold question of when that search is *triggered*. The issue, in other words, is whether the arrest of an occupant or recent occupant of an automobile triggers—without further inquiry—an automatic SITA of the entire passen-

---

[57] Id at 1719, 1723.

[58] *Belton*, 453 US at 460 n 3; *Gant*, 129 S Ct at 1722–23, 1724–25 (Scalia, J, concurring), 1725 (Breyer, J, dissenting), 1727 (Alito, J, dissenting).

ger compartment or, alternatively, an arrest triggers a full passenger compartment search only after a case-by-case inquiry into
whether the particular arrestee was within reaching distance of
the automobile at the time of the search.

Justice Stevens's opinion for the majority in *Gant* acknowledged
that lower courts have widely read *Belton* to permit an automatic
vehicle SITA even if an arrestee is nowhere near the vehicle at
the time the search was conducted. Justice Stevens attributed this
reading of *Belton* not to anything in the Court's opinion but to
Justice Brennan's dissent. While in *Belton* the four arrestees were
unsecured at the time of the vehicle search, Brennan had argued
that under the majority's approach "the result would . . . be the
same even if [the officer] had handcuffed Belton and his compan-
ions in the patrol car" before conducting the search.[59] As Justice
Stevens rightly observed, Justice Brennan's reading of *Belton* had
been adopted by most of the courts of appeals. To read *Belton* this
way, Justice Stevens objected, "untether[s] the rule from the justifications underlying the *Chimel* exception—a result clearly in-
compatible with our statement in *Belton* that it 'in no way alters
the fundamental principles established in the *Chimel* case regarding
the basic scope of searches incident to lawful custodial arrests.'"[60]
After twenty-eight years of experience applying *Belton*, Stevens
continued, "we now know that articles inside the passenger compartment are rarely 'within the area into which the arrestee might
reach' and blind adherence to *Belton*'s faulty assumptions would
authorize myriad unconstitutional searches."[61] Thus, Justice Stevens concluded that police may not conduct a *Belton* search unless
the arrestee is *actually* within grabbing distance of the automobile.

There is language in *Belton* to support Justice Stevens's reading
of the case. *Chimel* was a scope (not a threshold) case, and the
basic line of analysis from *Chimel* to *Belton* is that the *Belton* rule
is merely a bright-line version of the *Chimel* standard for determining the scope of a SITA for arrests in automobiles. As the
Court reasoned in *Belton*:

> No straightforward rule has emerged from the litigated cases
> respecting . . . the proper *scope* of the search of the interior of

---

[59] *Belton*, 453 US at 468.

[60] *Gant*, 129 S Ct at 1719.

[61] Id at 1723, quoting *Belton*, 453 US at 460.

> an automobile incident to a lawful arrest of its occupants. . . .
> While the *Chimel* case established that a search incident to
> arrest may not stray beyond "the area within the immediate
> control of the arrestee," courts have found no workable defi-
> nition . . . when that area arguably includes the interior of an
> automobile. . . . Our reading of the cases suggests the gen-
> eralization that articles within the relatively narrow compass of
> the passenger compartment of an automobile are in fact gen-
> erally, even if not inevitably, within the "area into which an
> arrestee might reach in order to grab a weapon or evidentiary
> ite[m.]"[62]

As Justice Alito pointed out for the *Gant* dissenters, however,
the "precise holding" in *Belton*, which appears immediately after
the language quoted above, is itself quite broad: "We hold that
when a policeman has made a lawful custodial arrest of the occupant of an automobile, he may, as a contemporaneous incident
of that arrest, search the passenger compartment of that automobile."[63] The *Belton* Court did not qualify this statement with
the requirement that the arrestee must actually be within reaching
distance of the passenger compartment, although the Court did
require that the SITA be contemporaneous with the arrest. The
broader reading is also supported by the factual question that the
Belton Court purported to be addressing: whether a police officer
who arrests the occupants of an automobile may conduct a SITA
of the "inside [of] the automobile *after the arrestees are no longer
in it*."[64] The Court's factual analysis was similarly broad, permitting a search of the arrestee's jacket because it was "located inside
the passenger compartment of the car in which the respondent
had been a passenger *just before he was arrested*."[65] Moreover, while
Justice Stevens made much of the fact that the officer in *Belton*
was solely responsible for four arrestees, the *Belton* Court did not
purport to be basing its decision on the precise facts at issue in
Belton.

Also in support of Justice Alito's reading of *Belton*, the Court
in *Belton* had quoted liberally from *United States v Robinson*[66] to

---

[62] *Belton*, 453 US at 459–60 (emphasis added).

[63] Id at 460.

[64] Id at 459 (emphasis added).

[65] Id at 462 (emphasis added).

[66] In *Robinson*, 414 US 218, the Supreme Court held that upon arrest, police may do

explain the advantages of a bright-line rule over a case-by-case determination. The *Belton* majority noted that in choosing a "straightforward rule, easily applied and predictably enforced," *Robinson* had "rejected the suggestion that there must be litigated in each case the issue of whether or not there was present one of the reasons supporting the authority for a search of the person incident to arrest." In support of its conclusion that the SITA of an arrestee's automobile—like a SITA of the arrestee's person—includes containers, the *Belton* Court quoted the following language from *Robinson*:

> The authority to search the person incident to a lawful custodial arrest, while based upon the need to disarm and to discover evidence, does not depend on what a court may later decide was the probability *in a particular arrest situation* that weapons or evidence would *in fact* be found upon the person of the suspect. A custodial arrest of a suspect based on probable cause is a reasonable intrusion under the Fourth Amendment; that intrusion being lawful, a search incident to arrest requires no additional justification.[67]

These quotations support the dissent's claim that *Belton*'s actual holding, rather that Justice Brennan's prediction, is the reason why the vast majority of lower courts read *Belton* to permit an automatic SITA of the entire passenger compartment regardless of whether the arrestee could have accessed the automobile at the time of the search.

More fundamentally, however, the scope/threshold ambiguity—though framed a bit differently—actually goes back to *Chimel* itself. In *Chimel*, the Court purported to be addressing the "permissible scope under the Fourth Amendment of a search incident to arrest"[68] but the Court failed to answer the crucial question of whether the scope determination should be made at the time of the *arrest* or at the time of the *search*. This is another way of asking the question whether an arrest triggers an automatic search even if—at the time of the search—the arrestee has been secured or even removed from the area where he was arrested.

---

an automatic and virtually unlimited SITA of the person of the arrestee. It likely does not include body cavity or other such intrusive searches.

[67] *Belton*, 453 US at 459, 461, quoting Robinson, 414 US at 235.

[68] *Chimel*, 395 US at 753.

The *Chimel* Court treated the SITA as an exigency search that was necessitated by the *fact* of the arrest:

> When an arrest is made, it is reasonable for the arresting officer to search the person in order to remove any weapons that the latter might seek to use in order to resist arrest or effect his escape . . . [and] to search for and seize any evidence on the arrestee's person in order to prevent its concealment or destruction. And the area into which an arrestee might reach in order to grab a weapon or evidentiary items must, of course, be governed by a like rule. A gun on a table or in a drawer in front of one who is arrested can be as dangerous to the arresting officer as one concealed in the clothing of the person arrested.[69]

As the quotation above makes clear, the Court envisioned that police officers would use the SITA to remove from the arrestee and his immediate environs weapons he might use against them and evidence he might seek to destroy *while they are in the process of arresting and securing him*. In other words, the Court implicitly assumed that the arrest and the search incident to arrest of person and surroundings would be immediately contemporaneous with one another. It turns out, however, that the arrest and SITA almost never occur at the same time. Police officers virtually always handcuff the arrestee and place him in a secure location before they are prepared to conduct a SITA of the place of arrest. As a result, *Chimel* left unanswered a crucial question: Is the scope of the SITA determined at the place of the arrest (even if the arrestee has been secured and moved) or at the place (and time) of the actual search?

In his dissent in *Gant*, Justice Alito asserted that the *Chimel* Court must have intended that the scope analysis take place at the time of the arrest even if the search occurs after the arrestee has been moved to a secure location. Otherwise, the dissent reasoned, *Chimel* would have had virtually no application: the Court must have known that police always secure arrestees before searching the premises. Similarly, Justice Alito argued, Justice Stewart's reasoning in *Belton* that the passenger compartment is "generally, even if not inevitably" within the arrestee's reach suggests that he too was applying the analysis at the time of the arrest, lest, again, *Belton* have no application in the real world in which police officers

---

[69] Id at 762–63. See *Robinson*, 414 US 218, 235 (holding that the SITA is "not only an exception to the warrant requirement of the Fourth Amendment but is also a 'reasonable' search under that Amendment").

actually function. Whether Justice Alito is correct—or whether the Court was simply not thinking about the gap between arrest and search—he is surely correct that unless the scope analysis is measured at the time and place of arrest, *Belton* and *Chimel* searches form a null set.

Justice Alito also argued at length that (contrary to the majority's claim) *Gant* had overruled *Belton* and *Thornton*, and that the overruling is not justified by ordinary rules of stare decisis. He reasoned that considerations of reliance, workability, and consistency with later cases argue against overruling *Belton*.[70] Justice Alito joined issue with the majority on its argument that *Belton* was badly reasoned. Justice Stevens had argued that *Belton*'s passenger-compartment-search rule was based on the "faulty assumption" that articles within the passenger compartment of an automobile are generally within the grabbing area of a person arrested in an automobile, which we now know they are not. As Justice Alito rightly pointed out, however, the so-called erroneous reasoning that gave rise to *Belton* traces back to *Chimel*, which has long been read to permit a SITA of the grabbing area determined as of the time of the arrest, even if the suspect has been moved. Thus, there is no more reason to overrule *Belton* than there is to overrule *Chimel*, and doing only the former "leaves the law [governing SITA] in a confused and unstable state."[71] The majority insisted that it was not overruling *Belton* and left Justice Alito's stare decisis argument largely unanswered.

Justice Scalia and Justice Breyer each wrote separately in *Gant*. Both Justice Scalia in his concurring opinion and Justice Breyer in his dissenting opinion agreed with Justice Alito's reading of *Belton* as authorizing an automatic SITA of an automobile after the arrest of a recent occupant even if the arrestee has been handcuffed and removed from the vehicle.[72] They also agreed with the majority, however, that the asserted officer-safety rationale for the SITA cannot justify vehicle searches under these circumstances.[73] After these agreements they parted company. Justice Scalia would have abandoned both *Belton* and *Chimel* as applied to vehicle searches and adopted a rule allowing automobile searches incident

---

[70] *Gant*, 129 S Ct at 1728–29 (Alito, J, dissenting).

[71] Id at 1731.

[72] Id at 1724 (Scalia, J, concurring); id at 1725 (Breyer, J, dissenting).

[73] Id.

to arrest only when "the object of the search is evidence of the crime for which the arrest was made, or of another crime that the officer has probable cause to believe occurred."[74] Under Justice Scalia's rule, the search of Gant would have been unlawful because there was no reason to believe that there would be evidence of the crime of arrest—driving without a license—in the vehicle. Justice Scalia joined the majority in order to avoid a "4-to-1-to-4 opinion that leaves the governing rule uncertain."[75] Justice Breyer said that, were the question one of first impression, he would have abandoned the *Belton* rule. He declined to join the majority on the grounds that the burden for changing a "well established legal precedent" had not been met.[76]

II. The Future of Automobile Searches

A. THE PROBLEM OF EXPLORATORY SEARCHES

One of the primary arguments that had been offered by the respondents' amici in *Gant* for overruling or modifying *Belton* was that doing so would limit police officers' ability to conduct purely exploratory searches.[77] The facts of *Gant* illustrate this strategy. Recall that police officers first encountered Rodney Gant when he opened the door of a home they suspected was being used to sell drugs. Immediately following this conversation, police ran a check of his traffic record. As their interaction with Gant would have given police no reason to suspect him of traffic violations, they conducted the record check in the hope that they could later use a traffic stop as a justification to stop and investigate his possible connection to the drug activity. When Gant returned to the home in his vehicle, the officers would have had no grounds to detain him if they had not discovered the outstanding traffic warrant. The arrest for the traffic violation, in turn, permitted police to conduct an automatic search of his person and the passenger compartment of his vehicle. The search was permissible even

---

[74] Id at 1725 (Scalia, J, concurring).

[75] Id.

[76] Id at 1726 (Breyer, J, dissenting). Justice Breyer joined Justice Alito's dissent except as to Part II-E, which defended *Belton* and *Chimel*.

[77] See Brief Amicus Curiae of the ACLU and the ACLU of Florida in Support of Respondent, *Arizona v Gant*, No 07-542, *17–19 (S Ct filed Oct 19, 2007); Brief for Amicus Curiae National Association of Criminal Defense Lawyers in Support of Respondent, *Arizona v Gant*, No 07-542, *8–11, 15–25 (S Ct filed Oct 19, 2007).

though police lacked probable cause to believe that there were drugs in Gant's car and they had no reason to think Gant would have evidence of the crime of arrest—the traffic offense—on his person or in his vehicle.

By the time *Gant* came before the Supreme Court, this strategy of using traffic stops to conduct searches for non-traffic-related evidence was entrenched and widespread.[78] Two factors made so-called pretext stops possible. The first is that police can stop, arrest, and search almost any motorist by simply waiting for him or her to commit one of a myriad of minor traffic offenses. As state laws criminalize infractions such as failing to pay attention to the road, failing to signal a turn, or neglecting to come to a full stop at a stop sign, police officers are assured of catching a driver in a traffic violation if they observe him long enough. Once the suspect has been stopped, even for a very minor offense, police can arrest (and conduct a SITA) under *Atwater v City of Lago Vista*.[79] This rule holds even if the arrest itself was unlawful under state law.[80] Second, however, police neither will nor can enforce all minor traffic laws against all violators. This means police have unbridled discretion to use a traffic stop, arrest, and SITA to get a free search for evidence unrelated to the traffic violation that formally justified the stop. That their actual motivations for the stop, arrest, and search may be pretextual is irrelevant under *Whren v United States*.[81]

There are two possible objections to this practice. First, it allows police to avoid the requirement that they have probable cause to believe there is evidence of crime in the place to be searched. Police can use a traffic stop to detain a driver when they suspect criminal activity but have insufficient evidence to conduct a search based on probable cause. Without the traffic offense—which has nothing to do with the crime police are really interested in—there could be no stop. If we care about requiring police to search only

---

[78] See Harris, *Car Wars*, 66 Geo Wash L Rev at 567–76 (cited in note 22); see LaFave, 3 *Search and Seizure* § 5.2(e), (f), (g) at 114–25 (cited in note 50) (discussing problem of pretext search and possible solutions).

[79] 532 US 318 (2001) (holding that the Fourth Amendment permits a suspect to be arrested for a non-jailable criminal offense such as failure to wear a seatbelt).

[80] *Virginia v Moore*, 553 US 164 (2008) (holding that a police arrest in violation of a state law making a particular violation subject to citation only does not require exclusion of evidence under the Fourth Amendment).

[81] 517 US 806 (1996).

when they have a good reason to suspect criminal activity, then this practice is an end-run around the Fourth Amendment.

Second, police can use traffic stops to target motorists on the basis of race or other impermissible factors. Evidence suggests that, in fact, minority motorists are being stopped and searched in disproportionate numbers.[82] Randall Kennedy calls this the "racial tax."[83] Others call it the crime of "Driving While Black."[84] There are many possible reasons for this disproportion—racial prejudice, racial profiling, overrepresentation of some groups in particular criminal activity. The important point, however, is that pretext stops make it impossible to know whether police are motivated by appropriate or inappropriate goals. Under current Fourth Amendment law, racial motivations remain almost entirely hidden. If police wish to investigate a minority driver, they need only wait until the individual commits a traffic offense. They need not articulate any additional justification, and their actual motivations for the stop are irrelevant under Fourth Amendment law.[85] The danger of racially motivated pretextual stops is arguably the more serious objection.

Prior to *Gant*, there were at least three possible ways to have addressed the problem of pretextual stops. One way would have been to attack the pretext directly. This solution was foreclosed in *Whren v United States*,[86] a case with facts perfectly suited to a pretext challenge.[87] In *Whren*, plainclothes vice-squad officers patrolling in a "high drug area" became suspicious of the youthful occupants of a truck. When police officers made a U-turn heading toward the truck, it made a turn without signaling and sped off. Police pulled the driver over for speeding and failing to signal and observed through the car window two large plastic bags of crack cocaine. The defendants complained that police officers would not

---

[82] See, for example, Randall Kennedy, *Race, Crime, and the Law* 137 (1997) (arguing that police use race as evidence of the increased risk of criminal conduct); Sheri Lynn Johnson, *Race and the Decision to Detain a Suspect*, 93 Yale L J 214, 220, 236–39 (1983) (criticizing the use of race as a signal of involvement in criminal activity); Angela J. Davis, *Race, Cops, and Traffic Stops*, 51 Miami L Rev 425, 431 (1997) ("Empirical evidence suggests that race is frequently a defining factor in pretextual traffic stops.").

[83] Randall Kennedy, *Blind Spot*, Atlantic Monthly 24 (Apr 2002).

[84] See, for example, Harris, *Driving While Black*, 87 J Crim L & Criminol at 572 (cited in note 22).

[85] See *Whren v United States*, 517 US 806 (1996).

[86] Id.

[87] Id.

have stopped their truck for the traffic offense unless they had been looking for drugs. They argued that since police "will almost invariably be able to catch any given motorist in a technical violation" they will be tempted "to use traffic stops as a means of investigating other law violations, as to which no probable cause or reasonable suspicion exists."[88] In addition, defendants, who were African American, argued that police officers could stop motorists based on impermissible factors such as race by hiding behind a traffic stop. The Supreme Court held that as the officers had probable cause to believe the defendants had violated a traffic law, the officers' subjective motivations were irrelevant. In a nod to the defendants' concern about racially motivated stops, the Supreme Court directed them to the Equal Protection Clause.[89] There is widespread agreement, however, that suits challenging pretext stops under the Equal Protection Clause do not offer a comparable solution. Not only are such suits unlikely to be brought and difficult to win, but most importantly there is no exclusionary rule under the Equal Protection Clause.[90]

A second strategy for putting an end to pretextual stops would have been to limit the kinds of crimes for which police can arrest (thereby limiting the availability of the SITA). This route was foreclosed by the Supreme Court in *Atwater v City of Lago Vista*.[91] Gail Atwater was stopped for a seatbelt violation, a misdemeanor offense for which there was no jail time but for which police could arrest under state law. When Atwater failed to produce her license and registration, the officer arrested her and took her to the police station. She was subsequently released and paid a $50 fine for the seatbelt offense. Atwater argued that the Fourth Amendment should be read to prohibit warrantless arrests for convictions that would carry no jail time, unless police have a compelling need for immediate detention. In affirming the lawfulness of Atwater's arrest, the majority declined to acknowledge the broader significance of the case: Arrests for fine-only offenses give police officers almost complete discretion to search motorists without articulating any

---

[88] Id at 810.

[89] Id at 813.

[90] See, for example, Pamela S. Karlan, *Race, Rights, and Remedies in Criminal Adjudication*, 96 Mich L Rev 2001 (2001) (describing the barriers facing § 1983 suits for damages or injunctions under the Equal Protection Clause).

[91] 532 US 318 (2001).

reason beyond the traffic violation.[92] Whatever the majority meant by its assertion that there is no "epidemic of unnecessary minor-offense arrests,"[93] the reality is that police routinely use traffic stops for the purpose of conducting exploratory searches. And the dissent objected that after *Whren* had put subjective considerations beyond review, the only way to prevent the use of minor offenses to conduct such searches was to disallow arrests for minor offenses, a route now also foreclosed.

The final strategy for limiting pretextual stops—the one partially adopted by *Gant*—would have been to eliminate the incentive to do such stops: the promise of an automatic SITA regardless of the crime of arrest. Here it is useful to conceive of the SITA as comprising two parts: the search of the arrestee's *person* and the search of the arrestee's *grabbing area*.[94] As to the arrestee's person the Supreme Court declined to eliminate the automatic search incentive in *United States v Robinson*,[95] upholding a SITA of an individual who was stopped and arrested for driving on a revoked license. During the post-arrest search of the defendant, police found in his pocket a crumpled cigarette package containing cocaine. The lower court had held that the search of the arrestee's pocket and the opening of the cigarette package were unlawful as an incident of a traffic arrest. The court reasoned that police could have ensured their own safety by using a *Terry* frisk and there was no other justification for the more intrusive search.[96]

The Supreme Court reversed, holding that officers may do an automatic search of the arrestee's person incident to arrest, including garment pockets and containers, regardless of the offense for which the individual was arrested. The Court's reasoning for the automatic search was twofold: First, the Court noted that due to the "danger to the police officer flow[ing] from the fact of the arrest, and its attendant proximity, stress, and uncertainty" police

---

[92] See id at 371–72 (O'Connor, J, dissenting).

[93] Id at 353.

[94] See *United States v Robinson*, 414 US 218, 224 (1973) (opining that the search incident to arrest is comprised of "two distinct propositions . . . that a search may be made of the person of the arrestee . . . . [and] that a search may be made of the area within the control of the arrestee").

[95] Id.

[96] Police did not claim that the cigarette package felt like a weapon, which would have justified removing and perhaps opening it under the "plain feel" doctrine. See *Minnesota v Dickerson*, 508 US 366 (1993).

are justified in making sure that any suspect is disarmed.[97] Thus, every arrest—regardless of the underlying crime—triggers a SITA. Second, as to the scope of the SITA, the Court reasoned that an arrest is more dangerous and uncertain with regard to officer safety than a *Terry* stop. Accordingly, while a *Terry* frisk requires police officers to demonstrate they reasonably believed the suspect was armed and dangerous, a post-arrest search of the suspect's person does not call for a factual showing that the suspect was likely to resort to violence or destroy evidence. The SITA requires no justification save the arrest itself. Also unlike a *Terry* frisk, which requires police to justify each step in the search, a SITA of the suspect's person automatically includes pockets and containers. The Court rejected the *Terry* analysis in the arrest context on the grounds that the increased risk and uncertainty posed by an arrest call for a bright-line rule rather than a case-by-case analysis.[98]

It is arguable, however, that neither of these reasons justified the seizure and subsequent search of the cigarette package found in Robinson's pocket (and, as we shall see, neither justifies the SITA of the grabbing area). Even if the search for weapons or evidence is automatic, it need not include places where these items could not plausibly be found. Police did not claim that the cigarette package could have contained a weapon. In addition, there was no cause for thinking that the suspect, arrested for driving on a suspended license, would have evidence of crime on his person. The Court's single sentence explaining the lawfulness of the search was a conclusion rather than a reason: "Having in the course of a *lawful search* come upon the crumpled package of cigarettes, [the police officer] was entitled to inspect it" and seize the contraband found inside.[99] What this statement confirms is that the scope of the SITA of the person is not limited to places where a weapon (or evidence of crime) could plausibly be. Why this would be so is not clear, and, moreover, it contradicts a central premise of the Court's Fourth Amendment jurisprudence: that the scope of a lawful search is limited by its justification. As a practical matter, of course, police would surely have seized and opened the cigarette package at the police station pursuant to a routine inventory of

---

[97] *Robinson*, 414 US at 234 & n 5.

[98] Id at 235.

[99] Id at 236 (emphasis added).

the arrestee's possessions. If so, the discovery of the cocaine was only a matter of time, and perhaps this fact is an adequate explanation for the Court's holding.

None of these rationales, however, ultimately justifies an *automatic* SITA of the arrestee's grabbing area (as *Belton* and sometimes *Chimel* have been read to authorize).[100] The asserted rationales for the grabbing area search, like the SITA of the person, are safety and destruction of evidence. In order to effectively disarm the arrestee, the Court reasoned in *Chimel*, police must have the power to remove any weapons that the suspect might be able to reach. "A gun on a table or in a drawer in front of one who is arrested can be as dangerous to the arresting officer as one concealed in the clothing of the person arrested."[101] Similarly, a gun on or under the seat or within reaching distance in the passenger compartment could be grabbed and used against an officer seeking to arrest a suspect in an automobile.

Stated this way the rationale makes perfect sense. The problem is that the rationale does not fit the circumstances of real-world arrests. Regardless of the location of the arrest, police officers virtually always search the arrestee and secure him *before* conducting a search of the location in which the suspect was arrested. While it is theoretically true that a gun within reaching distance is as dangerous as a gun on the arrestee's person—and if a gun were within reach police could surely seize it—in most circumstances the best strategy is to secure the arrestee so that he cannot grab anything nearby. But once police have done so, the justification for a safety-based grabbing area search or seizure—that goes beyond weapons or contraband in plain view—no longer applies. Similarly, the need for an emergency-based bright-line search rule has also ceased. Moreover, unlike items on the arrestee's person, which will be subject to seizure and search during inventory, the same cannot be said about items in the arrestee's grabbing area. Obviously the grabbing area in a residence is not subject to inventory, and police may or may not have the authority to impound and inventory the arrestee's automobile.[102] Thus, unlike the search

---

[100] See notes 135–37 and accompanying text (discussing lower courts' application of *Chimel*).

[101] *Chimel v California*, 395 US 752, 763 (1969).

[102] See note 113 and accompanying text.

of the arrestee's person, it cannot be said that the seizure of items in the grabbing area is "just a matter of time."

The only rationale that could justify an automatic SITA of the arrestee's grabbing area—after the arrestee has been secured and/ or moved—is that an arrestee has a reduced expectation of privacy in areas that could contain evidence of contraband. (The pre-*Chimel* SITA cases had this flavor, although a number of them involved individuals who at the time of arrest were engaged in criminal activity.) Justice Scalia made this point in his concurrence in *Thornton v United States*,[103] where he argued that the only justification for an *automatic* SITA of the passenger compartment of an automobile is that it might contain evidence relevant to the crime for which the suspect was arrested.[104] As he sensibly points out, it is "not illogical to assume that evidence of crime is most likely to be found where the suspect was apprehended."[105]

Of course, this rationale does nothing to justify an automatic grabbing area search when the underlying offense is a traffic violation. And it is precisely this search that gives rise to the problem of police officers using traffic stops to conduct exploratory searches for evidence of other crimes. The obvious solution—and the one ultimately adopted by the Supreme Court in *Gant*—is to limit the grabbing area search during traffic stops to situations that pose an actual risk of danger or destruction of evidence.

It bears noting that the best answer to Justice Alito's stare decisis argument in *Gant*, and the one the majority failed to make, is precisely the intractability of the exploratory search problem. What *had* changed since *Belton* is not the factual premise for the grabbing area search, as the *Gant* majority claimed, but that subsequent Supreme Court holdings had transformed the SITA into a strategy for conducting exploratory searches of virtually any motorist. *Atwater* permitted police to arrest for offenses so minor that any motorist could be subject to a SITA of their automobile, and *Whren* made police motivation irrelevant. These post-*Belton* holdings gave police almost unlimited discretion to stop, arrest, and search motorists. The best argument for overruling *Belton* was that

---

[103] 541 US 615, 630 (2003).

[104] Id at 630 (Scalia, J, concurring).

[105] Id.

limiting the SITA of the grabbing area was the only remaining strategy for reining in the exploratory search.

B. NARROWING THE BELTON RULE: GANT'S FIRST HOLDING

While police organizations worried that limiting the *Belton* search would be disastrous for law enforcement and the defense bar predicted that it would be a victory against exploratory searches, the truth is much more nuanced and probably somewhere in between. Recall the *Gant* majority held that police may do a *Belton* search only if the arrestee is "unsecured and within reaching distance of the passenger compartment at the time of the search"[106] *or* it is "reasonable to believe that evidence of the offense of arrest might be found in the vehicle."[107] As a formal matter, this holding means that police will have little incentive to conduct traffic stops motivated by the desire to conduct exploratory searches. When police officers arrest a suspect, the safest course of action is to remove the suspect from the vehicle, place him in handcuffs, and move him to a secure location away from the vehicle. Once they take these actions, police are not permitted to conduct a search incident to arrest of the vehicle under *Gant*'s first holding. And *Gant*'s second holding is also of no help in these circumstances as it is not "reasonable to believe" that evidence of a traffic offense will be found in the vehicle.

Thus, at first glance, it appears that *Gant*'s narrowing of the *Belton* rule could significantly narrow police ability to do automobile searches and, in particular, their power to use traffic arrests to search for evidence of other crimes. As a number of observers have already pointed out, however, *Gant* left police with alternative ways to justify automobile searches. And many of these alternatives are easily manipulated to use a traffic stop to obtain an exploratory search. Which of these judgments is ultimately correct will depend in large part on the accuracy of the claim that police can accomplish substantially the same searches using different rationales. This in turn requires a detailed analysis of the alleged alternative strategies and the extent to which they are, in fact, equivalent to the old search incident to arrest. I turn to this task below.

First, it bears noting that *Gant* will have no effect at all on

---

[106] *Arizona v Gant*, 129 S Ct 1710, 1719 (2009).

[107] Id at 1714.

pretextual *stops*, which remain unreviewable for Fourth Amendment purposes under *Whren* and *Atwater*. Moreover, once the vehicle has been stopped police officers have multiple ways to gain access to the vehicle and its passengers. Perhaps the easiest and least costly option is for police to simply ask the driver for permission to search. According to national and state statistics on police justifications for automobile stops and searches, consent searches make up a large proportion of police searches.[108] It turns out that once an individual has been stopped by police, he will usually consent to a search of the vehicle. This is true even if there is evidence of crime in the automobile and police are likely to find it. It appears that guilty drivers consent because they fear that failure to consent will make them look guilty to police or in hope that if they do consent they will look innocent and police will decide not to take the time to search. In addition, individuals who have been stopped, subjected to a license and registration check, and asked whether they have drugs or weapons in their automobiles may not realize that they still have the right to say no when police ask to search. And police officers are under no constitutional obligation to apprise citizens that they may refuse consent or to tell them when a stop has ended and they are free to go.[109] *Gant* has nothing to say about the use of pretext traffic stops in order to obtain consent to search.

Second, if the driver or owner refuses consent, police can still arrest for the traffic offense under *Atwater*.[110] While, after *Gant*,

---

[108] A 2005 report by the Bureau of Justice Statistics found that 57.6 percent of all searches of drivers or their vehicles during a traffic stop were conducted with the consent of the driver. Bureau of Justice Statistics, *Contacts Between the Police and the Public* 2005, 6 (2007). The Texas Department of Safety has collected four years of data on traffic searches. In the third and fourth year of the study, when the department kept the most comprehensive statistics, it reported that approximately 36 percent of searches were conducted pursuant to consent. Steven R. Wolfson, *Racial Profiling in the Texas Department of Public Safety Traffic Stops: Race Aware or Race Benign?* 8 Scholar 117, 172–73 (2006). See also Dennis Rosenbaum and Alexander Weiss, *Illinois Traffic Stops Statistics Study: 2008 Annual Report* 10 (2008) (finding that 91 percent of drivers gave police their consent to search); Robin Engel et al, *Project on Police-Citizen Contacts: Final Report* 2006, 53 (2006) (a 2006 report on traffic stops in Philadelphia found that consent searches made up 68.5 percent of total searches and 41 percent of drivers were searched based solely on consent).

[109] *Schneckloth v Bustamonte*, 412 US 218 (1973) (holding that a person's knowledge that he has the right not to consent is only one factor to be taken into account in determining whether his consent was voluntary); *Ohio v Robinette*, 519 US 33 (1996) (holding that a suspect who has been lawfully seized need not be advised that he is "free to leave" before his consent to search will be found voluntary).

[110] If police tell the arrestee that they can (and will) arrest the driver and impound the vehicle if consent is not forthcoming, this statement of fact is unlikely to be treated as a

arrest for a traffic violation no longer affords the right to an automatic search of the *vehicle*, it still guarantees an automatic SITA of the *person* of the arrestee under *Robinson*. Recall the Supreme Court held in *Robinson* that the post-arrest search of the person is justified regardless of whether there is reason to believe that weapons or evidence of crime will "in fact be found upon the person of the suspect."[111] The search incident to arrest of the person requires nothing except the *fact* of the arrest.

While the reasoning in *Gant* could be viewed as undermining the *Robinson* guarantee of an automatic SITA, I believe the best reading of *Gant* leaves *Robinson* undisturbed. The argument to the contrary goes like this: The *Gant* majority emphasized that searches incident to arrest must be no broader than their rationale, which is either to prevent the arrestee from securing weapons or to prevent him from destroying or concealing evidence. Thus, a SITA of the vehicle is justified only if the arrestee is in a position from which it is likely that he can, in fact, secure weapons or evidence of the crime. The *Robinson* Court upheld a search of an arrested traffic offender, during which police found drugs inside a crumpled cigarette package in the arrestee's pocket. As the arrest was for driving with a revoked license and there was no reason to think the package contained a weapon or contraband, the search of the cigarette package was not justified by either of the rationales deemed essential in *Gant*. Applying *Gant* to the SITA of the arrestee's person would mean that police could search for weapons but not for evidence of crime.

The better reading of *Gant*, however, is that its analysis is limited to the search of the arrestee's grabbing area. There are good reasons to treat the SITA of the person differently from the SITA of vehicles or premises. Most importantly, police officers have more compelling reasons for doing an automatic search of the arrestee's person than they do his vehicle. As police will continue to be in close proximity with the arrestee himself while securing and transporting him, it makes sense to permit a full search of his person without additional justification. The safety rationale arguably justifies the seizure of Robinson's cigarette package, as it could have contained a razor or small knife. Of course, once police

---

threat for Fourth Amendment purposes. See LaFave, *Search and Seizure* § 8.2(c) at 69–75 (cited in note 50).

[111] *Robinson*, 414 US at 235.

officers had secured the cigarette package, Robinson could no longer have accessed any weapon inside so there was no immediate justification for opening it. Even so, however, Robinson would have been required to empty his pockets upon arrival at the place of custody both for safety reasons and to permit his personal effects to be inventoried for safekeeping (including opening containers). Thus, as it was only a matter of time before the illegal drugs would have been discovered, it makes little difference whether the discovery is made at the point of the arrest or in the police station. The same cannot be said of the automobile; while the arrestee will always be taken into custody, the car may or may not be impounded and inventoried even if the driver is arrested. Authority for impoundment and inventory is a matter of state law, and the police may in any event choose not to take the time and trouble to do it.

Assuming then that *Gant* leaves *Robinson* undisturbed, police can continue to stop and arrest motorists for traffic offenses and get an automatic SITA of the arrestee's person. If this search yields evidence of crime—or if police see evidence in plain view as they did in *Whren*—this may give them probable cause to search the automobile under *California v Acevedo*.[112] Alternatively, these searches might provide evidence of an additional arrestable offense, which could lead to a SITA of at least the passenger compartment of the vehicle under *Gant*'s second holding, which I discuss in more detail below.

But suppose police officers find no evidence of crime on the arrestee's person or in plain view. And suppose further that there is no justification under *Terry* to do a frisk of the automobile. Police officers still have one final option if state law permits: to impound the arrestee's automobile and inventory the contents. Impoundments and inventories are viewed as purely administrative actions. The lawfulness (including the constitutionality) of these actions depends upon compliance with regularized state procedures and a purpose of furthering the interests of public safety and community caretaking.[113] As long as police follow predeter-

---

[112] 500 US 565 (1991) (authorizing a search of the entire vehicle if police have probable cause to believe there is evidence of crime within).

[113] See *South Dakota v Opperman*, 428 US 364, 368 (1976); *Colorado v Bertine*, 479 US 367, 375 (1987). In analyzing impoundments, lower federal courts carefully scrutinize the existence and sufficiency of standardized impoundment policies and most require an affirmative showing that impoundment was justified by public safety or community care-

mined procedures that reflect such interests, impoundments and inventories are largely immune from review for alleged pretext. Moreover, police may inventory the entire automobile (not just the passenger compartment) and any evidence of crime they might find may be seized and used in a criminal case against the suspect. While some have predicted that impoundments and inventories are the best substitutes for the now unavailable *Belton* searches, these actions are costly substitutes. Impoundments and inventories are time consuming and compliance with regularized procedures means that police cannot pick and choose their targets based on the likelihood of finding evidence of crime. This is an area that is likely to see more litigation in the aftermath of *Arizona v Gant*.

One final observation is that *Gant*'s first holding creates an interesting irony: With the possible exception of circumstances involving multiple occupants of a vehicle, police officers have more power to search an automobile when they conduct a *Terry* stop than when they conduct a custodial arrest. Officers may "frisk" an automobile if they reasonably believe the suspect is dangerous and may gain immediate control of weapons, a situation that may occur if the suspect is stopped but later released and permitted to return to his automobile.

C. "REASONABLE TO BELIEVE": GANT'S SECOND HOLDING

While *Gant*'s first holding has gotten more attention, its second holding may turn out to be more important. The Court held that a SITA of an arrestee's automobile is permissible if it is "reasonable to believe that evidence of the offense of arrest might be found in the vehicle."[114] Unfortunately, Justice Stevens's opinion provides absolutely no insight into what he meant by the "reasonable to believe" standard, except to say that the justification for his new rule does not flow from the safety and destruction of evidence rationales of *Chimel*.[115] Moreover, the language used by Justice

---

taking purposes. See, for example, *United States v Bridges*, 245 F Supp 2d 1034, 1034–35 (SD Iowa 2003) (finding impoundment unlawful where no written policies and purpose not related to public safety or community caretaking); *United States v Donnelly*, 885 F Supp 300 (D Mass 1995) (finding impoundment unlawful because policies did not adequately constrain police discretion to impound); *United States v Best*, 415 F Supp 2d 50 (D Conn 2006) (finding impoundment lawful because ordered pursuant to standardized procedures and for legitimate community caretaking purposes).

[114] *Gant*, 129 S Ct at 1714.

[115] Id at 1732–24.

Stevens tracks neither of the two established Fourth Amendment standards: probable cause and reasonable suspicion. Justice Stevens explicitly borrowed this language from Justice Scalia's concurrence in *Thornton*. The concurrence does provide a more detailed account of what the language might mean, but no other Justice joined Justice Scalia's opinion.

By using the term "reasonable to believe," the Court explicitly precluded searches for evidence when there is no plausible reason to believe that there would be evidence in the car—as would be true for most if not all traffic stops. In this way, *Gant*'s twin holdings removed much of the incentive for police to conduct pretextual traffic stops. On the other hand, it seems clear that the *Gant* Court did not mean the "reasonable to believe" standard to require probable cause. "Probable cause" is a term of art that echoes the precise constitutional language of the Fourth Amendment itself.[116] Surely the Court would have used this explicit term if this is what it meant. Perhaps it was just sloppy drafting. But this seems implausible, as the precise phrase "reasonable to believe" was repeated verbatim three times: twice by Justice Stevens in *Gant*[117] and once in Justice Scalia's concurrence in *Thornton*.[118] In any event, police can already conduct a warrantless search of a car if they have probable cause to believe it contains evidence of crime.[119] It would have been odd if the Supreme Court had reiterated this settled principle using different language without explanation. Perhaps anticipating potential confusion between the new *Gant* rule and the automobile exception, Justice Stevens explicitly distinguished the rule in *California v Acevedo* and *United States v Ross*, which he described as another "established exception to the warrant requirement." He explained that *Ross* permits "searches for evidence relevant to offenses other than the offense of arrest, and the scope of the search authorized is broader."[120]

---

[116] US Const, Amend IV. While Fourth Amendment cases use various phrases to explain the meaning of probable cause, virtually all Fourth Amendment holdings use this precise term except in cases where only reasonable suspicion is required.

[117] *Gant*, 129 S Ct at 1714, 1721, 1723. I am assuming that "reason to believe" and "reasonable to believe" mean the same thing.

[118] *Thornton*, 541 US at 632.

[119] See *California v Acevedo*, 500 US 565 (1991).

[120] *Gant*, 129 S Ct at 1721 (citing *United States v Ross*, 456 US 798, 820–21 (1982)). The dissent also seems to agree that the majority's test is not equivalent to probable cause. *Gant*, 129 S Ct at 1731 (Alito, J, dissenting).

The remaining question is whether an arrest for a crime as to which evidence might possibly be found—such as the drug crime at issue in *Gant*—automatically justifies a search of the car even if there is no *additional reason* to think there might be evidence in the car. Justice Scalia's concurring opinion in *Gant* might suggest this conclusion. He described the rule at issue in *Gant* as "the rule *automatically* permitting a search when the driver or an occupant is arrested."[121] Justice Scalia explained that he would have preferred to overrule *Belton* and adopt something akin to *Gant*'s second holding. He would have held that "a vehicle search incident to arrest is *ipso facto* 'reasonable' only when the *object of the search* is evidence of the crime for which the arrest was made or of another crime that the officer has probable cause to believe occurred."[122] By contrast, where there has been no arrest, officers must have "reason to believe"—by which Justice Scalia means reasonable suspicion—"that the suspect is dangerous and may gain immediate control of weapons."[123]

The term "reasonable to believe," however, does suggest that in addition to having probable cause to arrest the suspect, police must have some additional reason to think there may be evidence of that crime in the automobile. Under some circumstances this might not require much. For example, in *Thornton* police conducted a consensual search of a suspect who had just alighted from his automobile, finding marijuana and cocaine. The officers then conducted a SITA of the passenger compartment of the suspect's vehicle and found a handgun. In his concurrence—the template for *Gant*'s second holding—Justice Scalia concluded that the SITA was justified because it was "reasonable . . . to believe that further contraband or similar evidence relevant to the crime for which he had been arrested might be found in the vehicle from which he had just alighted and which was still within his vicinity at the time of the arrest."[124] Justice Scalia explained that the post-arrest premises search was not a "general or exploratory [search] for whatever might be turned up" because it is logical to "assume" that evidence of his crime is "most likely to be found where the suspect was apprehended." The "fact of the arrest distinguishes the arrestee

[121] Id at 1724.

[122] Id at 1725 (emphasis added).

[123] Id at 1724 (quoting *Michigan v Long*, 463 US 1032, 1049 (1983)).

[124] *Thornton*, 541 US at 632.

from society at large, and distinguishes a search for evidence of *his* crime from general rummaging."[125] As this was the entirety of Justice Scalia's analysis of the legality of the SITA, it appears the only thing that mattered was the nature of the crime of arrest. On the other hand, in *Thornton* cocaine had been discovered on the arrestee's person, which might have suggested that more drugs would be found in the automobile. It is not clear whether Justice Scalia was calling for a showing of articulable facts of the sort required by *Terry v Ohio*,[126] or whether the nature of the crime was enough. The former would be something akin to reasonable suspicion. The latter would mean that an arrest for some kinds of recent or ongoing crimes could lead to an automatic search of the vehicle in or near which an individual was arrested.

On the other hand, it is easy to imagine cases in which a person is arrested in a car for an offense that might suggest evidence could be found in the automobile but where police have no *independent* reason to believe the automobile contains evidence. This might be true, for example, of arrests for certain white-collar offenses, arrests for violent crimes not connected to the automobile, or arrests of high-level drug dealers who do not themselves handle the contraband. In such cases, *Gant* seems to prohibit a car search incident to arrest unless police officers have something more than probable cause for the arrest. But how much more is unclear.

Unaccountably, the Supreme Court declined to commit itself to either of the two familiar Fourth Amendment standards ordinarily required to justify governmental action: probable cause and reasonable suspicion. Lower courts will not have the luxury of leaving the standard undefined, but they have little to go on. The

---

[125] Id at 630 (emphasis added). Justice Scalia's reasoning in *Thornton* harkened back to a pre-*Chimel* line of cases in which post-arrest searches relied on a "more general interest in gathering evidence" relevant to the crime of arrest. Id (citing *United States v Rabinowitz*, 339 US 56 (1950)). In applying the *Rabinowitz* rule, most lower courts required only probable cause for the arrest without regard to the likelihood that evidence of the crime of arrest would actually be found at the place of arrest. Thus the arresting officer was permitted to conduct a search of the entire premises in which the arrestee had a "possessory interest" as long as the defendant was arrested on the premises and not elsewhere. See generally LaFave, 3 *Search and Seizure* § 6.3(b) at 348–50 (cited in note 50). A few lower courts treated the arrest and search as separate events and held that the post-arrest search was justified only if police had reason to believe that "articles subject to seizure are concealed at the place of arrest" but most did not. Id (quoting *United States v Antonelli Fireworks Co.*, 53 F Supp 870 (WDNY 1943)).

[126] 392 US 1, 21 (1968) (holding that police must be able to identify *"articulable facts* which, taken together with rational inferences from these facts, reasonably warrant" the stop or frisk).

courts could opt for a reasonable suspicion standard—or something less—based on Justice Scalia's concurrence in *Thornton*. Or, given that the Supreme Court declined to use either of the two familiar terms, probable cause or reasonable suspicion, they might opt for something in between. The Supreme Court can be faulted for leaving the lower courts with virtually no guidance for applying *Gant*'s second holding.

It is also not clear what the *scope* of these new evidentiary searches is or should be. On the one hand, Justice Stevens's opinion for the majority purports to limit rather than to overrule *Belton*. As *Belton* permitted an automatic search of only the passenger compartment, perhaps the "reason to believe" search is so limited. But it's hard to think why this would be. The *Gant* search is for evidence of a particular crime and thus it follows that the scope of the search should be dictated not by the old *Belton* rule, but by the object of the search, which would include anywhere the evidence sought could be hidden. There is no logical reason to limit the scope of such a search to the passenger compartment if evidence of the crime of arrest could be found in the trunk. While permitting a full SITA of an automobile in connection with the crime of arrest could create some overlap with the automobile exception, one could imagine cases where police would not have probable cause to search the automobile but they would have probable cause to arrest the driver.

With the somewhat unusual lineup in *Gant*—Justices Stevens, Souter, Thomas, Ginsburg, and Scalia for the Court—it is a little hard to predict what any or all of them actually meant by the "reasonable to believe" rule. Indeed, it is likely that Justice Stevens deliberately left the standard undefined in order to garner the necessary votes to reach a majority. This makes it even more difficult to predict what the Court will hold in the inevitable supplementary cases necessary to define its obscure holding.

III. Broader Implications of Gant

Although *Gant*'s formal holding is limited to the automobile context, its reasoning has broader implications. I suggest three.

A. THE WARRANTLESS WORLD OF INTEREST BALANCING

On the one hand, *Gant* represents a narrowing of police officers' search authority: They can no longer use traffic offenses as an excuse to search the passenger compartment. Instead, they get a passenger compartment search only if the arrestee is unsecured and within grabbing range of the automobile, which—as we have seen—will be almost never. While the search incident to arrest is no longer automatic, I have argued that *Gant* will limit police officers less than *Gant*'s supporters would like to think. *Gant*'s second holding, authorizing a vehicle search for evidence of the crime of arrest, also appears to narrow police authority because it disallows evidentiary searches in connection with traffic arrests. On the other hand, however, the Court inexplicably declined to use either of the familiar Fourth Amendment standards that ordinarily define the quantity and quality of evidence necessary to justify searches and seizures. It is difficult to know what to make of the Court's Delphic holding, but it could open the door to a more explicit under-all-the-circumstances balancing approach in contrast to the existing, two-tier reasonable suspicion/probable cause analysis. It may be yet another sign that the Court is moving toward an ever more fluid Fourth Amendment based on reasonableness balancing rather than warrants and probable cause.

Ever since the Supreme Court's decisions in *Camara v Municipal Court*[127] and *Terry v Ohio*,[128] Fourth Amendment law has been moving further and further from its monolithic starting point where probable cause had a unified meaning and searches and seizures were all or nothing affairs.[129] In these cases, the Court invoked a balancing test to determine the reasonableness of a search, holding for the first time that a lesser intrusion on individual privacy interests requires a lesser governmental interest. In *Camara*, the Court cabined its interest balancing analysis to noncriminal, administrative searches, but in the landmark case of *Terry v Ohio*, the Court extended its sliding-scale approach to traditional criminal investigations.

Following *Terry*, the Supreme Court has continued to invoke

---

[127] 387 US 523 (1967).

[128] 392 US 1 (1968).

[129] See also Anthony Amsterdam, *Perspectives on the Fourth Amendment*, 58 Minn L Rev 349, 388 (1974) (calling the Fourth Amendment "monolithic").

the language of interest balancing in more and more contexts.[130] While "probable cause" requires—at least theoretically—some fixed quantum of evidence, the degree of certainty required to satisfy reasonable suspicion depends upon what police are looking for and what kind of investigation they propose to do. For example, in *Florida v J.L.*,[131] the Court held that an anonymous tip that police would find a young black male wearing a plaid shirt standing at the bus stop and carrying a gun was not sufficient under *Terry* to justify a stop and frisk.[132] The Court went on to say, however, that if the same tip had been about the location of a bomb rather than a gun, it might have been enough. A more serious governmental interest—the greater risk to the public from a bomb and the lack of innocent reasons for possessing one—might require a lesser showing to justify the same or greater level of intrusion. The Court in *J.L.* also stated that less reliable information might justify a search in contexts involving lesser expectations of privacy, like airports and schools.[133] Moreover, not only does the required quantum of evidence vary depending on the circumstances—what the government is looking for and where it is looking—but it also determines the range of investigatory activities that are permitted. In describing how to analyze the permissible length of a *Terry* stop, the Court has held that the method of investigation must be designed to "confirm or dispel [the officer's] suspicions quickly" and must last no longer than necessary to effectuate that purpose.[134]

That the Supreme Court already refers to administrative searches, school and airport searches, and searches for weapons during a *Terry* stop not as separate categories but as examples of the same balancing analysis signals a functional, if not a formal move toward a world in which interest balancing is the rule rather than the exception. What is striking about *Gant*'s second holding is that the Court opted for reasonableness language without invoking either of the two familiar Fourth Amendment standards.

---

[130] See, for example, *Mich. Dep't of State Police v Sitz*, 496 US 444 (1990) (roadblocks); *NJ v TLO*, 469 US 325 (1985) (searches of students by school officials); *Vernonia School District 47J v Acton*, 515 US 646 (1995) (random urinalysis drug testing of students).

[131] 529 US 266 (2000).

[132] Id at 268.

[133] Id at 273–74.

[134] *United States v Sharpe*, 470 US 675 (1985).

While probable cause and reasonable suspicion have been viewed as embodying roughly two different quantities (and qualities) of evidence—a full search requires more (and better) evidence of criminal activity than a *Terry* frisk—the phrase "reasonable to be-lieve" could suggest a case-by-case, under-all-the-circumstances balancing analysis. As a functional matter, the Supreme Court has already moved a long way in this direction; however, a formal embrace of the case-by-case approach would have important im-plications for Fourth Amendment analysis surrounding new and innovative technologies that raise widely varying privacy concerns.

B. GANT AND CHIMEL SEARCHES

While the *Gant* majority made clear that its *holding* is limited to vehicle searches incident to arrest, the *rationale* for its holding has implications for searches incident to arrest in homes as well. First, *Gant* made clear that *Chimel* searches are strictly limited to their justification: to prevent suspects from accessing weapons or destroying or concealing evidence. This part of the majority's rea-soning surely applies to searches incident to arrest in houses as well as in cars. Just as an arrestee who is secured in a patrol car is no longer within grabbing distance of the passenger compart-ment, an arrestee who has been handcuffed and moved to a secure location is no longer within grabbing distance of the location where he was arrested. If *Gant* applies it would resolve a split in the lower courts on the lawful scope of a *Chimel* search in a house. Courts are divided on whether the scope of the search incident to arrest should be determined as of the time of the *arrest* (even if the arrestee has been moved or secured) or at the time of the *search*.[135] Many courts have adopted a *Belton*-like search rule for SITAs in the home, permitting searches of the hypothetical grab-bing area surrounding the suspect at the time he was arrested even if he has already been secured and even moved. Because the ques-tion is counterfactual, the analysis has usually resulted in a nearly bright-line rule permitting a search of the arrestee's hypothetical "wingspan."[136] Other courts have taken the view that the scope question should be asked at the time of the search. These courts

---

[135] See generally Moskovitz, 2002 Wis L Rev at 657 (cited in note 15).

[136] Id at 682–85 (citing cases). See, for example, *United States v Turner*, 926 F2d 883 (9th Cir 1991); *State v Murdock*, 455 NW2d 618 (1990).

almost never uphold a search under the SITA doctrine.[137]

The question at issue in these home-arrest cases is precisely the same question the *Gant* Court addressed in the context of vehicle searches, and the resolution should be the same. In homes, as in vehicles, police generally arrest, handcuff, and move arrestees to a secure location before conducting a *Chimel* search. But once they have done so, the justification for a *Chimel* search has evaporated, and *Gant* makes clear that no search incident to arrest is justified. As the dissent in *Gant* predicted, applying *Chimel* (as interpreted in *Gant*) to searches incident to arrest in homes will virtually eliminate such searches.[138]

The possibility that *Gant*'s second holding—that police may search a vehicle if they have reason to believe it may contain evidence of the crime of arrest—could apply to SITAs in homes is more remote and would be more controversial. While the Court explicitly limited this holding to the vehicle context, the rationale articulated in *Thornton* for permitting a search of the premises where a suspect is arrested is actually much broader. Harkening back to the pre-*Chimel* line of cases, Justice Scalia reasoned that "there is nothing irrational about broader police authority to search for evidence when and where the perpetrator of a crime is lawfully arrested." The "fact" of the arrest "distinguishes the arrestee from society at large, and distinguishes the search for evidence of *his* crime from general rummaging." It is "not illogical to assume that evidence of crime is most likely to be found where the suspect was apprehended."[139]

In this part of his *Thornton* concurrence, Justice Scalia's goal was to provide a more "honest" rationale for the automatic *Belton* vehicle search. His reasoning, however, is as true of arrests in homes as it is of arrests in vehicles. In the arrestee's home as in his vehicle, it makes sense to assume that "evidence of crime is most likely to be found where the suspect was apprehended." Would Justice Scalia approve the application of his *Gant* analysis to residential arrests, given the strong commitment to protecting

---

[137] Moskovitz, 2002 Wis L Rev at 685–88 (cited in note 15) (citing cases). See, for example, *People v Summers*, 86 Cal Rptr 2d 388 (Ct App 1999); *Stackhouse v State*, 468 A2d 333 (Md 1983).

[138] See *Arizona v Gant*, 129 S Ct 1710, 1730–31 (2009) (Alito, J, dissenting) (assuming that Gant's first holding should apply to "all arrestees" and noting that if scope of a search is determined at the time of the search, the *Chimel* rule will "rarely come into play").

[139] *Thornton*, 541 US at 630.

the privacy of the home demonstrated in his opinion in *Kyllo v United States*?[140] It is hard to know. One important difference between *Kyllo* and the SITA cases, however, is that when conducting a SITA in a home police would already be acting pursuant to a warrant (or in exigent circumstances) and with probable cause. The warrant to arrest sets the arrestee apart from society at large and "distinguishes the search for evidence of *his* crime from general rummaging." Thus, while Justice Scalia seems committed to the warrant requirement for searches of the home, it is not clear whether he would require a search warrant—in addition to an arrest warrant—to justify a search of the residence for evidence of the crime of arrest.[141]

C. BRIGHT-LINE RULES AND OFFICER SAFETY

The discussions surrounding *Belton* and *Gant* focused largely on questions having to do with officer safety, and in particular on the importance of bright-line rules that avoid requiring police officers to make difficult judgments in dangerous and uncertain circumstances. The connection between police safety and clear rules is a familiar refrain. While Fourth Amendment doctrine generally requires case-by-case determinations,[142] when it comes to officer safety the Supreme Court has opted for rules instead. So, for example, in *Pennsylvania v Mimms*[143] and *Maryland v Wilson*,[144] the Supreme Court held that when police officers stop a vehicle they

---

[140] 533 US 27 (2001). In *Kyllo*, Justice Scalia wrote for the Court that the use of a thermal imager to detect infrared radiation inside of a house constituted a Fourth Amendment search requiring probable cause and a warrant.

[141] See *Payton v New York*, 445 US 573 (1980). *Payton*, which held that police need an arrest warrant in order to enter a suspect's home to arrest him, was decided before Justice Scalia was on the Supreme Court. Of the Justices who were on the Court when *Payton* was decided, only Justice Stevens remains.

[142] See, for example, *Rakas v Illinois*, 439 US 128 (1978) ("This is not an area of the law in which any 'bright line rule' would safeguard both Fourth Amendment rights and the public interest in a fair and effective criminal justice system. The range of variables in the fact situations of search and seizure is almost infinite."); *Ohio v Robinette*, 519 US 33 (1996) ("In applying [the reasonableness] test we have consistently eschewed bright line rules, instead emphasizing the fact-specific nature of the reasonableness inquiry."); *Michigan v Chesternut*, 486 US 567 (1988) ("Both petitioner and respondent . . . in their attempts to fashion a bright-line rule applicable to all investigatory pursuits, have failed to heed this Court's clear direction that any assessment as to whether police conduct applies to a seizure implicating the Fourth Amendment must take into account all of the circumstances surrounding the incident in each individual case.").

[143] 434 US 106 (1977).

[144] 519 US 408 (1977).

may automatically order the driver and passengers, respectively, to get out of the car. The Court accepted the government's argument that police officers remove occupants from their automobiles to diminish the risk that they will make unobserved movements to secure weapons.[145] Similarly, the rule in *United States v Robinson*[146] that police get an automatic post-arrest search of the suspect, without regard to whether weapons or evidence are likely to be found on the suspect, seeks to avoid step-by-step justifications for safety-related decisions.

The Supreme Court explained the need for the *Belton* passenger compartment rule on precisely these grounds. In *Chimel* the Court had held that police officers may search the area into which an arrestee might be able to reach and grab a weapon or evidence. In applying this rule to arrests in automobiles, the *Belton* Court concluded that police officers needed a clear rule for what constituted the relevant grabbing area. The Court emphasized that police officers cannot be hampered by "a highly sophisticated set of rules, qualified by all kinds of ifs, ands, and buts and requiring the drawing of subtle nuances and hairline distinctions . . . which may be literally impossible of application by the officer in the field."[147] As an individual who is arrested in an automobile would likely be able to reach into most parts of the passenger compartment, the Court adopted a bright-line rule that permitted an automatic search of this entire area incident to arrest.

The *Gant* Court rejected the factual generalization underpinning *Belton*—that items inside the automobile are always within the arrestee's grabbing distance—because the Court recognized that police generally secure arrestees outside of the vehicle before searching.[148] Ironically, in *Belton* itself the arrestees were probably not within reach of the passenger compartment as they had been removed from their automobile and placed in separate locations on the highway. The only reason there was any risk that the suspects would have been able to grab weapons from the vehicle was that the officer was alone and had only one set of handcuffs for

---

[145] *Mimms*, 434 US at 110. See also *Wilson*, 519 US 408 (reasoning that passengers as well as drivers may employ violence to prevent police from discovering contraband in their automobiles).

[146] 414 US 218 (1973).

[147] *New York v Belton*, 453 US 454, 458 (1981).

[148] *Gant*, 129 S Ct at 1723.

four arrestees! (If the officer had had backup and four sets of handcuffs, perhaps there never would have been a *Belton* case.)[149] Whatever the benefits of the automatic *Belton* search, it was probably unnecessary to assuring police safety in the very case that created the rule (or it was necessary only because of the unrepresentative facts at issue in the case). More importantly, the *Belton* rule was so poorly matched to the factual circumstances surrounding an arrest precisely because the Court either did not know or did not acknowledge how police actually behave on the ground. The Court worried that without an automatic search, police officers would be forced to "draw[] subtle nuances and [make] hairline distinctions" about the lawfulness of searches for weapons.[150] What we now know, however, is that prior to *Belton* police officers already had their own clear rule: remove the suspect from the automobile, search his person, and put him in the patrol car. The officer in *Belton* probably searched the automobile because he had four suspects to control without backup and without enough handcuffs to go around. He didn't need *Belton* to tell him how to secure the scene.

What this analysis suggests is that, contrary to the Supreme Court's familiar refrain, bright-line rules are actually the *least* necessary when the issue is police safety. Police officers handcuff and secure arrestees before they search vehicles because it would compromise their own safety (and perhaps the safety of the public) to search a vehicle with the arrestee still inside or otherwise unsecured. Similarly, police officers who arrest suspects inside their homes handcuff their arrestees and move them to a secure location before they search any part of the premises where the arrest took place. Police conduct in confronting and securing suspects is determined much more by their own desire for self-preservation—and police "best practices" that reflect this commitment—than it is by constitutional rules, bright-line or otherwise.[151] Police offi-

---

[149] Of course, this depends upon whether you accept Justice Stevens's reading or Justice Alito's reading of *Belton*. See notes 59–67 and accompanying text. Although the specific facts in *Belton* were important to some members of the lower court, see notes 45–49 and accompanying text, the Supreme Court did not base its holding on the precise facts at issue.

[150] *Belton*, 453 US at 458 (citing Wayne R. LaFave, *"Case-by-Case Adjudication" versus "Standardized Procedures": The Robinson Dilemma*, 1974 Supreme Court Review 127, 142).

[151] See generally Rachel A. Harmon, *When Is Police Violence Justified?* 102 Nw U L Rev 1119 (2008) (arguing for a doctrine of excessive force that takes account of police officers' individual and institutional regard for their own safety).

cers will take these defensive actions regardless of what the Supreme Court says about whether or not a search of the grabbing area is lawful under the Fourth Amendment.

The claim has often been made that limiting *Belton* searches to instances in which the suspect is within grabbing distance of the vehicle will create perverse incentives for police officers to leave arrestees unsecured in order to get a search of the vehicle.[152] As any good police officer will tell you, however, this alleged risk is fanciful in the extreme. While police officers often ask drivers to remain in their vehicles during traffic stops resulting in tickets, they always ask vehicle occupants to step out of the automobile before placing them under arrest.[153] The rationale for these differing practices is that an arrest is more likely to provoke a violent confrontation with the suspect and ordering the suspect out of the automobile gives the officer better visibility and control should the arrestee try to access a weapon.

While bright-line rules are generally unnecessary to ensure that police officers can protect themselves, there is a good argument for adopting Fourth Amendment doctrines that avoid penalizing police officers for the actions they virtually always take—and we want them to take—as a matter of good police practice. For example, it makes good sense to hold that when police officers conduct a traffic stop or arrest they should have the authority to remove the driver and passengers from the vehicle without committing an unlawful seizure. For similar reasons, it makes sense to hold that police officers who conduct an automatic search of an arrestee's person for weapons and destructible evidence can do so consistent with the Fourth Amendment. But if so, the reason is not that the rules are necessary to guide police conduct but that police practices reasonably necessary to ensure their protection should not be deemed "unreasonable" within the meaning of the Fourth Amendment.

IV. CONCLUSION

In the end it is hard to predict precisely how much *Arizona*

---

[152] See *Gant*, 129 S Ct at 1730 (Alito, J, dissenting).

[153] The dissent in *Mimms* claimed that police generally require vehicle occupants to remain in their automobiles during a traffic *stop*, see 434 US at 119–20 (Stevens, J, dissenting); however, the practice is to remove the occupants prior to announcing and executing a custodial *arrest*. I have confirmed this point in multiple conversations with police officers and prosecutors.

v Gant[154] will matter. It may have a significant effect on Fourth Amendment law—and on police practices on the ground—or it may not make much difference at all. The answer will depend upon such yet to be answered questions as whether police have viable alternatives to the previously automatic *Belton* search and how these alternatives will affect police incentives to use exploratory searches. This in turn will depend on how these alternatives are litigated as they become more numerous. The answer will also be affected by how the lower courts apply *Gant*'s "reasonable to believe" standard and whether the Supreme Court clarifies what it meant in future cases. In addition, *Gant* may have broader effects, such as changing the way the courts analyze SITAs in the home and moving Fourth Amendment analysis toward a more explicit under-all-the-circumstances interest-balancing approach.

Gant's effect will also depend upon the resolution of other ambiguities in the Court's opinion. For example, does the majority's claim that it will be "the rare case" in which police are unable to prevent access to the automobile mean that police officers *must* secure a suspect if it is possible to do so? Assuming there are such "rare cases," what factual circumstances will warrant a *Belton* search on the grounds that the arrestee could "access the interior of the vehicle"? Suppose there are other passengers or civilians who remain unsecured: could this justify a search of the passenger compartment even if the arrestee is secured? (Recall, the majority in *Gant* distinguished *Belton* on precisely these grounds, namely, that in *Belton* one officer had to secure four arrestees.)

Finally, *Gant* implicitly calls into question the now familiar refrain that bright-line rules are necessary to ensure police safety. Police officers have much more compelling reasons to take action to preserve their own safety and that of the public than to ensure compliance with Fourth Amendment search-and-seizure rules. If bright-line rules make sense in such situations it is because we should avoid case-by-case adjudications that could risk penalizing police officers for taking actions that are safe and appropriate, not in order to make sure they do.

---

[154] 129 S Ct 1710 (2009).

ROSALIND DIXON

UPDATING CONSTITUTIONAL RULES

I. Introduction

In the United States, the dominant mode of "updating" constitutional meaning[1] is via a process of judicial interpretation.[2] In a smaller subset of cases constitutional meaning is also updated via "super-statutes" enacted by Congress.[3] The virtual impossibility of formal amendment to the Constitution under Article V[4]

Rosalind Dixon is Assistant Professor, University of Chicago Law School.

AUTHOR'S NOTE: Thanks to Gregg Bloche, Adam Cox, Richard Epstein, Lee Fennell, Jake Gersen, Tom Ginsburg, Dennis Hutchinson, Alison LaCroix, Saul Levmore, Anup Malani, Richard McAdams, Martha Nussbaum, Randy Picker, Eric Posner, Laura Rosenbury, Adam Samaha, Lior Strahilevitz, and David Strauss, and other participants in the University of Chicago Law School Work-in-Progress Luncheon, for helpful discussions and comments on earlier versions of this and related papers. Thanks to Galina Fomenkova, Emily Tancer, and David Tanury for outstanding research assistance in relation to the entire project, and to Peter Mulcahy in relation to the issue of constitutional ages. Special thanks are also due to Richard Holden for helpful discussions and permission to use the calculations in Part II derived from joint work on constitutional amendment.

[1] By updating, I mean to suggest the idea of a constitutional interpreter adopting a new understanding of a constitutional provision, designed to better accord with contemporary attitudes and priorities than a prior understanding, but also anchored in some way in some prior constitutional text, purpose, or practice. Contrast Adrian Vermeule, *Constitutional Amendments and the Common Law*, in Richard W. Bauman and Tsvi Kahana, eds, *The Least Examined Branch: The Role of Legislatures in the Constitutional State* 230 (Cambridge, 2006). Compare also T. Alexander Aleinikoff, *Updating Statutory Interpretation*, 87 Mich L Rev 20 (1988). The term, however, is obviously itself one which raises complex problems of boundary definition.

[2] David Strauss, *The Irrelevance of Constitutional Amendments*, 114 Harv L Rev 1457, 1487 (2001) (hereafter *Irrelevance*).

[3] William Eskridge, Jr., and John Ferejohn, *Super-Statutes*, 50 Duke L J 1215 (2001).

[4] See Donald S. Lutz, *Toward a Theory of Constitutional Amendment*, in Sanford Levinson, ed, *Responding to Imperfection: The Theory and Practice of Constitutional Amendment* 237

is thus deemed by many to be more or less irrelevant.[5]

A key difficulty with this picture, however, is that it leaves out of account the degree to which against this background there is a serious gap in our ability to update, rather than in some cases more provisionally "work around,"[6] core constitutional "rules" as opposed to "standards."[7] When it considers such rules the Supreme Court almost always applies a literal as opposed to evolutionary approach to constitutional interpretation.[8] Academic commentators also consistently defend such an approach on the part of the Court, as the preferred one.[9]

In the context of constitutional standards, constitutional scholars make at least four arguments in favor of a present-focused approach to the interpretation of the Constitution: one based on arguments from democracy,[10] another on concerns about constitutional stability,[11] a third based on the potential for constitutional "learning" over time,[12] and a fourth based on more pragmatic considerations

---

(Princeton, 1995); Rosalind Dixon, *Partial Constitutional Amendment* (Working Paper 2010) (on file with author).

[5] Strauss, *Irrelevance*, 114 Harv L Rev 1457 (cited in note 2).

[6] See Mark Tushnet, *Constitutional Workarounds*, 87 Tex L Rev 1499 (2009).

[7] On the rules-standards distinction, especially in a doctrinal setting, see, e.g., Kathleen Sullivan, *Foreword: The Justices of Rules and Standards*, 106 Harv L Rev 22 (1992).

[8] No one seriously predicts, for example, that the Court will uphold the recent challenge to the apportionment of Congress on the basis that (on a functional or evolutionary reading of US Const, Art I, § 2, cl 3) the current size of the House violates the assumptions of the Framers about the appropriate ratio of citizens to representatives in Congress: see Ashby Jones, *Does Congress Need More Members? A Lawsuit Says Yes. Lots More*, Wall St J Law Blog (Sept 16, 2009), online at: http://blogs.wsj.com/law/2009/09/18/should-we-double-the-size-of-the-house-a-lawsuit-says-yes/. There are, of course, some instances in which the political branches adopt certain constitutional "workarounds" designed to update the effective operation of such rules, and for one reason or another, these workarounds escape judicial consideration: see Tushnet, 87 Tex L Rev 1499 (cited in note 6). However, in many cases, the validity of such workarounds will ultimately come before the Court for consideration in a way that does then raise this same problem of constitutional rule updating.

[9] For a defense of this position from a generally conservative, textualist approach to interpretation, see, e.g., Frank Easterbrook, *Statute's Domains*, 50 U Chi L Rev 533 (1983); and for the defense of this position by liberal constitutional scholars, see notes 10–12 and accompanying text.

[10] See Jack M. Balkin, *Original Meaning and Constitutional Redemption*, 24 Const Comm 427 (2007) (hereafter *Constitutional Redemption*); Jack M. Balkin, *Abortion and Original Meaning*, 24 Const Comm 291, 301 (2007) (hereafter *Original Meaning*); Robert Post and Reva Siegel, *Roe Rage: Democratic Constitutionalism and Backlash*, 42 Harv CR-CL L Rev 373 (2007).

[11] Post and Siegel, 42 Harv CR-CL L Rev (cited in note 10).

[12] David Strauss, *Common Law Constitutional Interpretation*, 63 U Chi L Rev 877 (1996) (hereafter *Constitutional Interpretation*).

relating to the need to respond to changing technologies and social circumstances.[13] However, when it comes to constitutional rules, these same scholars suggest that, because of concerns about "fidelity" and also institutional capacity, the literal meaning of the text of the Constitution should almost always be controlling.[14]

Yet at the same time, in many cases the literal application of particular constitutional rules has the potential to impose serious error costs.[15] Not only do changes in social circumstances and understandings over time mean that, from a contemporary perspective, a number of core constitutional rules are now no longer optimal.[16] Because such rules often prescribe structures or procedures that affect a variety of substantive legal outcomes, in many cases the error costs involved are also quite significant.

In part because of this, Congress, state legislatures, and even state voters have in several instances sought to design new small "c" constitutional rules aimed at reducing such error costs. In several contexts, such as those involving the Treaty Clause and congressional-executive agreements, the attempt by Congress to pass such "updating legislation" has also enjoyed significant success. However, in other cases, such as *Clinton v New York*[17] and *United States Term Limits Inc. v Thornton*,[18] similar attempts at legislative updating have been far less successful. This is in large part because the Supreme Court has held that, no matter how outmoded they be, the mere presence of certain rules in the original Constitution by itself blocks the enactment of such updating legislation.

There is, however, a clear way to address at least part of this problem: in cases where Congress, state legislatures, or even state voters seek in good faith to offset the error costs associated with constitutional rules, the Court should apply an additional margin of deference to determining the constitutional validity of such ac-

---

[13] Balkin, *Original Meaning*, 24 Const Comm at 301 (cited in note 10).

[14] See Strauss, *Constitutional Interpretation*, 63 U Chi L Rev at 881 (cited in note 12); Balkin, *Original Meaning*, 24 Const Comm at 305 (cited in note 10).

[15] The Constitution's numerical provisions are some of the most extreme instances of rule-like norms, but other examples of potential ongoing significance also include the Emoluments Clause, the clause preventing members of Congress holding any other office (Art I, § 6, cl 2) (including membership in the National Guard), the Natural Born Citizen Clause (Art II, § 1, cl 5), and the Appointments and Removal Clause (Art II, § 2, cl 2).

[16] Contrast William J. Brennan, Jr., *Construing the Constitution*, 19 UC Davis L Rev 2 (1985).

[17] 24 US 417 (1998).

[18] 514 US 779 (1995).

tion—either by way of an additional margin of avoidance, or by way of substantive deference on the merits of a constitutional question, or both.[19]

In some cases, where the constitutionality of a measure is clear, such additional deference will simply serve to confirm the validity of the measure. In other cases, where there is little plausible constitutional basis for upholding federal or state action under existing text or precedent, there will also be no capacity to affect the Court's decision, but for the opposite reason: the case for constitutional invalidity was clear. It is thus only in an intermediate category of case, where there is some real doubt or argument as to constitutional validity, that such a plus factor would have the potential to be decisive and therefore lead to a form of "indirect updating" by the Court. Nonetheless, in a number of important cases, such indirect updating would have a clear capacity to help address current constitutional error costs.

Objections to constitutional rule updating by the Court will also have limited force as applied to this kind of indirect, as opposed to direct, form of constitutional rule updating. Arguments about the need for fidelity to the text of the Constitution have almost no force when applied to indirect updating, because the Court under such an approach is acting in full compliance with the literal requirements of the text of the Constitution. Concerns about judicial error also have far less force, because the relevant process of updating involves a process of cooperation between the Court and legislatures, and also tends to be far more reversible than direct forms of updating.

The argument develops in four parts. Part II sets out the error costs associated with core constitutional numerical rules, such as the two Senators rule and two-thirds majority voting requirement in the Treaty Clause. Part III considers the ways in which Congress and state legislatures (and even voters) have arguably attempted to counter such error costs, and the mixed record of success for such attempts at constitutional rule updating by legislatures. It also outlines the core normative proposal offered by the article, according to which the Court would apply an additional margin of deference to attempts by legislatures to update constitutional rules. Part IV considers objections to constitutional rule updating by the Court,

---

[19] For sympathetic proposals, albeit restricted to the interpretation of Article II of the Constitution, compare Abner S. Greene, *Checks and Balances in an Era of Presidential Lawmaking*, 61 U Chi L Rev 123 (1994).

and shows why such objections have limited applicability to such indirect, as opposed to direct, modes of constitutional rule updating. Part V concludes by considering arguments that the error costs associated with various constitutional rules should instead be addressed by renewed attempts to rely on a process of constitutional amendment, either under Article V or otherwise.

II. Constitutional Rules and Error Costs

In noting the literal interpretation given by the Court to most constitutional rules, constitutional scholars such as David Strauss suggest that one justification for this approach on the part of the Court is that for many constitutional rules, it "is more important that [they] . . . be settled than that they be settled right" or optimally.[20] One potential reason for this is that constitutional rules may address questions the particular answer to which is relatively unimportant to individuals, both subjectively and as a more objective matter, considering the welfare and distributive stakes involved.[21] Strauss likens this situation to a form of pure "coordination game," or cooperative game with multiple equilibria, in which parties are ultimately indifferent between two different strategies, but the payoff to each is much greater if they can "match" that strategy with that of another player.[22]

One of the defining features of constitutional rules is also undoubtedly that a number of them do involve a form of pure coordination game. One plausible example of such a provision, which Strauss points to, is Section I of the Twentieth Amendment, which sets 12 noon on January 20 as the time at which the President and Vice-President Elect assume authority under Article II.[23] Almost no one in America seems likely to mind whether the President is inaugurated on January 19 or 20, or at 12 noon or 1 p.m., but most Americans will care a great deal about having agreement on what the relevant date and time are. The opportunities for watching the inauguration, or selling hotel rooms to those who wish to, seem likely to be almost precisely the same whether the inauguration is held on January 19 or 20; whereas if there is uncertainty as to which

[20] Strauss, *Constitutional Interpretation*, 63 U Chi L Rev at 907 (cited in note 12).
[21] Id.
[22] Id at 910.
[23] Strauss, *Irrelevance*, 114 Harv L Rev at 1487 (cited in note 2).

date and time apply, there could be a serious constitutional crisis.[24] In such cases, there will also be little capacity from a contemporary perspective for a static or literal reading of constitutional rules to impose error costs, or losses to social welfare (however defined) associated with a suboptimal choice of substantive constitutional norm.[25]

However, in many instances, constitutional rules help create co-ordination against a very different background, where parties do have strong preferences about the substance of particular consti-tutional norms, or at least about the results they produce. In such cases, the form of constitutional coordination involved is far closer to a "battle of the sexes" than a pure coordination game,[26] where parties prefer coordination to noncoordination, but each also prefers a different basis for coordination.[27] (Think of a married couple who wish to spend the evening together, one of whom wishes to go the opera, the other to a wrestling match.) There will thus also be far greater potential for the particular choice of constitutional rules made by the Framers to involve error costs, when judged from a contemporary perspective.

Take two core constitutional numerical rules: the two Senators rule and the requirement in the Treaty Clause that treaties be rat-ified by two-thirds of the Senate. The application of each rule has in recent years had major economic and social consequences, and has created clear "winners" and "losers" on issues which are in fact highly charged "as a matter of morality or public policy."[28]

In recent years, political scientists have shown that there is a consistent bias in federal spending toward small as opposed to large states.[29] They have also shown that this disparity is almost impos-

---

[24] Id.

[25] Richard A. Posner, *An Economic Approach to Legal Procedure and Judicial Administration*, 2 J Legal Stud 399 (1973); Adam M. Samaha, *Undue Process*, 59 Stan L Rev 601 (2006–2007).

[26] Compare Adam Samaha, *Originalism's Expiration Date*, 30 Cardozo L Rev 1295, 1354–63 (2008).

[27] Douglas Baird et al, *Game Theory and the Law* (Harvard, 1994).

[28] Contrast Strauss, *Constitutional Interpretation*, 63 U Chi L Rev at 916–17 (cited in note 12) (suggesting few Constitutional rules are likely to involve issues that are charged in this way).

[29] In 1995, for example, they have shown that the federal "balance of payments" was negative in six of the then largest states, but positive in eight out of the 10 smallest states: see discussion in Lynn A. Baker and Samuel H. Dinkin, *The Senate: An Institution Whose Time Has Come?* 13 J L & Pol 21, 41 (1997) (citing KSG study).

sible to explain other than by reference to the power of Senators in small states to advance special legislation favoring their state, or legislation, the benefits of which are expected to exceed the costs for citizens in that state, but not the nation as a whole.[30] The two Senators rule also plays a critical role in this because, while the Senate is checked by the House in its capacity to pass such special interest legislation, there is still a clear, statistically significant overall correlation between a state's voting power in Congress and the share it receives of federal government spending.[31]

In the context of the Treaty Clause, the requirements it imposes for successful ratification of a treaty also have major implications for the likelihood that the United States will ratify treaties of major public policy significance. Take two major treaties rejected by the Senate over the last decade: the Comprehensive Nuclear Test Ban Treaty (CNTBT) and the Convention on the Law of the Sea (UNCLOS).[32] The ratification of the CNTBT was rejected by a narrow majority of the Senate in 1999 (48 votes for, and 51 against, ratification), but many commentators suggest that under an ordinary majority rule, it would in fact have prevailed, owing to the potential for increased lobbying efforts by the President.[33] The Law of the Sea Convention, in turn, gained clear supermajority support in the Senate (49 yea votes as opposed to 30 nays), but failed just short of the two-thirds supermajority support required for successful ratification. The failure by the Senate to ratify each treaty has also clearly had major military and economic consequences.

The failure to ratify the CNTBT has, from a military perspective,

---

[30] Id at 41–42. It cannot, for example, be explained by any principled concern to redistribute resources from rich to poor states. Another potentially important distributive consequence of the two Senators rule is that it tends to reduce at least the "descriptive" or visible representation of minority voters in the Senate: see id at 43–47; Neil Malhotra and Connor Raso, *Racial Representation and the U.S. Senate Apportionment*, 88 Soc Sci Q 1038, 1046 (2007).

[31] Baker and Dinkin, 13 J L & Pol at 45 (cited in note 29) (reporting a statistically significant correlation at the 5 percent level). The measure of voting power they use in this context is the "Per Capita Shapley-Shubik Index."

[32] Comprehensive Nuclear Test Ban Treaty, Sept 24, 1996, 35 ILM 1443; United Nations Convention on the Law of the Sea, Dec 10, 1982, 21 ILM 1261. For discussion of the Comprehensive Nuclear Test Ban Treaty (CNTBT) and U.S. ratification efforts, see Editorial, *The Test Ban Treaty*, NY Times A18 (May 25, 2009). For discussion of the United Nations Convention on the Law of the Sea (UNCLOS) and U.S. ratification efforts, see Michael A. Becker, *International Law of the Sea*, 43 Intl Law 915, 915–21 (2009).

[33] John K. Setear, *The President's Rational Choice of a Treaty's Preratification Pathway: Article II, Congressional-Executive Agreement, or Executive Agreement*, 31 J Legal Stud S5, S6 (2002). But see Editorial, *Banning the Ban*, The Nation (Nov 8, 1999).

undermined efforts to persuade other nuclear states, such as China, North Korea, India, Pakistan, Indonesia, Iran, Israel, and Egypt, to participate in the regime established by the treaty and has thereby increased the ability of North Korea and India to detonate nuclear weapons without the fear of effective international sanctions.[34] In a domestic context, it has also strengthened the argument for alternatives to the CNTBT regime, such as proposals for a national missile defense system, that themselves have cost billions of dollars and altered the terms of the general foreign policy debate.[35] Economically, failure to ratify the CNTBT has implied the failure to reap the full benefits of past expenditures in anticipation of the CNTBT's taking effect, such as the United States' contribution to a $1 billion International Monitoring System designed to enforce the CNTBT, and hundreds of millions of dollars of domestic expenditure on a "Stockpile Stewardship" program designed to maintain the safety and integrity of the United States' nuclear arsenal without the use of nuclear testing.[36]

As to the Law of the Sea Convention, the failure to ratify the treaty has been defended as protecting U.S. sovereignty and specifically the integrity of U.S. military operations under the Proliferation Security Initiative (PSI), which authorizes the U.S. military to interdict vessels engaged in the traffic of weapons of mass destruction.[37] Supporters of the Convention, on the other hand, suggest that the United States' failure to ratify the Convention has undermined, rather than helped, promote the effectiveness of the PSI, and also put the United States in a position of strategic weakness in relation to the use of key maritime passages such as in Indonesia where, without a treaty, it must depend on bilateral consent for use of such passages.[38] The economic stakes behind the

---

[34] Editorial, *The Test Ban Treaty*, NY Times at A18 (cited in note 32).

[35] Editorial, *Rules of the Game*, NY Times A28 (Jan 30, 2009).

[36] Associated Press, *Bomb "Sniffers" Await Ban Treaty*, Newsday A31 (May 24, 2009); *On Target, Finally; The National Ignition Facility*, The Economist (U.S. edition) (May 30, 2009).

[37] For general discussion of PSI, see Becker, 43 Intl Law at 923–24 (cited in note 32). For arguments against UNCLOS ratification on U.S. sovereignty grounds, see Editorial, *A Sinkable Treaty*, Wall St J A8 (Nov 3, 2007); Frank Gaffney, Jr., Editorial, *LOST Justice*, Wash Times A17 (Oct 16, 2007).

[38] On UNCLOS ratification strengthening PSI, see Editorial, *Unbury This Treaty; The Senate Can Protect American Interests by Ratifying the Law of the Sea Convention*, Wash Post A18 (Oct 31, 2007); Becker, 43 Intl Law at 923–24 (cited in note 32). For maritime passage, see James A. Baker and George P. Shultz, *Why the "Law of the Sea" Is a Good Deal*, Wall St J A21 (Sept 26, 2007).

Convention are also high: they include not only the costs associated with the increased risk of environmental damage to the Arctic without the treaty, but also how major new oil reserves in the Arctic are divided among nations such as Russia, Denmark, Canada, and the United States, in relation to which the longer the United States delays ratifying the treaty, the less likely it is to be able successfully to claim such reserves without serious opposition from these other nations.[39]

Whatever their ultimate view of the two treaties, most commentators therefore agree that, by leading to the defeat of these treaties as part of U.S. law, the Treaty Clause has not only had some distributional consequences, but has also decided issues of significant national importance. In both contexts, demographic changes have also been sufficiently great since 1789 that, from a contemporary perspective, the two Senators rule and Treaty Clause now almost certainly impose literal requirements that are either over- or underinclusive.

In the context of the two Senators rule, increases in population have occurred at substantially higher rates in large as compared to small states. (In 1790, for example, the three smallest states in the union, Delaware, Rhode Island, and Georgia, contained 6 percent of the national population,[40] whereas in 2000, the three smallest states, Wyoming, Vermont, and Alaska, were home to a mere 0.6 percent of voters.[41]) This has meant that voters in small states now have a vastly more disproportionate say in national legislation decision making compared to voters in large states, even when compared to 1790.[42] In the Treaty Clause context, the admission of new states and the increase this has caused in the overall size of the Senate since 1789 has also been such that, even if one assumes that the clause was optimal when it was adopted, from a contemporary

---

[39] One estimate is that, under the treaty, the United States would stand to claim an additional 500,000 square kilometers north of the Arctic Circle as a potential additional oil reserve: see Trevor Cole, *Poles Apart; America's "We're Special" Attitude Is Freezing Out Other Countries—and Big Business—in the Arctic*, The Globe and Mail (Canada) 30 (Oct 26, 2007). Others claim that the United States would do even better absent a treaty. See, e.g., David R. Sands, *Treaty Sparks Rivalries; Senate Fight Looms Amid Race to North Pole*, Wash Times A01 (Nov 12, 2007).

[40] See U.S. Census Bureau, *Census of Population and Housing: 1790 Census*, online at http://www2.census.gov/prod2/decennial/documents/1790a-02.pdf.

[41] See U.S. Census Bureau, *Summary Population and Housing Characteristics Part 1, Table 1: Age and Sex: 2000*, online at http://www.census.gov/prod/cen2000/phc-1-1-pt1.pdf.

[42] Baker and Dinkin, 13 J L & Pol 21 (cited in note 29).

perspective, it almost certainly imposes error costs in the direction of under-ratification of treaties.

The size of a voting body will have the potential to influence the effective difficulty of obtaining a supermajority in that body for two interrelated reasons: one having to do with the increase in decision costs associated with larger decision-making bodies, and the other with the statistical likelihood that a supermajority of at least quasi-independent decision makers will favor a particular proposal.[43] Decision costs alone can take at least two forms: those opportunity costs implicit in the time taken to debate and vote on a particular proposal, and those costs associated with the potential for "hold-up" or a veto by some members of a collective decision-making body.[44] Both forms of decision cost will also tend to increase consistently with any increase in the size of a representative decision-making body, such as the Senate.[45]

As I have shown elsewhere with Richard Holden, the law of large numbers is another reason why, in larger voting bodies, it may be harder to obtain the supermajority of votes necessary for a particular proposal, such as a proposal that a particular treaty be ratified.[46] Under a supermajority voting rule, the law of large numbers means that, even absent any change in decision costs, in a large decision-making body it is far less likely than in a smaller body that there will be an idiosyncratic draw of preferences or types in favor of such a proposal.

This can be demonstrated by a simple example involving a series of coin tosses in which "heads" is treated as a vote in favor of ratifying a treaty, and "tails" as a vote against ratification. For a voting body with (say) three or six members, the probability of successful ratification is 50 percent or 34 percent, respectively, whereas for a voting body of even 12 or 24, the probability is as low as 19 percent or 8 percent. For a voting body with 100 members,

---

[43] Rosalind Dixon and Richard Holden, *Designing Constitutional Amendment Rules—to Scale* (paper for University of Chicago Conference on Constitutional Design, 2009), online at: http://faculty.chicagobooth.edu/richard.holden/papers/DH.pdf (hereafter *Designing Constitutional Amendment Rules*).

[44] Gordon Tullock and James Buchanan, *The Calculus of Consent: Logical Foundations of Constitutional Democracy* (Michigan, 1965).

[45] Id.

[46] Dixon and Holden, *Designing Constitutional Amendment Rules* (cited in note 43).

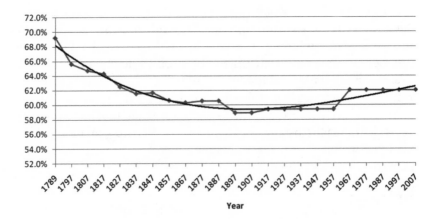

Fig. 1.—Functional equivalent over time to a two-thirds majority voting rule in the original senate (adjusting for increases in senate size).

the probability of successful ratification falls below 1 percent.[47]

If one makes certain stylized assumptions about voting patterns on the ratification of treaties (i.e., that (1) the median U.S. voter is more or less indifferent about whether or not to ratify international treaties in the abstract, (2) the views of the median voter in this context have remained more or less constant over time, and (3) the views of particular members of the Senate on questions of treaty ratification are drawn at least semirandomly from the voting population as a whole, relative to that of the median voter) one can in fact quantify quite concretely the increase this implies over time in the effective difficulty of treaty ratification under the Treaty Clause.

Figure 1, for example, sets out one calculation of the functional equivalent to the original trade-off made by the Framers between what one might call "flexibility" and "rigidity" costs when it came to adopting the requirement of two-thirds majority support for the ratification of treaties for progressive changes in the size of the Senate. (The dotted line shows the "adjusted" supermajority rule for each change in the size of the Senate, which would maintain the original functional trade-off made by the Framers between rel-

---

[47] This effect is also quite general and does not depend on the binary nature of outcomes in the "coin flip" setting. It applies even where there is a continuum of voter preferences and policy choices: see Richard Holden, *Supermajority Rules* (Working Paper, 2009), available online at: http://faculty.chicagobooth.edu/Richard.holden/papers/index.html.

evant competing costs, and its shape reflects not only the gradual "deflation" in the adjusted supermajority rule but also the tie-breaking, or integer-rounding, problem created by there being an even number of Senators at all times. The solid line shows the (third-order polynomial) trend line in the adjusted supermajority rule over time.) The potential error costs these calculations imply from a contemporary perspective are also evident when one considers that several important treaties rejected by the Senate—including UN-CLOS—would almost certainly have passed under such an adjusted supermajority threshold.[48]

III. CONSTITUTIONAL RULE UPDATING—BY LEGISLATURES

In the face of these error costs, the Supreme Court has (for good reason, Part IV suggests) taken almost no steps actively to update various constitutional rules. However, Congress, state legislatures, and indeed even voters have consistently attempted to do so—and in several cases, enjoyed significant success in the passage of such updating legislation. The most prominent example of successful legislative rule updating of this kind in fact involves the Treaty Clause itself and the development by Congress of "congressional-executive agreements" as an alternative pathway to international lawmaking under Article I.

As the effective difficulty of ratifying treaties under the Treaty Clause has increased over the last two centuries in the way figure 1 identifies, so too has the use of executive agreements steadily increased. From the 1890s onward, there has also been a particularly distinct shift in the use of such agreements relative to the treaty form in that, since that time, the United States has not only come to rely more heavily on executive agreements than on treaties;[49]

---

[48] See U.S. Senate, *Rejected Treaties*, online at: http://www.senate.gov/artandhistory/history/common/briefing/Treaties.htm#5 (noting 49 votes for, and 30 votes against, ratification of the Law of the Sea Convention in 1960—and thus 62 percent supermajority support for ratification). This, of course, ignores the possibility of strategic voting in the shadow of such an adjusted rule, both in 1960 and subsequently, but such a concern seems largely inapplicable in this context: see, e.g., Mike D. Shear, *The Trail: The Law of the Sea: Almost Swimming in Support*, Wash Post A4 (Nov 1, 2007) (noting increasing bipartisan support for the treaty); Setear, 31 J Legal Stud at 6 (cited in note 33) (suggesting that this and other important treaties would likely have been brought to a successful floor vote under a lower supermajority rule).

[49] Between 1803 and 1838, the ratio of treaties to executive agreements signed by the United States was roughly 2:1 (60 treaties and 27 executive agreements), and between 1840 and 1888 1:1 (215 treaties and 238 executive agreements), whereas thereafter it was at least 1:2. See *Treaties and Other International Agreements: The Role of the United States*

Congress has also developed new forms of executive agreement, based on the model of the McKinley Tariff Act of 1890 and Dingley Tariff Act of 1897, which give the President broad ex ante authority to negotiate internationally on behalf of the United States.[50] Whether coincidental or not, this shift has also occurred in close parallel to changes in the relationship between the actual super-majority requirements of the Treaty Clause and the adjusted su-permajority rule set out in figure 1, given that in the 1890s, the gap between these two requirements was at its greatest.[51]

At least one way in which to understand the increasing use of congressional-executive agreements, as opposed to treaties, over the last century is, therefore, as a response by Congress to the increasing error costs associated with the literal requirements of the Treaty Clause.[52] It is also now well settled that the use by Congress and the President of such congressional-executive agreements is con-sistent with both Articles I and II of the Constitution, so that there is little doubt that, if this is the case, Congress has in fact succeeded in using ordinary legislative means to update constitutional meaning (i.e., the supermajority voting rule found in Article II).[53]

In other cases, by contrast, attempts by Congress and other po-litical actors to pass such updating legislation have met with far less success—in large part because the Court has been far less willing to defer to Congress or state legislatures (and voters) in their en-actment of substitute constitutional rules. Consider one arguable instance of an attempt by Congress to reduce the practical effect

Senate, *a Study Prepared for the Committee on Foreign Relations United States Senate by the Congressional Research Service Library of Congress*, S Rep No 106-71 at 39, 106th Cong, 2d Sess (Jan 2001).

[50] For discussion of the effect of the two Acts, see, e.g., Bruce Ackerman and David Golove, *Is NAFTA Constitutional?* 108 Harv L Rev 799, 821–26 (1994–95); Oona A. Hath-away, *Treaties' End: The Past Present and Future of International Lawmaking in the United States*, 117 Yale L J 1236, 1293–94 (2008).

[51] Of course, the use of such congressional executive agreements also greatly increased from the 1930s and 1940s onward, both in the trade context and also much more broadly. This has led some commentators to argue that the overall shift in international lawmaking processes, from treaties to congressional-executive agreements, in fact constitutes a distinct informal Constitutional *amendment* to the Treaty Clause, which occurred around 1944–45. See Ackerman and Golove, 108 Harv L Rev at 873–900 (cited in note 50).

[52] But see id at 873–900 (advancing an entirely different theory of why congressional-executive agreements have been recognized as valid in the latter part of the twentieth century, based on a theory of informal Constitutional amendment).

[53] For the general acceptance of the interchangeability of treaties and congressional-executive agreements, see, e.g., Hathaway, 117 Yale L J at 1239 (cited in note 50); Ackerman and Golove, 108 Harv L Rev at 806–08 (cited in note 50).

of the error costs, from a contemporary perspective, of a core Constitutional rule, namely, the enactment of a presidential line-item
veto as a means of mitigating the effect of a two Senators rule. A
presidential line-item veto clearly does not have an unlimited capacity to reduce disparities in federal spending between small and
large states[54] because it is likely to be used by the President for
these purposes only in those small states that are not competitive
in presidential elections, and even then most likely only in a subset
of those states that vote against the incumbent President.[55] However, at least in this subset of cases it does have the potential to
reduce the fiscal distortion caused by such a rule. Its actual tendency
to do so may also be far from trivial, considering that, on this basis,
every Democratic President since 1960, bar one, could potentially
have vetoed spending measures in Alaska, Idaho, North and South
Dakota, and Wyoming—or five of the twelve smallest states; and
every Republican President since Nixon could have vetoed measures
in Hawaii and for the most part also Rhode Island.[56]

At the same time, for some Justices at least, there is a real question
whether, as a form of purely legislative rule, a line-item veto is
consistent with other constitutional provisions, such as those in
Article I, Section 7 governing the exercise of a presidential veto.
In *Clinton v New York*,[57] a majority of the Court also ultimately
rejected the validity of the line-item veto as inconsistent with the
procedures in Article I, Section 7. In writing for the Court, Justice
Stevens held that there were "important differences between the
President's 'return' of a bill pursuant to Article I § 7, and the exercise
of the President's cancellation authority pursuant to the Line Item
Veto Act," including in the timing and comprehensiveness of the
relevant power.[58] Stevens noted further that, although the Constitution expressly authorizes the President's action in the former case,

---

[54] For doubts about the effectiveness of a line-item veto, though mostly as a means of
reducing overall spending, rather than malapportioned spending, see, e.g., Baker and
Dinkin, 13 J L & Pol at 34 (cited in note 29).

[55] Exercising the veto in a small state that has voted for the President's party, while not
directly harming the President's reelection chances, could still significantly harm the reelection chances of congressional representatives from the President's party.

[56] Only Presidents Reagan and Nixon, in their second Terms, would not confidently
have used such a veto, given their overwhelming national reelection returns which put
Rhode Island in the Republican column. The exception to the Democratic pattern was
President Johnson, because of his overwhelming victory nationally.

[57] 524 US 417 (1998).

[58] Id at 438–39.

it is silent in the latter; and given both this history and ordinary principles of constitutional construction, there were "powerful reasons for construing constitutional silence as equivalent to an express prohibition."[59]

An even starker example of where attempts of this kind at legislative updating have failed involves the Qualifications Clauses, and the arguable attempt by state voters to offset the increasing length of congressional tenure allowed by the "deflation" of the age floors in Article I, Section 2, Clause 2. While it certainly seems plausible to think that these age requirements were in part designed to ensure a certain level of maturity or experience on the part of candidates for office, another presupposition of the Framers may have been that they would serve to limit the total number of years that representative served, on average.[60] In the early Republic there was, for example, a strong norm of voluntary retirement or "rotation in office." Life expectancies, even if somewhat higher for elected officials than the population at large, were also radically lower than now. (For example, in 1789 one calculation suggests that, conditional on living to age 30, average life expectancy was 60—or 30 years beyond the time at which one could first be elected; whereas in 2004, the National Vital Statistic Report shows that, conditional on reaching the ages of 25 or 30, relevant to Qualifications Clauses in Article I, average life expectancy was 79–80—or 54 to 49 years beyond the time of first possible election.) The combined result was that in the decades after the Constitution was first enacted, average congressional tenure was 2–3 years, whereas now it is more than 10 years in the House and 12 years in the Senate.

On this reading, the literal requirements of the Qualifications Clauses have also, progressively, become too low to serve the purposes for which they were enacted. On the Supreme Court's interpretation of them, they have also directly blocked the possibility of renewal by Congress, state legislatures, and state voters of the relevant eligibility floor.

---

[59] Id at 439 (the relevant principles being those relating to the interpretation of text reflecting the product of "great debate" and "finely wrought compromises").

[60] See, e.g., Madison, *Notes of Debates in the Federal Convention 1787* 109–11 (Athens, 1966) (noting relationship between debate on the age requirements for the Senate and debate over term limits). See also Patrick J. Fett and Daniel E. Ponder, *Congressional Term Limits, State Legislative Turnover: A Theory of Change*, [1993] PS: Pol Sci & Politics 211 (June 1993); Edward J. Lopez, *Congressional Voting on Term Limits*, 112 Public Choice 405, 406 (2001); W. Robert Reed and D. Eric Schansberg, *The House Under Term Limits: What Would It Look Like*, 76 Soc Sci Q 699, 699–70 (1995).

In *United States v Thornton*,[61] in considering a state law imposing term limits on members of Congress, the Court held that the literal requirements of the Qualifications Clauses not only "fix" the eligibility requirements for Congress vis-à-vis candidates' age. It also held that, according to the principle *expressio unius est exclusio alterius* (the specific excludes the general), which was known to the Framers,[62] these requirements exhaust the full range of qualifications that may legitimately be imposed on members of Congress so that neither the states nor Congress could seek to increase rotation in electoral office by adding to or "supplementing" those qualifications.[63]

The Court applied a similar analysis in *Clinton v New York*, in the context of line-item veto legislation. In the treaty context itself, Professor Larry Tribe has also made cogent arguments, to similar effect, against recognizing broad scope for Congress under Article I to pass congressional-executive agreements—thereby bypassing Article II, Clause 2.[64] For legislative attempts to update constitutional rules to succeed consistently, therefore, what is needed, I argue, is for the Court to afford some additional margin of deference to such legislation—at least equal in force to this *expressio unius* presumption.

In cases where the constitutionality of a measure is clear, such deference may simply serve to confirm the validity of that measure. In other cases, where there is little plausible constitutional basis for upholding federal or state action, under existing text or precedent, such a plus factor will also have no capacity to affect the Court's decision, but for the opposite reason: that the case for constitutional invalidity is clear (think, here, of Article I congressional-executive agreements before 1937). Only in an intermediate category of case, where there is some real doubt or argument as to constitutional validity, will the constitutional "plus" provided by such a principle potentially be decisive, and even then it must be weighed with other

---

[61] 514 US 779 (1995).

[62] Id at 779, 792 n 9. The Court also placed significant reliance on broader historical arguments, considered in *Powell v McCormack*, 395 US 486 (1969), about the specific purposes of the Framers in this context. For a critical analysis of this part of the judgment, see, e.g., Harry H. Wellington, *Term Limits: History, Democracy and Constitutional Interpretation*, 40 NY L Sch L Rev 833 (1996).

[63] 514 US 779, 797.

[64] Lawrence Tribe, *Taking Text and Structure Seriously: Reflections on Free-Form Method in Constitutional Interpretation*, 108 Harv L Rev 1221, 1239–45 (1995).

factors before the Justices can decide how to resolve a particular case.[65]

Notwithstanding this, if the Court were to recognize a principle of indirect updating, this could still be highly significant to the chances of successful legislative updating by Congress and state legislatures in the future.[66] Historically, there is clear support for the significance of the Court showing such deference in the context of the Treaty Clause and congressional-executive agreements, where both the Supreme Court and lower federal courts level have historically shown what is quite clearly a combination of both deliberate constitutional avoidance,[67] and also substantive deference on the merits, when determining the scope of Congress's authority under Article I to enact such agreements.[68]

A further example of the Justices adopting such an approach is also found in the dissenting judgment of Justice Breyer in *Clinton v New York* upholding the constitutionality of a Presidential line-item veto. Not only, for example, did Justice Breyer in this context reject arguments based on the formal gap between the literal requirements of Article I, Section 7 and the line item, on the basis that where "the question is one of literal violation of the law," the

---

[65] See, e.g., *Roper v Simmons*, 543 US 551, 555 (2005) (Kennedy, J) (suggesting that international practice served merely to "confirm" the Court's finding that the juvenile death penalty is unconstitutional); *Roper v Simmons*, 543 US at 587 (O'Connor, J, dissenting) (suggesting that domestic norms were such that no international consensus could tip the balance toward invalidity); *Knight v Florida* 528 US 990, 993 (1999) (Breyer, J, dissenting from the denial of certiorari) (suggesting that international consensus was sufficient to tip the balance in favor of a grant of certiorari). In this sense, the deference due to legislative attempts to update constitutional rules under such an approach will closely resemble the weight given by the Court in recent cases to evidence of a foreign or international legal consensus in a particular constitutional area.

[66] Compare Dixon, Working Paper 2010 (cited in note 4). In some cases, of course, there is also a further question as to how significant Court judgments themselves are to ultimate constitutional outcomes. See, e.g., debates over the significance of constitutional judgments such as *INS v Chadha* concerning legislative vetoes: see Adam Samaha, *Low Stakes* (paper prepared for the symposium: The Judiciary and the Popular Will, University of Pennsylvania Journal of Constitutional Law, 2010) (on file with author).

[67] In a context such as the Treaty Clause, involving core separation of powers issues, Constitutional avoidance by courts is particularly valuable because it allows Congress and the President to adopt new practices that can themselves act as a "gloss" on the meaning of the text of the Constitution: see *Youngstown Sheet & Tube Co. v Sawyer*, 343 US 579 (1952) (Frankfurter, J, concurring).

[68] For examples of avoidance, see, e.g., *Ernest E. Marks Co. v United States*, 117 F2d 542, 546 (CCPC 1941); *Wislar v United States*, 97 F2d 152 (1938), cert denied 305 US 629 (1938). For instances of deference in the application of the nondelegation doctrine prior to 1944, in the particular context of early congressional-executive agreements as substitutes for the treaty form: see, e.g., *Field v Clark*, 143 US 649 (1892); *United States v Curtiss-Wright Export Corp.*, 299 US 304 (1936).

Court should not seek to parse compliance as a matter of degree;[69] he also held that even though the relevant veto power "skirt[ed] a constitutional edge" when it came to (more functional) separation of powers and nondelegation principles, it should be afforded an additional margin of deference as "an experiment that may, or may not, help representative government work better,"[70] thereby implicitly connecting such deference to the desirability of offsetting some of the disparities in federal spending caused by the two Senators rule.[71] Moreover, no Justice was willing to uphold the relevant legislation without also endorsing at least some of Justice Breyer's reasoning in this context.[72]

In the future, the likelihood that many cases involving attempts at legislative rule updating will be "hard" or otherwise evenly balanced also means that, even if some members of the Court are willing to endorse such a principle, this could significantly increase the chances that such rules will successfully survive a judicial challenge.[73] In many of these cases, the importance of the issues involved—such as, for example, in the context of the two Senators rule—will also only add to the overall significance of any such result.

IV. Objections to Updated Constitutional Rules: Direct versus Indirect Updating

Defenders of the constitutional status quo (in which the Court adopts an evolutionary approach to constitutional standards

---

[69] 524 US 417, 473 (Breyer, J, dissenting).

[70] Id at 498.

[71] Id at 468–73 (workable government), 498 (representative government).

[72] See id at 497 (O'Connor and Scalia, JJ, dissenting (and concurring in part III of Breyer's reasoning rejecting automatic application of an *expressio unius* principle)).

[73] Two areas in which such a principle might possibly apply, in addition to those already mentioned, are, for example, attempts by Congress to reduce the racially disparate impact of the two Senators rule or to reduce the resource implications, for the federal courts, of the Twenty Dollars Clause. (On the potential present-day error costs associated with such rules, see, e.g., Malhotra and Raso, 88 Soc Sci Quarterly at 1046 (cited in note 30); Note, *The Twenty Dollars Clause*, 118 Harv L Rev 1665 (2004–2005).) In both cases, there is also a real question as to the scope of Congress's power under Article I to engage in forms of legislative rule updating by, for example, attempting to create increased minority representation in the House, under the Voting Rights Act of 1965 (VRA), as a partial substitute for representation in the Senate, or Article I as opposed to Article III courts: see, e.g., *Northwest Austin Municipal Utility District Number One v Holder*, 129 S Ct 2504, 2508 (2009) (raising doubts about, though not ruling on, the constitutionality of certain provisions of the VRA); *Northern Pipeline Construction Co. v Marathon Pipe Line Co.*, 458 US 50, 67 (1982) (suggesting clear limits to the scope of Congress's power to establish Article I courts beyond cases involving pure public rights).

but not rules) make two broad arguments against more direct forms of constitutional rule updating by the Court: one based on a concern about fidelity by the Justices to the text of the Constitution and the costs of disrupting settled expectations about the meaning of constitutional rules,[74] and a second based on a concern about institutional competence and the capacity for judicial error costs in the process of updating.[75]

The first argument is the simplest and most absolute, and turns on the idea that where the text is relatively "rule-like, concrete and specific," notions of interpretive fidelity on the part of the Justices mean that the text necessarily controls constitutional meaning.[76] A related argument is that if the Court departs from such specific textual provisions in one case, especially those with high public salience, it "greatly increase[s] the risk that the [current] valuable consensus on the text will dissolve generally, increasing the potential for disruption and for outcomes that are, even to those who dislike [the substance of the rule], worse still."[77] The costs associated with disruption of this kind will also tend, so the argument goes, to be even greater for constitutional rules than standards, because a key function of constitutional rules is to settle constitutional conflict, or to provide a "focal point" for various forms of socially valuable coordination.[78]

The second argument is also straightforward. It turns on the idea that in many areas involving constitutional rules, the subject matter of those rules is such that the Court lacks relevant expertise and information and therefore may misjudge the capacity of the particular rule to advance given objectives, or impose other unintended

---

[74] On fidelity, see Balkin, *Original Meaning*, 24 Const Comm 291 (cited in note 10); and on the costs of disrupting settled expectations, see Posner, 2 J Legal Stud at 401 (cited in note 25); Samaha, *Undue Process*, 59 Stan L Rev at 614–20 (cited in note 25); Strauss, *Constitutional Interpretation*, 63 U Chi L Rev 877 (cited in note 12).

[75] Posner, 2 J Legal Stud at 401 (cited in note 25); Samaha, *Undue Process*, 59 Stan L Rev at 614–20 (cited in note 25).

[76] Balkin, *Original Meaning*, 24 Const Comm at 305 (cited in note 10). See also Richard H. Fallon, Jr., *A Constructivist Coherence Theory of Constitutional Interpretation*, 100 Harv L Rev 1189, 1282–84 (1986–87); Ronald Dworkin, *Taking Rights Seriously* 121–23 (Harvard, 1977) (setting out the idea of "enactment force" as opposed to "gravitational force").

[77] See Strauss, *Constitutional Interpretation*, 63 U Chi L Rev at 919 (cited in note 12).

[78] Id at 910; Samaha, *Undue Process*, 59 Stan L Rev at 621–23 (cited in note 25); Richard H. McAdams, *Beyond the Prisoner's Dilemma: Coordination, Game Theory, and Law*, 82 S Cal L Rev 209, 240–41 (2009).

costs.[79] Related to this will also be the degree to which, if the Court does err in a particular context in being willing to engage in a form of constitutional rule updating, such error costs are likely to be practically reversible by Congress or state legislatures via ordinary legislative means.

In many, if not all, situations these arguments together also provide a powerful case against the desirability of direct updating of constitutional rules by the Court.[80] However, the force of these arguments simply does not hold when applied to indirect as opposed to direct modes of constitutional rule updating by the Court.

A decision by the Court to apply additional deference to particular legislation, under an indirect updating approach, in no way involves a decision to disregard the text of the Constitution, literally construed. In fact, because it depends for its operation on consideration of the full range of other constitutional sources that provide support for the validity of particular legislative action, it encourages careful attention by the Court to the entire text of the Constitution. Unlike more direct forms of updating, such an approach therefore raises neither any real concern about fidelity in particular cases nor, on slippery-slope grounds, about fidelity to the constitutional text as a whole.

With respect to fears about judicial error costs, such concerns will be vastly less applicable to indirect as opposed to direct approaches to constitutional rule updating. The fact that Congress or state legislatures have primary responsibility under such an approach for designing replacement constitutional rules means that, simply by virtue of the law of large numbers, there is a greater chance that the relevant rules will be well designed from the outset.[81] In some cases, at least, Congress will also have important advantages over the Court in terms of both internal diversity and access to relevant information.[82] For constitutional procedural rules such as the Treaty Clause that touch directly on processes internal to Con-

---

[79] On the idea of error costs in the process of Constitutional decision making by the Court, see, e.g., Cass R. Sunstein, *Supreme Court 1995 Term, Foreword: Leaving Things Undecided*, 110 Harv L Rev 4 (1996).

[80] As Note, 118 Harv L Rev 1665 (cited in note 73) suggests, one arguable exception might involve the Twenty Dollars Clause in the Seventh Amendment.

[81] Adrian Vermeule, *Law and the Limits of Reason* 90 (Oxford, 2008).

[82] Id.

gress, access to such information will also be particularly valuable.[83]

Even if the Court does in fact err in the process of constitutional rule updating, under an indirect as opposed to direct approach, there will be the added safeguard of a much greater chance of Congress or the states being able to reverse such errors—by ordinary legislative means.

Take a potential decision by the Court to read the word "two" in Article I, Section 3, Clause 1 in a functional way so as to give California, New York, and Texas twelve Senators, Wyoming two Senators, and most other states some number in between (a twelve Senators rule), and thereby preserve the underlying ratio of large to small state representation on which the two Senators rule was based,[84] and compare this to (say) the line-item veto as a more indirect response by Congress to the error costs associated with the two Senators rule.

Assuming a twelve Senators rule were actually implemented, such a decision by the Court would be very difficult to reverse.[85] The main reason for this is that, if the Senate were enlarged so as to give greater representation to large states, Senators who thereby gained office would likely tend to oppose further rounds of reapportionment aimed at reducing the size of the Senate. For such Senators to support such measures would almost certainly mean putting their own office at risk, and broader studies of congressional voting patterns suggest that this means later reapportionment is, at best, unlikely.[86] Another obstacle to reversing such a decision would

---

[83] Evidence of this is arguably the decision by Congress to exempt trade-related international agreements, but not most other agreements, from the operation of the filibuster: see, e.g., Hathaway, 117 Yale L J at 1261 (cited in note 50). Striking in this context is also the parallel between changes in the requirements for a motion for cloture under Senate Rule 22, and the adjusted supermajority rule set out in figure 1: see Sarah A. Binder and Steven S. Smith, *Politics or Principle? Filibustering in the United States Senate* (Brookings, 1997).

[84] This would preserve the ratio between the population of the largest and smallest three states in 1789 (as measured by the 1790 census). See notes 40–41.

[85] This understanding was, for example, implicit in the attempt by Sen. Dirksen in 1964 to "freeze" the implementation of the Court's reapportionment decisions: see Robert B. McKay, *Reapportionment: Success Story of the Warren Court*, 67 Mich L Rev 223, 228 (1968–69). For how political dynamics of this kind can lead to the de facto entrenchment of Constitutional norms or decisions, see Daryl Levinson, *Political Commitment, Entrenchment, and Self-Enforcement in Constitutional Law*, paper presented to University of Chicago Law School, Law and Politics Workshop, May 13, 2009 (on file with author). On these informal norms, see Ernest A. Young, *The Constitution Outside the Constitution*, 117 Yale L J 408 (2007).

[86] Fett and Ponder, [1993] PS: Pol Sci & Politics 211, 213 (cited in note 60) (showing

be the potential for collective action problems, given that the potential error costs associated with such a decision (relating to the
quality of Senate deliberation and the distinctiveness of the Senate
relative to the House) would tend to be borne by Americans generally, rather than by a subset of voters in small or large states or
in one party or another.[87]

In the context of line-item veto, by contrast, if Congress at any
time came to the view that the line-item veto was not serving its
purpose, it could simply undo the error made by the Court in
upholding it by repealing the relevant statute that authorized it.
The same position would apply in the treaty context if the Senate
came to the view that, as a means of international lawmaking, congressional-executive agreements were being overused relative to the
treaty form. In key areas of national significance such as those involving human rights or multinational security cooperation, even a
minority of Senators could reassert their prior privileges under the
Treaty Clause by use of the filibuster.[88] In other contexts, if they
were able to gain a majority in favor of their view, Senators could
also reassert the need to give broader scope to the Treaty Clause
simply by blocking passage of various congressional-executive
agreements. At the level of fidelity, judicial error, and the reversi-
bility of any such errors, there is, therefore, a crucial difference
between indirect and more direct modes of updating when it comes
to objections to the idea of constitutional rule updating by the
Court.

V. Amending versus Updating

For some, any form of constitutional updating by the Court
will nonetheless be ruled out by the fact that Article V, or least
equivalent processes of constitutional amendment, are understood
to provide the exclusive mode of legitimate constitutional updating.[89] In some countries, where the requirements for successful constitutional amendment are less demanding than in the United States,

that recently elected members of the House are far more likely to support congressional
term-limit proposals than longer-serving members).

[87] Mancur Olson, *The Logic of Collective Action: Public Goods and the Theory of Groups*
(Harvard, 1965).

[88] See Hathaway, 117 Yale L J at 1304–05 (cited in note 50).

[89] Many though not all scholars in this category are originalists: see, e.g., Raoul Berger,
Originalist Theories of Constitutional Interpretation, 73 Cornell L Rev 350 (1987–88); Antonin
Scalia, *A Matter of Interpretation* (Princeton, 1997).

such a response seems a quite plausible response to the potential error costs associated with various constitutional rules.

Consider, for example, rules in the Irish and Indian Constitutions governing the ratification of treaties or the size of government, which are somewhat parallel to the two-thirds supermajority requirement in the Treaty Clause or two Senators requirement in Article II. In Ireland, against the backdrop of strong desire for independence from the United Kingdom, the original 1937 Irish Constitution affirmed "the inalienable, indefeasible, and sovereign right" of the Irish nation "to determine its relations with other nations . . . in accordance with its own genius and traditions," and the right of the Irish people "to decide all questions of national policy, according to the requirements of the common good"; it also specifically provided that "the executive power of the state in or in connection with its external affairs . . . be exercised by or on the authority of the [Irish] government."[90] Fifty years on, the Irish Supreme Court held that the specificity of these pro-independence rules was such that, despite significant public support in Ireland for increased integration with Europe, correctly interpreted these were a direct bar to Ireland being part of such efforts.[91] This did not mean, however, that such rules ultimately led to any long-term constitutional error costs in Ireland, because under the relatively permissive requirements for amendment established by Article 46 of the Irish Constitution, an amendment to these rules designed to allow ratification of the Single European Act passed comfortably in the same year that the Irish Court handed down its decision.[92]

In India, a similar position has applied in the context of constitutional rules such as those governing the size of government. Because the original Constitution in India contained no explicit provisions regarding the size of the executive, it effectively adopted a "rule" permitting extremely large cabinets.[93] Over subsequent decades this rule proved to involve substantial error costs in terms of

---

[90] Irish Constitution, Arts 1, 5, 29.

[91] See, e.g., *Crotty v An Taioseach* [1987] IR 713 (Walsh, Henchy, Hederman, JJ) (holding that in unamended form Articles 1, 5, and 29 absolutely prevented Ireland from ratifying the Single European Act 1986).

[92] Tenth Amendment to the Constitution of Ireland (passed by clear legislative majority, and 70 percent of voters).

[93] Constitution of India 1949.

its effect on the stability of government.[94] Legislative measures designed to address this problem also proved largely ineffectual.[95] However, because in most instances the constitutional amendment process under Article 368 of the Indian Constitution requires the support of only a simple majority of the Indian parliament, the parliament in 2004 was able to relatively easily pass an amendment to the Indian Constitution seeking to address these error costs by establishing a rule limiting the size of national and state governments to 15 percent of the relevant legislature.[96]

In the United States, by contrast, the difficulty of formal constitutional amendment under Article V of the Constitution means that constitutional amendment is a far less realistic response to the present-day error costs of parallel constitutional rules. The hurdles imposed by Article V are such that, of 11,000 attempts to amend the Constitution over the last 200 years, only 27 (at most) have actually succeeded.[97] On most measures, these hurdles mean that, in global terms, the U.S. Constitution is now either the most or second most difficult to amend.[98] For constitutional rules such as the two Senators rule, the specific requirements prescribed by Article V are also even more demanding than in respect of other constitutional norms, because Article V specifically provides "that no State, without its Consent, shall be deprived of its equal Suffrage in the Senate."[99]

---

[94] Because governments in India are often minority or coalition governments, there is an inherent tendency for government instability. By creating broad scope for opposition parties to use cabinet posts as a means of promoting defection by members of the governing party, the original Constitution also greatly increased this potential for instability. See *The National Commission to Review the Working of the Constitution*, Final Report, par 4.19 (2002).

[95] See discussion in T. V. R. Shenoy, *There Is No Substitute for Vigilance*, Rediff India Abroad (July 9, 2004) (discussing limits to the Anti-Defection Act 1985).

[96] Indian Constitution 1969, 91st Amendment. For discussion see Mohan Guruswamy, *91st Constitutional Amendment: Not Quite Adequate*, Hindu Business Line (July 20, 2004).

[97] See, e.g., John R. Vile, *Encyclopedia of Constitutional Amendments, Proposed Amendments, and Amending Issues, 1789–2002* (ABC-CLIO, 2003).

[98] Lutz, *Toward a Theory of Constitutional Amendment* 237 (cited in note 4); Zachary Elkins, Tom Ginsburg, and James Melton, *The Endurance of National Constitutions* (Cambridge, 2009).

[99] This makes amendment of Article 1, Section 3, Clause 1, within the confines of the Constitution, close to, if not actually, impossible. One possibility, canvassed by Lynn Baker and Samuel Dinkin (see 13 J L & Pol 21, cited in note 29), is that Article V could be amended in order to remove this requirement of unanimous consent, but such an argument encounters severe difficulties in how it treats the relationship between the general and specific requirements of a particular constitutional clause: see Sanford Levinson, *The Political Implications of Amending Clauses*, 13 Const Comm 107 (1996).

For both the two Senators rule and the Treaty Clause, political realities further mean that, even if these formal legal hurdles to amendment did not exist, it would still be extremely difficult to rely on Article V in order to amend these rules. As Baker and Dinkin argue in the context of Article I, Section 3, Clause 1, "any state that currently receives disproportionately great representation in the Senate relative to its share of the nation's population benefits from the existing allocation of representation and therefore should have little interest in changing it," and "the number of such over-represented states has always exceeded the one-third-plus-one necessary to block the mere proposal of any constitutional amendment."[100] Accordingly, it also follows that Senators from small states will be extremely unlikely to support any amendment which might make it easier to amend Article I, Section 3, Clause 1 and especially one as broad as an amendment to Article V itself.[101]

This same argument holds for use of Article V to amend the Treaty Clause. Why, one might ask, would two-thirds of Senators, other than in the most exceptional cases, vote to remove the right of two-thirds of Senators to decide whether or not to ratify a treaty? As Edwin Corwin suggested in 1940 in criticizing the Treaty Clause, there seems not "the least likelihood that . . . two thirds of the Senate [will] consent to relax that body's powers" especially in an area of such potential significance.[102] I have shown elsewhere that because it contains the same two-thirds supermajority requirement for congressional approval as the Treaty Clause, Article V is itself one of the most prominent examples of a constitutional rule that, from a contemporary perspective, likely involves error costs.[103] For either the two Senators rule or the Treaty Clause to be successfully amended, the only realistic route for proponents of such change will therefore be informal amendment to the Constitution, other than via Article V, where these problems of endogeneity may be less severe.

Bruce Ackerman, in developing what it is perhaps the leading account of informal amendment in the United States, identifies two

---

[100] Baker and Dinkin, 13 J L & Pol at 71 (cited in note 29).

[101] Id at 72.

[102] Edward S. Corwin, *The President: Office and Powers: History and Analysis of Practice and Opinion* 232–40 (NYU, 1940). The events of 1945 support this interpretation: see Ackerman and Golove, 108 Harv L Rev at 889–90 (cited in note 50).

[103] See Dixon Working Paper 2010 (cited in note 4).

instances of large-scale constitutional change outside Article V, namely, the Reconstruction Amendments and the New Deal expansion in federal regulatory power.[104] From these "constitutional moments," Ackerman concludes that informal constitutional change can occur in the United States where three conditions are met: (1) there is a proposal for small "c" constitutional change; (2) there is a "triggering election," in which that proposal or analogs to it are centrally at issue; and (3) there is subsequent legislative "ratification" of the proposal by Congress.[105] Ackerman therefore posits that, while the House and Senate certainly have a central role to play in the process of constitutional change, that role will tend to turn on the outcome of ordinary, and not supermajority, voting procedures. This means that informal amendments will tend both to overcome the current small state veto over amendment and also, to a large degree, be as likely in a Congress of today's size as in 1789.[106]

At the same time, as a solution to the problem of constitutional rule updating, the difficulty with such a process of informal amendment is at least twofold. The first is that many scholars do not acknowledge that such processes exist. Instead, many favor the view that while such constitutional moments clearly involved major constitutional change and were legitimate as a matter of political principle, they occurred almost wholly outside the terms of the Constitution or involved extraconstitutional, not constitutional, processes of change.[107] The second, related difficulty is that, at least as initially formulated, Ackerman's theory implies extremely infrequent scope for constitutional updating—indeed, it points to amendment at an even slower rate than under Article V.[108] The more Ackerman has been willing to expand his theory to identify further constitutional moments,[109] the more difficult it has also become to delineate such moments from more ordinary moments of

---

[104] Bruce Ackerman, *We the People*, vol 1, *Foundations* (Belknap, 1993).

[105] Id.

[106] On the relative stability of a 50 percent majority rule, see Dixon and Holden, *Designing Constitutional Amendment Rules* (cited in note 43).

[107] See, e.g., David R. Dow, *The Plain Meaning of Article V*, in Sanford Levinson, ed, *Responding to Imperfection: The Theory and Practice of Constitutional Amendment* 117 (Princeton, 1995). See also Tribe, 108 Harv L Rev at 1286–88 (cited in note 64).

[108] For criticisms of Ackerman's theory as underinclusive in this context, see, e.g., Michael W. McConnell, *The Forgotten Constitutional Moment*, 11 Const Comm 115 (1994).

[109] See, e.g., Bruce Ackerman, *The Storrs Lectures: Discovering the Constitution*, 93 Yale L J 1013 (1983–84).

constitutional contestation, or "dialogue," in which the Court sees itself as having a central role to play in deciding whether and to what degree constitutional change occurs.

Other proposals designed to overcome the difficulty of formal constitutional amendment under Article V also encounter difficulties when applied to many constitutional rules. One proposal, by Akhil Amar, is that Americans should be free to amend the Constitution via a national referendum process.[110] Whatever its general merits, the difficulty with this proposal as applied to most constitutional rules is that it assumes a degree of popular interest in proposed amendment that simply will not exist in the case of many specific, technical constitutional provisions, such as the Treaty Clause or even the two Senators rule.[111]

A second proposal I have developed elsewhere is that the Court should give some degree of positive force to proposed and failed, as well as successful, constitutional amendments, according to the degree of support they receive in Congress and state legislatures.[112] By enlisting Congress, rather than voters, as the initiator of constitutional change under Article V, my approach is also clearly less sensitive than Amar's to the need for popular interest in the error costs associated with specific constitutional rules. By adjusting the level of deference enjoyed by congressional or state legislation to the degree of support a proposed amendment enjoys in Congress and state legislatures, my proposal also encounters some of this same difficulty, albeit in less acute form.

No matter how one conceives of applying or redesigning the constitutional amendment process, therefore, it is almost inevitable that an insistence on reliance on such processes as a means of constitutional updating will be simply to endorse, rather than address, the current deficit regarding the updating of constitutional rules. If one takes seriously, as many proponents of amendment exclusivity do, this deficit and its effects in areas such as federal spending,[113] it may therefore be that for the foreseeable future indirect consti-

---

[110] See Akhil Amar, *Consent of the Governed: Constitutional Amendment Outside Article V*, 94 Colum L Rev 457 (1994).

[111] For other criticisms of Amar's proposal, see Henry P. Monaghan, *Our Perfect Constitution*, 56 NYU L Rev 353 (1981).

[112] Rosalind Dixon, Working Paper 2010 (cited in note 4).

[113] For criticism by Constitutional conservatives of decisions such as *Clinton v New York* and *Thornton*, see, e.g., Steven G. Calabresi and Christopher S. Yoo, *The Unitary Executive: Presidential Power from Washington to Bush* (Yale, 2008).

tutional rule updating is the option which for constitutional conservatives, as well as liberals, is actually the least worst of the available alternatives.

TONY A. FREYER

WHAT WAS WARREN COURT
ANTITRUST?

The Warren Court's antitrust jurisprudence provoked caricature, both as "coonskin cap" frontier law and as sentimental guardianship of mom and pop stores in an age of managerial capitalism.[1] In fact, early Court decisions, exemplified by *Brown Shoe* in 1962, embraced multiple antitrust goals, which reflected an ongoing dialogue in the legal and business world over exactly what antitrust should do, a dialogue occurring not only in law reviews but mainly in the pages of *Fortune* magazine. At the outset, multiple goals for multiple reasons were absorbed by the Court, but as time went on, the Court fragmented, and what appeared from the outside to be ambivalence was in fact growing internal consensus on how the activist majority prioritized the goals of antitrust. The internal deliberation over

Tony A. Freyer is University Research Professor of History and Law, University of Alabama.

AUTHOR'S NOTE: For insights I am grateful to Shahar Dillbary, William Brewbaker, Dennis J. Hutchinson, and Lois Rae Carlson. For research I wish to thank the staffs at the Library of Congress Manuscripts Division; American Heritage Center, University of Wyoming; Seeley G. Mudd Manuscript Library, Princeton University; David Warrington, Special Collections, Harvard Law School; Robert Marshall and Penny Gibson, University of Alabama School of Law Library; Jonathan Ray, History, and Sarah Rutledge, Law, University of Alabama. For financial support I thank the Tobin Project; the Earhart Foundation; the University of Alabama Law School Foundation and the Edward Brett Randolph Fund, and Law School Dean Kenneth C. Randall; Robert Olin, Dean, College of Arts and Sciences, and Michael Mendle, Chair, History Department; and Office of Academic Affairs, University of Alabama. I also thank my secretary, Mrs. Jenny Rieth.

[1] *Antitrust in a Coonskin Cap*, Fortune 65 (July 1966); *Antitrust: The Sacred Cow Needs a Vet*, Fortune 104 (Nov 1962).

Brown Shoe provides the lens through which this development can be understood. The Court's internal deliberations occurred within a forgotten public debate over the soul of antitrust—played out especially in *Fortune* and by leading advocates such as Thurman Arnold—which this article reclaims.

Free-market critics insisted that the Warren Court protected small business competitors rather than truly efficient "imperfect" competition.[2] As the critics contributed to *Fortune*'s ongoing antitrust dialogue, they confronted opposing behavior-oriented economic theories advocated by legal realists like Thurman Arnold and other antitrust experts.[3] Reflecting these economic and legal theories, the Warren Court's inner decision-making process implemented multiple antitrust policy goals beyond those the critics rejected.[4] This article places Warren Court antitrust within two major postwar trends: a "Managerial Revolution . . . quite fatal to profit maximization" and a new market for antitrust expertise.[5] These trends converged in a new media market embracing the Supreme Court, which *Fortune*'s reporting exemplified.[6] Despite internal tensions between activists and moderates, Warren Court antitrust doctrine exploited divided business opinion while it enforced the policy goals Arnold epitomized.[7] This historical understanding suggests policy

---

[2] Max Ways, *Antitrust in an Era of Radical Change*, Fortune 128–30, 214, 216, 221, 222, 224 (March 1966); Herbert Hovenkamp, *The Antitrust Enterprise Principle and Execution* 31–45 (Harvard, 2005); Milton Handler, *Introduction*, Theodore Kovaleff, *Historical Perspective: An Introduction*, and Donald Dewey, *Economists and Antitrust: The Circular Road*, in Theodore P. Kovaleff, ed, 1 *The Antitrust Impulse: An Economic, Historical, and Legal Analysis* xxiii–xxxiii, 3–19, 103–26 (Sharp, 1994); Rudolph J. R. Peritz, *Competition Policy in America, 1888–1992* 236, 258–62 (Oxford, 1996); Tony Freyer, *Antitrust and Global Capitalism, 1930–2004* 102–34 (Cambridge, 2006).

[3] Spencer Weber Waller, *Thurman Arnold: A Biography* 151–84 (New York, 2005) (cited hereafter as Waller).

[4] Compare text and notes Sections III–IV to Warren Court antitrust references: Lucas A. Powe, Jr., *The Warren Court and American Politics* 121–23, 180–81, 461 (Harvard, 2000); Bernard Schwartz, *Super Chief: Earl Warren and His Supreme Court—A Judicial Biography* 162–64, 195–96, 222–24, 376–77, 384, 437–38, 475–79 (New York, 1983), and biographies or autobiographies cited below.

[5] Robin Marris, *The Economic Theory of "Managerial" Capitalism* 46 (Free Press, 1964); Alfred D. Chandler, Jr., *The Visible Hand: The Managerial Revolution in American Business* 455–500 (Harvard, 1977); Neil Fligstein, *The Transformation of Corporate Control* 191–314 (Harvard, 1990); Freyer, *Antitrust and Global Capitalism* at 102–34 (cited in note 2).

[6] Tony Freyer, *The Warren Court as History*, in Daniel Hamilton and Alfred L. Brophy, eds, *Transformations in American Legal History II: Essays in Honor of Morton J. Horwitz* (Harvard, forthcoming) (includes discussion, Anthony Lewis interview, May 8, 2008, Cambridge, MA).

[7] As discussed in Sections II and III, multiple antitrust policy goals include managerial accountability—especially concerning administered prices—limits upon market domi-

goals that could address current antitrust issues, such as managerial accountability, the limits of price theories, and "[d]istinguishing attacks on rivals that harm consumers from those that benefit consumers."[8]

I. FORTUNE'S CHANGING ANTITRUST

Warren Court antitrust decisions coincided with historic developments in American managerial capitalism which *Fortune* chronicled. The liberal state and managerial capitalism emerging from the Great Depression unleashed enormous productivity during World War II, continuing through the first phase of the Cold War until 1973.[9] By the 1960s, as postwar Wall Street volumes reached new heights, corporate management's general policy of fighting for market share—especially through advertising—rather than maximizing profits for investors was the least risky pricing strategy most executive managers pursued under oligopolistic competition. A major study supported statistically the "main theorem" that "various pressures lead managers to maximize the rate of growth of the firm they are employed in subject to a constraint imposed by the security motive." Critic John Kenneth Galbraith and defender Peter Drucker agreed that profit maximization was secondary to the manager's personal motivations involved in winning power and creative influence identified with running a bigger division or groups of divisions.[10] *Fortune*'s analysis of these historic trends challenged managers, antitrust enforcement authorities, and the Warren Court itself.

The Eisenhower administration's antitrust activist was Robert A. Bicks. During his eighteen-month tenure leading the Antitrust Division (1959–60), *Fortune* reported that Bicks was the "most vigorous trust buster" since the consummate activist Thurman Arnold (1938–43). Indeed, Bicks filed the most antitrust cases since Arnold,

---

nance, and defense of small business opportunity; compare "populist overtones," Terry Calvani and Michael L. Sibarium, *Antitrust Today: Maturity or Decline*, in Kovaleff, ed, 2 *Antitrust Impulse* at 608–10 (cited in note 2).

[8] William H. Page and John E. Lopatka, *The Microsoft Case Antitrust, High Technology, and Consumer Welfare* 118 (Chicago, 2007).

[9] Thomas K. McCraw, *American Capitalism*, in Thomas K. McCraw, ed, *Creating Modern Capitalism* 340–43 (Harvard, 2000).

[10] Marris, *Economic Theory of "Managerial" Capitalism* at 47 (cited in note 5); Freyer, *Antitrust and Global Capitalism* at 110–12 (cited in note 2); Daniel J. Boorstin, *The Image: A Guide to Pseudo-Events in America* 211–28 (Colophon, 1964).

and against major corporations such as General Electric and General Motors, as well as firms in various other market sectors ranging from shoes and dairy foods to construction, finance, machinery, the Salk vaccine, and Big Oil. Although Bicks and his staff lost the last two cases, his overall record of victory included the momentous electrical conspiracy litigation that established a new standard of business criminal liability. His enforcement activism embraced not only the Sherman Act's antimonopoly provision (section 2), but also galvanized the Clayton Act's section 7 proviso prohibiting merger investments in particular markets that "lessen competition." Aided by the Warren Court's controversial construction of the latter provision in *DuPont/GM*, Bicks initiated in *Brown Shoe* and other cases new legal challenges to the enormous postwar corporate restructuring of American capitalism and consumer society.[11]

Fortune articles endorsed Bicks's activist enforcement. Denouncing the management breakdown in his own and other companies engendering the massive electrical conspiracy, GE board chairman Ralph J. Cordiner declared that the nation's productive economy resulted from a favorable "business atmosphere . . . founded on free markets and intense competition at the market place. Any arrangement that tends toward a system of cartels or price control or regulations by competitors is recognized by the citizens of this country as a deterrent to the present and future growth of our country." Due to "this basic reason" American "public opinion has obliged the government, regardless of the party in power, to enforce the antitrust laws aggressively—in the public interest." While this *Fortune* article declared that Cordiner and Bicks saw that antitrust activism was essential, it also attributed to Eisenhower's two attorney generals the view that Bicks's "vigor of antirust activity has quenched any Democratic charge of" Justice Department "favoritism to big business." Still more candidly, the article concluded, "Vigorous trust busting under a man like Bicks is the price that business pays to keep the lid on a veritable Pandora's box of wild-eyed programs masquerading as antitrust."[12]

---

[11] Richard Austin Smith, *What Antitrust Means Under Mr. Bicks*, Fortune 120, 121, 256, 261, 262, 264, 266, 270 (March 1960); Theodore Philip Kovaleff, *Business and Government During the Eisenhower Administration: A Study of the Antitrust Policy of the Antitrust Division of the Justice Department* 113–38 (Ohio, 1980); *Brown Shoe Co., Inc. v U.S.*, 370 US 294 (1962); *U.S. v E. I. DuPont de Nemours and Co.*, 353 US 586 (1957).

[12] Smith, Fortune at 123, 120, 270 (cited in note 11); Richard Austin Smith, *The Incredible Electrical Conspiracy: Part I*, Fortune 132–37, 170, 172, 175, 176, 179, 180 (April 1961);

Bicks's enforcement strategy reflected these diverse business views. Congressman Emanuel Celler and Senator Estes Kefauver, coauthors of the 1950 amendment strengthening the Clayton Act, exemplified a vocal public opinion endeavoring to protect small business from steadily mounting corporate concentration. Relentlessly expanding big business thus was bad for America. Leading industrial organization theories rejected this express condemnation of big business. Still, in what *Fortune* described as a "disturbing book," the proponents of these theories, Harvard professors Carl Kaysen and Donald Turner, argued that Congress could address "unreasonable market power" resulting from corporate concentration by enacting a new antitrust court and agency. Bicks rebutted all this. Echoing Arnold's often-expressed sentiments on the subject, Bicks asserted: "Absolute size is absolutely irrelevant. Material instead is whatever power to control market price, and market entry, that may come through *relative* size gauged in the context of a particular market." Again like Arnold, Bicks aimed to achieve results by vigorously enforcing existing antitrust laws and, wherever necessary, winning new interpretations from the Supreme Court.[13]

The amended Clayton Act was a significant focus of enforcement. The Supreme Court's 1957 *DuPont/GM* decision overturned a lower court decision in favor of DuPont. Applying the Clayton Act's 1950 amendment prohibiting conduct in a particular market "tending to lessen competition," the Court decided against the powerful company. Employing such precedents, Bicks pursued a case-by-case litigation strategy in order to resolve big business "uncertainty" concerning the scope of the 1950 Celler-Kefauver amendment on mergers. He wanted "judicial support for . . . [the] belief that Section 7 prohibits a company with a dominant position in its market from acquiring a profitable company to which it sells." Second, Bicks and his staff sought to remove the claim of "efficiency" as a "*complete* defense" in section 7 cases, "since almost invariably it is easier and quicker to buy know-how and management than to develop it from scratch." Bicks and his associates accepted "[t]he 'efficiency' or 'economies' defense . . . only in those cases where defendants can prove that the efficiencies or economies could not be

---

id Smith, *Part II*, Fortune 161–64, 210, 212, 217, 218, 221, 224 (May 1961); compare Ruth Sheldon Knowles, *Oil, Vaccine, and Mr. Bicks*, Fortune 168, 169, 170, 256, 261, 262, 267, 268, 270 (June 1960).

[13] On legislative history, see *Brown Shoe*, 370 US 294, 311–23 (1962); Smith, Fortune at 262, 266 (cited in note 11) (italics in original).

obtained except by the challenged merger." Bicks and his staff tested this theory in the *Brown Shoe* case.[14]

Fortune's examination of Bicks's enforcement regime established the pattern for its antitrust articles throughout the 1960s. Business attitudes toward antitrust in principle repeatedly affirmed the assumption that "irreparable damage will be done if the idea gets around that corporations take a cynical view of the laws they live by, or are tolerant of wrong doers." Such individuals were "to be condemned not because they sought profit, which is the vital spark of enterprise, but because they flagrantly broke the competitive rules that make the profit system an effective servant of the people." Moreover—undoubtedly influenced by the unprecedented media images of imprisoned corporate executives in the electric conspiracy cases—business diffused the "self-righteous attacks of 'anti-business' factions in both organized labor and the political left" by acknowledging "clear breakdowns of management responsibility." Finally, business contended that antitrust was among those areas where "it is getting increasingly hard to know what's right or wrong about a lot of business practices. Business has become so complex that many of its ramifications have gone beyond the understanding of our moral instructors, the clergy, and the moral understanding of businessmen themselves."[15]

Although business endorsement of antitrust in principle persisted, attitudes toward merger policy shifted. *Fortune* commentators increasingly disputed continuing Bicks's policy of limiting the "efficiency" or "economies" defense, where a firm's purchase of a company that was also its customer established the former firm's dominance within the same market.[16] A noteworthy case in point was the contradictory analysis appearing in articles regarding the Supreme Court's affirmation of Bicks's theory in the *Brown Shoe* case (1962).[17] Even so, *Fortune* writers readily perceived that the

---

[14] *Brown Shoe*, 370 US 294 (1962); *DuPont/GM*, 353 US 586 (1957); Smith, Fortune at 266 (cited in note 11) (italics in original).

[15] Editorial, *The Price-Fixing Case*, Fortune at 102, 104 (March 1961) (see further articles discussed below).

[16] Smith, Fortune at 262, 266 (cited in note 11).

[17] Robert H. Bork and Ward S. Bowman, Jr., *The Crisis in Antitrust*, Fortune 138–40, 192, 197, 198, 201 (Dec 1963); Harlan M. Blake and William K. Jones, *In Defense of Antitrust*, Fortune 135, 171, 172, 174, 176 (Aug 1964); Milton Handler and Stanley D. Robinson, *The Supreme Court vs. Corporate Mergers*, Fortune 164–65, 174, 176, 178 (Jan 1965).

legal "criteria" establishing "such definitions and standards are useful only if applied to a specific set of circumstances." Similarly, an
editorial addressing the Sherman Act's section 2 during the early
Kennedy administration endorsed balanced yet vigorous enforcement. "Big companies" were "required . . . not to use their market
power to drive weaker competitors out of business. This is as it
should be, and a considerable amount of self-policing is expected
of them. But in the final analysis, enforcement of Section 2, the
most difficult and most important part of the Sherman Act, is and
should remain the responsibility of the cop on the antitrust beat."[18]

Essentially, *Fortune*'s articles involving mergers searched for predictability. Criticism of the Kennedy administration's first antitrust
enforcer, Lee Loevinger, emphasized his abrasive rhetoric. Yet the
Supreme Court's 1962 *Brown Shoe* decision vindicated Bicks's activism, though he had left office.[19] Even so, *Fortune* quoted Attorney
General Robert Kennedy's assistant Byron White, saying, "I think
most of us around here feel that the antitrust laws represent national
policy and should be applied with wisdom and good will on a case-
by-case basis, and in a fair way, with justification found in the general
purpose and intent of the antitrust laws." White's affirmation that
he expressed the "antitrust mainstream" echoed Bicks, and also,
inferentially, Thurman Arnold.[20] By the mid-1960s, amidst the Supreme Court's increasingly controversial antimerger decisions, *Fortune* reported that establishing greater "certainty" in U.S. merger
law was the third most important policy upon which business urged
action from the Johnson administration. Struggles over the Vietnam
War and urban racial unrest, however, as well equivocal business
support for the Great Society programs, made antitrust a "missing
campaign issue" in 1968.[21]

Big corporations' growing investment through diversification, especially conglomerates, engendered controversy over "reciprocal"

---

[18] Editorial, *How Low Is Reasonable?* Fortune 120 (July 1961).

[19] George Bookman, *Loevinger vs. Big Business*, Fortune 93–95, 114 (Jan 1962); Lee
Loevinger, *Antitrust Is Pro-Business*, Fortune 96, 97, 126, 128, 130, 135, 136 (Aug 1962);
Tony Freyer, *Regulating Big Business Antitrust in Great Britain and America 1880-1990*
304–07 (Cambridge, 1992).

[20] Bookman, Fortune at 114 (cited in note 19); Dennis J. Hutchinson, *The Man Who
Once Was Whizzer White: A Portrait of Justice Byron R. White* 265–66 (Free Press, 1998)
(and on Thurman Arnold, see Section II below).

[21] Edmund K. Faltermayer, *What Business Wants from Lyndon Johnson*, Fortune 122–25,
228, 230, 230, 234 (Feb 1965); Editorial, *The Missing Campaign Issues*, Fortune 73–74 (Aug
1968).

relations or "reciprocity." Consistent with *DuPont/GM*, the Court's 1960s decisions challenged merger investment to achieve "vertical growth" as well as the "horizontal" purchase of firms competing directly in the same industry. As a result, *Fortune* reported, giant firms "branched out horizontally into other industries, becoming more and more diversified until they have found themselves with a long list of suppliers in one hand and a long list of products for sale in the other." The expanding investment in computer technology during the same period created a new "centralization of policymaking authority . . . helping to ensure that deals will not be made, or strangled, by salesmen or purchasing agents in the boondocks, where views of company interests are liable to be parochial." Computer tracking of volume buyers and sellers enabled a new management role dubbed the "trade-relations" (TR) person. TR people so aggressively pursued interpersonal or "reciprocal" relationships that *Fortune* considered whether the American "economy might end up completely dominated by conglomerates happily trading with each other in a new kind of cartel system."[22]

Conglomerates especially divided business opinion. A 1965 *Fortune* article noted business critics professing "to be shocked" at a TR manager's "tactics." Moreover, in "giant conglomerates" reciprocity evidenced "trade relations" that "tend to close a business circle. Left out are firms with narrow product lines; as patterns of trade and trading partners emerge between particular groups of companies, entry by newcomers becomes more difficult." Indeed, hypothetical "conglomerate cartels" were "constantly being broken up by technological advances: new products and processes lure companies away from stable relationships. Competition from foreign companies also works against a hardening of trade patterns." As a result, *Fortune* observed, antitrust authorities were "not directly attacking all aspects of the practice of reciprocity." Instead, like Bicks's challenge to the "efficiency defense" under the Clayton Act's section 7, antitrust enforcers targeted the "process of diversification by merger. When a powerful company acquires a smaller one, the smaller, which now has a parent bristling with reciprocal strength, may come to dominate its industry."[23]

---

[22] Freyer, *Regulating Big Business* at 308 (cited in note 19); *DuPont/GM*, 353 US 586 (1957); Edward McCreary, Jr., and Walter Guzzardi, Jr., *A Customer Is a Company's Best Friend*, Fortune 180, 181, 194 (June 1965).

[23] McCreary and Guzzardi, Fortune at 181, 194 (cited in note 22).

From 1962 to 1969, *Fortune* promoted an antitrust dialogue addressing American capitalism's "historic change" identified with corporate diversification. Corporate America's "traditional orientation around products" was being restructured into "new alignments . . . based on management capabilities and the ability to mobilize capital." But managers' and investors' efforts to attain massive corporate restructuring through "mergers and acquisitions cannot be based strictly on what makes good business sense" in the face of an "unpredictable obstacle course prepared by the agencies enforcing the antitrust laws." Thus, *Fortune* "repeatedly" urged "an overhaul" of antitrust so that "enforcement agencies and the courts" had a "new definition of what constitutes a threat to competition— a definition based on the economic realities of today." Moreover, *Fortune* urged, business should "call politicians to account" and thereby overcome the "amazing immunity from politics" antitrust "enjoyed" concerning the "single most serious problem in the whole arena of business' relations with government." *Fortune*'s own articles demonstrated, however, that business proved itself to be divided regarding conglomerates; as a result, the call for political mobilization failed.[24]

The campaign to redefine "competition" became the focus of controversy. In 1962 and 1969 articles, *Fortune* noted that when "analysis proceeds from classical perfect-competition economics" it "does not always accurately correspond to what actually goes on in particular industries." Indeed, *Fortune* rejected such economic rationales that urged abolition of antitrust on the ground that it held— through Warren Court decisions like *Brown Shoe*—"free enterprise" in a "strangling grip."[25] By contrast, *Fortune* pursued an antitrust dialogue seeking imperfect "competition theories" that favored business realities. Thus, a 1962 editorial declared, "Antitrust: The Sacred Cow Needs a Vet." Generally, articles criticized the Federal Trade Commission for failure to follow a consistent economic the-

---

[24] Editorial, *Missing Campaign Issue*, Fortune 73–74 (Aug 1968); Allan T. Demaree, *What Business Wants from President Nixon*, Fortune 84–86, 130, 132 (Feb 1968); Robert H. Bork, *Antitrust in Dubious Battle*, Fortune 102–04, 160, 164, 165 (Sept 1969) (for earlier articles, see above citations).

[25] Editorial, *Antitrust's Pregnant Silence*, Fortune 86 (Sept 1969); compare *Antitrust: The Sacred Cow Needs a Vet*, Fortune 104 (cited in note 1) (noting earlier eras when antitrust laws applied "allowing full freedom to the legitimate evolution," defeat of cartels, and western Europe adopted antitrust; but see extreme conservative defense of free market practices in Sylvester Petro, *The Growing Threat of Antitrust*, Fortune 128–30, 188, 191, 192, 197, 198, 203, 204, at 208 (Nov 1962); see note 17 above).

ory. Adhocracy was a problem. The Warren Court received criticism for decisions embodying archaic theories dubbed "Antitrust in a Coonskin Cap." Regarding Justice Department antitrust enforcement, *Fortune* articles condemned Kennedy's officials as simply antibusiness, altogether lacking economic understanding. Johnson's appointee Donald Turner was still more problematic; he represented Harvard's industrial organization theories that resisted corporate concentration.[26]

Eventually, *Fortune* preferred Robert H. Bork's antitrust competition theories. In 1963 Yale law professors Bork and Ward S. Bowman credited University of Chicago economist Aaron Director with theories showing prevailing antitrust doctrines of "exclusionary dealing" to be "demonstrably fallacious in concept and visibly hurtful in application." Applying the same theoretical rigor, Bork and Bowman condemned the Supreme Court's and federal agencies' current antimonopoly and merger decisions. Singled out for particular criticism was the Court's 1962 *Brown Shoe* decision and the theories it affirmed limiting the "efficiency defense" and restricting markets that had originated with Bicks. Bork and Bowman did support the Court's long course of decisions condemning price-fixing practices. In 1969, following *Fortune*'s endorsement of views articulated in earlier articles, Bork distilled three fundamental points: (1) *"The only legitimate goal of our present statutes is the maximization of consumer welfare."* (2) *"Efficiency-motivated mergers deserve the law's protection. The market will penalize those that do not in fact create efficiency."* (3) "[I]njury to *competitors* is irrelevant to the question of injury to competition and consumer welfare."[27]

Still, *Fortune* recognized that Bork's theories were not those business, antitrust authorities, or the courts generally accepted as "imperfect competition." Broadly identified with industrial organization economists such as Harvard's Edward Mason, the prevailing theories addressed "a basic paradox in business motivation" in which the "market economy relies on the self-interest of the businessman, in seeking to maximize profits, as the dynamic force of the system."

---

[26] See note 1 above; Harold B. Meyers, *The Root of the FTC's Confusion*, Fortune 114–15, 152, 154, 156, 158 (Aug 1963); Ways, Fortune at 128–30, 214, 216, 221, 222, 224 (cited in note 2); Max Ways, Editorial, *A New "Worst" in Antitrust*, Donald F. Turner, *The Antitrust Chief Dissents*, Fortune 111–12, 113–14 (April 1966); Robert H. Bork, *The Supreme Court Versus Corporate Efficiency*, Fortune 92–94, 155 (Aug 1967).

[27] See note 17; Bork, Fortune at 92–94, 155 (cited in note 26); Bork, Fortune at 103 (cited in note 24) (emphasis in original).

In addition, however, "businessmen may seek to increase profits by methods that do nothing to improve resource utilization or efficiency or to increase consumer satisfactions in relation to the price paid."[28] Although challenging editor Max Ways's critique of such "mainstream" antitrust theories, Turner agreed with him that antitrust laws should condemn price-fixing conspiracies. Moreover, Turner expressly did not accept Celler's, Kefauver's, and others' view that antitrust laws were intended as "weapons against bigness per se." Instead, the "principal purpose of antimerger law is to forestall the creation of, or an increase in, market power." Even so, "an active merger policy intended to limit increases in market concentration is unlikely to result in lower efficiency, that an antimerger policy and efficiency are not in conflict."[29]

The "traditional reasons" for targeting "market power" were to "preserve competitively structured markets" and thereby "achieve better market performance." This "structure-conduct-performance analysis" conformed to business realities during the 1960s. Yet Ways, Bork, and others contended that corporate concentration essentially was irrelevant because there was always "inter-product" competition, "new" market competition centered on "managerial brains," and mergers creating scale economies were usually efficient, especially if they facilitated research and development. Turner presented empirical evidence published by Joe S. Bain and others showing that these assumptions underestimated or ignored obstacles to market entry. Moreover, *Fortune*'s articles showed, managers within or trading with corporations undergoing diversification complained of abuses.[30] Evidence also showed that internal managerial control could encourage managers to practice such abuses, including manipulated pricing practices. Inferentially, Turner's characterization of "mainstream" antitrust goals echoed Bicks's recognition that "market" definition and the "complete" efficiency defense raised difficult problems of proof if abuse of market power was to be rejected.[31]

In 1965 *Fortune* published an assessment of the Supreme Court's merger cases consistent with Bicks's and Turner's competition the-

---

[28] Blake and Jones, Fortune at 135 (cited in note 17). For Edward Mason, see Section II below.

[29] Turner, Fortune at 113, 114 (cited in note 26).

[30] Id.

[31] See notes 11–14, 16.

ories. Antitrust lawyers Milton Handler and Stanley D. Robinson addressed the Supreme Court's recent controversial decisions. Bork and others uniformly condemned the Court's merger and monopoly opinions for merely protecting competitors instead of efficient competition. Handler and Robinson praised, however, Chief Justice Warren's *Brown Shoe* decision. It effectively addressed, they said, the "sharp" twelve-year "controversy" arising from the Celler-Kefauver amendment "over the standards to be applied in resolving the two principle issues in merger litigation: market definition and competitive effects." The authors lauded the decision for affirming that the determination of "competitive effects" depended upon the facts delineating the operation of a "unique" industry within particular product markets. In "drawing market boundaries," many "such 'practical indicia' were to be weighed and a balance struck." Finally, Handler and Robinson contrasted this emphasis upon multiple evidence and goals with the Court's subsequent departures from *Brown Shoe* that primarily targeted the threat of corporate concentration.[32]

Fortune's "antitrust dialogue" from Bicks to Bork was dynamic. Business opinion accepted Bicks's activist enforcement in order to defuse political support for "wild" antitrust policies. Amidst the electrical conspiracy litigation, business opinion supported Bicks's attack on price fixing. Yet some business opinion also accepted, at least in principle, Bicks's aggressive antimerger cases such as *Brown Shoe*. Thus reporting on massive corporate restructuring, *Fortune* did not articulate antimonopoly or merger issues solely in terms of market concentration. Similarly, Turner's defense of "mainstream" antitrust conceded that worry about concentration alone was not the sole reason for pursuing an active antimerger policy. Rather, Bicks and Turner suggested, protecting consumer choice and product quality—as well as curbing managerial abuse of market dominance that undercut consumer protection—also were legitimate policy goals attainable through active enforcement. Bork and Max Ways denied these multiple enforcement goals; they recast the Bicks-Turner "imperfect" competition theories as nothing more than the protection of "competitors" over competition itself.[33]

---

[32] Handler and Robinson, Fortune at 164, 165, 178 (cited in note 17).

[33] See notes 26, 28, 29, 31.

Thurman Arnold further exposed Bicks's versus Bork's conflicted antitrust fundamentals.

II. THURMAN ARNOLD AND THE ADVOCACY OF MULTIPLE ANTITRUST POLICY GOALS

Thurman Arnold and the quintessential Washington, D.C., law firm he established with Paul Porter were in the forefront of a dynamic market for antitrust expertise.[34] During the Warren Court years, government actions steadily expanded the reach of the 1950 Clayton Act's antimerger amendment; following the massive electrical equipment cases, private litigation also proliferated. The same years witnessed, too, the "flowering of a plaintiff's antitrust Bar." Thus, antitrust corporate defendants confronted a new class of private plaintiffs, including the "country's largest investor-owned electric utilities, state and local and even foreign governments, and important industrial companies." Before the 1950s, business tended to "call on his counsel for advice after the ship has already entered perilous waters," former ABA president Bernard G. Segal observed. "Today, when a company is contemplating a merger, acquisition, joint venture, or other action having antitrust overtones . . . the antitrust lawyer . . . [is] called upon promptly. Often, the negotiations are shaped by his advice." Representing the same business firms as both plaintiffs and defendants encouraged lawyers to advocate multiple antitrust policy goals; in court and public addresses Arnold articulated these same goals.[35]

In 1954, representing a Denver independent theater against Loew's Co., which included Twentieth Century Fox, Arnold stated antitrust fundamentals. He told a federal district court jury, "The anti-trust laws are distinctly an American institution. America believes in freedom of competitive opportunity, that the freedom of competitive opportunity should be protected and those who prevented competitive opportunity of individual business men should be penalized." Arnold emphasized that the corporation's size was irrelevant. "Now, many people think that the anti-trust laws are aimed to prevent American business from growing big. That is not

---

[34] Waller at 124–204 (cited in note 3).

[35] Id; Freyer, *Regulating Big Business* at 281–82 (cited in note 19); Bernard G. Segal, "A Lawyer Looks at the Antitrust Client," in *Economic Facts and Antitrust Goals; Inputs for Corporate Planning: Tenth Conference on Antitrust Issues in Today's Economy* 39–47, at 41, 42, 45 (New York, 1971); Calvani and Sibarium, *Antitrust Today* at 605–99 (cited in note 7).

the purpose of the anti-trust laws," he insisted. Indeed, the "great nationwide concerns, of which the defendants are examples, have been one of America's principal contributions to the efficiency of our economy and to our economic leadership." Moreover, "Properly utilized, without combinations against individual businesses, these great concerns give not only to the consumers, but to individual businessmen goods and services which individual businessmen need, at cheaper cost." Accordingly, "we are not going to introduce any evidence complaining about the size of these corporate defendants."[36]

Given that the defendant's size raised no legal question, what was the antitrust issue? Arnold answered: "What the anti-trust laws are principally aimed at is preventing, ladies and gentlemen of the jury, combinations among great nationwide concerns which deprive the local individual business man of a fair chance to get the products they sell at terms which they can profitably compete at." Thus, the "combination of these businesses . . . will be the subject matter of the case, and . . . we will attempt to show you, that they did, by their concerted action, not by the action of any single one of them, deprive the Broadway Theater of any chance of a fair competitive market." Assisted by Denver counsel and future Supreme Court Justice Byron White, Arnold won from the jury a $100,000 damage award, which on appeal was upheld. Clearly, the plaintiff's case required proving a conspiracy resulting in a violation of the Clayton Act, rather than the different proofs showing, for example, whether a merger was reasonable. Nevertheless, Arnold insisted, a corporation's size was irrelevant and protection of "freedom of competitive opportunity" of both "national" and the "local independent businessman" were essential goals common to antitrust cases.[37]

The *Loew's* case coincided with Arnold reappraising the antitrust laws in a public forum at the University of Chicago Law School. Noting the demise of the "idea of competition" in the "minds of European businessmen," Arnold emphasized "that the idea of competition" was "still alive in this country." Since the 1930s, certain business and public opinion leaders urged "schemes of rationalizing competition" through planning or a "regulatory agency." Arnold

---

[36] Waller at 157, 158 (cited in note 3); *Loew's, Inc. et al. v Cinema Amusements, Inc.*, 210 F2d 86 (10th Cir 1954).

[37] Waller at 158, 156 (cited in note 3); 210 F2d 95 (1954); Hutchinson, *The Man Who Once Was Whizzer White* at 226 (cited in note 20).

nonetheless argued that American antitrust laws embodied "our dominant ideal . . . of just freedom, not regulation," promoting "a free·competitive economy." Depending on the effectiveness of federal enforcers and the courts—including the Supreme Court—antitrust imposed "a tough philosophy. It gives no security to anyone. It does not protect the small businessman. It pays no regard to that new freedom which so many people are now advocating—freedom from business risks. It is tough for labor . . . . for the sugar industry [and] . . . . for the farmers." Suggesting *Fortune*'s public discourse contesting antitrust from Bicks to Bork during 1960s, Arnold declared, "[e]verywhere you turn you find that the idea of freedom from competitive risk seems to be paramount in our unique thinking."[38]

In *Loew's*, Arnold represented an independent firm; from his client Coca-Cola he understood big organizational efficiencies such as economies of scale. The postwar American economy led the entire world, he said, in "tremendously expanding production." The "great modern corporation" was the "great contribution which Americans made to the world revolution" attained through the "art of organization." American antitrust had "only one purpose . . . to defeat all schemes which restrict production." Large-scale organization not only enabled "big corporations . . . to do" what "they do best—producing basic supplies—but they have wanted to own the distributors in the various" U.S. "communities." Coca-Cola, however, represented the "types of great organizations of the future." Rather than own "sugar plantations" or bottlers, Coca-Cola relied on competitive contracts to "creat[e] wealth in outlying communities . . . . in the people who serve it, and it also creates wealth in its competition" with Pepsi-Cola. "Now here, I think, is the pattern of the great corporation, limited to its functions of serving independent business and exporting capital," contrary to "mercantilistic corporations which want to own, want to control, the supplies, want to control the people."[39]

Since his tenure at the Antitrust Division, Arnold reiterated these antitrust fundamentals. He ranked himself among those "practical

---

[38] Thurman Arnold, "A Reappraisal of the Antitrust Laws," in *Conference on Freedom and the Law, the Law School, the University of Chicago Conference Series Number 13, Fiftieth Anniversary Celebration, May 7, 1953* at 98–102 (Chicago, 1953). Professor Aaron Director spoke during the morning session; John Kenneth Galbraith and Arnold spoke during, respectively, the afternoon and evening sessions.

[39] Arnold, *Reappraisal* at 101–02 (cited in note 38).

reformers" who "always ha[d] to fight not only reactionary opposition to reform, but also the politically impractical ideas of liberal
economic planners." Neither group grasped that business, government, and political "institutions respond to pressures, not logical
thinking. They are like human personalities. The direction they
take depends on the necessity of adjustment to outside forces. If
you are going to make that adjustment easier and less painful, you
must use methods which do not create fear and distrust by attacking
revered traditions. And there lies the strength of the Sherman Act,"
Arnold declared. "It is a symbol of our traditional ideals."[40] Testifying in 1964 before the Senate's Antitrust and Monopoly subcommittee, he distinguished "bigness" from "two principal evils of concentrated economic power in a democracy. The first is the power
of concentrated industry to charge administered prices [like exclusion agreements enforced] rather than prices based on competitive
demand. A second is the tendency of such empires to swallow up
local businesses and drain away local capital," instead of investing
in local communities as did his client Coca-Cola.[41]

These comments reflected the lawyer targeting *provable* illegal
practices. Thus, in the *Loew's* case, Arnold told the members of the
jury about the irrelevance of size to the "purposes" of the antitrust
laws because otherwise "you cannot follow the evidence very well."[42]
The need to present evidence in this wide context was consistent,
moreover, with Arnold's legal-realist behavioral assumption "that
the only instrument which has a chance to preserve competition in
America is antitrust enforcement through the courts." Like antitrust
itself, Americans "[t]raditionally . . . accept the courts as an institution which cannot be criticized or badgered as we badger an
administrative bureau," or, for that matter, legislatures and executives. "Unfortunately, all antitrust law enforcement under any plan
depends on the public attitude," evidencing "a strong demand,"
Arnold declared. "There was such a demand when I was in office."
Amidst the immediate postwar environment, however, "in an economy entirely dependent on government spending we are sufficiently

---

[40] Thurman W. Arnold, *The Bottlenecks of Business* 92 (Reynal, 1940).

[41] Statement of Thurman Arnold to the Subcommittee on Antitrust and Monopoly of
the Senate Committee on the Judiciary, July 29, 1964, quoted at 22 (typescript), the
Thurman W. Arnold Collection, Accession No. 0627, Box 5, addresses, speeches, statements, 1959–68, American Heritage Center University of Wyoming (cited hereafter as
TWAP).

[42] Waller at 157 (cited in note 3).

prosperous that there is little demand. However, I expect the demand to grow as the consequences of the present centralization of economic power makes themselves felt in the business world."[43]

As a famous antitrust enforcer and then successful partner in one of the nation's leading law firms, Arnold selectively used economics to establish legal proofs in antitrust cases. Since the 1930s, lawyers and judges gradually incorporated theories of imperfect competition into their analysis. At the same time, only certain economists adapted such theories to the evidence procedures and standards of proof courts employed.[44] In the Antitrust Division, Arnold pioneered the expanded employment of economists. A leader in these developments associated with industrial organization theories was Harvard's Edward Mason. He began reshaping economic theory to develop legal "tests" of the sort lawyers and judges used in litigation, especially to establish whether the "existence of price discrimination, of price rigidity, advertising expenditures, price leadership and other practices are sufficient to indicate the presence of monopoly elements."[45] Regarding the evidence addressing monopoly under the Sherman and Clayton Acts, a prominent example of Mason's influence was his support of Joe S. Bain's seminal empirical study of the bearing antitrust had on market structure and entry.[46]

Arnold indicated the uncertainties inherent in economic theories. Certain economists, such as the University of Chicago's Aaron Director, taught students that rigorous micro-economic analysis clearly refuted antimonopoly theories like Bain's.[47] By contrast, Mason emphasized that even though "measure[ing] *conceptually* departures from pure competition in various ways such as ratio of price to marginal costs, ratio of actual to competitive profits, ratio of

---

[43] Thurman Arnold, *The Effectiveness of Antitrust*, in Edwin Mansfield, ed, *Monopoly Power and Economic Performance: The Problem of Industrial Concentration* at 151, 152 (Norton, 1968); see note 6 for influence of legal-realist behavioral assumptions.

[44] Freyer, *Antitrust and Global Capitalism* at 27–28 (cited in note 2).

[45] Edward S. Mason, *Monopoly in Law and Economics*, 47 Yale L J 34–35, 47, 49 (1937); Edward S. Mason, *A Life in Development: An Autobiography* (unpublished, n.d., Harvard University Archives).

[46] Joseph Bain, *Barriers to New Competition: Their Character and Consequences in Manufacturing Industries* at viii (Harvard, 1956) (Bain thanks for "generous support" from the "Merrill Foundation, provided through the grant to the Research and Policy Group on Monopoly Policy at Harvard University, as Directed by Dean Edward S. Mason."); and see note 29 above (Turner cites Bain's study).

[47] Aaron Director, "The Parity of the Economic Market Place," in *Conference on Freedom and the Law* at 16–25 (cited in note 38); Bork and Bowman, Fortune 138–40 (cited in note 17); Freyer, *Regulating Big Business* at 278, 320 (cited in note 19).

actual to competitive out put" were "possible," taken separately "each of these conceptual measures is firstly only a partial measure on its own terms and assuming static conditions, and secondly, is not susceptible to statistical application."[48] Arnold observed in 1968 that such tensions regarding the applications of economics constituted the "one struggle which I faced in my tenure which [the current Antitrust Division head] Don[ald] Turner faces today." For academic economists the "antitrust concept" was "too fuzzy either for those," like Mason's colleague John Kenneth Galbraith, "who want to plan the nation's economy or those," such as Chicago's Aaron Director, "who want to construct a set of principles which if followed automatically govern the economy without Government interference."[49]

Arnold's use of economic data in standards of proof partly involved straightforward common law pragmatism. Unlike the economist favoring either planning or the uninhibited free market, the "lawyer realizes that the case-by-case method of dealing with changes in our economic structures is the only effective way of adapting economic change to present reality," Arnold said in the 1968 New York State Bar address. "The lawyer is like a gardener who wants his trees to grow as fast as they can and then prune them into the shapes which fit a formal garden." Economists such as Galbraith or Director "want to throw away the pruning shears and devise a seed which will make the trees grow automatically into the proper shape." Moreover, in 1938–43, "antitrust prosecution was far easier than it is now. Since most business executives believed that what they were doing was legitimate, there was little attempt to conceal things. The files of corporate defendants and trade associations were filled with candid memoranda which no longer exist in corporate files today. Evidence was easy to obtain." But in 1968, "both corporate management and trade associations understand the antitrust laws, and their counsel guard them against obvious violations."[50]

Arnold also understood changes in American corporations' struc-

---

[48] Edward S. Mason, *The Effectiveness of the Antitrust Laws*, in Mansfield, ed, *Monopoly Power and Economic Performance* at 160 (cited in note 43).

[49] Thurman Arnold, *Antitrust, Then and Now—A Reminiscence*, annual dinner of the Antitrust Law Section of the New York State Bar Association, Wednesday, January 24, 1968, New York City at 19 (TWAP, Box 5, speeches, etc., 1959–68). See note 38 above for Arnold's contact with economists Director and Galbraith.

[50] Id at 17–18, 19.

ture and prices since the 1930s. Antitrust Division head Donald
Turner confronted "legal problems . . . more complex and difficult
than they were in my day." Thirty years before, "business management did not have the slightest interest in conglomerate mergers.
They were happy with vertical and horizontal ones. The name
'conglomerate' had not been coined. Management techniques before 1950 had not sufficiently advanced to make conglomerate
mergers profitable."[51] For Arnold, the conspicuous example of effective corporate management embracing antitrust fundamentals
throughout the global market in the postwar era was his client, the
Coca-Cola Company. It produced the "most widely advertised and
distributed single product that the world has ever known." The
research and development of the product "for over half a century
is its most valuable property." The management's creative development and marketing enabled Coca-Cola to pursue stable yet competitive prices: it "does not fix prices (a first-class hotel can get 50
cents for a drink if it wants)" but the company "nevertheless keeps
that market alive and expanding by seeing to it that the corner
drugstore can make money selling it at a nickel."[52]

Above all, Arnold insisted, Coca-Cola exemplified the "dynamic
process" accommodating investment and profitability to local, national, and global markets. The company "builds up its own markets
by leaving the profits of bottling and selling its product to local
enterprises. This is the most important factor in the strength of
Coca-Cola at home and abroad." Across the globe and within "every
state of the Union, these [local] businesses . . . prosper" because
of "Coca-Cola's markets" and "its low cost mass production of
goods which supply those markets." This postwar managerial and
market decentralization contrasted sharply with the period before
the Great Depression when "[g]reat businesses used their power to
acquire local businesses which processed or distributed their product. They created a system of absentee ownership of local enterprises which often drained capital away from outlying areas instead
of creating new independent purchasing power there." Coca-Cola's
growth since the Depression revealed, by contrast, the future of
American enterprise's "corporate growth" whereby the "true capital
of the twentieth century is its industrial potential constructively

---

[51] Id at 18.

[52] Thurman Arnold, *Depression—Not in Your Lifetime*, Collier's at 26, 28 (April 25, 1953).

directed and dynamically inspired by private industry."[53]

Other factors vindicated channeling economic issues through anti-trust litigation, especially to the Warren Court. According to Swed-ish scholar Hans Thorelli's leading historical study, Arnold knew, "It was the tradition of the American common law that the relation between business and government should be based on some broad common-law principle which would acquire definite meaning through a series of court decisions. The Sherman Act followed that tradition."[54] By the 1960s, moreover, European authorities who by World War II had expressly rejected American antitrust in favor of massive cartels "recognize[ed] the need for case-by-case enforce-ment of antitrust policy."[55] This international emergence of antitrust broadly resonated with the many "cases of national significance," including antitrust, which the Supreme Court decided. Such cases "have their roots in the economic and moral attitudes of the times. Since these attitudes change, the Supreme Court's opinions must change with them if the Court is to articulate effectively the fun-damental, economic, and moral basis of our laws . . . ." Finally, such considerations fortified Arnold's "conviction that the Supreme Court under Chief Justice Warren will go down as the greatest Court in our history."[56]

Arnold's public discourse on antitrust thus suggested multiple policy goals. Insistent that antitrust did not address a firm's size in order to attain economic, managerial, or consumer "efficiency," he emphasized the value of "facts" in a case record established through the judicial adversarial process.[57] This approach he shared with cer-tain legal realists and such prominent antitrust authorities as Milton Handler. Antitrust students and professionals, Handler wrote in 1967, "may be disturbed at the prospect of converting a trial into an economic inquest. I submit, however, that it is preferable to have policy made on the basis of a record in which views of the theorists are tested in the fire of cross-examination and where wishful spec-ulation can be differentiated from solid fact."[58] Arnold's legal-realist

[53] Id.

[54] See note 41 at 12–13; Hans B. Thorelli, *The Federal Antitrust Policy* (Baltimore, 1955).

[55] See note 49 at 21.

[56] Speech of Thurman Arnold Before the Lawyers Association of Kansas City, Missouri, January 13, 1965 at 1, 8, Box 5, TWAP.

[57] See notes 36, 37, 43 above.

[58] Milton Handler, *The Supreme Court and the Antitrust Laws: A Critic's Viewpoint*, 1 Ga L Rev 344, 359 (1967).

behavioral assumptions also reinforced his belief that business paid attention to antitrust when there was public demand preferring active enforcement. Finally, employing Coca-Cola's promotion of decentralized market efficiency as proof, he concluded that "in the United States the antitrust concept" remained the "most effective brake against the development of a distorted and unbalanced business structure which can be found in the industrial world."[59]

Arnold, the "practical reformer," knew that economists gave multiple antitrust policy goals a mixed reception. Free marketers such as Director advocated micro-economic price theories of imperfect competition, claiming that, generally, oligopolies resulted from management efficiencies such as scale economies and technological innovation. Ultimately, managerial "efficiencies" determined consumer prices. Thus, Chicago law and economics theories eventually condoned enforcing antitrust against price fixing and various other cartel practices; by contrast, such theories resisted applying the Sherman or Clayton Acts' monopoly provisions to interfere with mergers.[60] Harvard's Edward Mason, however, chaired a group including lawyers and economists which, through ongoing debate, produced studies challenging increased corporate concentration, like Bain's work and Carl Kaysen and Donald F. Turner's *Antitrust Policy: An Economic and Legal Analysis* (1959).[61] The book articulated what became the structure-conduct-performance analysis opposing high corporate concentration based upon "unreasonable market power." Mason nonetheless noted that this standard was difficult to prove, much like the Chicago theories accepting oligopolistic markets as virtually "inevitable."[62]

Phillip Areeda's development of the prominent antitrust course at Harvard Law School was consistent with the multiple antitrust policy goals Arnold defended. As a Harvard undergraduate in economics, Areeda was undoubtedly influenced by Mason's industrial organi-

[59] See notes 43, and 49 at 21.

[60] See note 47.

[61] Lawyer-Economist Group, Mason chaired, noted in *Foreword*, and Edward S. Mason, *Preface*, in Carl Kaysen and Donald F. Turner, eds, *Antitrust Policy: An Economic and Legal Analysis* v–vi, xi–xxiii (Harvard, 1959), similar to Bain's reference cited in note 46 above. See also Mason, *A Life in Development* at 33, 59, 80 (cited in note 45).

[62] Mason, *Preface* at xx (cited in note 61); Hovenkamp, *Antitrust Enterprise* at 36 (cited in note 2); Freyer, *Antitrust and Global Capitalism* at 120–25 (cited in note 2); Mason, *Effectiveness of Antitrust*, in Edwin Mansfield, ed, *Monopoly Power and Economic Performance* at 158–61 (cited in note 48).

zation theories.[63] During Areeda's Harvard Law School years, 1951–54, Robert Bowie and Kingman Brewster taught the then standard antitrust courses in which antitrust was one of several policies targeting "government control" or "regulation of business." In Areeda's last year, Bowie taught, with economists Mason and Carl Kaysen, an antitrust seminar; it examined "legal-economic problems involved in the construction and enforcement of antitrust laws as a vehicle for the maintenance of 'workable competition' in the American economy."[64] By the mid-1960s Donald Turner, Derek Bok, and others taught antitrust within a more business–government relations approach. After serving the Eisenhower administration, in 1961 Areeda returned to Harvard, where he developed new antitrust courses. By 1967 he published the first edition of what became the leading antitrust case book, *Antitrust Analysis: Problems, Text, Cases.* The text's analytical questions and problems emphasized a case's record and facts, like Arnold's advocacy.[65]

Areeda's teaching and case book accentuated contingencies. Aaron Director's influential teaching of antitrust cases at the University of Chicago expressly urged free-market theories. Harvard's Edward Mason, however, essentially conceded Arnold's point that no economic theory could formally "prove" a given antitrust court decision. Such industrial organization theories undoubtedly influenced Areeda. Even so, his teaching and case book emphasized the contingency of economic theory within antitrust law and policy.[66] The course description for an antirust seminar Areeda taught with MIT economist Morris A. Adelman in 1967–68 read: "Antitrust law is concerned with business size and market structure when it

[63] The Economics Department, Harvard University, declines to give registration information about its undergraduate students. I am informed, however, that most undergraduates during the late 1940s to early 1950s, when Phillip Areeda was enrolled, took John Kenneth Galbraith's Industrial Organization (including antitrust and monopoly issues) course, which was the "undergraduate" counterpart of a graduate seminar Mason taught (John Kenneth Galbraith interview, May 9, 2003).

[64] In the *Harvard University Law School Register Catalogue*, for every year from Areeda's first year in law school 1951–52 to 1968–69, I have traced the Government Regulation and Antitrust curriculum (Manuscripts Special Collections, Harvard Law School). The quoted phrases and references to *Antitrust Seminar* at 46, vol 50, April 15, 1953, for academic year 1953–54, *Catalogue*, instructors, Bowie, Mason, and Kaysen. Concerning Brewster, see Freyer, *Antitrust and Global Capitalism* at 120–21 (cited in note 2).

[65] Interview (phone), Professor Derek Bok, June 22, 2009; Professor Bok's comments confirmed the course listings in *Catalogue*, 1961–69 (cited in note 64). Phillip Areeda, *Antitrust Analysis Problems, Text, Cases* (Brown, 1967). I am grateful to Herbert Hovenkamp for further insight into Professor Areeda's book.

[66] Id, and cited in notes 45–47, 63.

deals with problems such as mergers, price leadership, and patent aggregations. The law's approach to many such issues depends on *predispositions* and/or *knowledge* about the significance of 'bigness' and its 'contributions,' and 'threats.'"[67] Thus, Areeda affirmed, corporate-concentration issues engendered "effects" beyond firm size which in turn involved value judgments subject to multiple legal and economic proofs of efficiency. The Supreme Court's 1962 *Brown Shoe* decision tested the legal proofs of these conditional effects.

III. THE BROWN SHOE DECISION AND MULTIPLE ANTITRUST POLICY GOALS

The Warren Court's *Brown Shoe* decision, Bork and other *Fortune* critics claimed, protected competitors rather than competition.[68] The critics emphasized that the Court "held illegal a merger" in which the "respective shares of the nation's shoe output were 4 percent and 0.5 percent. Kinney," the nation's largest family shoe retailer, "had 1.2 percent of total national retail shoe sales by dollar volume," whereas Brown was the fourth largest manufacturer by dollar volume. "[T]ogether the companies had 2.3 percent of total retail outlets." Such market shares were too trivial to warrant prosecution. Moreover, since there were "over 800 shoe manufacturers the industry was close to pure competition."[69] Nevertheless, Chief Justice Warren's express holding on the merits for a unanimous Court was that Congress intended in the Clayton Act's section 7 to "protect *competition* not *competitors*." Also, asserting that only "social values" favoring small business were at issue, the critics underestimated the Court's analysis of Brown's problematic tie-in agreements. Inside the Court, however, antitrust activist William J. Brennan and moderate John M. Harlan viewed the tie-in issues in terms of multiple antitrust efficiency goals advocated by Bicks, Arnold, and other antitrust practitioners.[70]

---

[67] "Antitrust Seminar" in *Catalogue, LXIV*, April 3, 1967, for 1967–68 at 80–81 (cited in note 64) (italics added).

[68] 370 US 294 (1962); see notes 17, 25 above.

[69] Bork and Bowman, Fortune 192, 197 (cited in note 17).

[70] In Warren's opinion, compare two contrasting passages employing "competition not competitors" phraseology: 370 US 320 (italics in original) applies to section 7 only, with no reference to small business, whereas 370 US 344 does include small-business language. Bork and Bowman, Fortune at 197 (cited in note 17), interpret only the latter passage,

By 1961 the Warren Court's four antitrust activists were established.[71] In 1956, Warren, Black, and Douglas dissented from a
majority including Felix Frankfurter which upheld DuPont's dominance in the cellophane products market.[72] The next year, however,
in *DuPont/GM*, new appointee William J. Brennan joined Warren,
Black, and Douglas to strike down stock investments that made GM
dependent on DuPont in the market for automobile finishing products. Frankfurter and Harold Burton dissented. The case was controversial in part because the Court affirmed the government's position applying the Clayton Act's section 7 to vertical financial
investments that had been initiated decades earlier. Moderates John
Marshall Harlan, Tom Clark, and Charles E. Whittaker did not
participate in the 1957 *DuPont/GM*.[73] And neither Harlan nor Clark
took part in the aggressive 1961 remedial decree against DuPont,
whereas Brennan wrote for the activist majority of four. Frankfurter—joined by Potter Stewart and Whittaker—wrote a powerful
dissent urging affirmation of the lower court's more limited order.[74]
The *DuPont/GM* decisions thus confirmed how difficult it was for
the antitrust activists to gain votes among the moderates by the
1961 October Term, when the Brown-Kinney merger reached the
Court.[75]

Yet in *Brown Shoe* both the activists and moderates agreed unanimously upon an expansive reading of the Clayton Act's section 7,
overturning a controversial merger. In the Court's December 9,

---

and thus they ignore the contrary interpretation offered below in the discussion of Brennan's and Harlan's roles in drafting Warren's opinion.

[71] My use and categorization of antitrust "activists," except for Tom Clark, follows Justice
Douglas, *The Court Years 1939-1975: The Autobiography of William O. Douglas* 162 (Vintage,
1981). Justice Clark did not participate in the three DuPont decisions and concurred in
Brown Shoe, responding to Justice Harlan (all discussed below). Also as discussed below
in those same decisions, I think antitrust "moderate" conforms more fittingly to Justices
Harlan, Stewart, Whittaker, Clark, and Frankfurter than does "conservative," Lucas A.
Powe, Jr., *Warren Court and American Politics* at 181 (Belknap, 2002).

[72] *U.S. v E. I. DuPont de Nemours & Co.*, 351 US 377 (1956). Nonparticipation due to
Clark being involved in the government bringing the case and Harlan was DuPont's
defense counsel. See also Box 89, Felix Frankfurter Papers, Manuscripts Special Collections, Harvard Law School (cited hereafter as FFP) (also on microfilm Reel 20).

[73] *U.S. v E. I. DuPont de Nemours & Co.*, 353 US 586 (1957); Box I, William J. Brennan
Papers, Manuscript Division, Library of Congress (cited hereafter as WJBP); and Box 96,
FFP (also on microfilm Reel 26).

[74] Indicating strength of support for Frankfurter's dissent, see May 18, 1961: *Dear Felix:
I thoroughly agree with and join your excellent dissenting opinion. Sincerely C.E.W*[hittaker];
May 18, 1961, *Dear Felix, I'd appreciate your noting my concurrence in your excellent dissenting
opinion. Sincerely yours, P.S.*, Box 148, FFP (also on microfilm Reel 72).

[75] *Brown Shoe Co. v U.S.*, 370 US 294 (1962).

1961 conference, the four antitrust activists joined moderates Harlan, Clark, Stewart, Whittaker, and Frankfurter to uphold the Missouri federal district court's decision striking down the merger between Brown and Kinney. Warren assigned writing the opinion to Whittaker.[76] The factual evidence concerning shoe manufacturing and retail markets at issue in the case was nonetheless sufficiently complex that Warren's memorandum to the Brethren stated, "Our print shop is not equipped to do the tables, so they must be prepared in the Government Printing Office."[77] Indeed, the lower court's decision was important enough that the Supreme Court authorized expedited appeal, thereby avoiding intermediate review by the court of appeals.[78] Between April and June 1962, Whittaker succumbed to clinically diagnosed, long-term depression and Frankfurter suffered a stroke, resulting in their retirement. Kennedy appointees Byron White and Arthur Goldberg took their seats too late to participate in *Brown Shoe*; amidst these difficulties Warren took over writing the opinion.[79]

Why did the Court agree unanimously on the merits? In April 1961, simmering personal tensions became public in another case: In open court, a *Washington Daily News* headline announced, a "bitter squabble" flared between Frankfurter and Warren.[80] Months later, however, *Brown Shoe* stirred neither legal nor personal issues disrupting unanimity. Black favored small business.[81] Warren joined him primarily because of opposition to big-business, abusive market dominance grounded upon California progressivism. Douglas held similar views. Brennan's organized labor background also encouraged distrust of market dominance.[82] Clark and Stewart—as well as the departed Whittaker and Frankfurter—could go along with the activists, by contrast, because Brown's problematic motivation for

---

[76] Id; Schwartz, *Super Chief: Earl Warren and His Supreme Court* at 438–39 (cited in note 4); Craig Alan Smith, *Failing Justice Charles Evans Whittaker on the Supreme Court* 212–14 (McFarland, 2005).

[77] "June 1, 1962 Memorandum For the Brethren [from E.W.] Re: No. 4–Brown Shoe v. U.S.", Box I, WJBP.

[78] 370 US 294 (1962).

[79] Compare Smith, *Failing Justice* at 212–14 (cited in note 76); Schwartz, *Super Chief* at 438–39 (cited in note 4).

[80] *Frankfurter Warren Squabble*, Washington Daily News front page headline (April 24, 1961).

[81] Powe, *Warren Court* at 181, 461 (cited in note 4).

[82] Jim Newton, *Justice for All: Earl Warren and the Nation He Made* at 346 (Riverhead, 2006); Douglas, *Autobiography* at 161–64 (cited in note 71).

acquiring Kinney comported with the admittedly ambiguous congressional purposes shaping the provisions of the 1950 amendment.[83] Harlan's participation in unanimity was more complex. As counsel for corporate giants, he had little or no express concern for small business; he clearly resisted, however, big-business managers pursuing sharp investment practices of the sort he had successfully defended against as DuPont's counsel.[84]

Thus, during spring-summer 1962, Warren's draft opinions maintained unanimity upholding the lower court's invalidation of the Brown-Kinney merger.[85] In late 1955, the government had filed the case seeking to enjoin Brown Shoe's acquisition of Kinney under the Clayton Act's section 7. The trial judge's preliminary order allowed Brown's purchase of Kinney to proceed as long as Kinney preserved its independent operations. In July 1956, the trial judge died, delaying the court's decision until 1959. Meanwhile, the court considered a massive record of evidence testing Bicks's and the Justice Department's theory limiting the "complete efficiency" defense, which depended in turn on complex statistical data defining geographic and product markets. The government, the new judge decided, had carried the burden of proof under section 7. Thus, Brown's investment established managerial dominance over the prices Kinney charged consumers and thereby "substantially lessened competition" in the manufacture and sales of shoes as a "line of commerce," within a "section of the country" defined as the nation and metropolitan areas of some 10,000 people. Brown appealed to the Supreme Court; the Kennedy Justice Department largely adopted as its own Bicks's argument.[86]

Warren circulated several opinion drafts by late June.[87] Each member of the Court accepted the drafts' deference to the various Congressional purposes shaping the provisions of the 1950 Clayton

---

[83] Powe, *Warren Court* at 461 (cited in note 4); *Brown Shoe*, "Legislative History," 370 US 311–23.

[84] Tinsley E. Yarbrough, *John Marshall Harlan: Great Dissenter of the Warren Court* 134–35, 340–41 (Oxford, 1992).

[85] The following summarizes *United States v Brown Shoe Co. and G.R. Kinney Co.*, 179 F Supp 721 (Missouri, ED 1959).

[86] Id; 370 US 294; Freyer, *Regulating Big Business* at 304, 306 (cited in note 19).

[87] "No. 4, Brown Shoe Co. v. United States," "Assigned [change from] Whittaker [to] Chief Justice, Date [change] Dec. 18, 1961" to "Jan. 22, 1962, Date Circulated 5-31-62, 6-18-62, 6-21-62," "Harlan, J. 6/1/6 Harlan to Cir[.] sep[arate] opn[.], Brennan, J. 6-21-62, Agree," "Announced 6-25-62." Box I, WJBP.

Act Amendment.[88] Even so, Warren worked from the assumption stated in the December conference that the trial "judge did a pretty good job. His findings may not have been up to the best standard, but they sufficed." Compared to the *DuPont Cellophane* case, which arose under section 2 of the Sherman Act, Warren said, "I don't think we have to be as tight" regarding Clayton Act, section 7. "The record showed that Brown was in the acquisition business and this added up to a substantial part" of retail shoe sales. Also, "I think men's, women's, and children's shoes was an adequate breakdown of lines of commerce."[89] Thus, following one strand of congressional purpose, Warren's draft decided against Brown's dominance over Kinney; such dominance enabled managerial control rather than market competition to set shoe prices the two firms either together or separately charged consumers.[90]

Warren's first draft opinion circulated on 5/31 received Brennan's comments. The draft stated that Congress sought in the 1950 Amendment to protect multiple policy goals, including efficient price competition set through market competition rather than managerial control, a decentralized market economy, and, where possible, the preservation of an independent-business "way of life."[91] The draft rejected Harlan's contention that the Court should have awaited court-of-appeals review before accepting the case. Warren's draft expressed marginal concern, however, about corporate size, even though Brown's purchase of Kinney, the nation's "largest family shoe retailer," made Brown the third biggest U.S. shoe company.[92] Brennan expressed doubts about the need to define the product markets below the national level, scribbling in the draft's margin: "But the market is one, nationwide: admittedly, three [shoe] products, but why not keep it clear that there is one market in this case?"[93] He also questioned the need to address horizontal merg-

---

[88] Compare *Brown Shoe*, "Legislative History," 370 US 311–23; Box I, WJBP; "No. 4–Brown Shoe Co. v. U.S. O.T. 1961 June 25, 1962," MC071 Box 133, John Marshall Harlan Papers, Seeley G. Mudd Manuscript Library, Princeton University (cited hereafter as JMHP).

[89] *DuPont Cellophane Case*, 351 US 377 (1956); Schwartz, *Super Chief* at 437, 438 (cited in note 4); Smith *Failing Justice* 212–14 (cited in note 76).

[90] My text construes, Opinion Draft, Brown Shoe, circulated May 31, 1962, Section "I," at 1–9, "III. Legislative History" at 15–29, JMHP.

[91] Opinion Draft Brown Shoe, circulated May 31, 1962, at 21, Box I, WJBP.

[92] Id, "II. Jurisdiction," 9–15, and at 7, 21.

[93] Id, Brennan's handwritten comments at 39.

ers.[94] Brennan concurred in Warren's support for Bicks's lower court argument that mergers should be examined in light of particular industries operating within the national market, but questioned the inclusion of submarkets constituting some 10,000 people.[95]

Brennan's marginal notes on the first circulated draft also stressed the evidence of intent to form a tie-in agreement. Warren's draft stipulated that the "use of a tying device can rarely be harmonized with the strictures of the antitrust laws, which are intended primarily to preserve competition."[96] Exceptionally, "a [tie-in] requirement contract may escape censure" where "only a small share of the market is involved, if the purpose of the agreement" was "to insure to the customer a sufficient supply of a commodity vital to the customer's trade or to insure to the supplier a market for his output and if there" was "no trend toward concentration in the industry." Brennan queried, "Isn't the whole handling of the [lawful] distinction very conclusory [sic]?"[97] The essential point, Brennan stated, was that manufacturing and retail industries such as shoes, though locally decentralized at present, were nonetheless undergoing ever increasing market concentration through merger. Moreover, Brown's "past behavior" and the "testimony of Brown's President" confirmed "that Brown would use its ownership of Kinney to force Brown shoes into Kinney stores." Thus, Brennan wrote, it was "more to the point" that "remaining vigor cannot immunize a merger if the trend in that industry is toward oligopoly."[98]

Brennan endorsed the phrase protecting "*competition* not *competitors*" due to congressional intent and the tie-in agreement, but expressed no direct concern for small business.[99] Warren's three circulated drafts each included five subjects in the following order: facts defining markets and the merger itself, jurisdiction (about truncated appeal), ambiguous congressional intent in legislative history of the 1950 amendment, effects of vertical merger (proving tie-in),

[94] Id at 1.

[95] Id 3–6.

[96] Id 29–39, at 35.

[97] Id at 35 (Warren draft text quoted and Brennan handwritten query).

[98] Id at 36, 37 (Warren draft text and Brennan handwritten note).

[99] Id at Draft p. 26 (Brennan did not comment directly upon "*competition* not *competitors*" phrase, which is 370 US 320, but he did accept the "III. Legislative History," in which quote appears).

and effects of horizontal merger (concentration trends harm small business). On the first page of the May 31 draft Brennan wrote: "What form did merger take? Why Part V?"[100] The first query involved the complex interconnected investment and market definition issues.[101] The second query suggested, however, that Brennan could have overturned the merger without considering the horizontal or concentration effects engendering the gradual elimination of small business.[102] Thus, Brennan condemned the merger because the proven facts revealed that Brown engaged in the tie-in agreement, which thereby foreclosed "*competition*" in violation of various congressional purposes shaping section 7. The phrase linking "competition" and "competitors" to small business appears in the "horizontal" effects section which Brennan questioned and could have dropped.[103]

Brennan did not "agree" to join Warren's opinion until the third draft circulated on June 21.[104] On that date he wrote, "Dear Chief: After having had a chance to study the separate concurrences of John Harlan and Tom Clark, I have concluded that I shall join your opinion."[105] The two moderates' position on the jurisdictional issue of appellate review may have influenced Brennan's wait. In a handwritten note to Harlan, Clark had admitted, "My face is red" because of inattention to the jurisdictional issue.[106] Still, since Clark left Harlan alone in dissent regarding the jurisdictional point, Brennan probably paid most attention to Harlan's reasons for joining Warren's opinion opposing the merger on the merits.[107] The day after Warren's first circulated draft, Harlan wrote, "Dear Brethren: I shall in due course circulate a separate opinion in this case, dissenting on the jurisdictional point. Pending further study of the Chief Justice's opinion, I have not yet decided whether I should add some-

---

[100] Id at 1 (including the two handwritten comments).

[101] Id "I" at 1–9.

[102] Id at 1, 39–51 (compare handwritten query and "Section V" of Draft).

[103] Id, and see notes 99, 100.

[104] See note 87.

[105] Id, "June 21, 1962 Re: No. 4 Brown Shoe Co. v. United States."

[106] "No. 4–Brown Shoe Co. v. U.S. O.T. 1961," "Memoranda," file includes handwritten note Clark to Harlan (n.d.), at p. 2, Box 133, JMHP.

[107] I admit speculation on this point.

thing further on the merits."[108] Prior to the Court's December 9, 1961 conference on *Brown Shoe*, Harlan's law clerks began preparing memos; these memos were the basis for Harlan's concurring opinion, which in turn prompted Brennan's June 21 note agreeing to join Warren's final opinion.[109]

"Since I am alone on the Jurisdictional Question," Harlan's handwritten notes stated, "[I] deem it a duty to express my view on the merits of this important case." Thus, regarding the decision overturning the Brown-Kinney merger, "I agree with the Court that this [lower court] judgment must be affirmed."[110] Harlan "Rest[ed] on" the evidence showing the "vertical" tie-in enabling Brown to achieve growing dominance over shoe prices in various "line[s] of commerce" through control of Kinney's retail operations in product and geographical markets.[111] The vertical outcome of the merger thus would increasingly foreclose those markets to many "independent" firms that traditionally competed for the same business.[112] Still, the financial concentration extinguishing independent firms concerned Harlan less than Brown's stated intent to assert its managerial control in order to foreclose competition through tie-in agreements imposed on Kinney. Finally, Harlan concluded, there was "Much doubt about 'the [merger's] horizontal' [dimensions]— Record very inadequate on that score."[113] Harlan's published concurring opinion on the merits expanded upon these notes, drawing from his law clerks' memos, which relied on evidence presented in both parties' briefs.[114]

The clerk's memos guided Harlan's answer to the issue whether the "effect" of Brown acquiring Kinney violated section 7.[115] Brown,

[108] "No. 4–Brown Shoe Co. v. U.S. O.T. 1961," "Memoranda," file, "June 1, 1962 Memorandum For The Conference Re: No. 4–Brown Shoe Dear Brethren:" signed "J.M.H." Box 133, JMHP.

[109] Id. "Memoranda File" also includes Brennan's letter to Warren, cited in note 105 above. In the "Memoranda File" there is also memo, "Brown Shoe Co. v. United States No. 4 Appeal from E.D. Mo. Bench Memo." The date is 12/5/61; initialed by "NL." Other "Bench Memos" are included.

[110] Id at 3 (Harlan's handwritten outline, "Brown Shoe").

[111] Id (Harlan's handwritten marginal note, "line of commerce" "Bench Memo," 12/5/61 "NL").

[112] Id at 1 ("Bench Memo," 12/5/61 "NL").

[113] See note 110 above.

[114] 370 US 365–74.

[115] "No. 4 Brown Shoe Co. v. U.S. O.T. 1961" in "Memoranda" file, "Bench Memo," 12/5/61, "NL," at 1, Box 133, JMHP.

the nation's number three "(in dollar volume)" shoe manufacturer, sought through investment to control Kinney, the "then largest independent retail chain of family-style shoe stores." The trial judge affirmed the government's argument construing the Clayton Act, holding that the "vertical and horizontal effects" of the "acquisition 'may be substantially to lessen competition, or tend to create a monopoly' in a definable 'line of commerce' within . . . one or more 'section[s] of the country.'" The lower court decision, as well as the government and Brown's lawyers, based their analysis on market data and structure showing the "various activities of the two firms in the manufacturing and selling ends of the shoe business." The evidence also sustained the government's contention that Brown controlled from 584 to 645 "franchise dealers" which were "not permitted to carry competing lines of shoes." During arguments before the Court, Brown's counsel nonetheless denied that his client followed such a restrictive policy, Harlan noted on the memo, because the franchise agreements were "cancellable at any time."[116]

The analysis shaped Harlan's opinion that interconnected "horizontal" and "vertical" dimensions of the merger presented difficulties for overturning it. Harlan underlined the memo's affirmation that "it is important to note that the [District Judge] did not rest his holding on a finding that the merger of [Brown's large and Kinney's small] manufacturing divisions (i.e., the horizontal combination on the manufacturing level) violated § 7." Had Brown bought "only" Kinney's few "manufacturing plants," it's "increment of .4% of production of shoes throughout the country" was too trivial to justify "break up" by the government. Even so, the "horizontal manufacturing combination" was significant for the government's case, Harlan underlined, "only to the extent that it adds to the leverage Brown has over its suppliers." Admittedly, Brown's horizontal control of Kinney's manufacturing capacity was "puny" within the national market. Nevertheless, in conjunction with "expanding vertically by taking over Kinney" Brown established itself, the government said, as "the 'supplier of much if not all of the pre-merger Kinney market'—and [so] . . . this horizontal growth, re-

---

[116] Id, in the following, Harlan's handwritten marginal notes, and quoted passages he underlined all quoted from the "Bench Memo."

sulting from its vertical expansion, enable[d] it to demand greater concessions from suppliers."[117]

Harlan marked the law clerk's analysis of further difficulties arising from how the government and the court handled the "horizontal" merger issues. The district judge and the Antitrust Division emphasized the "trend towards oligopoly in the shoe business. To the extent that any large shoe manufacturer swallows up . . . a small competitor this trend is enhanced," the memo conceded. Still, the "problem with all the 'trend to oligopoly' cases is precisely where the line ought to be drawn; each merger alone seems harmless, but if each is allowed, there will soon be no one but a handful left in the market." Harlan nonetheless marked his law clerk's conclusion that the Supreme Court need not address "this difficult issue in the present case" because the "vertical aspects of this merger more than adequately support the result" of the lower court's decision. Harlan also marked the memo's view that the horizontal combination of Brown's and Kinney's "two substantial retail chains, which had previously competed in cities where both had stores (thus giving the public the benefit of vigorous competition at the retail level) . . . would certainly 'lessen competition'" in "line[s] of commerce" designated men's, women's, and children's shoes within a metropolitan "section of the country."[118]

Harlan read the "line of commerce" provision in light of competitive consumer prices and demand. Essentially, the memo endorsed the views of Bicks and Arnold, promoting price competition determined through consumer behavior, rather than, as Bork and others contended, the efficiency costs of managerial control. The memo emphasized that Brown admitted the evidence showing "7 of 24 witnesses thought of the Brown and Kinney outlets as being in competition with one another." The government would have won had the district judge "based his finding on this testimony alone," and, the clerk declared, "I think that it is . . . clearly right." The evidence assembled in the government's tables showed, Harlan underlined, "that there was overlap in the price and style of shoes sold by the outlets . . . . I cannot imagine that 'low-priced' shoes and 'medium-priced' shoes are not some what interchangeable and therefore in competition under the doctrine of the [*Cellophane*] case.

---

[117] Id at 2.

[118] Id at 3.

Certainly the ordinary shoe buyer does not tell himself that he will buy only" either a "low" or a "medium-priced" shoe. "He usually does some window-shopping, compares values, and then forks up a little more or spends a little less depending on what his judgment advises."[119]

Ultimately, the "effects of the vertical merger are so obviously within . . . § 7," the memo concluded, "that I think an affirmance is inescapable." Harlan's markings indicated agreement. He scribbled in the margin Brown's contention that there was "no evidence that any independent manufacturer could be displaced . . . as suppliers of Kinney." The remark appeared alongside the memo's comment that the "merger effectively forecloses other independent manufacturers from producing shoes to be sold by the Kinney stores. The evidence revealed," Harlan underlined, "that only 20% of Kinney's sales were shoes that it had produced, the remainder were 'made up' by small manufacturers. Before the merger, Kinney purchased no shoes from Brown; by 1957—just two years after the merger—Kinney was getting 7.9% of its shoe sales from Brown." This pattern of increasing exclusion closely paralleled what happened to a leading franchise dealer, "whose purchase of Brown shoes shot up from approximately 12% to 33% within 7 years after its merger with Brown." Harlan marked the "effect of" Brown's "purchase of a large number of retail shoe stores is to lessen competition throughout the country for . . . access to Kinney stores. This is precisely what § 7 prohibits."[120]

The demise of smaller firms concerned Harlan less than Brown's intent to dominate competition expressly through managerial control over prices and production. Throughout the memo Harlan noted the inconsistency between Brown's contention that its tie-in agreements did not foreclose independents, and the evidence in the record showing that Brown's management effectively admitted intent to foreclose Kinney's suppliers. Indeed, Harlan marked the analysis of evidence showing Brown's admission "that shoe manufacturing plants are easily adapted to the manufacture of different styles, types, and grades of shoes." Thus, "if Brown can adapt its plants to supply the shoes needed by Kinney, it would be naïve to suppose that it would not do so forthwith in order to avail itself of

---

[119] Id at 3–4, 4.
[120] Id at 5.

this *captive market* [emphasis added]." Accordingly, "insofar as" the merger "provide[d] the opportunity for Brown to foreclose other manufacturers by entering onto production of 'low-priced' shoes," the merger was "one which <u>may</u> lessen competition." Moreover, under section 7 there was "certainly no statutory authorization to wait and see whether Brown does supply these shoes; the merger is either void now so as to nip the lessening of competition in the bud, or it is valid because no lessening of competition is likely."[121]

Harlan rejected Brown's insistence that possible foreclosure of "all Kinney outlets" was irrelevant because it involved "a bare 1%" share of national "retail shoe" sales. Harlan marked evidence showing "that many of the retail shoe outlets" upon which the "1% figure" was "computed are already committed by reason of ownership or control by one of the [few] large shoe manufacturers." Thus, Harlan underlined, the "percentage of the *available* market which independent shoe manufacturers had prior to this merger by reason of Kinney's independence (and which has been removed by the merger) is much more substantial than 1%." Moreover, the record revealed, "manufacturers whose business entirely depended on supplying Kinney," as well as "retailers competing with Kinney," were all "effectively ousted by the merger." Perhaps the merger facilitated cost efficiencies enabling Brown sometimes to charge marginally lower prices; nevertheless, it was not free-market competition, but managerial control susceptible to abuse that determined such prices. Finally, although a few large firms remained competitive with Brown-Kinney, there still was "harm" done free-market competition. "If the existence of more powerful entities would justify such a merger," Harlan underlined, "oligopoly could never be prevented."[122]

Harlan did not dispute his clerk's conclusion: "I think this is an open-and-shut case."[123] Like Brennan, Harlan believed that it was unnecessary for Warren's opinion to address the conflicted horizontal-merger issues involving demise of small business and advancing market concentration.[124] Essentially, not unlike Brennan, Harlan rejected Brown's intent to achieve market dominance through what Bicks called the acquisition of managerial talent,

---

[121] Id at 6.

[122] Id at 6, 7.

[123] Id at 7.

[124] See notes 94, 102, 103, 110, 112, 113.

rather than developing it from within the existing organization. Thus, consistent with Bicks's declared purpose for trying the case in the first place, Harlan and Brennan targeted the "full efficiency defense" Brown raised to deny evidence that the tie-in agreements created section 7 violations.[125] Bork and other critics dismissed such evidence, arguing it did not offset the merger's cost efficiencies resulting from economies of scale leading to lower shoe prices for consumers.[126] As an experienced antitrust defense council, Harlan's support for Warren's opinion on the merits also may have sought to undercut corporate managers' incentives for pursuing mergers through sharp practices. As DuPont's defense counsel prior to 1955, Harlan had learned to distinguish between what he considered legitimate or improper management intention in such cases.[127]

The consensus points Harlan and Brennan shared suggested the multiple antitrust goals pervading the Court's *Brown Shoe* decision. To be sure, following one strand of congressional purpose shaping the Clayton Act's section 7, Warren's opinion endorsed small-business values.[128] In addition, however, antitrust attorney Conrad W. Oberdorfer praised the Court for "very definitely" affirming that "each merger presented a unique situation and that no slide rule or mechanical formula ought to be applied." Moreover, the "antitrust defense bar" understood a merger required "an appraisal of the particular industrial situation involved," and its "effect on the strength of competition rather than on the number of competitors."[129] Echoing Arnold's realist-behavioral definition of consumer prices, Gordon B. Spivack recognized that, notwithstanding the various tests the Court employed to define the essential "product" market and "geographic area," the "real test of a market is a group of sales, a monopoly of which would give the monopolist substantial power over the price." Even so, "you have to define a market in terms of the alternatives available to competitors. Once you start talking about power over

---

[125] Id notes 11, 14, 16.

[126] See notes 68, 69.

[127] See note 84.

[128] See note 81.

[129] Gordon B. Spivack, Conrad W. Oberdorfer, and G. Richard Young, "Growth through External Expansion: Present-Day Tests for Horizontal, Vertical, and Conglomerate Acquisition: A Panel Discussion," in David F. Cavers, Jr., ed, *Primer on Horizontal Agreements and Other Restraints of Commerce: Second New England Antitrust Conference Sponsored by the Antitrust Committee, Boston Bar Association and the Greater Boston Chamber of Commerce, March 22, 1968* (Gorham & Lamont, 1969); Oberdorfer at 69, 74, 75.

price, or alternatives available to competitors, you are talking about matters of degree, not matters of kind."[130]

Thus, Spivack observed, *Brown Shoe* concerned no "single market" but "a great many . . . markets and sub-markets" encompassing "different groupings of sales." Any "monopoly" involving market sales ensured "different amounts of power over price, because there are different alternatives available to competitors, depending upon how readily they are available, how expensive they are, and how much time it would take to get to those alternatives." Suggesting Arnold's advocacy, Spivack declared that as a result of *Brown Shoe* the courts "look at every realistic market and sub-market, and if in any commercially realistic market or sub-market the competitors are foreclosed from a substantial share of the market, the merger is held to be illegal." Also, applying the *DuPont/GM* precedent, the Supreme Court's construction of the Clayton Act's section 7 term "substantial" could be understood "as saying that 15 per cent or more of a market is substantial." The Court also partly rested its decision upon clear evidence of Brown's "intent" to purchase Kinney in order to "arbitrarily exclude [big or small] competitors from a substantial amount of business," or "to adversely affect market structures . . . even though very small market shares" were "involved."[131]

Proof of the tie-in agreement doomed the merger. Before the merger, Kinney's retail operations entailed shoe purchases from many "small manufacturers, " but Kinney bought no shoes from Brown. "Within two years after the merger occurred, and while the case was still pending, Brown became the single most important supplier of shoes to Kinney stores." Thus, the Court held that the merger was a "tie-in agreement, where you force the customer to take products he does not want." Spivack observed: "Tie-agreements are almost always illegal."[132] Even so, Bork's and other critics' emblematic claim that the Court's 1962 decision protected competitors, not competition, obscured Brown's choice of merger investment in order to implement restrictive tie-in agreements rather than develop managerial efficiencies within the firm.[133] Spivack thus focused on Harlan, "who [was] no antitrust zealot." Given "Brown's

---

[130] Id at 76 (Spivack).

[131] Id at 77, 78.

[132] Id at 78.

[133] See notes 68, 69.

purpose [which rested upon an illegal tie-in agreement] in buying
Kinney, the reasonable result of the merger was that those small
shoe manufacturers were going to be put out of business. And that
was substantial enough in his mind to strike down the merger *without regard to industry concentration or trends.*"[134]

Antitrust practitioners Handler and Robinson also indicated how
the Warren Court understood the *Brown Shoe* decision. In the broad
competition language of the 1950 Amendment, Congress delegated
to the Court the "role as the ultimate arbiter in the merger field,"
said Handler and Robinson. The "plain teaching of Brown Shoe
was that in merger litigation, the facts reign supreme and mathe-
matical tests are not controlling." A merger's "anticompetitive effects" required proving not only "market power" revealed by "statistical market shares" within the industry, but also other "factors,"
including "reasonable interchangeability of use, cross-elasticity of
demand, and production facilities, industry or public recognition,
peculiar characteristics and uses, unique production facilities, distinct customers, distinct prices, sensitivity to price changes, and
specialized vendors."[135] Harlan, Brennan, and other members of the
Court analyzed these factors applying multiple antitrust policy
goals; they defined "competition," consumers, and "competitors,"
selectively employing economic and behavioral principles such as
Arnold used to refute free marketers and regulation planners. The
Warren Court's activist-moderate antitrust consensus, however, did
not last.

IV. WHAT HAPPENED TO BROWN SHOE?

Several cases in early 1966 suggested that the activist-moderate antitrust consensus had fragmented. In *FTC v Brown Shoe Co.*
a unanimous Court supported Black's opinion upholding the FTC's
declaration that the "Brown Franchise Stores' Program" instituted
anticompetitive and unfair trade practices.[136] Clark's unpublished
draft of a concurring opinion nonetheless had altered Black's opinion.[137] With Justice Abe Fortas not participating, the Court divided

---

[134] See note 132 (in quote concerning Harlan, emphasis added).

[135] See note 32 at 165.

[136] *Federal Trade Commission v Brown Shoe Co.*, 384 US 316 (1966).

[137] Federal Trade Commissioner Petitioner v. Brown Shoe, Inc. [May, 1966], Mr. Justice
Clark, concurring in the result, in Box 388, Hugo L. Black Papers, Library of Congress
Manuscript Division (cited hereafter as HLBP), discussed below.

6–2 in favor of Black's opinion protecting small Los Angeles grocery stores from large ones in *U.S. v Von's Grocery Co.* Harlan and Stewart dissented, arguing that Black's opinion misapplied the 1962 *Brown Shoe* decision.[138] The Court's opinion-making in these two cases thus revealed grounds for dissents that emerged during late April to mid-June 1966.[139] These dissents resonated with Handler's and other practitioners' assertions that Warren Court antitrust exhibited inconsistent reasoning targeting corporate concentration.[140] *Fortune* critics Max Ways and Bork adamantly insisted, by contrast, that the Court persistently defended small competitors, thereby repudiating the realities of big business "imperfect" competition.[141]

Practitioners and consistent critics thus provided a context for understanding the Court's internal decision making following *Brown Shoe*. By 1968, various antitrust practitioners agreed that 1962 *Brown Shoe* provided a clear and reasonable standard, both for applying the Clayton Act section 7 and general merger policy during the massive corporate restructuring of the 1960s.[142] At issue was not the Court's unanimous 1962 decision, Handler insisted, but cases such as *Von's Grocery* "create[d] the false impression" that they were "the result of an inexorable progression from *Brown Shoe's* premises[.] Why pretend to a consistency which does not exist?" Handler further noted that the Antitrust Division's Donald Turner "defend[ed]" *Von's Grocery* because in effect it "transform[ed]" the Celler-Kefauver "antimerger law designed to protect competition into an anti-concentration measure without regard to competitive effects[.]"[143] Critics Ways and Bork, however, lumped together all Warren Court antitrust decisions as constituting a uniform policy protecting competitors rather than imperfect competition. Ironically, within the Court the rise of dissents signaled that the antitrust

[138] *U.S. v Von's Grocery Co.*, 384 US 270, 281 (1966).

[139] *Von's Grocery*, argued March 22, 1966—decided May 31, 1966; *FTC v Brown Shoe*, argued April 25, 1966—decided June 6, 1966; *United States v Pabst Brewing* Co., 384 US 546 (1966), argued April 27, 1966—decided June 13, 1966; *United States v Grinnell Corp.*, et al., 384 US 563 (1966), argued March 28–29, 1966—decided June 13, 1966; *Federal Trade Commission v Dean Foods Co.*, 384 US 597 (1966), argued March 28, 1966—decided June 13, 1966.

[140] Milton Handler, 1 Ga L Rev at 349–62 (cited in note 58); and note 129 above.

[141] See note 26 above.

[142] See notes 28, 32, 129–32 above.

[143] Handler, 1 Ga L Rev at 356, 357 (cited in note 58).

activists had prevailed sufficiently to facilitate the critics' claims.[144]

FTC v Brown Shoe (1966) arose seven years earlier, coinciding with Bicks's more well-known litigation targeting Brown Company. Whereas Bicks's *Brown Shoe* suit tested the Clayton Act's section 7, the FTC case challenged the commission's authority to prevent "unfair trade practices."[145] After "extensive hearings" in seven cities in five states and Washington, D.C., the FTC's order went against Brown. In 1964, however, the court of appeals overturned the FTC, holding that Brown's use of contract agreements with its retailers to exclude them from doing business with Brown's competitors did not constitute "unfair practices." The court of appeals distinguished the issue of the FTC's authority from the Supreme Court's 1962 *Brown Shoe* decision construing the Clayton Act section 7.[146] The FTC appealed. Black's opinion for the Supreme Court stated: "the question we have for decision" was "whether the Federal Trade Commission can declare it to be an unfair practice for Brown, the second largest manufacturer of shoes in the Nation, to pay a valuable consideration to hundreds of retail shoe purchasers in order to secure a contractual promise from them that they will deal primarily with Brown and will not purchase conflicting lines of shoes from Brown's competitors."[147]

From May 17 to June 2, 1966, Black circulated several opinion drafts culminating in the final decision delivered on June 6.[148] As to whether the burden of proof under the Clayton Act section 7 "competition" provisions should be applied in order to extend the FTC's authority over unfair trade practices, the Court's unanimous decision was: "We hold that the Commission acted well within its authority in declaring the Brown franchise program unfair whether it was completely full blown or not."[149] The drafts and the final opinion suggested Black's opposition to Brown as among the

---

[144] Compare sources and text, notes 1, 25–27 to following discussion in text and sources cited.

[145] Compare timing of Bicks's litigation discussed note, 14; and early stages of *Brown Shoe Company, Inc. v Federal Trade Commission*, 339 F2d 45, 46 (1964).

[146] 339 F2d 45, 47 (1964).

[147] 384 US 316, 320 (1966).

[148] Circulated draft opinions and handed-down opinion, dated, respectively, May 17, 25, June 2, and June 6, 1966, case file No. 118 O.t. 1965 FTC v. Brown Shoe Co., Box 388, HLBP.

[149] 384 US 316 at 322 (1964).

"world's largest manufacturers of shoes."[150] Nevertheless, the bulk of the draft and final opinions targeted the "franchise program" as imposing unfair, anticompetitive practices. Indeed, Black's earliest uncirculated draft memo dated May 6 included the handwritten note: "Brown's customers who entered into these restrictive franchise agreements . . . were given in return special treatment and valuable benefits which were not granted to Brown's customers who did not enter into the agreements."[151] Also, extensive handwritten notes headed "Brown Shoe v US 370 US 294" showed that Black's *final* opinion of June 6 enlarged the FTC's authority by analogizing the principles affirmed in the 1962 decision.[152]

Black's final opinion appearing in the *United States Reports* gave no hint that Clark had prepared a concurring opinion.[153] Following Black's first circulated opinion draft on May 17, Warren, Brennan, White, and Douglas readily confirmed their agreement. From May 25 to June 1, Clark, Stewart, Harlan, and Fortas notified Black that they too joined his opinion.[154] Even so, responding to the second circulated draft on May 25, Clark wrote marginal notes expressing agreement on the result; but he also suggested that Black should clarify the relationship between the Clayton Act provisions and the FTC's authority.[155] On May 27, Stewart wrote Black, "Unless somebody else writes separately, I shall go along with your opinion." Several days later Harlan was "glad to join your opinion as recirculated on May 26" which "removes the misgivings I had about one aspect of your original circulation."[156] The timing of these cryptic remarks implied reaction to a draft opinion Black received with the heading: "Mr. Justice Clark, concurring in the result." Since

---

[150] Quoted phrase appears on page I of each draft and final opinions cited in note 148; and 384 US 316 at 317 (1966).

[151] See note 148; typescript draft "October Term 1965 No. 118–Federal Trade Commission v. Brown Shoe., Inc. Cert. To C.A. 8. 5-6-66 HLB:fl Mr. Justice Black delivered the opinion of the Court." Quoted phrase insert 1A, in Box 388, HLBP.

[152] See note 148; "Brown Shoe v US 370 US 294," handwritten, ten numbered page notes, Box 388, HLBP.

[153] See notes 136, 137.

[154] Letters headed "Dear Hugo," giving notice of joining signed, respectively, E.W., May 19; Bill [Brennan], May 19; Byron [White], May 19; P[otter] S[tewart], May 27; A[be] F[ortas], June 6; J[ohn] M. H[arlan], all 1966. Justice Douglas is listed as joining on draft handwritten "cir. 5/26," Box 388, HLBP.

[155] Full cite in note 148, second Draft recirculated May 25, 1966; Clark's handwritten marginal note reads, "Dear Hugo, Here I am basic agree-xcuse [*sic*] please—but how about pp. 4, 5, 6, Thanks. TCC 5/25[.]"

[156] See note 154.

Black's opinion alone was reported as the Court's decision in *FTC v Brown Shoe*, he undoubtedly directly addressed Clark's concerns and, indirectly at least, also those raised by Harlan and Stewart.[157]

Comparison with Clark's unpublished concurring opinion revealed that Black's May 6 uncirculated draft memo did not mention 1962 *Brown Shoe*.[158] That precedent was cited, however, in Black's final opinion of *FTC v Brown Shoe* announced on June 6.[159] Clark's unpublished concurrence refers without date to May.[160] Clark expressly agreed to the *results* of Black's draft opinion recirculated on May 25; so, he probably gave the draft concurrence to Black sometime around that date.[161] Even so, Clark very likely influenced Black's undated, handwritten ten-page remarks titled "Brown Shoe v US 370 US 294," which in turn were incorporated into the Court's final decision.[162] Clark's concurrence stated that by omitting an analysis of 1962 *Brown Shoe*, Black's draft opinion "seems to imply" that the FTC had authority "to condemn, <u>per se</u>, exclusive dealing agreements without regard to the (1) relative bargaining power of the parties involved, (2) relevant market affected by the agreements, or (3) the extent, or existence, of anti-competitive market foreclosure."[163] The inclusion of 1962 *Brown Shoe* in Black's final opinion defused a per se rule, creating a decision more consistent with the views of the Court's antitrust moderates, though not necessarily practitioners like Handler.[164]

Black's opinion drafting of *FTC v Brown Shoe* coincided with the Court considering several other antitrust cases, especially *Von's Grocery*.[165] The FTC case defined Brown's franchise program as exclusive dealing, much like the tie-in agreements the Court's activists

---

[157] See notes 136, 137, 154.

[158] See notes 137, 152.

[159] 384 US 319 (1966).

[160] See note 137.

[161] See note 155.

[162] Juxtaposition of evidence developed above in notes 136, 137, 152, 155 supports this conclusion.

[163] Full cite, note 137, quoted phrase at p. 1.

[164] Id, and note 162; but see Handler, 1 Ga L Rev at 349 (cited in note 58), "the recent revolutionary ruling of the Court in the second *Brown Shoe* case . . . held that exclusive dealing arrangements may be forbidden by the Federal Trade Commission, even where there are no likely anticompetitive effects within the meaning of Section 3 of the Clayton Act. With this decision, the qualifying clause found in that legislation has for all practical purposes been obliterated."

[165] See note 139.

and moderates alike held to be illegal in 1962 *Brown Shoe*.[166] Regarding that same 1962 decision, *Fortune*'s antitrust critics, by contrast, had emphasized small competitors being protected from the Brown-Kinney merger, despite each firm's comparatively modest market share.[167] Merger issues involving small business and limited market share also arose in *Von's Grocery*, though there was no direct evidence of an illegal practice such as a tie-in agreement.[168] Thus, in the FTC case the Court agreed unanimously as Clark insisted upon following closely 1962 *Brown Shoe*. Moreover, Black was deflected from imposing a strict per se rule that could have been used to protect small business from growing corporate concentration.[169] During the same period in *Von's Grocery*, however, Black achieved a per se rule aimed at preserving small groceries imperiled by ever encroaching mergers in the rapidly growing Los Angeles market. But unlike the FTC case, Black's success engendered vigorous dissent.[170]

Von's Grocery originally arose during Bicks's litigation campaign applying Clayton Act section 7 "competition" provisions to major consumer markets.[171] Unlike the mixed merger-tie-in questions of *Brown Shoe*, the issue in *Von's Grocery* was whether two merging Los Angeles supermarket chains "ranking," respectively, "third" and "fifth in terms of total sales by grocery stores in [the] metropolitan area . . . would not probably lessen competition at time of merger or in foreseeable future." Following procedural maneuvers from 1960 to 1964, the trial judge accepted the defendants' market data showing that "competition appeared open to everyone, especially those with experience and training, and consumer was reaping full benefit."[172] The government appealed to the Supreme Court. Black's 1966 majority opinion stated that the "sole question" was "whether the District Court properly concluded on the facts before it that the government had failed to prove a violation of § 7."

---

[166] Compare discussion of each case, respectively, notes 145–64 and Section III above.

[167] Compare commentary, notes 26, 27.

[168] 384 US 270–79 (1966).

[169] See notes 161–64.

[170] Id; see notes, 139, 168; 384 US 281–304 (1966) (Stewart, J, dissenting).

[171] See Bicks's litigation cited in note 14 and the evolution of the litigation discussed in *United States v Von's Grocery Company*, 233 F Supp 977 (1964).

[172] Compare discussion 1962 *Brown Shoe* Section III above; and 233 F Supp 976–85 at 976 (1964).

Reversing the lower court, Black emphasized that the "steady decline in the number of individual grocery store owners" in the Los Angeles area was the "crucial point" of the factual evidence. It was "thus apparent that the District Court" employed "the term [market] 'concentration' in some sense other than a total decrease in the number of separate competitors."[173]

Between April 20 and May 24, 1966, Black circulated several opinion drafts of *Von's Grocery*, leading to a final opinion announced on the May 31.[174] His first uncirculated draft analyzed the trial court's factual evidence primarily within the legislative history of the Celler-Kefauver Amendment that focused on the intent to protect small business from escalating corporate concentrations. "This is exactly the evil which Congress sought to prevent by passing §7 of the Clayton Act," Black's handwritten insertion read, "as is shown in the legislative history . . . which this Court discussed fully in Brown Shoe Co. v. U.S., 370 U.S. 294, at pp. 311–323."[175] Indeed, during the drafting process Black worked from a typed memorandum summarizing a total of approximately sixteen quoted passages from House and Senate reports, Celler's and Kefauver's statements, and political party platforms, all of which tied the amendment to the protection of small business embattled by escalating corporate concentration.[176] Accordingly, Black's final opinion declared, "Congress sought to preserve competition among many small businesses by arresting a trend toward concentration in its incipiency before that trend developed to the point that a market was left in the grip of a few big companies."[177]

By late May, Warren, Brennan, Douglas, White, and Clark accepted Black's *Von's Grocery* opinion. Suggesting that he embraced Black's citation of 1962 *Brown Shoe* as the basis for construing section 7, Clark wrote on April 26: "Dear Hugo Okay—Well done as usual—join me." White, however, wrote a letter emphasizing that Black had written into section 7 an expansive per se rule which

---

[173] 384 US at 272, 273, 304.

[174] See circulated drafts and final opinion, dated, respectively, April 20, April 22, May 6, May 24, May 31, 1966, "United States v. Von's Grocery," Box 391, HLBP.

[175] Handwritten revisions of typed, uncirculated draft "No. 303–U.S. v. Von's Grocery 1965 t.," handwritten marginal insertion at 4C (underlined emphasis in original), Box 391, HLBP.

[176] "Relevant Legislative History to the Celler-Kefauver Anti-Merger Amendment to § 7 of the Clayton Act," Box 391, HLBP.

[177] 384 US 294 at 277.

"goes considerably farther than the Government contended in this case . . . or in any other that I know of. And it is farther, I think, than Congress intended to go." White "read" Black's "rule" to be "that once a trend towards concentration is established—that is, an excess of exits over entries which predictably will continue—any disappearance of a competitor by merger is barred by §7, at least where the disappearing competitor has 4% of the market and absent it being a failing company." White recognized that "some mergers justify others . . . especially where technology or marketing methods change and require larger entities with greater aggregations of credit and capital," which seems "to be true of the grocery business in Los Angeles and elsewhere." White concurred in the result, adding an opinion setting out "a more limited approach" to Black's rule.[178]

Stewart's dissent excoriated Black's expansive *Von's Grocery* majority opinion. Fundamentally, Stewart declared, the Court "turns its back on" the "two basic principles" Warren formulated in 1962 *Brown Shoe*: (1) section 7 "standards . . . require that every corporate acquisition be judged in light of the contemporary economic context of its industry." And (2) the "purpose of §7 is to protect competition, not to protect competitors, and every §7 case must be decided in the light of that clear statutory purpose." Indeed, Black's opinion ignored the phrase in *Brown Shoe* that highlighted protection of "*competition* not *competitors*." The Court "instead" focused on evidence showing the "number of individual competitors has decreased over the years, and apparently on the theory that the degree of competition is invariably proportional to the number of competitors, it holds that this historic reduction in the number of competing units is enough under §7 to invalidate a merger within the market." Rejecting *Brown Shoe*'s "two principles," the Court thereby created a "startling per se rule" that was "contrary not only to our previous decisions, but contrary to the language of §7, contrary to the legislative history of the 1950 amendment, and contrary to economic reality."[179]

---

[178] See concerning "Von's" to "Dear Hugo," from, respectively, Byron [White] (handwritten, n.d.), TCC, 4/26 (handwritten), Bill [Brennan], April 23, 1966, E[arl]. W[arren]. Douglas's joining inferred. Letter dated May 6, 1966, Re: No. 303–United States v. Von's Grocery to "Dear Hugo" from "Byron," at 1, 2, Box 391, HLBP; 384 US at 280–81 (White, J, concurring) follows closely the Justice's letter.

[179] 384 US at 281–304 (Stewart, J, dissenting) at 282–83. *Brown Shoe Co. v United States*, 370 US 294 at 320 (1962) (emphasis in original).

Since 1962 *Brown Shoe*, the "sole consistency" Stewart perceived in section 7 cases was that the "government always wins." He conceded that Congress intended section 7 to protect small business from "incipient" market concentration. Black's opinion ignored, however, that other stated congressional purposes were to limit nationally operating corporations removing capital from local communities and to promote efficient management investment strategies rather than legally problematic practices such as exclusive dealing. Even so, Von's Grocery's acquisition of Shopping Bag Food Stores was the purchase of one Los Angeles–based firm by another. In addition, both supermarket chains were family-owned enterprises pursuing sound management and investment strategies targeting the metropolitan area's spiraling population growth, interstate highway expansion, and reliance upon the automobile. Moreover, both supermarket chains competed against other chains and numerous smaller stores in distinct western and southeastern metropolitan submarkets. Also, throughout the Los Angeles area entry into the grocery business was not difficult; often, former managers from the supermarket chains started the new, smaller stores.[180]

Joining Stewart's dissent on May 19, Harlan added, "I think it is one of the best antitrust opinions that has emerged from this Court in a long time." Months earlier his clerk prepared a memorandum indicating the basis for Harlan's agreement. The Von's Grocery–Shopping Bag merger created "a combined" market "sales of 7.5%," the "merged firm became the largest in Los Angeles, and some competition was lost," especially given the long-term trend. Though these facts were reconcilable with *Brown Shoe* and other precedents, he wrote, "[a]s a merger I cannot see that this substantially impedes competition." Also "entry" was open, "and competition seems healthy. More important, I think it is unwise to use the antitrust laws to attempt to halt broad changes in merchandising techniques, such as the change from corner grocers to supermarkets. Especially in Los Angeles, a city designed for the automobile, the concept of the corner grocer" was "anachronistic. If that is the reason for the attack on this merger, it should not be sustained." Moreover, "[b]oth companies were family run," not "a national chain," and both operated primarily in separate city submarkets

---

[180] 384 US 281–304 at 301 (Stewart, J, dissenting).

where other chains competed. Independent "stores" buying "through cooperatives" also competed effectively.[181]

During April–June 1966, the Court's antitrust opinion-making confirmed the pattern of dissent. *FTC/Brown Shoe* and *Von's Grocery* indicated that once Clark was satisfied that 1962 *Brown Shoe* was properly applied, he voted with the antitrust activists.[182] Thus, Clark, Douglas, Brennan, and Warren joined Black's June 13 opinion overturning the district court's dismissal of Bicks's earlier case challenging Pabst Brewing Company's acquisition of Blatz Brewing Company. Although nine members of the Court agreed that the lower court erred in applying section 7, White concurred solely in that result.[183] Harlan joined by Stewart and Fortas alone concurred that the district court had erred in *Pabst Brewing*; but they also expressly rejected Black's application of 1962 *Brown Shoe* to section 7 market-definition issues.[184] In *Dean's Food Co.*, the four antitrust activists joined Clark's majority opinion expanding the FTC's authority to enjoin already completed mergers. White, Harlan, and Stewart joined Fortas's dissent.[185] Finally, Harlan alone and Fortas joined by Stewart dissented from Douglas's majority opinion holding that Grinnell Corporation's merger-growth through proven illegal conduct violated the principle that there was "no difference between the relevant market in Sherman Act and Clayton Act cases."[186]

Viewed from within, Warren Court antitrust was less ambivalent than antitrust practitioners and critics suggested. Practitioners understood accurately that 1962 *Brown Shoe* established for section 7

---

[181] Harlan's quote from May 19, 1966, Re: <u>No. 303—Von's Grocery Dear Potter</u>; Clerk's memorandum, "United States v. Von's Grocery Co. Appeal from S.D. Calif. No. 303," 8/27/65, at 1, 2 in MC071, Box 256, JMHP.

[182] See notes 158, 166, 169, 178.

[183] Full cite, note 138, 384 US 546 (1966) (Douglas, concurring, 553–55); (White, J, concurring, at 555, result bearing on national market).

[184] 384 US 546 (Harlan, joined by Stewart, concurring in result only, not market definition, 555–61) (Fortas, concurring in result, not market definition, 561–62).

[185] *Federal Trade Commission v Dean Foods Co.*, 384 US 597 (1966) (Fortas, J, joined by Harlan, J, Stewart, J, White, J, dissenting, 612–40).

[186] *United States v Grinnell Corp.*, 384 US 563 (1966) (Harlan, J, dissenting, 583–85, Fortas, J, joined by Stewart, J, 585–96, dissenting). *Grinnell* arose primarily under sections 1 and 2 of the Sherman Act; however, in part because Grinnell Corp. held financial control of three other companies, there were also Clayton Act section 7 issues. As a result, Douglas's majority opinion equated the Sherman Act section 2 and Clayton Act section 7 standards, as stated the quoted clerk's typed note to "Mr. Justice" [signed] "JBF," Box 1366, William O. Douglas Papers, Manuscript Division, Library of Congress.

cases the "practical indicia" which "may be selected or ignored or given more or less weight," by government or private lawyers "depending less on discernible objective factors than on the supposed exigencies of antitrust enforcement." These practitioners also correctly perceived a clear movement toward Black's per se rule in *Von's Grocery* targeting corporate concentration.[187] The Court's hidden decision making obscured, however, Clark's central role—which Douglas later acknowledged—in the attempt to maintain the multiple policy goals of *Brown Shoe*.[188] Thus Harlan's, Stewart's, Fortas's, and White's proliferating concurring and dissenting opinions did not resist small business. Nevertheless, those same opinions recognized that through market definition section 7 encouraged managers to make efficient investments that preserved local capital in decentralized markets.[189] Yet by the mid-1960s, Turner's Antitrust Division and the FTC embraced Warren Court antitrust activists' attacks on corporate concentration. As a result, *Fortune* critics' consistent assertion that the Court protected competitors not competition seemed to ring true.[190]

V. Conclusions

As the Warren Court ended, the apparent entrenchment of its antitrust precedents proved deceptive. In a 1969 *Fortune* article, Bork published a ringing defense of free-market antitrust theories. "Far from being personal or idiosyncratic, they represent, in their general outline," he declared, "a broad and growing school of thought about antitrust policy." Despite Bork's insistence that Richard Nixon's head of the Antitrust Division "start and focus a systematic discussion of antitrust goals and economics," initially the government pursued an activist antitrust regime.[191] Not until 1973–74—amidst the oil crisis, the onslaught of "stagflation," the termination of U.S. spending for the Vietnam War, and the Watergate crisis—did the Nixon administration embrace free-market efficiency antitrust theories. By the arrival of the Reagan admin-

---

[187] Oberdorfer, *Growth Through External Expansion* at 72 (cited in note 129); Handler, 1 Ga L Rev 347–60 (cited in note 58).

[188] See note 182; Douglas, *Court Years* at 162 (cited in note 71).

[189] See notes 178–86.

[190] See notes 141, 144, 187.

[191] Bork, Fortune at 165 (cited in note 24).

istration, in antitrust and all fields of government regulation, market fundamentalism triumphed. Following the 1987 stock market crash and the massive savings and loan bailouts, however, Republican as well as Democratic antitrust authorities urged a revival reminiscent of Warren Court antitrust.[192] As antitrust enforcement waxed and waned up to the financial crisis and 2008 presidential election, the Warren Court's antitrust heritage was ambiguous.

Fortune's antitrust dialogue and leading advocates like Arnold revealed wider meanings of Warren Court antitrust than critics allowed. The critics' mantra possessed persuasive power, claiming that *Brown Shoe* and other precedents protected small business competitors rather than efficient oligopolistic competition. Nevertheless, as *Fortune*'s and Arnold's commentary suggested, many big business leaders did not embrace the critics' views for two basic reasons. First, big business accepted in principle activist antitrust in order to deflect "wild," more aggressive antitrust policies being urged in Congress. Second, the pragmatic, case-by-case approach of government prosecutions and private actions—which the Warren Court upheld—may have facilitated "uncertainty," but it also reinforced the "imperfect competition" managers exploited to further their companies and their own welfare. Thus, the complex historic changes of postwar American capitalism were channeled into an adversarial judicial process, undercutting public support for both critics and antitrust extremists. Fundamentally, Warren Court antitrust imposed rules that constrained without subverting big business managers' identification of corporate growth with their own security.

Within this public context, antitrust advocates supported *Brown Shoe*'s multiple policy goals. The decision's problematic fifth section condemning horizontal concentration reflected "small business" values Black held. Warren opposed the merger because his California progressivism made him distrustful of big business dominance; Douglas also opposed such dominance. Moderates Clark and Stewart generally deferred to ambiguous congressional intentions shaping the 1950 Amendment. The decision's internal opinion-drafting process also demonstrated that neither Brennan nor Harlan

---

[192] Kovaleff, *The Reagan . . . REvolution*, in Kovaleff, ed, *Antitrust Impulse* 193–278 (cited in note 2); Hovenkamp, *Antitrust Enterprise* 31–56 (cited in note 2); Peritz, *Competition Policy* 229–303 (cited in note 2); Freyer, *Regulating Big Business* 317–23 (cited in note 19); Freyer, *Antitrust and Global Capitalism* 145–69 (cited in note 2).

was preoccupied with protecting small business. Rather, the activist and moderate agreed that the Brown-Kinney merger should be overturned because of the proven tie-in agreement. Handler and other antitrust lawyers praised the Court's decision for this holding, along with its clarification of market definition issues. These outcomes vindicated Bicks's original motivations seeking a limited "efficiency defense" and clarification of market definition. Thus, *Brown Shoe* not only supported small business and decentralized market opportunity; it also held managers responsible for avoiding abusive practices through merger investment implementing what Arnold called "administered" prices.

Multiple antitrust policy goals awaited revival. During the later 1960s, cases such as *Von's Grocery* agitated critics' claims that Warren Court antitrust merely protected small competitors. Still, oligopolistic competition advanced. Indeed, the government's first systematic "merger guidelines," which Turner announced in 1968, endorsed statistical concentration levels accepting oligopolistic competition in many industries. From the mid-1970s on, free-market antitrust theories, conservative Supreme Court decisions, and deregulation generally assumed that oligopolistic competition was inevitable. After the millennium, however, a Republican FTC Trade Commissioner "suggest[ed] that current antitrust doctrine needs to take larger account of nonprice competition, which ever way it cuts." Concerning mergers, he declared that "intangible efficiencies like quality of management or the compatibility of different corporate cultures may be more important than anything else, but we do not take formal account of them in our *Merger Guidelines*."[193] Amidst bipartisan demands for antitrust revival, "non-price competition" and broader managerial accountability were consistent with the Warren Court's multiple policy goals; as constituted in the Court's precedents, those goals offered a usable past.

---

[193] Thomas B. Leary, *The Bipartisan Legacy*, 80 Tulane L Rev No. 2 at 611, 613 (2005).